Tales from the
Cult Film Trenches

ALSO BY LOUIS PAUL

Italian Horror Film Directors (McFarland, 2005)

BY TOM LISANTI AND LOUIS PAUL

Film Fatales: Women in Espionage Films and Television, 1962–1973 (McFarland, 2002)

Tales from the Cult Film Trenches

Interviews with 36 Actors from Horror, Science Fiction and Exploitation Cinema

LOUIS PAUL

FOREWORD BY TOM WEAVER

McFarland & Company, Inc., Publishers
Jefferson, North Carolina, and London

LIBRARY OF CONGRESS CATALOGUING-IN-PUBLICATION DATA

Paul, Louis, 1960–
Tales from the cult film trenches : interviews with 36 actors from horror, science fiction and exploitation cinema / Louis Paul ; foreword by Tom Weaver.
p.   cm.

Includes bibliographical references and index.

ISBN-13: 978-0-7864-2994-3
softcover : 50# alkaline paper ∞

1. Horror films—United States—History and criticism.
2. Science fiction films—United States—History and criticism.
3. Exploitation films—United States—History and criticism.
4. Motion picture actors and actresses—United States—Interviews   I. Title.
PN1995.9.H6P343 2008   791.4302'8092273—dc22   [B]   2007027699

British Library cataloguing data are available

©2008 Louis Paul. All rights reserved

No part of this book may be reproduced or transmitted in any form or by any means, electronic or mechanical, including photocopying or recording, or by any information storage and retrieval system, without permission in writing from the publisher.

On the cover: Madeline Smith in a
publicity photo from 1973 film *Live and Let Die*
(Danjaq Productions/Eon Productions/United Artists/MGM)

Manufactured in the United States of America

*McFarland & Company, Inc., Publishers
Box 611, Jefferson, North Carolina 28640
www.mcfarlandpub.com*

Acknowledgments

Quite a number of people have had a hand in helping me with this project, but a very special thanks should go to Kevin Clement of *Chiller Theatre*; it is due to his unswerving dedication to genre film fandom, his insistence that everyone have a good time at his *Chiller Theatre* conventions (now in their 17th year!), his help getting me access to some of his guests, and his friendship, that I have been able to meet and interview a number of the interviewees in this book. I wish to thank him for his kind permission in allowing me to reprint a number of interviews that appeared previously in *Chiller Theatre* magazine, albeit in shorter, edited versions. I also want to extend a warm thank you to Ted Bohus, Phil Palmieri, Kevin Collins, Tom Johnson, and especially, Tom Weaver. Another large thank you to Thomas Lisanti for all his hard work and assistance on the Richard Herd interview, and for help with the Lana Wood and Celeste Yarnall entries. I'm also grateful to Tom for inviting me to be his co-author on the book *Film Fatales*, thereby beginning my association with an American publishing company. Of course, I wish to thank the thirty-six interviewees for their time and kindness.

I also wish to thank my former fellow colleagues at the Billy Rose Theatre Collection at the New York Public Library for the Performing Arts at Lincoln Center. I worked there for nearly thirty years, and it is partly due to its print resources that I have managed to complete this project to my complete satisfaction. I want to extend a special thank you to Robert Taylor, curator of the Billy Rose Theatre Collection, and, in particular, Christopher Frith, and Rhony Dostaly, who have given me much support over the years.

This project contains interviews conducted over a large span of time. Some of these interviews have appeared, in edited form, in *Chiller Theatre* magazine, but the bulk of them have not been published anywhere. The earliest interview dates back to 1994, and the most recent was conducted during the winter of 2006, with some final questions asked of the interviewees done in 2006. Finally, this project also closes a personal chapter in my life, and I want to dedicate this book to all the companion animals, present and past (Bruce, Kaspar, Emma, Henry, Panda, Gizmo, Pumpkin, and Petey) who have given me much joy and love over the years; to my father, Walter; to my mother Catherine; and the largest dedication I leave for my wife, Wendy, without whom I would not be.

Contents

Acknowledgments v
Foreword by Tom Weaver 1
Introduction 3

Tom Atkins	7	Valerie Leon	164
Adrienne Barbeau	16	Richard Lynch	172
Michael Berryman	24	Charles Napier	180
Samson Burke	32	Linnea Quigley	186
David Carradine	40	Steve Railsback	192
Robert Davi	53	Tura Satana	199
Brad Dourif	63	John Saxon	204
Keir Dullea	68	Madeline Smith	214
Sid Haig	75	William Smith	221
Tippi Hedren	80	Austin Stoker	234
Gloria Hendry	90	Don Stroud	239
Richard Herd	98	Cary-Hiroyuki Tagawa	254
David Hess	110	Dee Wallace Stone	262
Brion James	117	Mel Welles	269
Brigitte Lahaie	128	Fred Williamson	279
Ed Lauter	137	William Windom	293
Christopher Lee	144	Lana Wood	300
Marrie Lee	157	Celeste Yarnall	307

Bibliography 317
Index 321

Foreword
by Tom Weaver

Before I begin, I should take a moment to explain, for the benefit of the 99-point-something percent of you who never heard of me, that Louis Paul asked me to write this intro because we're in the same line of (what we laughingly call) work: Interviewing stars and supporting players known for their horror, science fiction and exploitation movies. The difference is that I've tried to specialize in players of the 1930s, '40s and '50s—and Louis picks up just about at the period of time where I drop out. (We didn't plan it that way—I'm not sure either of us *could* have planned anything like that quite so well!)

Concentrating as I do on older pictures, my "problem" is that many (most) of the top stars and character people had joined the heavenly choir before I ever loaded my first audiotape into my earliest recorder; before my questions about those old pictures had been born, most of the answers had died. So it's with a bit of (I admit it) envy that I look at Louis' lineup, which includes so many of the top people in these genres from this more modern era. And I marvel at Louis' ability to get these folks to really open up about their films, themselves and, juiciest of all, each other. It's been a real education, reading up on all these cult people—as I'm sure it will be for anyone who doesn't live and breathe this stuff the way Louis does. "The blunter the better" is the way I like interviewees to come across, and he certainly achieved that with Robert Davi, David Carradine, Don Stroud, Fred Williamson and so many of the other first-rate interviews (IMHO) in here.

Now that it's the twenty-first century, even some of *these* people aren't what you'd call spring chickens any more; in fact, two of 'em, Brion James and Mel Welles, have already gone on to their rewards. But now some of their best stories are on paper, amidst all these others—and I sure hope Louis goes on to a volume 2 and 3 and more, because there's no time like the present to preserve old-time movie memories. At the rate Louis is going, pretty soon it won't be easy for future film historians to write about these folks and their movies without also writing about Louis and his pioneering efforts, and quoting from his interviews... which will put him right in the middle of the exploitation movie scene himself.

Well, what better place for a guy who "lives and breathes" this stuff?

Introduction

This long in gestation project began as a series of interviews that I conducted with filmmakers and actors and intended to use in my own (now long defunct) small-press publication, *Blood Times*. My correspondence with other writers, editors, and publishers enabled me to begin writing for their genre-related publications; I spent much of the latter portion of the eighties and well into the early nineties contributing to a wealth of journals including Craig Ledbetter's *Euro Trash Cinema*, Hugh Gallagher's *Draculina*, and *World of Fandom*. In the mid-nineties, I began to write for *Chiller Theatre* magazine, the bi-annual film journal published by Kevin Clement, who also runs the *Chiller Theatre* film conventions on the East Coast of the United States, and managed to gain access to the guests who attended the show. It was a personal pleasure to meet many of these people, as I had enjoyed their work so much over the years. When time constraints, and other matters, did not allow in-person interviews, some were conducted via email or via telephone, although I must say that there is nothing like an in-person interview, when a typically innocent question can provoke either an unguarded or surprising response, leading the interview into areas not considered beforehand. It's this kind of spontaneous detour that I love encountering, and as you read through these pieces, you'll find a wealth of these entertaining moments unfold before your eyes, as they had before mine.

As a journalist associated with a variety of magazines, I have been interviewing people for many years, and have whittled down the number of interviews to the thirty-six that appear in this book. Casual television fans and moviegoers, and baby boomers especially, will be familiar with many of the performers I interviewed for this book. While the majority of these players may have not had their names emblazoned on theater marquees for the world to see, some have. Thus, inside this volume, for example, you will read the words of Christopher Lee, a horror film icon, David Carradine, the many-times-over comeback kid, along those of Marrie Lee, a relatively obscure Asian actress whose action movies' cult following includes Quentin Tarantino, and Valerie Leon, a British sex symbol of the seventies who had a thriving career capped with a starring role in one of the best-regarded horror films to come out the UK. I also found that once a subject relaxed, we not only became engaged in a great casual discussion about their work, likes, and dislikes, but at times, they revealed what it was that drew them into the acting profession in the first place.

While a great many of the interviewees have also become quite adept at playing supporting roles, and some have become known as character actors, some appear in leading roles as well. This same truism goes for a leading actor who may, in a long and varied career, flit back and forth between leading, supporting, and character roles; some fine examples are the aforementioned David Carradine, Christopher Lee, and Steve Railsback. A great many of these performers have portrayed heroes as well as villains. In one episode of a television series or in a movie, any one of these actors could be your best friend, lover, or savior; in another they could be your worst nightmare. Most of the performers have often shown the public the depth of their talents by portraying evil in one role, and good in another. After all, it's all acting anyway, isn't it?

Aren't the movies a great entertainment? I personally find genre films more interesting than straight serious dramas, but I do not belittle those in any way. There is a good amount of that fare that I respect and enjoy watching, Although I get more of a kick out of viewing a good action, comedy, horror or sci-fi film, I do like everything; it does not matter to me, as long as the entertainment is good. A lot of my interviewees appeared in a variety of roles, in a variety of entertainments. While some of the interviewees have said that the praise that they have received for their work is something that they really appreciate, I have found others who had no idea that anyone even recalled their career highs, and in some instances, lows. Some of the subjects have retired from the profession, and some have moved onto other endeavors in life. There is also a bit of sadness involved with a project with the scope that this one has. For instance, shortly after our interview in 1999, Brion James passed away; and more recently, mere months after conversing via email about updating his profile, Mel Welles passed away in 2005. I believe that readers will be entertained by what they had to say.

Other marvelous encounters involve people like Don Stroud, a Hawaiian beachcomber and surfer who become a surfing double, then a stunt double, and then made his way to Hollywood and a career that lasted for decades, and Charles Napier, who had an early interest in acting, but took a detour to become a journalist for a number of years, then became a truck driver, before he returned to acting fulltime. There are stories about beautiful women like Tippi Hedren, Madeline Smith, and Dee Wallace Stone who all worked in modeling positions in a variety of media, and eventually found their way to stardom. There are stories about actors who have struggled mightily, some even overcoming different forms of resistance. You'll meet David Carradine who went from being part of the Hollywood studio system during his early television career, to becoming an outspoken outsider, blazing his own path in Hollywood. You'll no doubt be entertained by the many stories told by Fred Williamson, who still fights the system as he continues to turn out independently-financed feature films that have appealed not only to his action fanbase, but to minorities as well. Even familiar movie villain Cary-Hiroyuki Tagawa had to overcome what seemed like Hollywood's continual resistance to hiring Asian actors for anything but supporting roles, and forge a career that went from portraying a baddie in the entertaining *Mortal Kombat* (1995) to appearing in a major supporting role in the critically acclaimed *Memoirs of a Geisha* (2005).

You will laugh along with perennial movie tough guys Ed Lauter and William Smith, who have a humorous outlook on life despite collectively appearing hundreds of times as villains. Unfortunately, not all the stories told by these actors have rosy glows. Tura Satana managed to survive physical abuse and a wild career as a stripper before becoming known as one of the toughest women in cinema history in director Russ Meyer's *Faster Pussycat, Kill Kill*. Brigitte Lahaie, the French actress, answered a modeling ad in a newspaper and began a career as an erotic film actress that lasted for well over a decade, before garnering respectful and positive reviews for her work with the French pioneering genre filmmaker Jean Rollin.

For me, besides bringing these little-known life stories to the public via written words, the most pleasure was enjoyed in the occasional special moments that might occur while working on this project, which included spending time alone with movie icon Christopher Lee. At eighty-six years of age, and with over two hundred fifty feature film credits and countless other roles in television programs, he is still a formidable presence in person. Another fine moment that brings memories of smiles is when I was contacted via email, from Singapore, by retired actress Marrie Lee, who played the leading role in a trio of fabulously entertaining '70s action movies (as the wondrously named Cleopatra Wong).

So, dear readers, please enjoy this collection of interviews with people who were Bible salesmen, body builders, composers, dancers, florists, models, soldiers, songwriters, strippers, stunt people, surfers, teachers, and truck drivers. These were the heroes and villains of our childhood, and some of them continue to work today. They entertain, sometimes they inform, but at all times, they're like you and me: They just want to have fun doing what it is they love to do.

Tom Atkins

Tom Atkins is an actor whose name you may not readily recognize, but you'll recognize his face if you were or are a fan of genre films of the eighties. If you are such a person, then you have seen him in such fare as *The Fog* (1980), *Escape from New York* (1981), *Creepshow* (1982), *Halloween III: Season of the Witch* (1982), *Night of the Creeps* (1986), *Maniac Cop* (1988), and *Two Evil Eyes* (1990), among others.

Like most of his fellow actors of the period, when Atkins was starting out he enjoyed performing live onstage. After receiving a degree in Journalism from Duquesne University, and a short stint in the *New York Times* advertising department, Atkins graduated from New York's prestigious American Academy of Dramatic Arts in 1967. He appeared in a number of plays, making his Broadway debut in *Keep It in the Family* in 1967. He made his cinematic debut alongside Frank Sinatra in the hard-boiled police procedural *The Detective* (1968).

Atkins spent the next dozen years of his professional life performing in minor roles in films, in addition to some television and theater work (chiefly performing at the Long Wharf Theatre in New Haven, Connecticut, and with local Pittsburgh repertory companies). A friendship with Adrienne Barbeau led to his relationship with John Carpenter, who signed him to star in *The Fog* and *Halloween III: Season of the Witch*. Carpenter also directed Atkins, in a supporting role, in *Escape from New York*. Another Atkins friend, fellow Pittsburgh native George A. Romero, cast him in an important supporting role in *Creepshow* and in the role of a policeman in, *Two Evil Eyes* and *Bruiser*.

A stoic, personable leading man, Atkins helped save the day in *The Fog* and *Halloween III: Season of the Witch*. In the former, his character managed to be one of the few to make it to the end alive. As Jamie Lee Curtis' boyfriend, he looked danger in the face while battling an encroaching fog that harbored the undead specters of murdered seamen. *Variety* noted in its 1/16/80 review that the "[r]ugged Atkins is well cast [as the hero]."

In *Halloween III: Season of the Witch*, he finally became a leading man. As Dr. Daniel Challis, investigating the case of a patient murdered in his hospital, Atkins pairs with Stacy Nelkin, who portrays the daughter of his patient. (Nelkin was the real-life inspiration for Mariel Hemingway's character in Woody Allen's *Manhattan*, as she and Allen had a much-publicized affair prior to that film.) Journeying to the quiet town of Santa Mira (home of Silver Shamrock, a Halloween novelty company), Atkins and Nelkin are horrified to learn that the owner of the novelty company, Conal Cochran (Dan O'Herlihy), is planning to use Halloween masks and black magic as one last great, macabre trick on children on Halloween. Although the character of seemingly unstoppable psychopathic killer, Michael Myers, was absent from this third installment of the series, genre fans were provided with a twist-laden thriller.

The 1986 film *Night of the Creeps* forever cemented Atkins as a genre fan favorite; he starred as a smirking, quip-spouting policeman investigating an alien invasion, zombies, and various other colorful oddities in a campus town packed with prankster students and nubile teens. Directed by Fred Dekker (*The Monster Squad*), *Night of the Creeps* was a knowing salute to the horror and sci-fi films of the fifties through the seventies, with Atkins delivering such then and now prized one-liners. His character, Detective Ray Cameron (notably based on the two-fisted western action star Rod Cameron whose career peak was in the forties and fifties), has much fun in the face of danger. Every time he answers the phone he says "Thrill me" as if waiting for someone to do just that. The director upped the cult factor ante by having supporting actors playing detective characters named Raimi and Landis, the actual names of cult favorite directors Sam Raimi (*The Evil Dead* series, *Spider-Man* 1–3) and John Landis (*An American Werewolf in London*, *The Blues Brothers*, etc.); he also had others in the cast sport the surnames Carpenter, Cronenberg, Romero and so on, as a tribute to other genre directors.

Although *Night of the Creeps* failed at the box-office, it became a major cult movie favorite, and it cries out for the full special features treatment on DVD. At the time of *Night of the Creeps'* theatrical release, Atkins related to *Fangoria* magazine (October 1986), that he was ripe for success as a horror leading man. "After doing [*Creeps*], I decided I wanted to be the next Vincent Price ... and that I [hoped I] would actively begin pursuing roles in horror films." *Variety* remarked (09/03/86), "Atkins' cynical remarks throughout the pic are the only comic relief."

Unfortunately for genre film cineastes, Atkins subsequently became stuck in character actor roles in movies, and his appearances on the big screen became less frequent. On television, he found steady work portraying supporting characters on the much-beloved series *Baretta*, *Harry-O* and *Quincy*. For a time he was a semi-regular on *The Rockford Files*, and returned to his supporting role during that show's brief incarnation as TV movie-of-the-week specials (1996 and 1999).

Nowadays, Tom Atkins' true love is the theater. Although he has appeared in a few episodes of the critical hit *Oz*, it is in the theater, onstage, live, and in the flesh, before an audience, where you can find him deriving the greatest satisfaction from plying his craft. In fact, it is the one place where his peers have justly recognized him. In 1973, he won the coveted Drama Desk Award for his performance in the Broadway production *The Changing Room*, about a rugby league team in the north of England. Although also nominated for the Tony award, he lost out to *Changing Room* co-star John Lithgow.

Atkins is currently involved in bringing his one-man show, *The Chief*, once again to Pittsburgh theater audiences. A play that tells the story of Pittsburgh and NFL legend Art Rooney, Sr., *The Chief* set box office records for ticket sales and met with great acclaim in its November 2003 world premiere at the Pittsburgh Public Theater. When it returned in December 2004 for a 17-performance run, the community response was again incredibly enthusiastic. *The Chief* was once again scheduled to return to Pittsburgh theaters in the winter of 2006.

Q: One of your very first film roles was in *The Detective* (1968) with Frank Sinatra...

Tom Atkins: That was the first film I ever worked. I think it was made in 1967 or

1968, somewhere around that time. We shot it in New York and I played a rookie cop. It was great to meet Sinatra and to get to work with him, as briefly as I did in the film. I had to audition for it with him. In addition, it was, to say the very least, very intimidating. To walk in a room and there is Frank Sinatra. But it went well. It rather played into the scenes we had together, my character being intimidated because he [Sinatra] was chewing me out for shooting somebody in a car that I was not supposed to have shot. My character thought that he was reaching for a gun, but he was reaching for his driver's license in the glove compartment. There were six black men in the car, and I shot the driver. Sinatra was chewing me out, so it was

Tom Atkins and Stacey Nelkin as pictured on the DVD release of *Halloween III: Season of the Witch* (1982) (Universal Pictures).

somewhat easy to play intimidated and fearful of him. It was great fun, and I really enjoyed it.

Q: Prior to that, you were primarily an actor on the stage.

Atkins: And I still am. Actually, appearing in *The Detective* was right at the beginning of my career, after my first time performing on Broadway. I had hardly started performing live on the stage. I had just got out of the American Academy of Dramatic Arts in 1967. The first audition I went on was a Broadway-bound show called *Keep It in the Family*, with Maureen O'Sullivan. It only ran four days. We had a wonderful time rehearsing that show, and playing up in Boston at the old Colonial theatre... a gorgeous place, I love Boston.

Keep It in the Family opened and closed in four days. The reviews were really bad in New York. They were good in Boston, but bad in New York. The then-influential theater critic Clive Barnes did not like it in particular ... and we folded. I was out of work, and out of an apartment, and I didn't know what the hell I was going to do, but I ended up doing *The Detective* in the fall, and then going up to the Long Wharf Theatre in New Haven. I ended up there for six seasons. Nevertheless, I would come into New York and we did things in-between. Years later, when we started *The Changing Room* in New Haven, at the Long Wharf Theatre, it was an American premiere; it had never been done over here before. It was a play by David Storey that had never been performed in America.

Q: I recall that it had a very large cast.

Atkins: There were something like twenty-two guys in it, and not one woman. The cast included the character of the owner of the team and his cohort, who were the two oldest actors, and the rest of the cast were the rugby players who I think were all in their thirties. George Hearn and John Lithgow were in it, it was a really good cast. It was great fun.

Q: Getting back to your work in movies, what can you recall about working in *The Ninth Configuration*, the film directed by *Exorcist* author William Peter Blatty?

Atkins: That movie was made in 1978, and filmed over in Budapest, Hungary. It was wacko! That was one of the most bizarre work experiences I have ever had in my life. If they had made a movie of the making of that movie, *that* movie would have been much better than the movie that they had ended up with. Honest to God, it is the truth. It was just crazy. Like *The Changing Room*, it had another large cast, about twenty guys. But unlike the play, there were a couple of women in it. Blatty's wife played a part in it, I think, and ended up leaving him. Blatty took twenty guys to Hungary for two and a half months even if they had a part which meant that they would only work a week. Blatty took everybody over there for a long, long time. A lot of the guys thought, "It's great. I'll go to Prague on my days off. I'll go to Moscow. I'll travel all over Europe...." But Blatty could not decide until midnight the night before what he was going to shoot the next day. So, as an actor, you could never plan to go anywhere. You were stuck there. Eventually, he ended up with a lot of really drunk actors, who did not want to work anymore. Many of them, also did not want to come out of their hotel rooms for the bus to take us to the castle location. The bus would arrive at six o'clock every morning to take everybody to the location. Three guys would have a few scenes in a room, but Blatty would call everybody. We would sit around outside the room where the scene was shot, in costume, just in case he decided to shoot something you were in.

Q: How did you become involved with John Carpenter?

Atkins: Through Adrienne Barbeau. She was dating John and she and I were already pals. She, my former wife, and some other people were all really good friends at that time. Adrienne was dating him, and we all went together to a screening of his movie, *Halloween*, in Hollywood, at the Directors Guild theatre. My wife, Adrienne, and another woman friend were on all sides of me with their hands in front of their eyes saying, "Can I look, can I look...?" I would say, "Yeah, yeah, it's OK to look." When it was over, my wife and her friend said, "It was so scary. We cannot let Adrienne marry that person... he is too weird." That is how I got involved with him, through Adrienne knowing him.

Q: What do you recall about the making of *The Fog*?

Atkins: It was wonderful, it was great. Jamie Lee Curtis was such a fresh young face on the scene; she was straight out of *Halloween*. Meeting her and her mom [Janet Leigh], it was great. We all went together to the locations in Inverness, California. We ended up shooting in a lot of scenic places, in Inverness, Petaluma, and Bodega Bay, where Hitchcock shot *The Birds*. It was all a great time.

Q: How did you deal with the May-December romance with Jamie Lee Curtis, as scripted? You were obviously a little older than she was at the time.

Atkins: Oh yeah. I think she was maybe nineteen or something like that. I was probably thirty-six. It was sweet to work with her, she was wide open to a lot of things and so was I, and we had a wonderful time. It was a great little movie.

Q: Your next genre appearance was in *Escape from New York*, where you had a smaller role, do you recall anything about working on that film, and appearing with Lee Van Cleef?

Atkins: Yes, I recall working with Lee Van Cleef. We shot most of our scenes in a jet propulsion lab out in Pasadena, California. This place had all this kind of equipment stuff, and gadget-type things there ... it was a stand-in, supposedly, for the futuristic base for the prison. The exterior of that, the prison, was shot out in Sepulveda Dam near San Fernando Valley. It had a great look to it, that movie; it was terrific the way it all came together. John also loved helicopters. He became a helicopter pilot, either while we doing that film or just afterwards. Anyway, in *Escape from New York* he had helicopters coming in and taking off while we were shooting the exteriors, to give the film a certain militaristic look. One of the things I remember most about that movie is the way we grabbed one particular shot. For some reason, I was in New York and he had set it up where if I had just happened to be in New York, that he might want to do an on-location pick-up shot for the movie. So, he called me, while I was in New York, and he said, "You're going to be in New York during such and such a time?" And, I said, "Yeah, that's right." Well, John said, "I want to grab a shot to open the film with the Statue of Liberty in the background, and you coming down the steps talking on the phone ... as if that's part of the base for the prison...." It turned out to be a wonderful shot. Not exactly spur-of-the-moment, but a grab-it-pretty-quick kind of thing, and it was a lot of fun too.

Q: *Halloween III: Season of the Witch* was a film that broke from the usual format of the *Halloween* series because it was an original film that did not follow the storyline of the previous two movies in the series. You had a powerful leading man part.

Atkins: John Carpenter and Debra Hill produced it, John wrote the score for it, Tommy Lee Wallace directed it; he had been John's right hand man for years before that. It was a great working experience; I had a lot of fun working on that film. I think it was John's intent when he started [the *Halloween* series], not to have the character of Michael Myers be in every *Halloween* movie, but to make a movie for every Halloween, and if you cannot make a movie for every Halloween, to have every *Halloween* movie be different, with a different story. But the first two films with Michael Myers went so over the top as far as success is concerned that after they did *Halloween III*, they went back to the Myers character for the rest of the series. I also remember Stacy Nelkin coming into the room to audition for her role. John and Tommy said, "Tom, we want you to come out to help audition five or six girls today. They're the final ones that we have selected. We want you to read some scenes with them." So I did, I showed up to read scenes with the actresses. Stacy Nelkin walked into the room, and she sat down and she read with us, and she thanked us, and left. We all sat around going, "We don't need to see anybody else because she is the one." Her audition was that good. She was terrific in that film. Nobody knows where she is anymore. I cannot figure out what happened to her.

Q: Miss Nelkin was a very pretty young woman, and it is interesting because in this film too, they cast you as the slightly older, world-weary–appearing leading man with an obviously younger leading woman. It worked out that way in *The Fog*, and the formula was repeated for *Halloween III*. In *The Fog*, Jamie Lee Curtis was a wanderer and you became the protector and then the lover. In *Halloween III* Stacy Nelkin was searching for her father's killer, you became the protector, and then the lover... but it works.

Atkins: It did, it did.

Q: I have to ask about *Night of the Creeps*, which has a cult following.

Atkins: That is my favorite, that is my very favorite role. I had more fun doing that than I had doing anything else. It has all the best lines in it: "I've got good news and bad news for you girls. The good news is that your dates are here. The bad news is that they're dead." And "Thrill Me," which I say every time my character answers the phone. I had the best time of my life doing that film. We shot it all over Los Angeles; I got to drive in this wonderful old Ford '49 Mercury. My character was that of a police officer who had a girl, only she died on me, or something, when my character was younger. That movie also had a young terrific director named Fred Dekker who filmed it. Unfortunately, it was not a commercial success, it really did not do that well, and I guess that is why he did not get much work after that.

Q: That movie almost instantly became a cult favorite when it was released. It has not appeared on DVD. It would certainly be welcome... of course with a Tom Atkins audio commentary!

Atkins: It should be put on DVD, because right now you cannot get it anywhere. I would love to do the audio commentary on that one.

Q: *Lethal Weapon* was your next film.

Atkins: Oh, I've got a story about *Lethal Weapon* for you. Fred Dekker directed *Night of the Creeps*, and while we were shooting that film, this kid, Shane Black, a friend of Fred's, kept hanging around the set. This kid always looked like he had a cloud over his head, always dark, always gloomy. He was hanging around drinking coffee, smoking cigarettes, watching us shoot, and I said to Fred, "Who is this guy?" He said, "Shane Black, he's a friend of mine. He has written a movie that they are thinking of doing over at Warner Bros. maybe, they are not sure. Would you want to read it?" I said, "Sure, I'd love to read it." The movie was *Lethal Weapon*, and the script was great. I said, "Oh man, that's terrific, I would love to play that crazy cop part." Well, that did not happen because Warner Bros. green-lit the film and decided to go big-budget all the way. They hired Mel Gibson, they hired Danny Glover, but then they invited me to play a small role as one of the characters that is killed in it, and it is nice that Shane Black remembered me. I only had two scenes, but I got work out of that because everybody has seen that movie at least ten times. It was a huge success for Warner Bros.

Q: And there were three sequels.

Atkins: Unfortunately Gary Busey killed me in the first one.

Q: What can you recall about director William Lustig's film *Maniac Cop*?

Atkins: There was an odd experience. It seemed to be shot at night all the time. I got killed a third of the way through the movie. I thought, "Shit, what's up with that? I don't mind getting killed, but let them throw me out of the window at the end but not so early on...."

Q: The director did a similar thing by killing off the leads to that film at the very beginning of one of the *Maniac Cop* sequels. Afterwards, you worked with George A. Romero in *Two Evil Eyes*.

Atkins: He is a Pittsburgh guy, I am a Pittsburgh guy, and we are good friends. I really love working with him. I am only sorry that I do not get enough chances to do it. He is just finishing off a new movie now in Toronto, *Land of the Dead*. He has been working on it for a long time, and I sure hope that this one is a big hit for him.

Q: You worked with him again in *Bruiser*.

Atkins: The very first time that I worked for him, was in *Creepshow*. It was a small part at the very beginning, and at the very end. I knew he had lived in Pittsburgh, and I had lived in Pittsburgh my whole life, when I met him in LA to audition for *Creepshow*. I said to him, "I would really like to play that guy who has shit growing all over him from out in the swamp." He said, "I can't. Stephen King's going to play that part." I said, "Just because he wrote it? He gets to do it?" But he said, "Will you do me a favor and play the dad who appears in the beginning and at the end with this young boy character, the father-and-son bookend [scenes]?" I said, "Sure, sure, I'd love to." It ended up being Stephen King's real-life son, Joey, who played the boy, and I had to hit him in the scene. Stephen King said, "Well, do what you have to do." Well, I know my way around in a scene, and I knew I was going to make some kind of contact with his face to make it look more real. It was a fun scene to do.

Bruiser was the last time I worked with George, up in Toronto. It was a departure for him, something a little different. I do not think the movie worked quite the way he hoped it would. It was about a man whose face was nothing but a blank, a mysterious blank, who used this anonymity to kill people. I kind of wish that they were able to make the face, the mask, better. I think it somehow was a special effect thing that needed to happen differently; that somehow, the way it works onscreen was not quite the way it was supposed to work.

Q: You worked with Bruce Willis in *Striking Distance*.

Atkins: Yeah, they came to Pittsburgh to film that movie. I played Willis' Uncle Fred in that. We had a big, heartfelt embrace in that movie. It was a scene set at a big party, where he has not seen me for a while. I played the brother of his father who just died. You do not always get a chance to work near where you live, and it was a pleasure to be able to get up and go to work near where I live and at the end of the day, drive home. It also turned out to be a longer shoot than originally intended. It was supposed to be a two-week job, and it probably should not have even been that long, but it rained very hard that summer, and it turned into a six-week job, which was a nice payday for me and I had a pleasant time. Dennis Farina was in it too; we had a good time together, got to know each other. Then there was Tom Sizemore, oh Jesus, Tom Sizemore. I don't know if he still *is*, but he was great fun to work with because you never knew what the hell he was going to do when he showed up on the set. We had to do this scene that caused many local Pittsburghers to get pissed off at the movie company because the filmmakers had to do this scene where the three rivers come together, and there's a big party, and everyone is drunk and wants to come salute each other, and Tom Sizemore had to get up on a table and make a speech with fireworks going off behind him. You know the thing with making movies? Everything takes time. It was supposed to happen when it got dark, around dusk, but it ended up happening sometime between two and four in the morning. Since his character was supposed to be drunk giving his speech, he got drunk and tried to give the speech. Dennis and I kept grabbing his leg when he got on the table ... he kept falling off the table, getting back up on the table. Then, they were shooting off the fireworks ... it was a little insane, but we all had such a great time. The people who lived up on Mt. Washington, near where the movie was shot, were very angry, many people were angry, because of the late night fireworks. But it was all in good fun in the end. I loved Rowdy Herrington, the director; he was good to work with, but I think he had some power struggle troubles with Bruce, and he didn't quite get the movie he wanted either.

Tom Atkins (left) and the author, October 2004.

Q: Have there been any feature film roles of late that I am not aware of?

Atkins: I have not done any feature films since I worked on *Bruiser* with George Romero. Film, television, and such, they do not invite me because I am based on the East Coast. I do not go looking for the roles either. I don't hang out in New York or LA, but that's not to say I don't work at all in those mediums. I did work on a couple of episodes of *Oz* recently.

Q: In the eighties, you were prominently featured in a number of films that did good box-office business or at the very least, became cult favorites. Why have we not seen Tom Atkins in more movies?

Atkins: If you are based in LA or in New York, you have a better chance of getting roles, because you are there, and you can go in and meet with the people. Sometime around 1985, I moved back to Pittsburgh, and then I got a call to come out to Hollywood to do *Night of the Creeps*. Afterwards, I went back to Pittsburgh, then I got a call to do *Lethal Weapon*, then I went back to Pittsburgh. For a while, I was going back and forth, and then I finally just stayed. However, occasionally, they do invite me to audition or cast me for a role. I did a couple of *Rockford Files* reunion television movies with James Garner, one of the sweetest and best people in the business, without a doubt. I have been doing a one-man play in Pittsburgh off and on for a while now. It is about the sports legend Art Rooney. He is the man who started the Pittsburgh Steelers in 1933, and his family has owned them ever since. It is a wonderful play and I have a great time doing it. The title is *The Chief*, because that is what they called him.

Credits: 1968: *The Detective*; 1970: *Where's Poppa?*; *The Owl and the Pussycat* (uncredited); 1974: *Get Christie Love: Market for Murder* (09/11/74) (television); *Harry-O* (television); *Rhoda: Pop Goes the Question* (10/14/74) (television); *The Rockford Files* (television); 1975: *Miles to Go Before I Sleep* (television); *The Rockford Files* (television); *The Rookies: Lamb to the Slaughter* (09/09/75) (television); 1976: *The Rockford Files* (television); *Serpico* (television); *Serpico: The Deadly Game* (television); *Special Delivery*; *Visions: Pennsylvania Lynch* (12/09/76) (television); 1977: *Baretta: It Goes With the Job* (12/21/77) (television); *Tarantulas: The Deadly Cargo* (television); 1978: *A Death in Canaan* (television); 1979: *Lou Grant:*

Fire (01/08/79) (television); 1980: *The Fog* (a.k.a. *John Carpenter's The Fog*); *The Ninth Configuration* (a.k.a. *Twinkle, Twinkle Killer Kane*); *Power* (television); *Skag* (television); 1981: *Escape from New York* (a.k.a. *John Carpenter's Escape from New York*); *Lou Grant: Strike* (02/16/81), *Drifters* (12/14/81) (television); *Sherlock Holmes* (a.k.a. *Sherlock Holmes: The Strange Case of Alice Faulkner*) (television); 1982: *Creepshow*; *Desperate Lives* (television); *Halloween III: Season of the Witch*; *M*A*S*H: The Tooth Shall Set You Free* (02/08/82) (television); *Quincy: Guns Don't Lie* (01/13/82), *The Last of the Leadbottom* (04/28/82) (television); *Skeezer* (television); 1983: *Murder Me, Murder You* (a.k.a. *Mickey Spillane's Mike Hammer: Murder Me, Murder You*) (television); *St. Elsewhere: Dog Day Hospital* (03/22/83) (television); 1984: *T.J. Hooker: Hooker's Run* (02/04/84) (television); 1985: *The Fall Guy: Skip Family Robinson* (03/06/85) (television); *The New Kids* (a.k.a. *Striking Back*); 1986: *Alfred Hitchcock Presents: Beast in View* (01/19/86) (television); *The Equalizer: Pretenders* (04/08/86) (television); *Night of the Creeps*; *Spenser: For Hire: White Knight* (10/18/86) (television); *Stingray: Sometimes You Gotta' Sing the Blues* (04/08/86) (television); 1987: *Lethal Weapon*; *A Stranger Waits* (television); 1988: *Lemmon Sky* (television); *Maniac Cop*; 1989: *Dead Man Out*; *The Heist*; 1990: *Two Evil Eyes* (a.k.a. *Due Occhi Diabolici* a.k.a. *The Facts in the Case of M. Valdemar*) [Italy-U.S.]; 1991: *Cry in the Wild: The Taking of Peggy Ann* (television); 1992: *Bob Roberts*; *What She Doesn't Know* (television); 1993: *Striking Distance*; *Sworn to Vengeance* (television); *Walker, Texas Ranger: Night of the Gladiator* (12/11/93) (television); 1996: *Dying to Be Perfect: The Ellen Hart Pena Story* (television); *The Rockford Files: If the Frame Fits...* (television); *Xena: Warrior Princess: Ties That Bind* (04/29/96) (television); 1997: *The Equalizer: Blood & Wine: Part 1/ Part 2* (09/23/97) (television); *Xena: Warrior Princess: The Furies* (09/29/97) (television); 1998: *Homicide: Life on the Street: The 20% Solution* (10/30/98) (television); 1999: *The Rockford Files: If It Bleeds... It Leads* (television); 2000: *Bruiser* [Canada-France]; 2001: *Out of the Black* (a.k.a. *Buried Lies*) (video); 2003: *Law & Order: Criminal Intent: Cold Comfort* (03/30/03) (television); *Oz: See No Evil, Hear No Evil, Smell No Evil* (01/12/03), *Sonata da Oz* (01/19/03) (television); 2004: *The Jury: Mail Order Mystery* (06/15/04); 2007: *Small Time Crime*.

Adrienne Barbeau

Adrienne Barbeau was born in Sacramento, California on June 11, 1945. The actress' film, television, stage, and recording credits span nearly forty years, and the still sprightly Ady, as her close friends lovingly call her, shows no signs of easing up her workload.

While Barbeau was still attending pre-school, she was encouraged by her mother to get a musical education. She was soon taking ballet lessons (at age three), and began vocal lessons a few years later. By the time she was in high school, music and dancing were a way of life for her and she never considered any other career. She began her professional performing career in 1963 with the San Jose Civic Light Opera Company; in 1968 she made her Broadway debut in *Fiddler on the Roof* alongside Bette Midler. She received a Tony award nomination for her performance in the role of Rizzo in the original Broadway run of *Grease* (1972), which led to her television career. She essayed the role of Carol, Bea Arthur's wisecracking daughter, in the hit series *Maude* (1972–1978).

Genre fans know the 5'5" actress primarily for her performances in such fare as John Carpenter's* *Someone's Watching Me!* (1978), *The Fog* (1980), and *Escape from New York* (1981), Wes Craven's *Swamp Thing* (1982), and George A. Romero's *Creepshow* (1983), and *Two Evil Eyes* (1990). On video, Barbeau jumped atop a fast motorcycle, with automatic weapons in hand, to save teens from demonic nuns in the camp, but fun horror-action film *The Convent* (2000). Barbeau even managed to rack up a number of notable reviews for her genre efforts. In a 3/24/82 *Variety* review of the film *Swamp Thing*, the journalist tapped into that special something that made Adrienne Barbeau work as a genre film icon: "The film's only asset for adult audiences is Adrienne Barbeau who is thoroughly believable and a feisty, rough 'n' tumble heroine, able to beat up most bad guys or outrun them through the swamp.... She also provides the necessary pulchritude for frequent 'damsel in distress' scenes."

In recent years, television audiences saw her in a recurring role on *The Drew Carey Show* (1998–2004) and on the HBO series *Carnivàle* (2003–2005), where she played the mature, still voluptuous, and definitely sinister snake charmer, Ruthie. More recently, Barbeau returned to the stage in the one-woman show, *The Property Known as Judy Garland*.

Q: How did you get your start in acting?

Adrienne Barbeau: When I came to New York, I was a struggling barmaid in a place just off Broadway on 49th Street. I was only 19 years old, and I did not know enough to be scared. There was this customer, a nice man. He would tip me well, and one night he

---

*She married Carpenter in 1979, and they divorced in 1984.

Bette Midler and Barbeau as sisters in an early, 1968 version of the hit musical *Fiddler on the Roof* (courtesy The Billy Rose Theatre Collection, The New York Public Library for the Performing Arts, Astor, Lenox and Tilden Foundations).

Barbeau as Bea Arthur's daughter in the smash seventies sitcom, *Maude*.

said he had been to the ballet. I had never been to the ballet, and said that I would have loved to have gone. He later returned with a ticket. That was very nice of him. He was Armenian, and I am of Armenian heritage. It was a very nice thing of him to do. Then, I believe it may have been 1964 or so, my friend sent me a Christmas card. Inside were $300 in checks and $300 in stocks. I tried to return the money, but he just wanted to help me out. He said that when his family had come from the old country, that an Armenian couple had tried to help him and his wife out, and that this was his way of returning the favor. I took the money and enrolled in acting school. I sent him cards, but after a while, they came back to me, which was sad at the time, but I will always be thankful to him.

Q: How did you come to appear in the hit television show *Maude*?

Barbeau: Norman Lear had seen me perform onstage in *Grease*, and was very taken with me. I was still performing in the show when he proposed the role of Carol in his new show *Maude*. I auditioned for him by memorizing three scenes that they gave me to read. I guess that impressed him, and they offered me the part. I moved to California and the rest is history. I think the one thing that helped was that Carol, my character on *Maude*, was not so very specific, or so much a character, a *type* let's say. She was written straight, and that's the way I played her. People who have had to play very strong or specific characters, like Sally Struthers did in *All in the Family*, had to overcome even more than I. Somewhere around the third year of doing *Maude*, I started to appear in more television movies, and other series, and for a while, I tried to only accept dramatic work, non-comedic roles. To me, that was a good way of helping to make people aware that I [could do more than just] comedy.

Q: There was a very famous poster of you in the seventies, and for a time, it seemed like every other male I knew had it on his bedroom or office wall....

Barbeau: I had appeared in an Off-Off-Broadway show called *Stag Movies*. It was an early role for me, a musical revue that spoofed the porno industry of the time. Anyway, the role called for some nudity, and we had to pose for some photos for the theatrical programs, publicity, whatever. Years later, some of those shots got out ... and it haunted me. I did not care for the way I looked back then. Frankly, I thought the pictures of me were ugly. So, I evened the score, somewhat, by posing in what I thought was a mildly sugges-

Adrienne Barbeau (left) in a photo from *The Fog* (Avco Embassy Pictures) (1980) with director John Carpenter, Jamie Lee Curtis and Janet Leigh.

tive manner, clothed of course, in a purple merry-widow corset type of thing, and I found that that poster nearly outsold the Farrah Fawcett, Cheryl Ladd, Suzanne Somers, and Cheryl Tiegs posters of the day. I wanted to show America a new image of myself. I wanted to say that I am not the girl next door, that I am me. It was the seventies.... I had been on *Maude* for five seasons, and I wanted to capitalize on my sensuality. I had great fun with that poster, and it became one of the best-selling posters right behind those women. You know, I did attempt to follow that poster with another idea. I posed, kind of like a sexy All-American girl, just wearing a *Rocky* t-shirt. But I did not like the background, so it did not happen after all. I guess that one successful poster was bound to be the big hit that it was for many reasons.

Q: How did you meet John Carpenter and get the opportunity to star in his television thriller *Someone's Watching Me!*?

Barbeau: I received a script for a television movie to be called *High Rise*. It was originally going to star Lauren Hutton, and it struck me, at the time, as one of the best scripts for television that I had ever read. Then, I was offered the leading role, and I went to meet the director; it was John. I liked him right away, and then I learned he already had a friend, so I never acknowledged any attraction, and did everything possible to make him unattractive in my mind. We worked together for several weeks, never really saying much to each other. At the end of the shoot, I was on my way to New York and he said, "When you come back to California, please give me a call. I have something I want to discuss with you." I thought he had another script with a role in mind for me. I came back and called, and he took me out to dinner and told me had fallen in love with me... the rest is history.

Q: What can you recall about the production of *The Fog*?

Barbeau: I believe that *The Fog* was a fine fun film for me. It was, after all, my first feature film as a leading actress. I also had the advantage of having that role [radio DJ Stevie Wayne] written expressly for me. I had of course worked in television before in leading roles, but yes, that was my very first appearance in a feature film, and I owe it all to John.

Q: Can you recall anything specific about the production of that film?

Barbeau: We filmed *The Fog* in an actual lighthouse located in Inverness, California, just north of San Francisco. We loved that part of the country. As a matter of fact, so much so that, after the film was completed, John and I bought a house there. Actually, most of my scenes were filmed on a set. Of course, the exteriors were at the lighthouse, which meant they had to lug all the equipment up and down something like 370 steps a day, several times a day, but it is a beautiful place, Inverness. I still go back there whenever I can.

Q: What can you recall about the making of *Escape from New York*?

Barbeau: I really do not think of *Escape from New York* as a science fiction film. It is an action picture. I enjoy action pictures, and maybe that is one reason why I had so much fun on *Swamp Thing*... they handed me a special effect M-16, I had a really good time lugging that thing around, but with that weapon in my hands, I felt like I was born for it.

Q: In Wes Craven's *Swamp Thing*, you were not only the damsel in distress, but you gave the villains their just deserts when it came time to protect yourself. It appears to have been an arduous low-budget production.

Barbeau: In *Swamp Thing*, my character was really physical. I fired guns, beat up 200-pound men; I loved that kind of role. In those years I was quite sturdy, still am. I could handle it well. It was probably my Armenian heritage coming to the forefront. Still, on that film there were some hard workdays. I would wake up in the middle of the night, unable to sleep because of the pain of being tossed around so much. My character was chased through fields, knocked to the ground, dragged into dungeons, and almost drowned in a murky swamp... naked. In addition, it was so humid, the heat, the insects.... But despite some production problems like not enough money, and some studio-enforced cuts, I think it is still a fun movie.

Q: What can you recall about working with George A. Romero?

Barbeau: In *Creepshow*, the George Romero–Stephen King film, I got to play a real bitch, someone who was always drunk and screeching. Hal Holbrook played my husband, and his character derived pleasure by daydreaming of ways to do me in. When his friend, Fritz Weaver, discovered an ancient monster in an old crate, Hal offered to take care of it for him ... after the monster took care of me. My character was just so outrageous in that thing. Funny thing, but I was recently asked what my favorite role is, and I had to think ... it might be in that film, as Billie.

Q: What was it like to work for John Carpenter as a director?

Barbeau: I would work with John and George Romeo again, any time. As directors, each one of them is wonderful.

Q: The action-horror movie *The Convent* seemed to have instant cult status stamped all over it. The story concerned a group of college students who break into an abandoned convent, which become possessed by demonic nuns. Your character saves the day on a motorcycle, armed with high-powered weapons.

Barbeau: I felt like it was my very own tribute to *Escape from New York*. Although it was a low-budget production, I felt it had a lot of talent connected to it, originality, and character. Sometimes, I would feel like Snake Plissken [Kurt Russell's character in *Escape from New York*], armed with another M-16 rifle. I'm sorry it didn't get a theatrical release because I always believed it to be a decent little film, a good picture, and a lot of fun.

Q: What can you tell me about your appearance on the HBO series *Carnivàle*?

Barbeau: I got a call for an audition by the producers. There was a role that I was somewhat interested in, the Tarot reader, but the producers suggested another part for me. I really did not know much about the show other than it took place in the thirties and that it something to do with Carnival workers... not that there was some mystical quality to it all. Finally, I read for the part of Ruthie, the snake charmer. I heard nothing for weeks, and then I received a call, and they told me that I had gotten the part... snakes and all. I love the part of Ruthie; it was such an incredible opportunity. Hardly anyone is writing such sensual and mysterious material for women my age. The way they write these scripts, for this show, I never know where my character is going. We usually got the scripts two, three weeks in advance of a shoot, then we do a reading with everyone involved, and then we go do the shoot. It's an interesting way to work, and even for television, I don't recall working this way before. But it keeps me sharp, and it makes my character still ... haunting. I do think that it is a strange show however, and something that can only be done on cable television. People seem to be catching on with the second season, it is becoming quite a cult phenomenon, and the third season... well, who knows how well that would do.

Q: Do you like performing in genre films?

Barbeau: No, not exceptionally. I really enjoy spy films, action movies. To be honest, I am not a big fan of horror films... funny, eh? And I was married to one of the greatest horror film directors.

Q: What have you been up to lately, besides appearing on *Carnivàle*?

Barbeau: Well, I had completed a stint doing voiceover work for animated shows for television. I was the voice of the Catwoman in a number of programs for the *Batman* series; I narrated the IMAX nature movie *The Living Sea*, and have just released a CD.

Q: What kind of music can we expect to hear on that?

Barbeau: Blues, jazz, and pop tunes. I perform in concert across the country when I can. I have done dates in West Coast venues like Harrah's in Las Vegas, the Hollywood Roosevelt Hotel, the Gardenia and the Moonlight Tango Cafe in Los Angeles.

Q: Will you be appearing in any more genre product in the near future?

Barbeau: I have just finished work on a horror film—see, there I go again—called *The Unholy*. It is an independent production, and I play a character in a family that gets involved in time travel, and invisibility experiments conducted by the U.S. government. We shot it in New York, in Queens actually, during one of the more recent East Coast cold spells. In fact, a blizzard struck the city when we were shooting exteriors out on Long Island, but we were all troupers. Then, I have a two-character play, which we are in preproduction on. My husband, Billy Van Zandt, wrote it and it is based on the life of Judy Garland, and it is called *The Property Known as Judy Garland*. It's about the very last performance that Judy Garland gave, in Copenhagen, in 1969. I hope to be performing that onstage in New York sometime soon. Either that, or it may be filmed for television, and then be performed onstage. I also have a memoir titled *There Are Worse Things That I Could Do*. Besides Cody, whose father is John, I had given birth in recent years [in 1997, at age fifty-two!] to two other boys, William and Walker, so I'm also a fulltime mom.

Credits: 1972: *Maude* (television); 1976: *The Great Houdini*; *Having Babies* (a.k.a. *Giving Birth*); 1977: *Eight Is Enough: Turnabout* (04/12/77) (television); *Hallmark Hall of Fame: Have I Got a Christmas for You* (12/16/77) (television); *Quincy: Let Me Light the Way* (05/27/77); *Red Alert* (television); 1978: *Crash* (a.k.a. *Crash of Flight 401*); *The Love Boat: Hollywood Royalty/The Caper/The Eyes of Love/The Masquerade Part 1/The Masquerade Part 2* (01/12/78) (television); *Return to Fantasy Island* (television); *Someone's Watching Me!* (a.k.a. *High Rise*) (television); 1979: *The Darker Side of Terror* (television); *Fantasy Island: The Pug/Class of '69* (11/24/79) (television); 1980: *The Fog* (a.k.a. *John Carpenter's The Fog*); *Top of the Hill* (television); *Tourist* (television); *Valentine: Magic on Love Island* (television); 1981: *The Cannonball Run*; *Escape from New York* (a.k.a. *John Carpenter's Escape from New York*); 1982: *Swamp Thing*; *The Thing* (a.k.a. *John Carpenter's The Thing*) (Voice only); *Creepshow*; 1983: *Fantasy Island: Midnight Waltz/Let Them Eat Cake* (02/12/83) (television); 1984: *Hotel: Tomorrows* (01/11/84) (television); *The Next One* (a.k.a. *The Time Travelers* a.k.a. *O Taxidiotis Tou Chronou*) [Greece-U.S.]; 1985: *Bridge Across Time* (a.k.a. *Arizona Ripper* a.k.a. *Terror at London Bridge*) (television); *Seduced* (television); *The Twilight Zone: Teacher's Aide/Paladin of the Lost Hour* (11/08/85) (television); 1986: *Back to School*; *Tomes and Talismans* (television); 1987: *Murder, She Wrote: The Bottom Line Is Murder* (02/15/87) (television); *Open House*; 1989: *Cannibal Women in the Avocado Jungle of Death* (a.k.a. *Piranha Women in the Avocado Jungle of Death*); *The Easter Story* (a.k.a. *The Greatest Adventure Stories from the Bible: The Easter Story*) (voice only) (video); *Monsters: All in a Day's Work* (05/06/89) (television); 1990: *Two Evil Eyes* (a.k.a. *Due Occhi Diabolici* a.k.a. *The Facts in the Case of M. Valdemar*) [Italy-U.S.]; 1991: *Blood River* (television); *Doublecrossed* (television); 1992: *Batman* (animated): *The Cat & the Claw: Part 1* (09/05/92), *The Cat & the Claw: Part 2* (09/12/92), *Perchance to Dream* (10/19/92), *Tyger, Tyger* (10/30/92), *Almost Got 'im* (11/10/92), *Cat Scratch Fever* (11/15/92) (voice only) (television); *The Burden of Proof* (television); *Dream On: Bad Girls* (07/11/92) (television); 1993: *Daddy Dearest: You Bet Your Life* (10/03/93) (television); *Father Hood*; *The Paisley Garden* (television); 1994: *Babylon 5: A Spider in the Web* (12/07/94) (television); *Batman* (animated): *Batgirl Returns* (11/12/94) (voice only) (television); *Jailbreakers* (television); *One West Waikiki: A Model for Murder* (08/25/94) (television); *Silk Degrees* (television); 1995: *Batman* (animated): *Catwalk* (09/13/95) (voice only) (television); *Burial of the Rats* (a.k.a. *Bram Stoker's Burial of the Rats*); 1996: *Flipper: Surf Gang* (02/05/96) (television); *The Wayans Bros.: New Lease on Life* (05/01/96) (television); 1997: *Batman: Gotham Knights* (animated): *You Scratch My Back* (11/15/97) (voice only) (television); *Bimbo Movie Bash*; *Weird Science: Show Chett* (02/16/97) (television); 1998: *Batman: Gotham Knights* (Animated): *Cult of the Cat*

(09/19/98) (television); *A Champion's Fight: A Moment of Truth Movie* (television); *Diagnosis Murder: Rain of Terror* (01/29/98) (television); *The Drew Carey Show: Cain and Mabel* (10/28/98), *My Best Friend's Wedding* (05/20/98) (television); *Scooby-Doo on Zombie Island* (animated) (voice only) (video); *Sliders: Oh Brother, Where Art Thou?* (07/06/98) (television); 1999: *Descent 3* (video game) (voice only); *The Drew Carey Show: Up on the Roof* (05/19/99); *The Love Boat: The Next Wave: Three Stages of Love* (02/19/99) (television); *Star Trek: Deep Space Nine: Inter Arma Enim Silent Leges* (03/03/99) (television); *A Wake in Providence*; 2000: *Across the Line*; *Batman Beyond* (animated): *Out of the Past* (10/21/00) (voice only) (television); *The Convent*; 2001: *Nash Bridges: Something Borrowed* (02/09/01) (television); *No Place Like Home*; *Sabrina, the Teenage Witch: The Gift of Gab* (11/02/01) (television); *Spring Break Lawyer* (television); 2002: *The Chronicle: Tears of a Clone* (01/25/02) (television); *The Drew Carey Show: Look Mom, One Hand!* (05/08/02) (television); *The Gotham Girls* (animated) (voice only); *The Santa Trap* (television); *Totally Spies!: Wild Styles* (03/16/02) (television); 2003: *Carnivàle* (television); 2004: *Carnivàle* (television); *The Drew Carey Show: Drew Hunts Silver Fox* (06/02/04), *Finale* (09/08/04) (television); *Ghost Rock* (a.k.a. *The Reckoning*); *Ring of Darkness* (television); *Totally Spies!: Fashion Faux Pas* (05/04/04) (television); 2006: *The Unholy*; *Christmas Do-Over* (television); 2007: *Halloween*.

Michael Berryman

Michael Berryman rose to genre film prominence with his portrayal of the killer Pluto in Wes Craven's influential horror film *The Hills Have Eyes* (1977). At the time of its release, the advertising used the actor's face, affected by actual birth defects, as the key visual item; it was promoted worldwide using his sneering glare.

Berryman was born on September 4, 1948 in Los Angeles, California to a family that consisted of his father, a brain surgeon, and his mother, a registered nurse. Medical science of the time could not correct Berryman's birth defects, and he grew to be a man with an unusual physical appearance. He continued on, graduating from California Polytech with a degree in veterinary sciences. Early on, he had an interest in the entertainment business. However, while working in a flower shop that he owned in the early seventies, he encountered the writer-producer-director George Pal, through Pal's son who owned an antique store on the same street. According to an interview with Berryman in *Fangoria* magazine in June of 1984, producer Pal asked if he was an actor, to which he replied, "No." Pal remarked, "You have a unique face. I think you'd work real well in my new film." The rest was movie history for Michael Berryman. The small part of an undertaker in Pal's big-screen flop *Doc Savage—The Man of Bronze* (1975) gave Berryman his first glimpse at the inside of the Hollywood dream machine, where anything was possible.

According to Berryman, "About nine months went by, then the same casting director from *Doc Savage*, Mike Fenton, who was now working on *One Flew Over the Cuckoo's Nest*, called me. He had me come down to meet Michael Douglas, the producer, and Milos Forman, the director." Berryman did not have an agent at the time; once he got one, he was awarded the part in *Cuckoo's Nest*.

"We worked for 128 days, six days a week, and it was like going back to school. We had two weeks of solid rehearsals.... I absorbed a wealth of knowledge." According to Berryman, the fastidiously (and strange) Forman "had two cameras running most of the time, but none of us knew which one actually had film in it. They did that to trick us. Milos would walk around trying to catch you off guard, and he would chastise you tremendously if you gave the slightest indication that you were aware of his presence."

Berryman's next film contained the iconic role with which he became most associated: *The Hills Have Eyes*. In this horrific thriller, a band of brain-fried, inbred cannibal killers terrorizes a family on a vacation. Eschewing the type of slick film production we are accustomed to, *The Hills Have Eyes* has a nailbiting, *Deliverance*-goes-to-hell nature. Audiences of the time could easily see themselves having to deal with such savage violence. *Variety* commented on the film (on December 27, 1978): "The Savages are a grotesque-featured bunch with more extravagance than credibility."

For his fourth film appearance, Berryman was given the chance to act as the heavy alongside a screen heavyweight (James Caan in one of his rare, heroic leading roles) in Claude Lelouch's western, *Another Man, Another Chance* (1977). "Early in that film, I kill Jimmy's wife. Seven years later, I'm riding with my band of desperados, and one of them is shot. The only person we can find to treat him is a veterinarian who turns out to be Jimmy. He recognizes a bracelet that I stole from his wife, and he jumps me, and kills me."

Some of Berryman's next characters were mental patients (*The Fifth Floor* [1978]), mutants (*My Science Project* [1985] and *Weird Science* [1985]) and just plain, weird killers (*Cut and Run* [1985]). Lucky enough to work again with Wes Craven, he was given major roles in *Deadly Blessings* (1981) and *The Hills Have Eyes: Part II* (1985). He had character parts in films as diverse as *Star Trek IV: The Voyage Home* (1986), *Solar Crisis* (1990), and *The Guyver* (1991). The *Hills Have Eyes* sequel's less-than-stellar box-office performance was summed up well by a February 19, 1986, review in *Variety*: "Pic was lensed in the fall of 1983 in California, and has been in territorial release since last summer. Craven, who has gone to bigger and better films, shows his contempt for the project in one very funny scene: after numerous flashbacks by characters recalling the first film's events, Craven runs out of survivors so suddenly the dog (named Beast) has a flashback of its own!"

Berryman co-starred as the Skull Cowboy in the original version of *The Crow* (1994) with Brandon Lee. Lee's demise while the film was in production necessitated that much of the movie be rewritten and the film restructured; all of Berryman's scenes were deleted. Much, if not all of this footage has made its way into the hands of collectors, but the footage has yet to appear as DVD bonus material despite numerous reissues of the film on DVD.

Berryman still performs in motion pictures including *Rebel Yell: The Billy Idol Story* (2000), the comedic adventure film *Spy Hard* (1996) alongside Leslie Nielsen, and the recent independent horror films *Slice* (2000) and *Satan's Playground* (2003). He attends genre film conventions as a welcome guest, and seeks opportunities to spread the word about animal rights activism.

Q: How do you feel about being identified with the horror genre?

Michael Berryman: I have done *The Hills Have Eyes I* and *II*, and *Cut and Run* is a very horrific film. Those are the three films that I would say were in that genre. I do not have a problem with being identified with the horror genre because I personally was there. I have always enjoyed horror films back to the old Universal horror films like *The Mummy's Curse* and so on. All those black-and-white horror films, I love them. It was like a dreamscape for me to appear in a horror film. I believe very strongly that if you have a dream, for instance, that they are opportunities. Everyone's own personal demons and fears are specific and, if we need to, we conquer our fears. To conquer our demons, and our fears, it means that we have analyzed why they bother us, and what is missing in our own personal make-up that enables us toward such actions. I do not have a problem with it at all, appearing in horror films. In fact, I am quite proud of acting in horror films. One of my proudest moments as an actor was appearing in an issue of *Fangoria* where they showed a picture of Boris Karloff posing as the executioner from the old movie, *Tower of London*, right next to a picture of me as the character of Pluto from one of the *Hills Have Eyes* movies, and the resemblance was, and remains, outstanding.

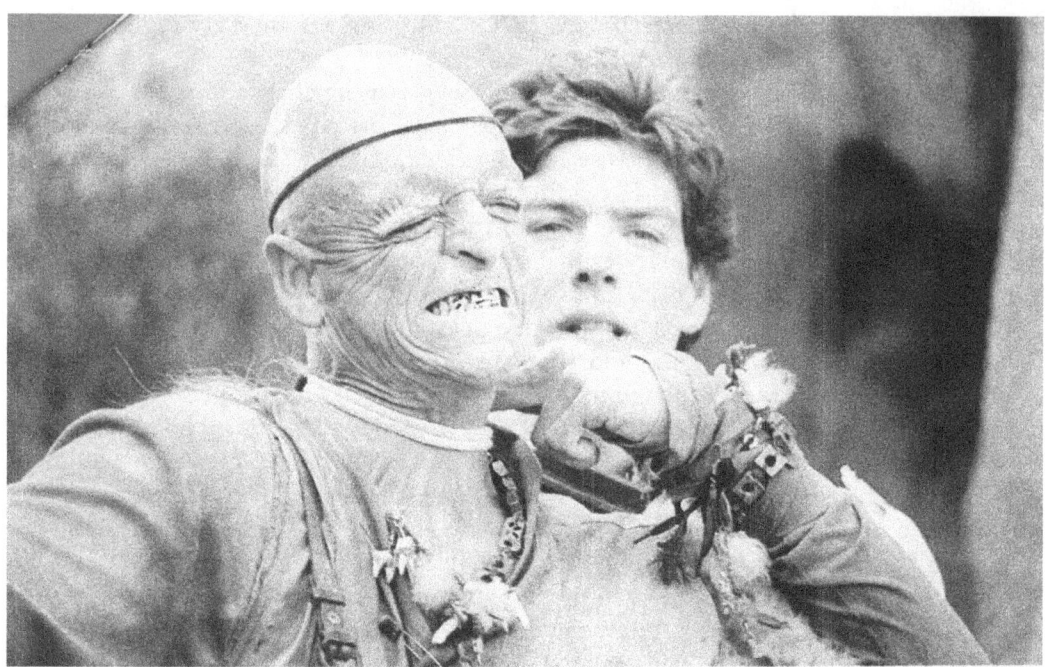

Michael Berryman (left) and Kevin Blair at the climax of Wes Craven's *The Hills Have Eyes* (1977) (Blood Relations Company/Vanguard/Anchor Bay).

Q: With cinema audiences now shifting away from the genre, would you really like to move on from horror films now?

Berryman: I will continue to do horror films because it addresses the thing about fear. Fear is a very interesting thing. I believe that real life horror goes on everywhere. Horror films allow people to deal with things that cause them fear. It allows the opportunity to balance real fear situations from fantasy situations. I will continue to appear in horror films as long as the parts are good. I won't say, for instance, that all the villainous parts I will do will be redeeming ones, redeeming in the sense that you have the victorious hero who battles the villain ... but, if the villain or the anti-hero is not someone of substance, then the audience has no one to root for, not the hero, or anti-hero, or the villain. In my roles, I embrace the dark side not because I would worship Satan; I embrace the dark side because we all have our dark sides within us. I have found that acting has become wonderful therapy because I cannot afford to go to a shrink, not that I need to, but therapy in itself allows us to know more about our individual selves. As for film roles, I do want to branch out, and do other things. But I love the horror film genre, I love getting scared, I love scaring people. I'm not a prankster but a movie that takes you somewhere dark, a movie that scares you, that's something that succeeds. Horror movies are supposed to scare you, at least the good ones.

Q: You looked like you had a lot of fun with *The Guyver*. Was your seeming ease with comedy in such a macabre role a result of the original script, the direction, or something that was improvised on location?

Berryman: The movie was designed to be kind of like the old *Batman* television series in the sixties, very much in a pop art, fantasy vein. Even the music had these kinds of weird stings to it. It was meant to be a humorous fantasy film. The dialogue, a lot of it, was ad-libbed on the spur of the moment. I really enjoyed the relationship between Spice Williams' character and my character. Especially in the scene where we are in the van, she's chewing gum, and I'm checking the mirror to make sure that my Guyvers are kidnapping the right person, and she says, "You never take me anywhere." My character, Lester, goes through all these little facial quirks and muscle pulls when he's irritated with this woman. "Oh, come on, we're doing a job here, we can discuss this later." But, oh no, she's insistent ... and I have this line where I say, "We'll go shopping in Brazil." This was all ad-libbed, and she goes, "Will you take me shopping?" In addition, my character has this pause: "...Yeah, shopping." Later in the film, when we go to kick some butt in real action-movie style, I say, "Let's go shopping." And she goes, "Well, you said Brazil!" Now that is humorous. I love the comedy portions of that movie. I enjoyed making *The Guyver*; we just had a field day with it. Of course, we also had the ace special effects and makeup genius Screaming Mad George with his wonderful production art and makeup. And the costumes were also just remarkable, they were works of art too.

Q: You have worked with many directors on a number of pictures... Wes Craven, Ruggero Deodato... who is your favorite?

Berryman: I very much enjoyed working on an obscure film with Claude Lelouche. I liked his camerawork, and I liked the way he captures you on the screen. He gives you very little direction, but he allows you to live in the moment. It was called *Another Man, Another Chance*, with Genevieve Bujold, James Caan, and Christopher Lloyd. Christopher Lloyd in that film went to the extreme of researching his character of Billy the Kid. The character of Billy in that film was just another character in the film, another person on Lelouche's stage, but Chris learned that his character had green eyes in real life, so he went out and bought green contact lenses for his part. The green eyes never read on camera, but it helped him and he got into his character. I like the European style of directing; I like what they do with light. In fact, I would like to see more films shot in black and white. I do not know if there will be a renaissance in that regard but I would like to see it. As far as horror films go, the best director that I have worked with ... I would say Wes Craven.

Q: Were you not supposed to appear in the aborted *The Hills Have Eyes III*?

Berryman: I have the original script at home, Wes Craven's son, Jonathan, wrote it. It was originally called *The Outpost*.* It was a very good script too; it would have been a roller coaster ride of fear. It would have been more like the original *Hills Have Eyes* movie. There was nothing in that script that was extemporaneous to the extent where you say, "Well, where did this come from? It doesn't fit in the flow of the action of the film." It would have grabbed you. It would have taken you for a ride. The buildup to the action was perfect. It would have been classic Craven. Here is the story: There is a scientist going on vacation with his family, and they are sidetracked and they have to go to an outpost and they have to take care of a problem ... genetic experimentation is running amok.

Q: Can you tell me about your involvement on *The Crow*?

Berryman: I worked on that film for quite a while. When I was in Wilmington, North Carolina, at Carolco Studios, where we were shooting the scenes, I made a point of going

---

*The Outpost *was rewritten by Jonathan Craven to have all of its overt* Hills Have Eyes *references removed. Directed by Joe Gayton, the film was titled* Mind Ripper, *and released to home video in 1995.*

Cowboy James Caan gets the drop on bandits Michael Berryman (far left), Lennie Geer (middle), and Charles Horvath (right) in the Claude Lelouch western, *Another Man, Another Chance* (1977) (Chartoff-Winkler Productions/Les Films 13/Les Films Ariane/Les Productions Artistes Associes/United Artists).

to the dailies every day. I think I worked there for about eight weeks, maybe more. Many of the scenes that Brandon Lee and I appeared in, he lived to see before his untimely death.

I recall that there was one scene that Brandon filmed that he never did see. He and his companion Eliza went out with some friends that night, and he did not attend the day's screening of footage. In the dailies for what was shot that day, there was a scene where he's walking on the sidewalk and some children run past him. They over-cranked the camera so the children are kind of dancing in a dreamscape slow motion all around him. They did not use this particular scene in the finished picture, but in the footage, Brandon turned and had this beautiful emotion showing on his face with a big, bright smile. At this same moment, a couple flakes of snow came across the landscape. It was a marvelous scene. I had dinner with him later that night and he was a little tired and he needed a pick-up so I said, "Brandon, you missed a real gem of a moment in the dailies tonight." He said, "Tell me about it." I told him about his expression in the film. Right there and then, he physically brought back the moment, and he explained to me what he saw and how he felt in that particular moment. When you are in character, in your mind, the action and the dialogue and everything that is going to happen. Then you can become an empty cup and you fill it with creativity, which comes from the inspiration of the moment. It is almost better for an actor to pretend or almost believe that you do not know your lines or what is about to happen next. It gets that adrenaline pumping and you get that little bit of butterflies in the stomach and you go with, what I call your trust. That's your insides working and then you get some magical moments. *The Crow*, the comic book, was adapted from James O'Barr's personal experiences, which led [him to write] the story to begin with; O'Barr also worked on the screenplay. The story... there is so much richness there that I believe most people who have seen the film at least two or three times always come back for the depth within that story. I am pleased with the film, although I had hoped that, when it did come out in its various home video incarnations [laser disc and DVD] that it would show all my footage, which was removed from the final cut of the film, not so much for myself and the effort that I put into it, but especially for Lance Sanderson and Scott Colter, the special effects team who created the Skull Cowboy character. They deserved to have that work of art seen. It was really a work of art.

Q: While the film was being re-structured after the tragedy, were a lot of your original lines that were cut from the film given to Rochelle Davis, the actress who played the young woman who becomes the movie's new narrator? Did they take those lines originally from your Skull Cowboy character?

Berryman: The narration that currently appears in the film, at the beginning, was done after Brandon's death. I believe David Schow might have written that. I never did ask Schow about that specifically at that time, because I didn't know what they were adding to the film until I saw it at a screening. In the original opening scene, Brandon and I were to be seen in a graveyard. It is raining and a crow lands on a tombstone. It pecks at the name ERIC DRAVEN on the tombstone, and blood comes running out of the tombstone. The camera follows the blood down to the flower that the girl puts there. Then his hand comes out of the ground and [Brandon Lee] crawls out of the grave literally and it is raining torrentially. The crow flies back to my arm and we turn the camera. We see the Skull Cowboy with wind and lightning effects all around us. The Crow [Lee] goes, "Who the hell are you?" And I say, "Interested? Then follow the Crow." I release the crow and it flies right over the camera. Then it starts from there. That was the original version of that scene. The scenes we had left to do included several where Brandon and I were in the loft, maybe three different scenes where I kept warning him, reminding him of the rules of the game which are that you may have your vengeance but if you get involved with any of the living, you will lose your powers. Some of my exact words of dialogue as originally written were "Quit screwing around." And he goes, "What?" You know, he is all upset, and I say, "If you don't do what I tell you, the blood will not return after you're shot." That is ironic because in the original version, when he is shot, the blood goes back and his wounds heal.... It did not happen that way ... in real life....

Q: How do you personally feel about filmmakers who have exploited your genetic physical defects, your appearance? Or are you at peace with that?

Berryman: When I was a small child, I went with my father to a Children's Hospital. My brain was growing larger and my skull was confined. I had a full craniotomy at age three, meaning that they cut through my skull and fabricated spaces with bone chips off of my hip to keep the brain separated so it would grow and I wouldn't go blind and die. They did a good job, but my hair never grew back. But this unique look got me into the movies. For years, I still wanted to be a veterinarian (which I became, later in life). At that time, I did not have the aptitude or maybe I was a little too lazy to get a tutor and work at my chemistry and things that were really giving me a difficult time. Then

When two villains collide, they show the world how sweet they really are! Gunnar Hansen (*The Texas Chainsaw Massacre*) and Berryman (*The Hills Have Eyes*) share a great moment at a 1993 Chiller Theatre convention.

when I was a veterinary assistant and I got into doing autopsies on animals and things of that nature, my fingers would crack open and split, which was another result of my birth defect, and I realized I would have problem in surgeries later on. So, there was a time when I was getting ready to leave California to move to another state, perhaps Alaska, to spend time with the environment, and animals. Then, I was discovered by George Pal and appeared in *Doc Savage* and the rest is, as they say, movie history. My stature as an actor also enables me to concentrate more on ecological concerns and animal activism, and to bring those concerns to others, to make them aware, which is really what I enable myself to spend more time on nowadays.

Credits: 1975: *Doc Savage: The Man of Bronze*; *One Flew Over the Cuckoo's Nest*; 1977: *Another Man, Another Chance* (a.k.a. *Un Autre Homme, Un Autre Chance*) [France]; *The Hills Have Eyes*; 1978: *The Fifth Floor*; 1980: *Co-Ed*; 1981: *Deadly Blessing*; 1983: *Likely Stories, Vol. 3* (television); *Mortuary*; 1984: *Invitation to Hell* (television); 1985: *Cut and Run* (a.k.a. *Inferno in Diretta*) [Italy]; *Highway to Heaven: The Devil and Jonathan Smith* (10/30/85) (television); *The Hills Have Eyes Part II*; *1st & Ten: Uneasy Lies the Head* (television); *My Science Project*; *Weird Science*; 1986: *Armed Response*; *The Fall Guy: War on Wheels* (04/11/86) (television); *Off the Mark*; *Star Trek IV: The Voyage Home*; 1987: *The Barbarians* (a.k.a. *E

Barbari and Company) [Italy]; *Highway to Heaven: I Was a Middle-Aged Werewolf* (10/28/87) (television); *The Highwayman*; *Kenny Rogers as The Gambler, Part III: The Legend Continues* (television); 1988: *ALF: We Are Family* (05/02/88) (television); *Saturday the 14th Strikes Back*; *Star Trek: The Next Generation: Conspiracy* (05/07/88) (television); *Voyage of the Rock Aliens*; 1989: *Oceano* (television) [Italy]; 1990: *Aftershock*; *Evil Spirits*; *Haunting Fear*; *Solar Crisis* (a.k.a. *Kuraishisu Niju-go Ju Nen*) [Japan]; 1991: *Beastmaster 2: Through the Portals of Time*; *The Guyver*; *Haunting Fear*; *The Secret of the Golden Eagle*; *Tales from the Crypt: The Reluctant Vampire* (07/10/91) (television); *Teenage Exorcist*; *Wizards of the Demon Sword*; 1992: *Little Sister*; 1993: *Auntie Lee's Meat Pies*; 1994: *The Crow* (scenes deleted); *Double Dragon*; 1995: *The X-Files: Revelations* (12/15/95) (television); 1996: *Mojave Moon*; *Spy Hard*; *We're No Angels* (a.k.a. *Noi Siamo Angeli*) (television) [Italy]; 2000: *Rebel Yell*; *Slice*; *Two Heads Are Better Than None* (television); 2003: *Area 23* (television); *Motley Crue: Greatest Video Hits* (video); *Satan's Playground*; 2004: *The Absence of Light*; 2005: *The Devil's Rejects* [U.S.-Germany]; *The Storyteller*; 2006: *Fallen Angels*; *Penny Dreadful*; 2007: *Brother's War*; *Brutal* (Video); *Dead Man's Hand*; *Ed Gein: The Butcher of Plainfield* (Video); *Nightmare Carnival*; *Outrage*.

Samson Burke

Samson Burke was born Samuel Burke in Montreal, Canada. As a young man, he became interested in bodybuilding and began the arduous task of sculpting, toning, and shaping his body. During his teenage years, part of his daily regimen included swimming, and he eventually became a competitive swimmer, winning a number of local physical fitness titles. Samuel's love of water also led to his joining a water polo team; he went on to take part in a number of national championships, and even represented Canada in the Olympics swimming competition. Before leaving his scholastic years behind, Burke was named Canada's Greatest All-Around Collegiate Athlete. Entering the world of bodybuilding, he won the title of Mr. Montreal, followed by other competitions where he won prizes for his hard work. In succession, he was named Mr. Canada, and Mr. Muscle Beach, and received from The Federation of Bodybuilders the much-coveted Top Amateur Athlete in the World prize.

Beginning his career as a wrestler, Samuel Burke renamed (Sammy Berg—Mr. Canada) spent several years in the ring. He racked up hundreds of wins, and as a tag team partner won the World Heavyweight Wrestling championship title in the late fifties by beating Buddy Rogers. Continuing with his wrestling career he also won (with then-wrestling partner Seymour Koenig) the International Television Tag Team title in the late fifties. It was at this point in his professional athletic career that Sammy Berg, wrestler, became Samson Burke, movie star.

After appearing as a dim-witted Hercules in the fantastic (and fun) film *The Three Stooges Meet Hercules* in 1962, Burke traveled to Europe and embarked on an equally exciting and varied career in a few influential muscleman or sword-and-sandal films (also known as peplums), adventures, and even a handful of westerns. When work in overseas genre films dried up, Burke returned to the States, specifically Hawaii, where he appeared in minor roles in a number of episodes of the television show *Magnum P.I.* Nowadays, Burke has returned to his true love, physical fitness, and owns and operates his own personal training business.

Q: I believe you were crowned Mr. Canada in 1953, Mr. Muscle Beach in 1960, and Mr. Professional Mr. Universe in 1961. You were a professional bodybuilder obviously; but what led you to the acting profession?

Samson Burke: As I began to sculpt my body, and became more aware of myself, I also began to build up quite a lot of self-assurance. Because of that, I think trying acting was a logical extension of competing in physical fitness trials, contests, etc. I eventually

Muscular Samson Burke surrounded by The Three Stooges (left to right: Joe De Rita, Larry Fine, and Moe Howard) in this posed photograph from *The Three Stooges Meet Hercules* **(1962) (Normandy Productions/Columbia Pictures).**

worked as an actor quite a bit when I went to Europe. In the United States, when I first got the role in the Columbia picture *The Three Stooges Meet Hercules*, that kind of encouraged me to take it further, because they were making the sword-and-sandal films over in Italy during this period. Therefore, after I finished the Three Stooges movie, I went over to Italy, and I eventually appeared in thirteen films over there.

Q: What can you recall about the making of the Three Stooges film?

Publicity shot for *The Three Stooges Meet Hercules* (1962) (Normandy Production/Columbia Pictures).

Burke: I used to ride with Moe Howard in the company car everyday, to the location at the Columbia Ranch where we were shooting. While we were making that film, the Stooges always kept me laughing from early in the morning, to late at night. Actually, I got more kicks out of that experience than anything else in filmmaking that followed. Moe always had so many one-liners ready; he was the funniest man I had ever met. He was naturally funny, and much funnier than you would see on the screen. He just kept me in stitches all the time; it made it easier to work, and contributed to a much more relaxed atmosphere on the set.

Q: In one of your first Italian films you played the character of Ursus.

Burke: I played Ursus in *The Vengeance of Ursus*. I was young, and to me it all was a great experience. I can only recall that I had a great time. The Italians were great people, and the food was unbelievable.

Q: Do you recall how you were cast in your first Italian film?

Burke: They were looking for somebody, preferably a tall person, because most of the people in the supporting cast were shorter. I was informed about the production, and I sent over many pictures from the Stooges movie. Then my Italian representative, my agent over there, dealt with the production company, and I got the part. It was not too hard actually, and that is how I got the role. By the time my plane landed in Italy, everything was already set, planned, and ready to go; all was arranged before I even got there. Luckily for me, I did not have much of a [language] problem because I spoke French fluently, and Italian is very close to French. I was able to pick up on the Italian language, and become fluent in it, in a short amount of time. Nowadays, I read and write in Italian as well.

Q: While working on these films, did you have to have to physically work out daily to keep your body in peak physical condition, to keep looking pumped-up?

Burke: We used to work out in the mornings for about six days a week, and take one day off for rest. We used to run two to three miles a day, spend hours in the gym or at the place where we were staying, and then go to the location and film all day long. Back in those days, when I would work out, I was not alone, and that helped a lot. There was Steve Reeves, Gordon Mitchell, and myself. The three of us lived in the same area, and we got together about three times a week as well. We kept in good physical shape by working out on a set schedule, and then working out with friends.

Q: Is it true that the elaborate sets used for that Ursus film were leftover from the epic *Cleopatra* film that Hollywood left standing?

Burke: *Cleopatra* was *still* shooting when we began production on the Ursus film, but we still used some of their sets. The *Cleopatra* production was only supposed to stay in Italy for a few months' time, but they ended up staying for an entire year, because of a variety of delays of one kind of another. I had a good chance to work on that film too, but I had already begun work on the Ursus film, so there was no way that I was going to be able to appear in both movies at the same time.

Q: What do you recall about appearing in *The Triumph of Robin Hood*?

Burke: I played Little John in that. It had a great cast of people. It seemed to take a long time to make that movie, but we all had a good time, a *great* time.

Q: You also co-starred with the popular Italian comedian Toto in *Toto Contro Maciste*, where you played the mythological hero Maciste. What can you recall about that film?

Burke: Toto was an extremely quiet person when he was off-screen. Although it was very pleasant to work with him, I remember him as extremely quiet and a little fragile because he was a much older man then. It was good to work with him because I was working with one of the top comedians in Italy, and this got you psyched up quite a bit as an actor.

Q: You also played the role of a king in a two-part German production of *Die Nibelungen*.

Burke: I played King Blo-Edin. It was based on an opera by Wagner. On that film, there was a lot of really hard horseback riding, and I had an elaborate costume, and a wig, and a big old fancy hat, and makeup that turned my eyes up and made me look like a Hun.

Q: That was pretty much of an epic film as well. It was split into two separate films when it was originally released to German television.

Burke: Yes, it certainly was an epic film. Some portions of the score were considered something not unlike the national anthem of Germany. I spent four months living in Belgrade, Yugoslavia working on that film. We used to work late into the night. We had a lot of heavy dialogue and I had never done anything like that before. It took a lot of preparation for me; I would be up until three o'clock in the morning studying, remembering my lines. It was quite an experience.

Q: You appeared with fellow bodybuilder-stuntman-actor Brad Harris in a German-Italian-Yugoslavian spy adventure film, *Three Green Dogs*, also known as *Death Trip*, which was partly filmed in Turkey. You performed a lot of vigorous-looking stunts, particularly one wild motorcycle chase.

Burke: I appeared as the villain in that film. We shot many motorcycle chases for that movie. I used to ride the whole of the mountainside, on the bike, sideways, and then climb the mountain. It is a very risky thing to do on the bike, climbing up the mountain, and then coming back down. I also flew out of a four-story building, with a safety belt on. In the scene, I flew out of the building to catch a gondola, and they lowered me down. I used to do all these stunts myself. I did not trust the other guys to do them, they may have gotten hurt. We did many interesting things, in terms of stunts, on that film because we were so far away from other major filmmaking capitals in Europe. We were working in the mountains and the hills of Godomie, in Turkey. I had one fight scene with Brad Harris where I was supposed to be chasing him down a mountain, and we were both on motorcycles. But the mountain was actually more like a giant beveled rock, a very smooth rock. We had leather seats put on our bikes, because the seats wore out by the time you got to the bottom, and you would have to put on new seats to ride back up the mountain. It's strange, but you see the beveled rock as you come down the mountain, so you slide your weight a little to the side, but my weight made my bike go faster, as I got into a curve. Then there was an opening, a cave of some sort, and I went doubly fast right into the cave, all the way down into the bottom. There was no way out except to be rescued. They had to throw a cord down, and I had to come up and out via rope. There was no other way to get out because I was stuck in the cavern. All told, it was an interesting and exciting experience working on that film. Then there was the time I was to be in another chase scene with Brad Harris and I went up in the gondola four stories high, and the thing slammed against the wall of a building, I will never forget that; I had bruises and marks all over my body for a long time afterwards. Sometimes working on adventure films in Europe, in the sixties, was very exciting, and a little risky, but I believe that working on that movie was worth the time.

Q: Did you know Brad Harris personally at the time that you were working in movies in Europe?

Burke: I have known Brad for a long time. In Italy, in the sixties, he used to work out with Gordon Mitchell and myself. We built a whole gym on a platform on the roof of the building where we lived, and we used to work out there every day. Brad used to come over, Steve Reeves used to come over; we would all work out together everyday.

Q: Did you appear in any other European-produced spy films besides that one?

Burke: I did appear in a television series, in Italy. I was very fortunate to have gotten that part. It was made for the Italian television network RAI-TV. I worked in Italian, strictly Italian, not English; by that time I was fluent in the Italian language so that did not pose a problem. It was interesting to do this role. I had to audition for it. I auditioned with many Italian theater actors who were simply fantastic; I never thought I had a chance. But in the end, I got the part over those guys; what a triumph that was.

Q: You also appeared in the role of Polyphemus in the RAI television program *The Odyssey*.

Burke: I had to go and get a plastic thing painted all over me like a frozen mask. It was interesting to do, but there wasn't too much to recall except that I had a lot of what's called humility-type lines to reproduce. Sometimes the dialogue was a little heavy, a little difficult for me. In one scene, there were these little lambs coming by and I was supposed to look like I was petting them, but I had my script right under them on the ground, and I read from the script for like three pages. I did not have to rehearse those heavy lines, thank goodness. Dino De Laurentiis produced that, and working for him, one thing led to another, so I got some other work because of that role.

Q: As the popularity of the sword-and-sandal films began to wane, you appeared with Klaus Kinski in a war film called *Five for Hell*.

Burke: I was supposed to be a commando who was also a knife thrower, an assassin with a blade. The film was about a bunch of soldiers, a bunch of guys who each specialize in different ways to kill people. I used to have a set of throwing knives, and I used to rehearse and rehearse. I learned how to throw them knives pretty good.

Q: Then you appeared in Italian westerns like the *Sartana* film. Was it difficult to move from the peplums, to the spy films, to the westerns?

Burke: No, not at all. As an actor, you just got a script, and then you read it, and you tried to focus on the part, you would put yourself in that character. Once you have that character started in your mind, you then have to believe that you are that character. It didn't matter what the genre was, what the role was, only that it was work that I was doing, that I was enjoying, that I was getting paid to do.

Q: I once read that you were supposed to star in an Italian western television series called *Cheyenne*. Was that ever completed and shown?

Burke: It never got off the ground because the producers backed out or something. It was one of those unfortunate things that happened in my career.

Q: You also appeared on American television programs like *I Spy* and *Magnum P.I.* Do you have any particular favorites of the U.S. television appearances that you made?

Burke: Actually, for the appearance in *I Spy*, I did not even have to leave Europe. That episode was shot in Greece, about six hours away from Athens. I played a priest who was also an arms smuggler. My role was the whole basis for that episode. What was interesting was, I had a Greek interpreter on the production who was feeding me my lines in Greek, and I did not have a clue what I was talking about. I did not know one word of Greek, so I had no idea what I was saying in that language. However, it was a very interesting experience nonetheless.

Samson Burke today.

Q: Of the movies that you have appeared in, do you have a favorite?

Burke: Actually, *The Three Stooges Meet Hercules* was one of the most favorite ones that I have done, and the most interesting. I had a lot of fun working on that film. Every day it was a pleasure to come to work.

My acting career was a lot of hard work that I enjoyed doing. Every time I had a new project to work on, I enjoyed doing it. All of us actors who were appearing in the sword-and-sandal films, we worked out every day to keep in shape physically to keep the weight down, we were just conscious that way, so health-wise, we were always in peak physical condition. Generally, I enjoyed every bit of it, and I was sorry when they stopped subsidizing films in Europe because, after a while, there was hardly any work around. I had to come back, and I didn't *want* to come back, I wanted to stay there in Europe, but the roles were becoming few and far between.

Credits: 1962: *The Three Stooges Meet Hercules*; *Toto Contro Maciste* (a.k.a. *Toto against Maciste* a.k.a. *Toto vs. Maciste*) [Italy]; *La Vendetta Di Ursus* (a.k.a. *The Mighty Ursus* a.k.a. *The Revenge of Ursus* a.k.a. *The Vengeance of Ursus*) [Italy]; 1963: *Il Trionfo Di Robin Hood* (a.k.a. *The Triumph of Robin Hood*) [Italy]; 1966: *Die Nibelungen Teil 1: Siegfried* (a.k.a. *Siegfried*) [West Germany–Yugoslavia]; *Die Nibelungen Teil 2: Die Krimhilde's Rache* (a.k.a. *The Revenge of Siegfried*) [West Germany–Yugoslavia]; 1967: *I Spy: Now You See Her, Now You Don't* (10/23/67) (television); *Kommissar X—Drei Grune Hunde* (a.k.a. *Kommissar X— The Three Green Dogs* a.k.a. *Commissioner X—The Three Green Dogs* a.k.a. *The Death Trip* a.k.a. *The Soft Kill*) [Italy–West Germany–France–Lebanon–Hungary]; 1968: *Arriva Dorellik* (a.k.a. *Here Comes Dorellik* a.k.a. *How to Kill 100 Duponts*) [Italy]; *Cinque Per L'Inferno* (a.k.a. *Five for Hell* a.k.a. *Five into Hell*) [Italy]; *L'Odissea* (a.k.a. *The Odyssey* a.k.a. *The Adventures of Ulysses* a.k.a. *The Adventures of Hercules* [Italy]; *Straziami, Ma Di Baci Saziami* (a.k.a. *Kill Me with Kisses* a.k.a. *Torture Me, But Kill Me with Kisses*) [Italy-France]; 1969: *Sono Sartana, Il Vostro Becchino* (a.k.a. *I Am Sartana, Your Angel of Death, I'll Dig Your Death, Sartana, Angel of Death, Sartana, the Gravedigger*) [Italy]; 1970: *Satiricossimo* [Italy].

David Carradine

David Carradine, the eldest son of veteran genre film icon John Carradine, has remained a favorite of martial arts and genre film fans for decades, primarily for his portrayal of the wise, philosophical, brutally honest, and deadly Kwai Chang Caine in the seminal television series *Kung Fu* (1972–75).

After aspiring to a number of occupations, and flitting through numerous pay-the-bill employment positions (including a door-to-door salesman hawking Bibles, sewing machines, etc.), Carradine settled on acting, his father's work. On his résumé, which he submitted to his representative agency in the early sixties, he listed his father as "John Carradine—itinerant actor."

The years 1957 through 1959 were spent acting with the San Francisco Semi-Professional Theatre group in numerous roles. He next worked with the San Francisco Tent Theatre, the Akron Shakespeare Festival and, during his two-year stint with the U.S. Army in 1960–1962, appeared in many U.S. Army special services' theatrical productions. Carradine had a starring role in the play *The Deputy* on Broadway in 1964 but a more notable role onstage was yet to come.

In 1965, he performed to great acclaim on the Broadway stage *The Royal Hunt of the Sun*. Critics for the *New York Times* and the *Herald Tribune* panned the play initially. But, the afternoon daily New York papers raved, and both the *Times* and *Herald Tribune* critics later backpedaled their reviews, due to the positive audience reaction, causing the show to last on the stage for a then-staggering six months. The play concerned the conquest by Pizarro, the Spanish explorer (as played by British actor Trevor Howard), of the Inca Empire, and their god named Atahualpa Capac (Carradine). For this major role, young Carradine's wardrobe consisted solely of Inca-type necklaces, hand and arm bracelets, and a loincloth. Interestingly, when represented by the firm of Byron Gordon and Associates to coincide with his appearance in *Royal Hunt of the Sun*, Carradine wrote his own lengthy bio, revealing much wit, charm, and liberal thinking. The following is an excerpt from that bio found in a scrapbook housed at The New York Public Library for the Performing Arts: "To begin with, I was born. On December 8, 1936, the year of the rat, at precisely 12 noon. The event took place in Hollywood, California; a fact which has marked me with permanent scars causing good people to shun my company, in the land of Nod and other civilized places. My father is an itinerant circus acrobat; my mother is an ex-housewife. In the manner of Hollywood marriages, I am my father's first of four sons, and my mother's second of two. I started acting when I was twenty-one, for no more reason than I couldn't seem to avoid it. Previously, I had aspired to be a magician, a Texas Ranger, a tap-dancer, an opera singer, a sculptor, and a composer; in that order. By way of formal education, I studied music sporadically for three years at several colleges around San Francisco; then quit to play around in the theatre. Specifically, I quit to mount a production of *Othello*. I directed, and played Iago. The co-director played Othello; he directed me, and I directed him. This didn't work out too well; we were an enormous failure. For the next couple of years, I served my apprenticeship playing all sorts of glorious roles in what we in San Francisco called semi-professional theatre; which means: someone got paid, and you can't prove it wasn't me. Eventually I escaped by way of a passing Shakespearean Tent repertory, and rode it to Hollywood. In Hollywood, I did one quick television show, in which I played a bohemian something or other who spent his evenings reading Shakespeare to jazz in coffee houses; an autobiographical piece. For the rest of the time I kept alive by painting murals in bars. When it became impossible to drink a beer without having to look at my lousy artwork, I hitchhiked to New York...."

Carradine garnered acclaim and positive critical notices in the television westerns *Taggart* (1965) and *Shane* (1966). In an interview with the *Newark Evening News* in June 1966 he stated, "I see [the character of] Shane as Ulysses. He is an old-fashioned Greek hero who wants to put roots down. Ulysses wanted to get back to Ithaca, but things kept getting in his way." Attempting to make this television version of the Alan Ladd feature film *Shane* different, Carradine said, "If [my character] was just another gunfighter trying to settle down, the show wouldn't last ten weeks. What makes Shane different is that he hasn't really shed the role of the gunslinger." However, *Shane* only lasted for one season. Carradine returned to the stage, working on the ill-received play *The Transgressor Rides Again* (about the second coming of Christ), which opened and closed on May 19, 1969. Supporting roles in the feature film westerns *The McMasters*, and *Macho Callahan* followed.

Carradine showed his penchant for portraying fiercely independent characters in roles like union boss Bill Shelly in Martin Scorsese's *Boxcar Bertha* (1972). This led to his starring role in the ABC television series *Kung Fu*. Originally, Asian actor Bruce Lee conceived the series as a starring vehicle for himself, and developed it, but ABC still prevented Asians from having leading roles on their television series. So Carradine was cast in the part instead. The *Kung Fu* pilot featured Carradine as Kwai Chang Caine, a withdrawn, quiet, stoic, and self-sufficient man with no regard for material things, just for his philosophy. The pilot was a hit, causing ABC to order three episodes. During this period, Carradine also directed his first feature film, *You and Me*. In a 1974 interview with *TV Guide* he expressed astonishment at the techniques displayed by the late martial artist-actor Bruce Lee in his last film *Enter the Dragon*, "That Bruce Lee, I get a thing from him, a spiritual essence. It's like you take from Nureyev, Valentino, Jesus Christ and Wilt Chamberlain. You look at them and see what they can do and you say, 'Man, there's hope for me.' That Bruce Lee, man, he's just too good. I must take from him and carry on ... the spiritual essence of the man."

Although the first *Kung Fu* series had a relatively short run (only three seasons), it influenced many viewers and helped pave the way for Asian actors to get a foothold in Hollywood. It also stoked the growing interest in Asian films, and possibly caused some easing of political tensions between the U.S. and China. Carradine downplayed his role as a martial arts master in a *New York Post* interview from October 1973: "It's all faked man, the fight scenes. They're like choreographed. I mean, I'm a dancer." Later in the same interview he claimed that his character Kwai Chang Caine was a martial arts master and a pacifist for a reason. "To me, acting is life. I don't differentiate between acting and living." Seemingly, Carradine was exaggerating, as he had been studying with martial arts master–philosopher Master Kam Yuen and become an avid student of his teachings, something he admitted years later when he authored the book *The Spirit of Shaolin*.

Carradine has also dabbled in other genre work like his interesting role as Frankenstein in Roger Corman's *Death Race 2000* (1975). *Variety* stated (on May 7, 1975) that "Carradine plays it cool and introspective, letting out occasional meditative remarks...." Other interesting roles followed in *Cannonball* (1976), *Deathsport* (1978), and Larry Cohen's *Q* (1982). In 1983, he co-starred with real-life martial artist and B-film star Chuck Norris in *Lone Wolf McQuade*. The film garnered some media attention prior to its release when Carradine insisted that the producers change, via editing, the outcome of Carradine's villainous character's fight with Norris' hero. Carradine sued the production company for breach of contract, claiming (in a *New York Post* article, dated September 29, 1982) that he "always plays the good guy" and had contracted to co-star in the film on the following three conditions: His character would not kill a woman in cold blood, would not die, and would not be defeated in hand-to-hand combat by Norris. After the film was shot, Carradine looked at a rough cut and found that his first two conditions had been met. But one scene, he said, had been changed through editing so that he lost a fight to Norris.

David Carradine as he appeared in the ABC television series *Kung Fu* (1972).

Carradine returned to a more heroic role by starring as Kain in the futuristic adventure film *The Warrior and the Sorceress* (1983). Returning to the Kwai Chang Caine character he made so famous years before, he appeared in a 1986 pilot designed to revive the *Kung Fu* series; *Kung Fu: The Movie* also featured the screen debut of Bruce Lee's son, Brandon. In 1987, he appeared in a television pilot, also featuring Lee, titled *Kung Fu: The Next Generation*. He appeared in yet another *Kung Fu* series which debuted in 1992, playing the great grandson of the original Caine character; *Kung Fu: The Legend Continues* lasted until 1997.

Outside of his genre film work, Carradine has portrayed folk music legend Woody Guthrie in Hal Ashby's *Bound for Glory* (1976). On December 19, 1976, he took a full-page ad in the *New York Times* stating his eagerness to continue with such good roles, and expressed his happiness about working on the Ashby film. Titled *This Train*, the piece read: "Once, many years ago, in a theatre off–Broadway, I tried to give the best performance of my life in a little play about the second coming of Christ. I spared nothing; of myself, the audience or the critics; took every chance and pulled no punches. The New York critics were unanimously brutal in their reaction. The only dissenter was a paper in

Carradine as Woody Guthrie in the film, *Bound for Glory* (1976) (MGM-United Artists).

New Jersey somewhere which called it a fine passion play and the best performance that reviewer had ever seen. The play closed in one night, and I more or less resolved never to give of myself so freely again. Now, Hal Ashby has given me in *Bound for Glory* the chance to do exactly as I believe, for once, with no censorship or opposition; and this time it seems the public is to be allowed to dig it. Maybe the critics are getting hipper. Maybe I'm getting better. I just want to thank everyone for the second chance to get out there with my real stuff. Now perhaps, I can finally get on with the work I was cut out for. This will be my nineteenth year in Show Business, and though there were some sunny seasons, most of it has been empty and cold. I have the New York stage to thank for my first helping hands, and I hope I can return the favor sometime soon. I exist up here on this silly silver screen only to serve you, the Audience. And more or less to thumb my nose at the moguls and satyrs who prey on you and me; an almost impossible position to maintain because of the old where-your-bread-is-buttered story, but I try it. For once, this time, everyone involved in this picture show, from the stand-by painter to the head of the studio, gave with all their hearts. I hope and pray this is a trend for all of us and not just a flash in the sky. Anyhow, better or worse, thank you for the chance to give and Merry Christmas to us all. December 8, 1976."

Of his role in the film, *Variety* stated (on October 27, 1976), "While Carradine-as-Guthrie is always prominent dramatic focus, the film averts completely the pitfalls of personal celebrity biography: instead Carradine is a Depression-era Everyman, acting upon, and reacting to the world around him."

Other notable roles were in Ingmar Bergman's *The Serpent's Egg* (1977) and the submarine thriller *Gray Lady Down* (1979). In the role of real-life gunfighter Cole Younger, he appeared with brothers Keith and Robert in Walter Hill's well-regarded western, *The Long Riders* (1980). He played the voyeur Leroy Jessup in the 1985 television remake of *The Bad Seed* and portrayed action heroes in *P.O.W. The Escape* (1986) and *Armed Response* (1986). He dueled with Mel Gibson in the big-budget major studio action comedy *Bird on a Wire* (1990), and portrayed what seemed to be a man playing a woman in drag, or something close to that, in the role of Pearl in the bizarre *Sonny Boy* (1990). After a decade toiling in bottom rung B and Z films, some of which went directly to video and cable, Carradine found his acting career resurrected by Quentin Tarantino, who cast him as the male lead in the two-part *Kill Bill* films, *Kill Bill: Volume One* (2003) and *Kill Bill: Volume Two* (2004). Also in 2003, he played a country-western singer in the movie *American Reel* and used his songwriting and performing skills onscreen.

As a maverick filmmaker, Carradine was instrumental in getting the metaphysical 1979 film *Circle of Iron* (a.k.a. *The Silent Flute*) produced; he also played four roles.* More impressive were his own film productions as producer, director, writer, composer, editor and star: *Free to be...You and Me* (1972), *Americana* (1981), and the still unfinished *Mata Hari* (which has been in production for decades). In *People* magazine (June 1978), he mentioned the long-in-production *Mata Hari:* "We're going to tell the story with my daughter Calista in the title role. She's 16, and see her grow older with the film. We're going to film the execution as a dream sequence this summer.... It would be awful to have to look forward to being shot for the next fifteen years." Almost 30 years later, the film is still in production.

Carradine marches to his own drummer. He composes his own original music and believes in the promotion of personal growth through individualism and Eastern beliefs. Assumed to have been a renegade actor for avoiding the Hollywood scene, he is far from that. He is an original thinker. The author of three books and the on-screen host of a number of martial arts instructional videos (including *David Carradine's Tai Chi Workout, David Carradine's Kung Fu Workout, Kickbox Workout for Beginners,* and *Shaolin Strength Workout for Beginners*), Carradine continues to act and maintains a high profile website (www.davidcarradine.com), where he offers download samples of his music and keeps fans apprised of his recent acting roles and other bits of information. He is a rare breed. Here is David Carradine unmasked.

Q: You very much seem to be a free-spirited individual and this comes across in your performances. Who were your childhood idols? And what are some of your musical interests?

David Carradine: For childhood idols I would say the western movie stars, and really not the big-timers. My grandmother, every Saturday, would take me on what we called the red car [trolley] in LA, from our house to Hollywood. There was a theater called The

---

*Carradine garnered one of his best reviews for his role in Circle of Iron, when Variety commented (on January 24, 1979), "[D]eriving from an idea by the late kung fu great Bruce Lee, and actor James Coburn, the Zen-oriented fable may not satisfy either the action or the art crowd [but] David Carradine, billed above the title here, assumes the role originally written for Lee, and he again demonstrates a forceful screen presence, playing four distinct parts with flair and acumen. Carradine is masterful in all of his roles, especially as the blind teacher, and the desert warrior."

Hitching Post. You went in through a turnstile and it cost you a quarter, and no adults were in there. My grandmother would take me there and give me two quarters, one of which would buy me a mountain of popcorn and candy and stuff like that. I would pay a quarter to get in and there was nobody in there but kids, and they would show you two westerns, four cartoons, and a serial. One of the serials I remember was called *Zorro's Black Whip* (1944). It featured a woman who was like a cowgirl. She was a nice girl, and when things went bad she would ride out to this cave where she had a black stallion. She would dress up in this black kind of Zorro-like costume with a mask, and then would go out and whip the bad guys. She had a boyfriend who was kind of a wimp and was usually seen tied to a chair. She would often have to go and rescue him, and why they were showing this to six-year-old kids I don't know, but I appreciated it. I loved those western heroes and I was also a freak for comic books, like *Superman* and *The Spirit*. But probably my favorite guy was Batman. I actually liked the darkness of him, and the fact that he was a real person. He didn't have super powers; he was able, through his intelligence and strength, to take on all the forces of evil.

I think when I became a teenager, I started to appreciate music, but it was still the western stuff that had influence on me. People like Roy Rogers. One of the things about Roy was he could actually ride Trigger, his horse, at a full gallop, and do all kinds of tricks on him. He was a great shot. I used to go skeet shooting with him, and he never missed. He could actually ride his horse Trigger and shoot straight, and play the guitar, and sing, all at the same time, he could really do it all. There was a story once about Gene Autry, somebody came up to Gene and said, "I don't get it. You're an ugly guy, you're bald, you're fat, you can't sing, you can't ride for shit, you can't shoot, and you're a lousy guitar player." And Gene said, "I don't have to do any of that stuff, I'm Gene Autry." I never really cared for Gene much. I would say that in my late teens, what I became interested in, really, was people like Thomas Jefferson, Albert Einstein... I guess that's when I began to think about values.

As far as music is concerned, I don't know, I probably made my first two babies to Frank Sinatra. My dad was an opera freak, and I used to dig opera. However, there was a moment in the mid-sixties when I suddenly discovered rock and roll, The Beatles, The Rolling Stones, and Bob Dylan. I decided that I should learn how to play the guitar. I had been a piano player all my life, but only somewhat casually. I learned how to play the guitar, and then went back and concentrated more on the piano and started to write my own songs. I would say that the inspiration for that was probably more John Lennon than anybody else, and it still is. I still think that John Lennon is the king of all musical statements made in the twentieth century. I cannot think of anybody else that hit us that hard, and is going to last that long.

Q: In your earlier years, say your late teens and early twenties, you rather stayed away from the Hollywood crowd.

Carradine: I still do. I have always stayed pretty far from the Hollywood crowd. I was not brought up as a Hollywood kid. I did not even know my father was an actor when I was a little kid. I thought he was a sea captain. That is all he seemed to care about. He was the skipper of a sixty-four-foot schooner he owned, and he was always dressed like that, like a seaman. That is all he ever talked about. I thought that's what he did.

Q: What can you recall about some of your earliest roles, like the television westerns *Taggart* and *Shane*?

Carradine: When I got out of the army, I was in New York. I got a good agent, and

I got a couple of parts in New York. I appeared in the last *Armstrong Circle Theater* live television program ever made. I had a one-scene bit—well, it was not exactly a bit, because I had a long speech, but that was it, one speech...

Q: Like a monologue?

Carradine: Not exactly a monologue. In the scene there's an investigator who's asking questions about something that's happened and he asks me a question and I give him a long answer and then they cut to something else, and this was all on live television. As I was sitting in my place, waiting for my scene to come, I saw the camera, which was on a dolly, getting hung-up on something, They couldn't move it because there was stuff in the way, and the wheels became all screwed-up. I was sitting there thinking that if they don't free that camera, my scene is cut and they'll go on to the next thing. The other camera was all set up and ready to go. I was sitting there wondering, and they got it to me just in time, and I got to make my debut.

Then I did an episode of *East Side/West Side* with George C. Scott, who was, almost, for that one week that I was with him; like a teacher to me. I remember that I was doing auditions all the time, and at one time, I was doing like fifty auditions in a row and then nothing happened for like a week or two. I called up my agent and I said, "How come I'm not doing any auditions?" And my agent said, "Well, David, you've auditioned for everybody in town and nobody wants you." He said, "Look, there's this one thing. Universal wants you to have an interview. They've got an office here in New York and they're interviewing people for a term contract." My dad did not want me to do that because he had labored under a term contract for five years and got paid nothing for some of his greatest work, and he did not want me to do it. The head agent, a guy named Milton Goldman, knew my dad. I remember walking down the street with my dad, and my dad walking beside Milton Goldman, and my dad saying to him, "He doesn't want it." And Milton saying, "Look, John, nobody else wants him. This is the only real chance he's got to get going." My dad then said, "OK, then you should do it." I went on and did a screen test in New York; there were six of us who got screen-tested, and only two of us got hired, to what they called a non-exclusive, multiple picture contract, where they guaranteed me at least five weeks work over a period of a year. Included in that contract was my appearance in *Taggart*. Then there was one in *Wagon Train*, there was a *Virginian* episode, and there were two episodes of *The Alfred Hitchcock Hour*. In one of the *Alfred Hitchcock* episodes, I was the guest star, with Sally Kellerman. I was the heavy, but I was also the lead in it. That was the whole contract. That was the story with *Taggart*. Now, with *Shane*, when I got out of the Universal contract after a year, and I was free, I got two Broadway leads, and the second Broadway lead [*The Royal Hunt of the Sun*] got me *Shane*. I actually had a choice between *Shane* and a thing called *Hawk*, which I turned down, and Burt Reynolds took. *Hawk* was a failure and so was *Shane*. The two of us, Burt Reynolds and I, just hung out and waited to see if anything else would happen. We all know what happened to Burt, and we all know what happened to me. It took four years after *Shane*—well, actually three years, because what happened before *Kung Fu* was *Boxcar Bertha*...

Q: With Martin Scorsese...

Carradine: Right, with Marty and that was his first picture he ever directed. I don't think anybody at the time really knew about it, but that was where the energy was. If you want to call it the mystical, the psychic, the destiny kind of energy, it was me and Marty Scorsese working together as real collaborators, which was what we were.

Q: That's what came across to me, which was as far as the creative process for that film was concerned, that it seemed to me that you had something more to do with the creation of that character...

Carradine: Well, it was more of a collaboration. That's what Marty always said, that we were collaborating, and we did, supporting each other. I kind of came into my own there. It was the first time that I actually sort of took control and did what I wanted to do; Marty let me do it. I wasn't going, "Now, what do I do?" I was kind of dictating what I was going to do. It's kind of interesting if you think about it: You look at that character Big Bill Shelly, and he is so similar to the *Kung Fu* character in a way. He's a union leader. That's kind of the way Caine was in the *Kung Fu* pilot. He's working on a railroad, and saying, "We gotta improve these conditions." He's an outlaw, and he's a fighter. It was also an opportunity for me, and you get a glimmer of this in *Boxcar Bertha,* you get no sense of it in *Shane,* or in the work I did on Broadway, or in *Taggart,* or any of that, but there was a comedic element that came into my performance, and it is subtle. But, from the very beginning, there was this big piece of like Stan Laurel in that character, in the *Kung Fu* character. There's also this kind of everyman thing, I guess there's some of it in Big Bill Shelly, but there's none of it in any of the work that I did before that, which was kind of a Henry Fonda–Jimmy Stewart–everyman kind of feeling, This skinny guy, who doesn't want to give anybody a hard time, doesn't want to fight, he's unassuming, and he's morally correct, all that kind of thing, and that was in my mind.

I should probably tell you, and you are not asking me this, but during that period between *Shane* and *Boxcar Bertha,* I did not work very much. I played some small heavy roles in movies and television. One of the things I did was a David Susskind special that was a remake of *Johnny Belinda* with Mia Farrow. I played the rapist who rapes Mia Farrow. I was standing in the hallway at CBS and Murray Susskind, who was David's brother, was talking to me, and he said, "If you were going to do another series, what would you want it to be?" I said, "I don't want to do another series." He said, "Yeah, but if you did, what would you want it to be about?" I said, "What it would be about is Cain, the first murderer, walking through the land of Nod, to the East of Eden, with the mark of God upon him, trying to atone for having killed his brother, and trying to do good." He stared at me and said, "I'm talking about a commercial television series." And I said, "So am I." He just shook his head and walked away. Three years later... bam! A script that was exactly that lands on my table, and that made me think. What it made me think about was that thing about being careful what you wish for because you'll probably get it. It was like I was predicting it. I always wondered what Murray Susskind must have thought years later.

Q: That series made you the star that you are today.

Carradine: There was a period right there when I had the most recognizable name in America, according to some surveys that they did. There was me, Steve McQueen was number two, and then there was the president, Richard Nixon. This was right after the series *Kung Fu.* There were articles that talked about me. There was one particular article that talked about me being the most American statement that there was, and I thought, "By Playing a Chinese?" Yeah, but I was huge, no doubt about it. As far as it being the beginning of my career, which some people surmise that it was, this thing premiered in 1972, I'd become a professional actor in 1958. I had been available to work with Marty Scorsese again, and he's a very loyal guy. He has always worked repeatedly with the same people. When he did *Mean Streets*, I was not available because of *Kung Fu*, but had some time for a tiny role. He shot the stuff I did in *Mean Streets* in one day, a Sunday; it was the only day that I was available. Otherwise, I might have been playing one of the other major roles, or he might have written something in for me, whatever. It was the moment. It was not so much the character in *Kung Fu*, it was the moment. It was bound to happen right then. I am somewhat glad that it happened the way it did because of the effect on the world, aside from the cult figure that I became and everything, I feel that I had something to do with the growing interest in martial arts and Eastern philosophy. I also feel partly responsible for the growing interest in health foods for that matter, and holistic medicine, maybe even détente with China. It was all happening right then. In fact, the pilot episode, the movie, the second showing of it, was pre-empted by Richard Nixon shaking hands with Mao Tse-tung to welcome him into the United Nations. Man, there was a synchronicity there that was something.

Q: *Kung Fu* came about when there was a lot of violence, including war protests, racial riots, etc. going on in America, and it showed people how to reach peaceful conclusions to potentially violent situations.

Carradine: We were ABC's token peace show, although we still had to kick ass twice a week. The network said we had to have two fights per episode, and the FCC said no more than two minutes of it, so we managed to pull that off somehow. I do not think that anybody ever realizes that there are only two minutes of kung fu fighting in any one of those episodes.

Q: At any point in time, did you ever meet Bruce Lee?
Carradine: No. I never did.

Q: How did you become involved with Roger Corman?
Carradine: When I left *Kung Fu*, when I walked off the series, I knew that I needed to make a movie right away; if I waited, it was going to be hard to get a movie. I had to start that going. The other thing I wanted to do was, I wanted to destroy the image of me as Caine. My manager said, "Read this script" [*Death Race 2000*]. Around page 30, there is a scene where I am driving in the car with a mask on, with a woman, and we're talking about how my face is all screwed up and I say, "You want to see my face, see it." And the girl takes off my mask, and goes, "Oh!" but it's just me, no scars, no disfigurement, I don't look like a monster, and I say, "What did you expect? Another pretty face?" I closed the script, picked up the phone, and said I wanted to do the movie. That's how my relationship with Roger began. As a result of that movie, we made a deal to do *Deathsport*, and then the thing with Ingmar Bergman came up when we were about to do *Deathsport*...

Q: *The Serpent's Egg*?
Carradine: *The Serpent's Egg*. I originally said, "I'm not available." And they said, "Try to see if Roger would let you go." I called up Roger and said, "I've been offered this movie with Ingmar Bergman..." And Roger said, "Yeah, sure." After I did the movie with Ingmar Bergman, he said, "I don't want you to do *Deathsport*." Roger said this. I said, "No, I really want to do it." I was really interested in the script. He said, "I don't think you should do it. I don't think it's right for you anymore." I said, "No, no, I want to do it." Now I had no idea that Roger was intending to make the movie one-quarter as good as *Death Race 2000*. He didn't do that either. He didn't realize what he needed to do in order to make that picture work. I got a review from one of the trade papers for that picture that

said, "Don't let the fact that David Carradine is terrific [in *Deathsport*] talk you into going to see it, because it is one of the worst movies ever made." That's the first time that I realized that you actually could not make a silk purse out of a sow's ear. No matter how good you are, you cannot make a bad movie work. Of course the director was a lunatic, and Roger was refusing to put any money into the picture. At one point when we were still shooting the film my manager called up Roger and said, "Roger, you've got to put some money into this picture." And Roger said, "I am. I'm paying David Carradine $350,000." His idea was that he was going to do this picture for the same budget as *Death Race 2000*. Well, I did *Death Race 2000* for $50,000 and 9.3 percent of the world's gross, after breaking even. I have made about $700,000 on that picture so far and I still make money on it. It also taught me something about that, which is don't steal money from a picture. Make money later on a picture, or make the picture just for love, or because people will think well of you and give you another part, but don't try to rob a picture for the money, which is of course *not* the philosophy that major stars have today.

Q: You have juggled major Hollywood productions like *Bird on a Wire* with lower budgeted films and your own martial arts instructional videos. As an actor and filmmaker, what do you find the most pleasurable and the most rewarding?

Carradine: The most rewarding, the most fulfilling thing is to be the centerpiece and the motivating force of a movie that's going to be seen by a whole lot of people. Man, when you know that, that is an incredible feeling. A television series comes close to that because it is seen by an incredible amount of people. The quality of the work is not quite as good because it has to be done so fast, and because there's censorship involved. But being central, and being involved in the script and the production, and making things work, that's exciting. Of course, my *own* movies...

Q: *Americana, Free to be You and Me,* and *Mata Hari.*

Carradine: Directing is the best job. It's not precisely the most fun, but it's the best job, there's no doubt about it. Maybe it is the most fun, I'm not sure. The other thing is the editing room and writing the scores myself, and the recording studios. Those areas are just an incredible amount of fun. They are also very peaceful. A movie set is frantic, but a recording studio or an editing room is very tranquil, almost meditative, *is* meditative really.

Q: Are these the films that you are the most pleased to have worked on considering that you have been working on them for so long?

Carradine: I think so. *Americana* and I'm still out to lunch on *Mata Hari*, and I really don't know if it will ever be finished, really. There was a moment when somebody said, "How do you know if your daughter is going to stick with it?" And I said, "Well, I don't. As a matter of fact, I expect that she will leave at some point, and then maybe come back." But, I say, "Hey, what's wrong with an unfinished symphony?" Considering that I made over one hundred feature films, twenty-something movies-of-the-week, and appeared in three or four miniseries I think, and three television series of my own, and done about thirty-five plays, having one unfinished masterpiece is not bad. It would be nice if somebody could see it because it is incredible stuff, but it is still unfinished. Things I am proud of... *Americana*, as I said I'm still out to lunch on *Mata Hari*, then there's *Bound for Glory*, and *The Long Riders*, and everything else kind of just follows along. There is *Kung Fu* of course, but there is so much of *Kung Fu* that you cannot focus on a couple of hours of it.

Credits: 1963: *Armstrong Circle Theatre: Secret Document* (06/05/63); *East Side/West Side: Go Fight City Hall* (11/11/63) (television); *Wagon Train: The Eli Bancroft Story* (12/11/63) (television); 1964: *Arrest and Trial: The Black Flower* (03/01/64) (television); *The Virginian: The Intruders* (03/04/64) (television); 1965: *The Alfred Hitchcock Hour: Thou Still Unravished Bride* (03/22/65) (television); *Bob Hope Presents the Chrysler Theater: The War and Eric Kurtz* (03/05/65) (television); *Bus Riley's Back in Town*; *Taggart* (television); 1966: *Shane* (television); *The Trials of O'Brien: The Greatest Game: Part 1* (03/04/66), *The Greatest Game: Part 2* (03/11/66) (television); 1967: *Cimarron Strip: The Hunted* (10/05/67) (television); *Coronet Blue: The Rebels* (08/21/67) (television); *Johnny Belinda* (television); *The Violent Ones*; 1969: *The Good Guys and the Bad Guys*; *Heaven with a Gun*; *Young, Billy Young*; 1970: *Ironside: Due Process of the Law* (02/13/70) (television); *Macho Callahan*; *The McMasters*; *Maybe I'll Come Home in the Spring* (television); *The Name of the Game: Tarot* (02/13/70) (television); 1971: *Gunsmoke: Lavery* (02/22/71) (television); *Night Gallery: The Phantom Farmhouse* (10/20/71) (television); 1972: *Boxcar Bertha*; *Kung Fu* (television); *You and Me* (a.k.a. *Free to Be You and Me* [also director]); 1973: *Kung Fu* (television); *Mean Streets*; *The Long Goodbye* (uncredited); 1974: *Kung Fu* (television); 1975: *Death Race 2000*; *The Family Holvak: Craw* (09/07/75) (television); *Kung Fu* (television); 1976: *Bound for Glory*; *Cannonball*; 1977: *The Serpent's Egg* (a.k.a. *Das Schlangenei*) [U.S.–West Germany]; *Thunder and Lightning*; 1978: *Deathsport*; *Gray Lady Down*; 1979: *Circle of Iron* (a.k.a. *The Silent Flute*); *Je Te Tiens, Tu Me Tiens Par La Barbette* (a.k.a. *I've Got You, Now You've Got Me by the Chin Hairs*) [France]; *Mr. Horn* (television); 1980: *Fast Charlie: The Moonbeam Rider*; *Gauguin the Savage* (television); *High Noon Part 2: The Return of Will Kane* (television); *Saturday Night Live* (television); 1981: *Americana* [also director]; *Cloud Dancer*; *Darkroom: The Partnership* (12/25/81) (television); *The Long Riders*; 1982: *Q* (a.k.a. *Q: The Winged Serpent*); *Safari 3000*; *Trick or Treats*; 1983: *The Fall Guy: To the Finish* (12/07/83) (television); *Lone Wolf McQuade*; 1984: *Airwolf: Mind of the Machines* (04/07/84) (television); *The Fall Guy: October the 31st* (10/31/84) (television); *Jealousy* (television); *On the Line* [U.S.-Spain]; *The Warrior and the Sorceress* [Argentina-U.S.]; 1985: *The Bad Seed* (television); *The Fall Guy: Dead Ringer* (09/26/85) (television); 1986: *Amazing Stories: Thanksgiving* (11/24/86) (television); *Armed Response*; *Behind Enemy Lines*; *Hammer House of Mystery and Suspense: A Distant Scream* (television) [Great Britain]; *Kung Fu: The Movie* (television); *North and South, North and South Book II* (television); *Oceans of Fire* (video); 1987: *Heartbeat* (video); *Matlock: The Country Boy* (12/15/87) (television); *The Misfit Brigade* (a.k.a. *Wheels of Terror*) [U.S.-Great Britain-Yugoslavia]; *Six Against the Rock* (television); 1988: *Animal Protector* [Sweden]; *Crime Zone* [U.S.-Peru]; *Fatal Secret* [Sweden]; *I Saw What You Did* (television); *Open Fire* [U.S.-Mexico]; *Run for Your Life* [Italy]; *Warlords*; *Wizards of the Lost Kingdom II*; 1989: *The Cover Girl and the Cop* (television); *Crimen De Crimenes* (a.k.a. *Crime of Crimes*) [Mexico-U.S.]; *The Mad Bunch* [Sweden]; *Matlock: The Prisoner: Part 1* (11/14/89), *The Prisoner: Part 2* (11/21/89) (television); *Nowhere to Run*; *Sundown: The Vampire in Retreat*; *Tropical Snow* [Columbia-U.S.]; *Try This One on For Size* [France-U.S.]; 1990: *Bird on a Wire*; *Children of the Night* (a.k.a. *Night Children*); *Dune Warriors* [Philippines-U.S.]; *Evil Toons*; *Future Force*; *Future Zone* (a.k.a. *Future Force 2*); *Las Huellas Del Lince* [Spain]; *Martial Law*; *The Ray Bradbury Theatre: And the Moon Be Still As Bright* (10/19/90) (television) [France-Great Britain-Canada-U.S.-New Zealand]; *Sonny Boy*; *Think Big*; *The Young Riders: Ghosts* (09/29/90) (television); 1991: *El Aguila Y El Caballo* [Canada-Mexico]; *The Brotherhood of the Gun* (television); *Capital Punishment* (a.k.a. *Kickbox Terminator*); *Deadly Surveillance* (television); *Field of Fire* [U.S.-Philip-

Carradine (flanked by brothers Robert and Keith, as he appeared in Walter Hill's western *The Long Riders* (1980) (Huka Productions/United Artists).

pines]; *The Gambler Returns: The Luck of the Draw* (television); *Karate Cop*; *Project Eliminator*; 1992: *Animal Instincts* [U.S.-Japan]; *Distant Justice*; *Double Trouble*; *Kung Fu: The Legend Continues* (television); *Night Rhythms*; *Roadside Prophets*; *Waxwork II: Lost in Time*; 1993: *Bitter End*; *Frontera Sur* (a.k.a. *Code Death*) [Mexico-U.S.]; *Kill Zone* [Philippines-U.S.]; *Kung Fu: The Legend Continues* (television); 1994: *Dead Center* (a.k.a. *Crazy Joe*) (video); 1997: *Brandon Lee: The E! True Hollywood Story* (television); *Captain Simian and the Space Monkeys* (animated): *The Mandrill Who Knew Too Much* (06/07/97), *Apepocalypse...A Little Later* (06/21/97) (voice only) (television); *Dr. Quinn, Medicine Woman: Hostage* (02/22/97) (television); *Full Blast* (video); *The Last Stand at Saber River* (television); *The Lost Treasure of Dos Santos* (television); *Macon County Jail*; *The Rage*; *Too Hot to Skate* (television); 1998: *An American Tail: The Treasure of Manhattan Island* (animated) (voice only) (video); *The Children of the Corn V: Fields of Terror*; *The Effects of Magic*; *Light Speed*; *Lovers and Liars* (a.k.a. *Criminal Desire*); *Martian Law* (television); *The New Swiss Family Robinson*; *Nosferatu: The First Vampire* (video); *Sublet* (a.k.a. *Codename: Jaguar*) (video) [Canada]; 1999: *Acapulco H.E.A.T.: Code Name: Flight 401* (05/29/99) (television) [Canada-U.S.]; *Charmed: déjà vu All Over Again* (05/26/99) (television); *Kiss of a Stranger* [Canada-U.S.]; *Knocking on Death's Door*; *Natural Selection* (a.k.a. *The Monster Hunter*); *Profiler: Inheritance* (02/06/99) (television); *Puzzle in the Air*; *Shepherd* (a.k.a. *Cybercity*); *Walking After Midnight* (television); *Zoo*; 2000: *By Dawn's Early Light* (television); *Claudia Jennings: The E! True Hollywood Story* (television); *Dangerous Curves* (a.k.a. *Stray Bullet*); *David Carradine: The E! True Hollywood Story* (television); *The Donor*; *Down 'n Dirty*;

Family Law: Going Home (10/23/00), *Telling Lies, Conclusion* (11/6/00), *For Love* (11/13/00) (television); *Nightfall* (a.k.a. *Isaac Asimov's Nightfall*); 2001: *The Defectors* (a.k.a. *Crime School*) (television) [Canada]; *G.O.D.*; *Jackie Chan Adventures: The Warrior Incarnate* (09/15/01), *Snake Hunt* (09/22/01) (animated) (voice only) (television); *Just Shoot Me: Brandi, You're a Fine Girl* (11/16/01) (television); *Largo Winch: The Heir: Revelations* (12/01/01) (television) [France-Germany-Canada-Belgium-U.S.]; *Lizzie McGuire: Between a Rock and a Bra Place* (05/11/01) (television); *Mad TV* (11/10/01) (television); *Out of the Wilderness* (television); *Queen of Swords: End of Days* (05/26/01) (television) [Spain–France–Great Britain–Canada–U.S.]; *Titus: Houseboat* (12/19/01) (television); *The Warden of Red Rock* (television); 2002: *Autograph: David Carradine* (10/14/02) (television); *Balto II: Wolf Quest* (animated) (voice only) (video); *The Outsider* (television); *Wheatfield with Crows* [Netherlands]; 2003: *Alias: Countdown* (04/27/03) (television); *American Reel*; *Bala Perdida* (a.k.a. *The Lost Bullet*) [Spain]; *Dead and Breakfast*; *Kill Bill: Volume One*; 2004: *Alias: Hourglass* (04/18/04) (television); *Carta de ajuste* (06/21/04) (television) [Spain]; *Hair High* (animated) (voice only); *Kill Bill: Volume Two*; *The Last Goodbye*; *Max Havoc: Curse of the Dragon*; *Mondo Things* (05/06/04) (television); 2005: *Brothers in Arms*; *The Contender: Rivals* (03/13/05) (television) (uncredited); *Cinema Mil* (07/16/05) (television) [Spain]; *Corazon de...* (09/14/05) (television) [Spain]; *Danny Phantom: The Ultimate Enemy* (09/16/05) (animated) (television) (voice only); *Eve: Kung Fu Divas* (02/08/05) (television); *Friday Night with Jonathan Ross* (04/01/05) [Great Britain]; *The Ghosts of Les Cheris*; *Miracle at Sage Creek*; *Richard & Judy* (04/04/05) (television) [Great Britain]; 2006: *Final Move*; *Homo Erectus*; *Richard III*; *Treasure Raiders* [Russia-U.S.]; *What We Did on Our Holidays?* [U.S.–Great Britain]; 2006: *The Last Hour*; *The Last Sect*; 2007: *Big Stan*; *Blizhiny Boy: The Ultimate Fighter*; *Buster's Class Project*; *Camille*; *Epic Movie*; *Fall Down Dead*; *How to Rob a Bank*; *Permanent Vacation*; *The Trident*.

Robert Davi

Robert Davi was born on June 26, 1954, in Astoria, Queens, New York. The actor is known throughout the world for a variety of roles. From his portrayal of James Bond villain Franz Sanchez in *Licence to Kill* (1989) to the FBI's Bailey Malone in the television series *Profiler* in the nineties, Davi has remained one of the most recognizable heroes *and* villains on big screen and small.

Davi's credits include appearances in well over sixty television and film productions with roles that show his tremendous range. He studied with the legendary Stella Adler, who also became his mentor; and he was a member of the Actors Studio where he studied with Lee Strasberg. Davi's big break came when he was cast opposite Frank Sinatra in the television film *Contract on Cherry Street* in 1977. Following that role, he has made appearances in a number of films that displayed his versatility, including *Terrorist on Trial: The United States vs. Salim Ajami.* His performance as a Palestinian terrorist in the award-winning miniseries garnered the actor much praise, and caught the attention of the producers of *Licence to Kill*, the last James Bond film to star Timothy Dalton; Davi brought the Bond movies kicking and screaming into the new millennium with his performance as the thoughtful, brutally dangerous drug czar Sanchez. The on-screen chemistry between Davi and Dalton was so intense that the film's climactic, extended mano-a-mano battle had initially received an R rating (the series' first) for its violence content, before it was cut to a more palatable PG-13. Davi also appeared in several episodes of television's mobster drama series *Wiseguy* in 1989.

As an actor, Davi also showed a variety of shadings with his characterizations in *The Goonies* (1985), *Raw Deal* (1986), *Die Hard* (1988), *Son of the Pink Panther* (1993), and *Showgirls* (1995), while working with a who's who of directorial talent (the likes of Steven Spielberg, Richard Donner, Blake Edwards, John McTiernan, and Paul Verhoeven).

More recently, Davi co-starred alongside Rodney Dangerfield in the comedian's last film, the romantic comedy *The 4th Tenor* (2002); can be seen in the Rob Schneider comedy *The Hot Chick* (2002); and produced and starred in *Hitters* (2002), an independent film that takes a realistic look at the struggles within a neighborhood mob crew. Although most audiences may identify the actor with his sometimes gruff, no-nonsense roles, he is a talented multi-faceted, almost chameleon-like actor. There is no telling what type of role you will see Robert Davi in next.

If you ever come across the man in person, I attest that he is the nicest bad guy you will ever meet. Besides working often, in the craft that he really loves, and raising his five children, Davi stays busy volunteering his time with many charities such as the Dream

Robert Davi, versatile screen actor and memorable movie villain of the eighties through today as he appeared in *License to Kill* (1989) (Danjaq Productions/Eon Productions/United Artists/MGM) (photograph courtesy Robert Davi).

Foundation, Exceptional Children's Foundation, Heart of a Child Foundation, the National Italian American Foundation, and Unico, and he is the national spokesperson for the organization I Save America. He also is the chairperson of his own independent film company, Sun Lion Films. In 2003, Davi became a real-life hero when he helped save his Los Angeles neighbors when their home caught fire in the middle of the night. It was widely reported in the media that he and two LAPD officers saved the family. He also recently directed and co-starred in the film *The Dukes*, about a fifties musical *a cappella* vocal group struggling to make a comeback.

Q: I read somewhere where you were quoted as saying that you were initially discovered while you were singing in school, by a nun, and that this nun brought your singing to the attention of your parents, which led eventually to a scholarship. Is this true?

Robert Davi: I was singing in the shower after football practice at my high school. The nun heard my voice emerging from the shower rooms in the hallway. She sent someone in after me and said, "Who's singing?" Then she said she wanted to speak to me, and she spoke to me. I was standing in the doorway with a towel wrapped around my waist while the nun was talking to me. She said, "You have a beautiful voice. Why don't you come join the Glee Club?" Unfortunately, I declined because it would have been a bit too much to take on at the time. I was already involved in athletics and drama. The name Glee Club also seemed a little bit nerdy to me. Then she called my parents, who encouraged me. My mother said, "Try it. If you don't like it, then you can drop it." I went and there were all these lovely young Irish Catholic girls there, and when they heard that I could sing, and that I was also an athlete, and involved in the drama club, that became something special for me.

Q: Eventually, that involvement in the Glee Club got you a variety of offers to sing, including one in Florence, Italy.

Davi: I studied there; I did a workshop in Florence. I also sang with the Lyric Opera Company in Long Island, and did a bunch of things like that.

Q: What made you want to become an actor?

Davi: I just remember watching these old movies with my mother. Spencer Tracy, Humphrey Bogart, actors like that, they always fascinated me, and watching them on television back in the old days... it *did* something to me. Those actors helped to develop that need to express myself, my wanting to be inside the movies I saw. There was just something that pulled me towards that. There was also my love for language, of poetry, of Shakespeare. I guess I was encouraged when I was in the fourth grade. I performed in a play when I was in the fourth grade, and I got very strong encouragement from that, and I remember enjoying it, and the expression of it.

Q: You studied at Hofstra University in New York, and earned a drama scholarship.

Davi: Then I went and studied with Stella Adler in New York. I got into the Actor's Studio; I worked with Lee Strasberg, and a host of people. To me it was a craft and I wanted to learn from everyone. Stella Adler was my main mentor, and she introduced me to the work of Michael Chekhov, who was dead by the time, but who had been a huge acting teacher, and a brilliant actor from the Moscow Art Theater. I started reading his acting books, and I tracked down one of the guys that started the technique with him in Russia. He was in his nineties when I met him, and I worked with him. I spoke to Anthony Quinn about the Chekhov techniques and to Jack Palance too. I also became involved with several people who were involved with maintaining an interest in the Chekhov acting techniques.

Q: One of your earliest onscreen acting credits was in the television film *Contract on Cherry Street*.

Davi: That was the first time that I appeared on camera in a film.

Q: Do you recall how you got that role?

Davi: In those days, I was living in New York, and I was studying acting here, doing my acting thing here. When *Contract on Cherry Street* came around, the big buzz with all of the New York actors was that Frank Sinatra was going to be filming a movie on the streets of New York. I asked my casting agent, "What about this film *Contract on Cherry Street*?" He said, "Sinatra's using all his friends." Or, "It's basically all cast." Just on a whim, I said to the agent, "Well, where are the production offices?" He said, "They're on 5th Avenue, Columbia Pictures." I said, "I'm going to go up there." He said, "Go ahead. What do you have to lose?" Therefore, I did. I walked right past the security guard, who just kind of waved at me. I took the elevator upstairs, to one of the floors. Two women were sitting behind a desk. I popped my head in the door and I said, "I hate to intrude, but I said, 'I know you're casting *Cherry Street*. I hear it's all cast, but I decided to come up anyway." They smiled, and they looked at me intensely, and said "No, not quite. Do you have a picture and a résumé?" I said, "No, not with me. I didn't want to be presumptuous." They said, "Come back tomorrow, and bring one." With that opening, I went and got a picture and résumé and I came back like twenty minutes later, and they were still there, and they laughed. The next morning, there was a voice mail on the actor phone, which was a voice mail service that we all had in New York at that time, and it said, "Call Columbia Studios immediately and talk to so and so...." I called them, and they said, "Hurry up, come in and pick up a script." I went in there, they said, "Here, here's the script. We want you to read this character. Come back at six o'clock tonight." I came back at six, I read and the casting director said, "One second, please." She went back into another room, she came out with a beaming smile on her face, and she said, "What are you doing this summer?" I said, "You tell me..." She said, "It is 99 percent yours. We will let you know on Monday." This was a Friday. And, that was that. I got the role.

Q: Did you ever interact with Frank Sinatra off the set?

Davi: Oh, yes. He was very gracious and generous. He was even a close friend of "Cubby" Broccoli. Later on in my life, people would tell me that while I was working, Sinatra was checking up on me, saying, "Hey, how's the kid doing?" I guess he referred to different people as *the kid*. In addition, people would tell me, "Sinatra likes your work." Someone would say to me, "Mr. Sinatra saw you in this or that and thought you were terrific. Blah, blah, blah..." On the set of *Cherry Street*, I remember one night especially. Here I am, an Italian-American, with Frank Sinatra, and we are in Little Italy on the corner of Mulberry and Hester Streets, at a social club at 2 AM, 3 AM, I am kind of checking out the scene. Observing, and being in the presence of whoever was there. Frank Sinatra, and Harry Guardino, those people were there...what a scene.

Q: After you moved to Hollywood, you appeared in a variety of roles in both television shows and in films, as a villain. Did you feel typecast?

Davi: Oddly enough, I have not played many gangsters. I may have played bad guys. I have stayed away from the Guido kind of bad guy as well. While I have played a gangster, I have done it very, very infrequently. For example, on *The Gangster Chronicles* I played a historic figure, Vito Genovese. In *White Hot*, the Thelma Todd film, I played Lucky Luciano. In the series *Wiseguy*, my character was very interesting, a gang leader possibly, but not a gangster. Those were really the only gangster type of characters that I have played. Otherwise, it has usually been the bad guy, from a Palestinian to a Columbian drug lord, to all different kinds of characters.

Q: Afterwards, you began to appear in films that later had cult followings, *The Goonies* and *Raw Deal* among others.

Davi: I was offered *First Blood Part 2* and *Goonies* at the same time, and we were trying to work out the shooting dates so I could be in both films. We could not work out the dates, unfortunately. I thought that would be a great one-two punch, to do a big action film, and to do a Steven Spielberg and Richard Donner film for the entire family. Spielberg did the second unit shooting for *The Goonies*. It was a great time. Dick Donner was wonderful to work with as a director. Frank Marshall did the third unit shooting, and Chris Columbus wrote the screenplay. There was some amazing talent involved with that film, and then there was the pirate ship set... just the whole experience of working on that movie was a lot of fun. Of course, the interplay between Joey Pantoliano and me was magic. We improvised a lot of that dialogue and the movements that we did. I improvised the opera singing, because they wanted the character to have some kind of particular traits. Whenever I play a bad person, I always look for something that is going to humanize the character, so I wanted to make this character someone that no one would listen to. Not even his deformed brother, when he was feeding him. It is as if you have to sing to be fed. However, here, you have to listen to me sing in order to get your supper. Moreover, when he would not listen... It was certain moments like that, that involved creative freedom that those people let me have...it was a great experience.

Q: And, *Raw Deal*?

Davi: That was when I first became friends with Arnold Schwarzenegger. I did not know him before then. John Irvin was the director on that film. We harassed each other, Arnie and me, on that set, always playing practical jokes on each other. We pulled a tremendous amount of practical jokes on one another.

Q: Do you still keep in contact with him?

Davi: We were tight up until 1996. Then I did the series *Profiler*, and my schedule got busy. Up until then, we became like best friends. Things happen...I just did not have the time. We used to work out every day, be over each other's house for dinner a couple of times a week. I did not have the time after a while.

Q: What do you recall about your small but important role in *Die Hard*? As Special FBI Agent Johnson (who is teamed with an African-American actor who is also portraying an FBI agent named ... Johnson), you have quite a bit of quotable dialogue as well as a couple of memorable moments onscreen.

Davi: Joel Silver and I had met; I thought John McTiernan, the director, was talented, having seen *Nomads* with Pierce Brosnan. But at that time, when production began, Bruce Willis was not as popular as he is now. He had a couple of pictures that were not performing well, and this film had to really perform at the box-office. No one knew that it was going do the business that it did; it went right through the roof. I did not even take billing. I remember I said to Joel Silver, "I'll do it, but don't even give me billing." because I knew that I had the Bond film to do at that time, and it was stupid of me. He said to me, "You have to take billing because you are SAG [Screen Actors Guild]. You're sure you don't want billing?" He had seen the film at that time, but I had no idea of the impact that the character had made. That was a fun film to work on. Joel Silver was terrific to work for, very creative. And McTiernan was great to work with, I had a good relationship with him.

Q: Was the role improvised at all? When you turn the hat around on your head, lean out of the helicopter, and decide to get all cocky?

Davi: Those were all improvised moments that we came up with, John McTiernan and myself, and some of the dialogue in the street... "I'm in charge here." All that stuff we worked out on the set.

Q: You played the villain Franz Sanchez in *Licence to Kill*, which is remembered by James Bond fans as not only one of the best films in the series, but as having one of the best and most realistic villains.

Davi: First, off, about how I got the role. I did a film, a movie-of-the-week called *Terrorist on Trial: The United States vs. Salim Ajami* with Ron Leibman and Sam Waterston and I had got tremendous, tremendous reviews. It was on the cover of every newspaper. It was huge at the time. I played a Palestinian kidnapped by the United States government to stand trial for acts of terrorism, whose defense attorney was Jewish, and was played by Ron Leibman. It was ahead of its time. Richard Levinson and William Link were the screenwriters. It was the last script that they wrote together; they had created the character of Colombo, which worked out well for Peter Falk, and had written *The Education of Private Slovik*. They were the major television writers of the time. The producer was George Englund who had produced *The Ugly American* and *The Shoes of the Fisherman*, he was a key figure in Marlon Brando's company, and he was one of Brando's closest friends. Therefore, that was an extremely high-quality project. When it was shown, Richard Maibaum, who had written the scripts for a number of the Bond movies in the seventies, and who had written the script for *Licence to Kill*, called up "Cubby Broccoli" and said, "Put on Channel 2." "Cubby" said, "I've got it on." Maibaum said, "I think that's the next Bond villain." "Cubby" said, "I agree." They called me in the next day, they offered me the part, and then they rather tailored it along the way for me. It was the last film with all of the original Bond creators involved. Richard Maibaum was there, "Cubby" Broccoli, Barbara Wilson, Michael Wilson, John Glen directed it, and of course, there was Timothy Dalton. There are many good memories associated with that film. With the Bond production family, it is like having a great family that is just a lot of fun. I also went around the world for four and half months promoting the film afterwards. The distributors wanted me to promote it. You will never do a press junket like the Bond films do. I do not care what film it is; the Bond film press junket goes all around the world, and is just incredible. It is a machine that everyone anticipates and it is much bigger in Europe than it is here.

Q: What can you recall about your fight scene with Timothy Dalton?

Davi: On the tractor-trailers? The French Remy brothers choreographed that. The Remy brothers are a French driving team that has choreographed some of the greatest stunt driving scenes in a lot of movies like the original *Italian Job* [1969], and then contributed to a number of movies with Jean-Paul Belmondo before working with the Bond people on a lot of Roger Moore's Bond films. They choreographed that scene. Those guys were geniuses with that stuff. Of course, you also work with the film's stunt crew, but wind up doing a lot of the stuff yourself. Choreographing, and improvising a bit of the stuff, like the scene with the machete, and basic structure, and movement, and all that for safety reasons. A lot of that is all choreographed, but on camera, it looks spontaneous.

Q: What was it like to work with Dalton, who was thought by some people to be among the best of the actors who portrayed Bond?

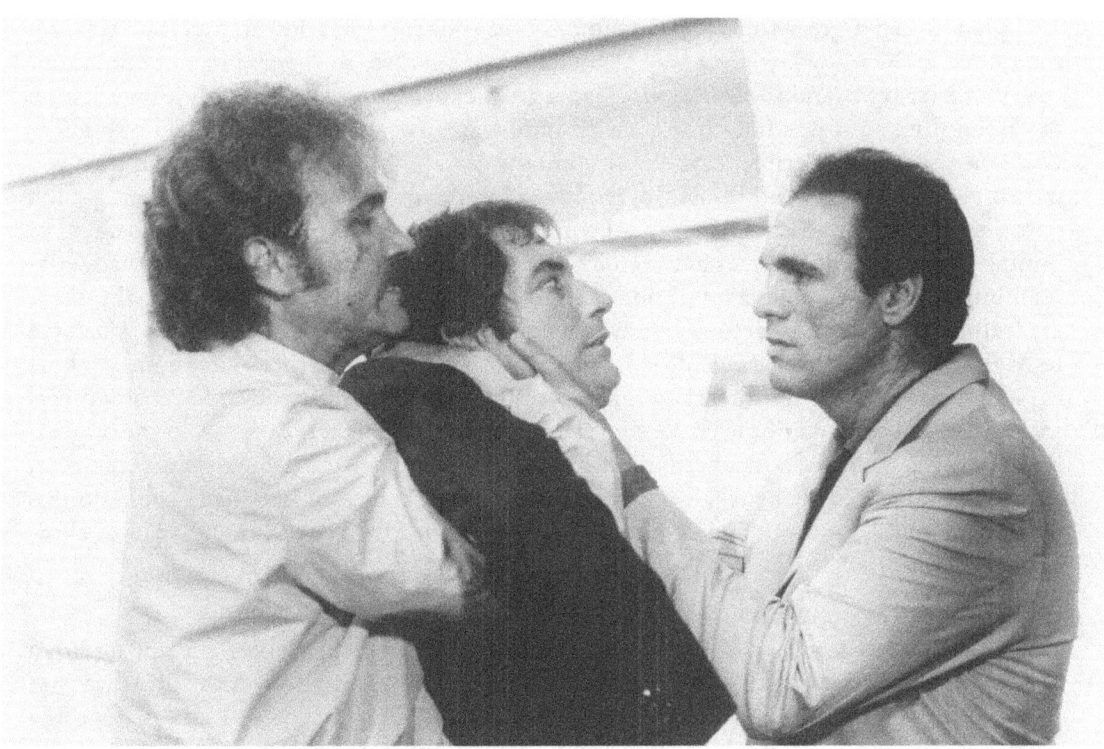

Davi threatens Timothy Dalton at the ferocious climax of the violent James Bond thriller, *Licence to Kill* (1989) (Danjaq Productions/Eon Productions/United Artists/MGM).

Davi: He and I got along great from the beginning because one of the things was the idea of going back to the feel of *Casino Royale*. I started researching Bond heavily, and read many of the books for the role, and in that early book, *Casino Royale*, Fleming had already stated that Bond and the villain of that particular piece shared a kinship in some way. I had spoken to Timothy and "Cubby" Broccoli about it, and subsequently Timothy brought it up, that in *Casino Royale*, Ian Fleming talks about how Bond and the villain are mirror images of each other. Going on that premise, thought and idea, I said, "Let's go back to that kind of thing." That is why, in a strange way, many people rooted for Bond, and many people rooted for Sanchez. I had people come up to me and tell me, after they saw the film, that if he was real, that they'd work for that guy [Sanchez] because one of the things that we put into the script was that business about loyalty, and how it was more important to my character than money. If you look at every act of violence that Sanchez commits, it's something that is done in response to something that has been done to him, every single one, from the whipping of the girl in the beginning. If you are playing by a certain set of rules, there are going to be consequences. Timothy and I had a very good time. It was mano-a-mano, two heavyweights. In addition, Benicio Del Toro and I became very close while working on that film. Later on, when I was working on *Christopher Columbus*, I suggested to [director] John Glen that we should get Benicio for a role, and they did.

Q: Speaking of *Christopher Columbus*, how was it to work on such an epic, grand-scale movie?

Davi: I had a great time. Years before, I had spoken to Marlon Brando one time on the phone in New York while I was at Stella Adler's house, so it was fun to be in a picture that Marlon Brando was in. I also had a great experience working with John Glen on the Bond film, so it was fine to work with him again. Also, Mario Puzo, who wrote *The Godfather*, wrote the script, so you're thinking those are two huge talents alone involved in this project, Brando and Puzo. But what was interesting was, when they offered me the part, I started doing research for my role immediately. I called John Glen and I said, "I'm finding a lot of inconsistencies between my real-life character, and the way Puzo had written him." I started making a lot of notes. I was playing this character, who in Spain, there are statues of him, there's actually a day devoted to him. Glen said, "Well, when you come to Malta, we'll talk about your ideas." I finally got to Spain, and there were some technical advisors who were on the set to make sure that we stuck fairly close to recorded history. So we talked and I got to make some changes to my character. Because, in the original script, my character was much...darker. It was fun to be in Malta, on a grand epic film, and with a great cast. For me, I was to the manor born. You could see that I could do this period epic piece, and not sound like a New York thug. It gave me the chance to show another color of what I can do.

Q: What can you recall about the production of *Predator 2*?

Davi: Danny Glover was already a friend of mine; we had worked previously in an episode of *Lou Grant* together. The producer, Joel Silver, was fun to work with. It was fun to mix it up. Again, like I said, I am known for the villains, but here I am, playing the chief of police, an FBI guy, I mixed it up. I decided not to try to repeat a character, and I have to say there are many fantastic, great actors but they play the same character, repeatedly. Although some of them do it very well and very successfully in many different movies, if you look at the body of my work you will see a variety of characters, even in the *Heidi Fleiss* movie. To my knowledge, there have only been a handful of people that have done that kind of thing, Anthony Quinn being one of them.

Q: Deciding not to repeat a character really shows in that great role you had in *Showgirls*.

Davi: I wanted to work with Paul Verhoeven, most assuredly. That was one director where I had really loved his work from *Soldier of Orange* through most of his films that he had made in Holland. Joe Eszterhas was a substantial writer; he wrote that script for *Basic Instinct* and wrote the script for *Showgirls*. *Showgirls* has a bit of a cult following, although I personally felt it was a bit forced, a bit risqué, and pushed the envelope at times. I really did not think it would get the negative press that it did at the time.

Q: Is it true that you met with real-life serial-killer profiler Robert Ressler prior to starting production on the television show *Profiler*?

Davi: I spoke to him, but the person I did meet who had much more of an effect on me, was a man that I met at Quantico, in Washington, DC, named Bill Hagenmeyer. He was running the child abduction serial killer unit. He was the profiler heading up the profiling unit. He has been retired since then. I sat with him, had extensive conversations with him, and researched the whole profiling thing up in Quantico. I was then able to have a conversation with Robert Ressler, and others who created the technique of profiling.

Q: Did you enjoy working on the show?

Davi: Yes and no, because there were a couple of frustrations. The producers did a terrific job, but I felt that we could have changed a few things. Me having been a stickler for research and reality, I had recommended to them in the first year that we should become procedural. There are seven steps to profiling...autopsy protocol, victimology, crime scene analysis...one thing I told them was that, "based on my research on the Internet from the fans, they're very, very interested in this sort of thing." Of course, this was in 1997, so it was way ahead of shows like *C.S.I.* Had they listened to me, things would have been different. It was interesting, I liked playing the part, I liked being engulfed in the FBI world, in the profiling world, and I thought it was very interesting.

Q: *Profiler* was two, three years too soon. It was ahead of the whole *C.S.I.* cycle of television shows. Now you look around, and there are a whole slew of similar shows.

Davi: We started the whole trend. We were a sensation on Saturday nights during the first season. No Saturday night show ever performed like that, we blew away all the competition that was put on opposite us. We blew away even the competition that ABC devised to stop us, like *The Practice*. There are different reasons why I think we didn't continue to do a bigger share of the ratings hold—we dropped off from a 19 share to a 16, to 14 share. What I believe happened was, when I originally signed on for the show, I was told that it would be me and her, Ally Walker, as the leads. Over time, the show became a little more balanced towards her, and my thing was, when you had the opening weekends, when we had the biggest share of the Saturday night audiences, who was the recognizable face? Who were people tuning in to see? I've been around for twenty years, been in different films, have a whole bunch of different fans...people were waiting for me to pop up and do something, maybe deliver something special with my characterizations. I always felt that with that show, regarding my character, that they had a horse that could run around a track, but they tied my legs together, and that is the truth about that. I used to say to them, "I never had to work so hard to play so dumb so I don't look stupid."

Q: Is there something that you have appeared in recently, that might not have received the attention it deserved?

Davi: I did this little kids' film, *The Sorcerer's Apprentice*, where I played Merlin the Magician with sort of a Welsh accent. It was a great little film for kids. In addition, it was such a sweet little film. Also, there is *The 4th Tenor* with Rodney Dangerfield. I played this Italian scoundrel, with an Italian accent, and this and that, a real scampino. It is not the greatest film in the world, but is it worth looking at, and having a smile? Yes, it is, for certain people, for a certain kind of audience, but it is obviously not a Quentin Tarantino film. As for the *Heidi Fleiss* film...if people knew who Ivan Nagy really was, their jaw would drop when they see my performance.

Q: What is your favorite role so far? And what do you believe makes a good villain and a good hero?

Davi: As for my favorite role, to be honest with you, I have not done it yet. What makes a good villain, and what makes a good hero? To me, I have never liked the cartoon kind of performance, although there is something to be said for that, for those who appreciate such things. What makes a good hero? A good hero is made by an audience commenting on the morality of the character as he is being played, not only by his actions. As it is said in *Richard III*, "Since I cannot prove a lover, I am determined to prove a villain." That character just made a choice to go after that. But, if a character has depth, and is multi-faceted, is a fine-cut multi-edged diamond, there is a lot to work with there. The best things concerning what makes a good hero and what makes a good villain is to try to find the humanity in each of those characters...or try to find the opposite. You try to find the good in the villain, and the bad in the hero.

Credits: 1977: *Contract on Cherry Street* (television); 1978: *Charlie's Angels: Mother Angel* (11/15/78) (television); 1979: *And Your Name Is Jonah* (television); *Barnaby Jones: False Witness* (11/29/79) (television); *From Here to Eternity* (television); *The Legend of the Golden Gun* (television); *The Incredible Hulk: The Slam* (10/19/79) (television); *Lou Grant: Slammer* (10/01/79) (television); *Trapper John M.D.: Licensed to Kill* (12/09/79); 1980: *Alcatraz: The Whole Shocking Story* (television); *The $5.20 an Hour Dream* (television); *Rage!* (television); 1981: *Dynasty: The Honeymoon* (01/19/81) (television); *The Gangster Chronicles* (a.k.a. *The Gangster Chronicles: An American Story*) (television); *Gangster Wars* (television); *Shannon: Gotham Swansong* (11/11/81) (television); 1982: *Hill Street Blues: Stan the Man* (11/04/82) (television); *T.J. Hooker: Second Chance* (09/25/82) (television); *St. Elsewhere: Samuels and the Kid* (11/30/82) (television), *Legionnaires: Part 2* (12/14/82) (television); 1983: *Bay City Blues: Zircons are Forever* (11/08/83) (television); *Bring 'Em Back Alive: The Shadow Women of Chung Tai* (01/29/83) (television); *The Fall Guy: The Molly Sue* (03/02/83) (television); 1984: *The A-Team: Sheriffs of Rivertown* (11/27/84) (television); *City Heat*; *The Fall Guy: Dead Bounty* (11/14/84) (television); *Hart to Hart: Always, Elizabeth* (05/15/84) (television); *T.J. Hooker: Exercise in Murder* (01/28/84) (television); 1985: *The Goonies*; *Hunter: Million Dollar Misunderstanding* (11/16/85) (television); 1986: *The Equalizer: Wash-Up* (01/29/86) (television); *Raw Deal*; 1987: *Wild Thing*; 1988: *Action Jackson*; *Die Hard*; *L.A. Law: Leapin' Lizards* (04/28/88) (television); *Terrorist on Trial: The United States vs. Salim Ajami* (television); *Traxx*; 1989: *Licence to Kill* [Great Britain–U.S.]; *Wiseguy: Battle of the Barge* (09/27/89), *Heir to the Throne* (10/11/89), *La Lacrime D'Amore: Part 2* (05/24/89), *A Rightful Place* (09/20/89), *Sins of the Father* (10/04/89) (television); 1990: *Amazon* [Finland–U.S.]; *Deceptions* (television); *Maniac Cop 2* (television); *Peacemaker*; *Predator 2*; 1991: *Legal Tender*; *The Taking of Beverly Hills*; *Under Surveillance*; *White Hot: The Mysterious Murder of Thelma Todd* (television); 1992: *Center of the Web*; *Christopher Columbus: The Discovery* [Great Britain–U.S.–Spain]; *Illicit Behavior* (a.k.a. *Criminal Intent*); *Wild Orchid II: Two Shades of Blue*; 1993: *Maniac Cop 3: Badge of Silence* (a.k.a. *Maniac Cop 3*); *Mardi Gras for the Devil* (a.k.a. *Night Trap*); *Quick*; *Son of the Pink Panther* [U.S.–Italy]; 1994: *Blind Justice*; *Cops and Robbersons*; *The Dangerous*; *No Contest* [Canada]; 1995: *Codename Silencer* (a.k.a. *Body Count*) [U.S.–Japan]; *Cyber Vengeance*; *Delta of Venus*; *Showgirls* [France–U.S.]; *The November Men* (uncredited); *V.R.5: Simon's Choice* (04/21/95) (television); 1996: *Absolute Aggression*; *For Which He Stands*; *An Occasional Hell*; *Profiler* (television); *The Zone* (a.k.a. *The Dogfighters*); 1997: *The Beneficiary* (television); 1988: *The Bad Pack*; 1999: *Batman Beyond* (animated): *Heroes* (02/21/99) (Voice only) (television); *My Little Assassin* (television); *The Pretender: End Game* (05/08/99) (television); 2000: *The Pretender: Spin Doctor* (02/05/00) (television); 2001: *Soulkeeper*; 2002: *Hitters*; *The Sorcerer's Apprentice* [South Africa]; *Verdict in Blood* (television) [Canada]; *Grand Theft Auto: Vice City* (a.k.a. *Vice City*) (video game) (voice only) [U.S.–Great Britain]; *The 4th Tenor*; *The Hot Chick*; 2003: *One Last Ride*; 2004: *Call Me: The Rise and Fall of Heidi Fleiss* (television); *Halo 2* (video game) (voice only); *Karen Sisco: No One's Girl* (04/07/04) (television); *Stargate: Atlantis: The Storm* (04/07/04) (television); 2005: *The Film Maker* [Great Britain]; *In the Mix*; *Scarface: The World Is Yours* (video game) (voice only); *Stargate: Atlantis: The Brotherhood* (02/25/05), *The Eye* (01/21/05) (television); 2006: *The Dukes*; 2007: *The Butcher*; *Magic*.

Brad Dourif

Brad Dourif was born Bradford Claude Dourif on March 18, 1950 in Huntington, West Virginia. He attended the Aiken Preparatory School in Aiken, South Carolina in the early sixties and then decided to become an actor at age sixteen, while working on sets and in bit parts in summer stock. He traveled to New York where he worked with the esteemed Circle Repertory Company theatrical company. He also taught acting at New York's equally renowned Columbia University.

Mainstream and genre movie audiences recall the unique-looking Dourif from a number of roles, including his film debut (in 1975) as Billy Bibbit in Milos Forman's powerful cinematic production of Ken Kesey's *One Flew Over the Cuckoo's Nest* (alongside star Jack Nicholson). Brad Dourif often found himself really going to the edge (and in some cases, over it) in terms of characterization when confronted by many of the roles presented to him. He worked with John Huston in *Wise Blood* (1979) (in the role of Hazel Moates, a religious zealot), Forman again in *Ragtime* (1981), David Lynch in *Dune* (1984) and *Blue Velvet* (1986), and Alan Parker in *Mississippi Burning* (1988). He began his genre film career with a bang by first appearing (in the flesh) as serial killer Charles Lee Ray, and then as Ray's reincarnated form, Chucky, the killer doll (featuring Dourif's distinctive voice only), in *Child's Play* (1988) (and its four sequels *Child's Play 2* [1990], *Child's Play 3* [1991], *The Bride of Chucky—Child's Play 4* [1998], and *Seed of Chucky* [2004]).

Other genre credits, including Dario Argento's *Trauma* (1992) (as Dr. Lloyd), the David Lynch–produced *Wild Palms* television miniseries (1994), Stephen Norrington's UK-made cyber thriller *Death Machine* (1995), Jean-Pierre Jeunet's *Alien Resurrection* (1997), and *The Progeny* (1999) have solidified Dourif's status as a genre film fave to audiences everywhere.

Besides distinctive turns in the television programs *The X-Files* (the 1995 episode *Beyond the Sea*), and recurring roles on *Babylon 5* (1994), *Star Trek: Voyager* (1995), and *Deadwood* (2004–), Dourif was seen in the role of Grima Wormtongue in two of the biggest epics ever produced, *The Lord of the Rings: The Two Towers* (2002) and *The Lord of the Rings: The Return of the King* (2003). Other interesting Dourif films are *The Eyes of Laura Mars* (1978), *Fatal Beauty* (987), the bizarre *Sonny Boy* (1988), *The Color of Night* (1994), *Nightwatch* (1998), and *Prophecy III: The Ascent* (2000).

Q: You are mainly thought of as an intense character actor. Which do you enjoy most, character actor parts, or leading roles?

Brad Dourif: Character actors do get a lot less money, but I did want to be a character actor. One of my heroes was Dustin Hoffman and other actors who could do a variety

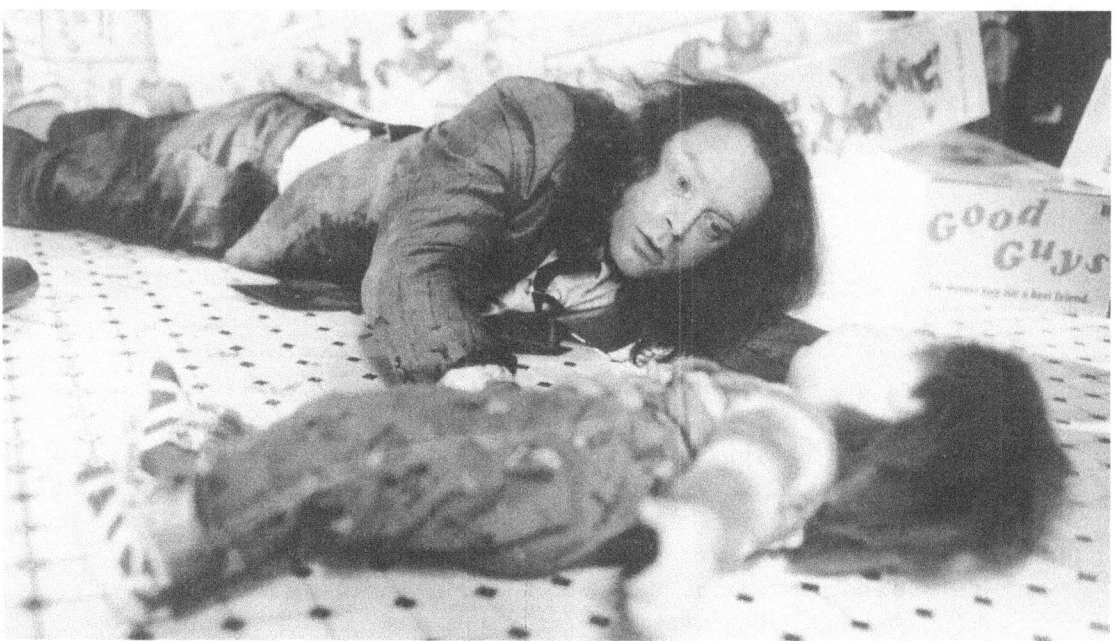

Brad Dourif prepares to mentally enter and animate the lifeless children's toy "Chucky" and then turn it into the murderous tool of his vengeance in *Child's Play* (1988) (United Artists).

of things, people who weren't considered leading actors. There are certain actors who have an edge, and I think I have an edge. I think actors who have a certain edge can play a variety of roles, different parts, than the non-leading roles.

Q: How do you feel about being considered a genre film specialist?

Dourif: Well, actually, it is nice to be remembered for your work, but I am trying to get out of these killer-type roles... the bad people. But different roles, different things about particular characters attract me to different parts at different times. It depends on the approach to the character in the script, by the writer, the director, and how I think I would approach the part.

Q: Do you find it taxing to portray characters more extreme than the norm?

Dourif: It can be more taxing to play somebody who is really off or extreme...

Q: Do you have a favorite director?

Dourif: I love David Lynch. He is one of the most original directors I have worked with. He has a unique vision.

Q: What about John Huston on *Wise Blood*?

Dourif: I had the leading role and I sometimes felt uncomfortable with it. At that time in my time, I had doubts about my abilities as an actor in a leading role.

Q: What can you tell me about Milos Forman and *Cuckoo's Nest*?

Dourif: Milos Forman was a very determined person. When you act in a film for Milos Forman, you know that you are going to be doing the best work that you can. Many people have said that the role of the Gemini Killer in *Exorcist III* was the best thing that I have ever done. I personally do not agree. I think my performance as Billy Bibbit from

One Flew Over the Cuckoo's Nest was better. As far as *Exorcist III* is concerned, acting with George C. Scott in that film was an intense experience, no question about that.

Q: What do you think when people recall your work nowadays and primarily mention the genre film work that you have done?

Dourif: I do many horror films now because that is what the people are watching, although, to be honest, I would like to broaden my horizons. I will continue to keep trying to do parts that are normal people, who are relaxed and have a sense of humor. I myself have intensity, which is both normal and natural. Do I think that I have become typecast? Absolutely, that is exactly what happened to me. However, I think one of the most impressive things I have done in recent years is a film called *Chain Dance* [1990], where I played a man with cerebral palsy.

Q: What about the *Child's Play* series?

Dourif: What kind of preparations can I do for a character like Chucky? He is not a real person, never was a real person... There is not a lot of preparation one can do for a role like Chucky. But I think one can have one whopping good time. It should be like primal scream therapy. You put yourself out there. I must say, though, that I enjoy playing Chucky. I go in and do all my vocal work, and then they match the puppet's lip moments to the dialogue I recorded. Sometimes, they have to keep re-recording the dialogue, matching my voice and what I am saying until it perfectly matches the puppet's movements.

Q: You have appeared in many television programs like *Star Trek: Voyager*, *The X-Files*, and *Babylon 5* to name but three. What are your favorite TV roles?

Dourif: The one I am currently a regular in right now, *Deadwood*, where I play a doctor who is far ahead of his time, and is into science. We will be starting our fourth season shortly. Let me say that I was a little reluctant at first to appear in episodic television, but my girlfriend encouraged me, and I'm glad she did because *Deadwood* is one of the best things I have ever appeared in and, I believe, one of the best television programs currently.

Q: Can you tell me how you approached your role in the two *Lord of the Rings* films?

Dourif: There was a period where I was playing killers and oddballs quite frequently, and it was too much. Playing

A handsome Dourif as he appeared in one of the supporting roles in Milos Forman's *Ragtime* (1981) (Dino De Laurentiis Productions/Sunley Productions Ltd./Paramount Pictures).

Grima Wormtongue in the *Lord of the Rings* films was different. This character is not a killer really, he is just a cowardly villain. There should be more footage of that character in the extended version of the film that [director] Peter Jackson prepared for the DVD release.

Q: Would you continue to provide the voice of Chucky if *Seed of Chucky* became a financial success rather than just a cult favorite?

Dourif: It's good work and I get paid. Frankly, as long as they keep making money, they will keep making them.

Credits: 1975: *One Flew Over the Cuckoo's Nest*; *W.W. and the Dixie Dancekings* (uncredited); 1976: *The Mound Builders* (television); 1977: *Gruppenbild Mit Dame* (a.k.a. *Group Portrait with a Lady*) [France–West Germany]; *Visions: The Gardener's Son* (01/06/77) (television); 1978: *The Eyes of Laura Mars*; *Sergeant Matlovich Vs. the U.S. Air Force* (television); 1979: *Studs Lonigan* (television); *Wise Blood* (a.k.a. *John Huston's Wise Blood*) [U.S.–West Germany]; 1980: *Guyana Tragedy: The Story of Jim Jones* (television); *Heaven's Gate*; 1981: *Ragtime*; 1982: *I, Desire* (a.k.a. *Desire, the Vampire*) (television); 1984: *Dune* [U.S.–Mexico]; *Tales of the Unexpected: Number Eight* (06/09/84) (television); 1985: *Impure Thoughts*; *Istanbul* [Belgium–Luxembourg–West Germany]; 1986: *Blue Velvet*; *The Equalizer: Out of the Past* (01/15/86) (television); *Moonlighting: All Creatures Great...and Not So Great* (11/11/86) (television); *Rage of Angels: The Story Continues* (television); *Spenser: For Hire: Rage* (04/01/86) (television); *Vengeance: The Story of Tony Cimino* (television); 1987: *Fatal Beauty* [U.S.-Japan]; *The Hitchhiker: The Legendary Billy B.* (02/13/87) (television); *Medium Rare* (television); *Miami Vice: Theresa* (02/13/87) (television); 1988: *Child's Play*; *Mississippi Burning*; 1989: *Desperado: The Outlaw Wars* (television); *Murder, She Wrote: Fire Burn, Cauldron Bubble* (02/19/89) (television); *Star Trek: The Next Generation: The Emissary* (06/04/89) (television); *Terror on Highway 91* (television); 1990: *Chaindance* [Canada]; *Child's Play 2* (a.k.a. *Child's Play 2: Chucky's Back*) (voice only); *The Exorcist III* (a.k.a. *The Exorcist III: Legion*); *Graveyard Shift* (a.k.a. *Stephen King's Graveyard Shift*) [U.S.-Japan]; *Grim Prairie Tales*; *Hidden Agenda* [Great Britain]; *Horseplayer*; *Murder Blues*; *Sonny Boy*; *Spontaneous Combustion*; 1991: *Body Parts*; *Cerro Torre: Schrei Aus Stein* (a.k.a. *Scream of Stone*) [Canada-Germany-France-Belgium]; *Child's Play 3* (voice only); *Critters 4*; *Jungle Fever*; *London Kills Me* [Great Britain]; 1992: *Final Judgment*; 1993: *Amos and Andrew*; *Tales from the Crypt: People Who Live in Brass Hearses* (10/13/93) (television); *Trauma* (a.k.a. *Dario Argento's Trauma*) [U.S.-Italy]; *Wild Palms* (television); 1994: *The Color of Night*; *Escape from Terror: The Teresa Stamper Story* (a.k.a. *Crimes of Passion: Escape from Terror: The Teresa Stamper Story*) (television); *A Worn Path*; *The X-Files: Beyond the Sea* (01/07/94) (television); 1995: *Babylon 5: Passing Through Gethsemane* (11/27/95) (television); *Bless This House: The Postman Always Moves Twice* (11/15/95) (television); *Death Machine* [Great Britain]; *Escape to Witch Mountain* (television); *Murder in the First* [U.S.-France]; 1996: *Black Out*; *If Looks Could Kill* (television); *A Step Toward Tomorrow*; *Star Trek: Voyager: Meld* (02/05/96), *Basics: Part 1* (05/20/96), *Basics: Part 2* (09/04/96) (television); *Sworn to Justice*; 1997: *Alien: Resurrection* (a.k.a. *Alien 4: Resurrection*); *Best Men*; *Jamaica Beat*; *Millennium: Force Majeure* (02/07/97) (television); *Nightwatch*; 1998: *Bride of Chucky*; *Brown's Requiem*; *Playing Patti*; *Progeny*; *Saturday Night Live* (10/17/98) (uncredited) (voice only) (television); *Senseless*; *Urban Legend* (uncredited); 1999: *A Tekerolantos Naploja* (a.k.a. *The Diary of the Hurdy-Gurdy Man*) [Hungary]; *Cypress Edge* [Greece]; *The Hunger: Sin Seer*

(11/07/99) (television); *Interceptors* (a.k.a. *Interceptor Force*) (video); *The Magnificent Seven: Chinatown* (06/09/99) (television); *The Norm Show: Norm and Shelly* (11/03/99) (television); *Silicon Towers*; *The Storytellers*; 2000: *Shadow Hours*; *The Prophecy 3: The Ascent* (a.k.a. *God's Army*); 2001: *Boogeymen: The Killer Compilation* (voice only) (video); *The Ghost* (a.k.a. *Code of the Dragon*); *Myst III: Exile* (video game) (voice); *Soulkeeper*; 2002: *The Alien Saga* (voice only) (television); *The Calling* (a.k.a. *Man of Faith*) (video); *The Lord of the Rings: The Two Towers* [U.S.–New Zealand–Germany]; *Ponderosa: Fugitive* (05/12/02) (television); *Run Like Hell* (video game) (voice only); 2003: *The Box*; *The Lord of the Rings: The Return of the King* [U.S.–New Zealand–Germany]; *Vlad*; 2004: *Deadwood* (television); *The Devil's Due at Midnight* (video) (unreleased?); *The Hazing* (a.k.a. *Dead Scared*); *El Padrino* (a.k.a. *El Padrino—Mexican Godfather*) [Mexico]; *The Lord of the Rings: The Third Age* (video game) (voice only); *Seed of Chucky* (voice only); 2005: *Brew*; *Deadwood* (television); *Drop Dead Sexy*; *The Great War of Magellan* (short film); *Gun* (video game) (voice only); *I'm Perfect*; 2007: *Halloween*; *Humboldt County*; *Sinner*; *Winston*; *The Wizard of Gore*.

Keir Dullea

Keir Dullea was born on May 30, 1936 in Cleveland, Ohio. In his earliest roles, the 6'1" actor seemed at ease essaying intense roles, chiefly communicating with his eyes. For later roles, he seemed to adjust his style of performing, and became equally comfortable relying solely on movement and physical gestures, and shutting down his expressive eyes (the windows to his soul), leaving little but a blank, vacant stare that made audiences uncomfortable and uneasy. One of his earliest roles was as a dangerously disillusioned youth in Irvin Kershner's *Hoodlum Priest* (1961). His performance was so notable that *Variety* remarked (in a 2/22/61 review), "The film's most moving portrayal is delivered by Keir Dullea."

In Frank Perry's controversial film *David and Lisa* (1962), Dullea appeared in the leading role (one that many star watchers believed should have catapulted him to stardom). In this movie, Dullea's David, a young man in a mental institution, slowly returns to sanity, among other inmates who have more pressing (and potentially dangerous) mental and emotional problems. He finds love with Lisa (Janet Margolin), a young woman suffering from schizophrenia; the deep sadness of the film lay in its denouement. Dullea was awarded a Golden Globe award for this performance as the Most Promising Newcomer—Male. *David and Lisa* received Oscar nominations for Best Director and Best Screenplay. A year later, he was nominated for a British Academy Award (BAFTA) as Most Promising Newcomer to Leading Film Roles (alongside co-star Margolin). In the U.S., reviewers lauded his work. In *Variety*'s 09/05/62 review, they remarked, "Keir Dullea has the knifelike frigid presence that is right [for his character] in his case of bottled up feelings that have made him fear death and any human emotions."

Audiences next saw Dullea as a tragic hero in *The Thin Red Line* (1964) an epic World War II tale based on a classic James Jones novel. In 1965, he essayed the role of Carol Lynley's creepy, possibly incestuous brother in the equally controversial *Bunny Lake Is Missing*. In the cult favorite, a woman (Lynley) who has recently settled in England with her young daughter Bunny goes to retrieve her after the girl's first day at school. However, no one at the school has seen her. When the police can find no trace that the girl ever existed, they begin to wonder if the child was a fantasy creation of the distraught mother who may, in fact, be mentally disturbed. Dullea was next cast in Stanley Kubrick's science fiction masterpiece *2001: A Space Odyssey*. Released in 1968, the film features a plot about the appearance of strange, white, sleek monoliths throughout time, beginning at the dawn of man. Astronauts Dave Bowman (Dullea) and Frank Poole (Gary Lockwood) have been sent to orbit the moons of Jupiter when another (now-thought alien) monolith appears in the stars. When their computer system (the HAL 9000 voiced by Douglas Rain) begins to distrust the space flight crew, it revolts. The two astronauts disconnect the HAL 9000; this results in the death of Poole and a journey for Bowman, who is left to face the ominous monolith alone, begins. Within a phantasma of pulsing, swirling colors and lights, he pilots an escape pod vehicle into deepest space towards the monolith orbiting Jupiter, and rapidly ages into an old man, and then his life seemingly ends. For Bowman, his final step in the evolutionary ladder is to transform into a new life form, a Star Child. While some audience members and critics scratched their heads, others applauded the curiously successful film adaptation of author Arthur C. Clarke's story, *The Sentinel*, as adapted by Clarke and Kubrick.

A promotional photograph of Keir Dullea from the seventies.

Dullea was never able to fully capitalize on the attention he received in his early career. His next major genre film, 1969's *De Sade*, a biography of the notorious Marquis De Sade, was plagued by problems (original director Cy Endfield took ill during production and was replaced by Roger Corman); it lost the vision of its original director and, along the way, any cohesiveness, and style. *De Sade* was greeted with indifference by both the media and audiences upon its release.

Dullea also appeared in the seldom-seen Italian thriller *Devil in the Brain* (1972) for director Sergio Sollima, and attempted to find meaningful, odd roles like the one he essayed in *Paperback Hero* (1973), where he portrayed a small-town hockey player whose own dementia had him confusing reality with the Wild West. *Starlost* (1973–74) was a Canadian miniseries about the title spaceship hurtling through space on a collision course with a star, years after the cataclysmic destruction of Earth; many viewers enjoyed the lo-tech adventures of the three main cast members (including Dullea as Ark leader Devon). In 1980, episodes of the 1973–1974, 16-episode show were re-edited into three feature-length movies for inclusion in a television syndication package. Part of *Starlost*'s appeal was that it echoed Douglas Trumbull's film *Silent Running*, and foreshadowed the British-American television series, *Space: 1999*.

Another prominent genre film for Dullea was Bob Clark's *Black Christmas* (1974), a nasty stalker flick (also made in Canada) about a small town where a killer is preying on students. Today, the film has quite a cult following, and is well recalled for its genre stunt casting of John Saxon (as the town sheriff) and an offbeat Margot Kidder as a rambunctious student. An equally strange genre effort for Dullea was the seldom-screened *Welcome to Blood City* (1977), a film obviously influenced by Michael Crichton's *Westworld* (1973); in it, a virtual reality experiment sends people to a violent representation of the Wild West

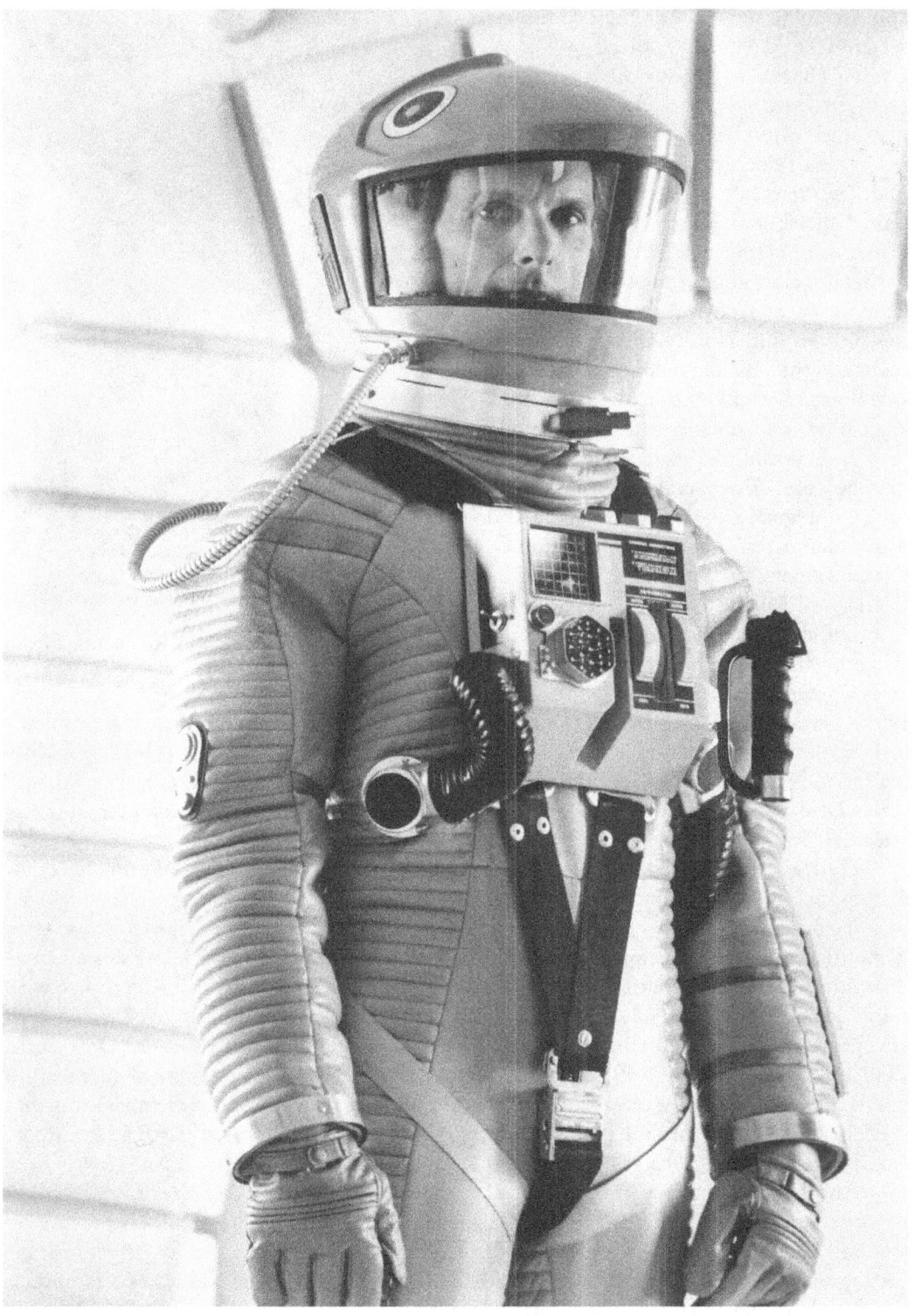

Keir Dullea in his iconic role as Astronaut Dave Bowman in Stanley Kubrick's *2001: A Space Odyssey* **(1968) (Polaris/MGM).**

complete with gunslingers. Next was his appearance as the husband of Mia Farrow in the haunting, psychologically exhausting supernatural horror film *Full Circle* (1977) directed by Richard Loncraine. In director Ulli Lommel's *Brainwaves* (1983), Dullea played a man who stood by his wife (Suzanna Love) after an accident causes her to lapse into a deadly coma. Medical experimenters devise a way to save her, with mixed results: She receives the brain waves from a murdered woman, and attempts to find the killer. That same year, Dullea with his then-wife Susie Fuller Dullea founded the Theater Artists Workshop of Westport, Connecticut. In Niko Mastorakis' bizarre thriller *The Next One*, Dullea starred as Glenn, a man with no past, but quite a future, as he appears from virtually nowhere as the potential resurrection of Jesus Christ. Or is he an alien life form?

He also co-starred as a physician in Mastorakis' bizarre *Blind Date* (1984), and appeared in the then-controversial television miniseries version of Aldous Huxley's novel, *Brave New World* (1980). In his most recent genre credit, he returned to the character of Dave Bowman in *2010*, in the 1984 film, co-scripted by Arthur C. Clarke and director Peter Hyams, from a novel by Clarke, a joint U.S. and Russian space flight to Jupiter restarts the HAL 9000 computer (again voiced by Douglas Rain) and attempts to learn what happened to the spaceship *Discovery* and its crew. Astronaut Bowman (Dullea) frequently appears and attempts to explain the origins of the monoliths. Always puzzled by his last transmission at the climax of *2001*, the new crew (led by Roy Scheider and John Lithgow) seeks to learn the reasons behind Bowman's then-last words "My God, it's full of stars...."

In the years since *2010*, Dullea has been active in feature films and on television, but his true love remains acting in the theater, where he finds the most challenges and enjoyment.

Q: *Bunny Lake Is Missing* has built up quite a cult following over the years. What are your remembrances of working on that motion picture?

Keir Dullea: The positive part of that film was working with Laurence Olivier. Carol Lynley was a lovely person, but working with Laurence Olivier was, in those days, any actor's dream. You are working with an icon, from an actor's point of view, and he was very nice to me. I actually got to meet Noël Coward who was in the film, although we did not have any scenes together. He coined a phrase, which in any other ordinary circumstances would not be the most positive thing to say to an actor, but given that it was Noël Coward, I did not mind. He was introduced to me, "Keir Dullea, this is Noël Coward, Noël Coward meet Keir Dullea." Coward said, "Oh, Keir Dullea and gone tomorrow." Nevertheless, overall it was a negative experience working on *Bunny Lake Is Missing*, because of the director, Otto Preminger. He was a horror to work with, he was a bully. Did you ever see the film *Stalag 17* [1953], where he played the commandant of the POW prison camp? That was Otto on a very, very nice day. He was a swine. They say, "Do not speak ill of the dead"—I will speak ill of him any time, he was a horror, and there was no excuse for it. I was a young actor, and I did certain things to protect myself. However, that should not be what it is about. Your energy should not be spent protecting yourself. In fact, it is the opposite. An actor has to open himself, and make himself vulnerable to use what he is. If you are busy closing yourself off, you cannot do your best work. Overall, it wasn't a very pleasant experience, but at least I went from hell to nirvana because my next film was *2001: A Space Odyssey*.

Q: Can you recall how you were cast in *2001*?

Dullea: While doing *Bunny Lake Is Missing* in London, I came home one day, and there was a message to call my agent in New York. I returned the call and he said, "Are you sitting down?" I said, "No." He said, "Sit down." and I did, He said, "You've just been offered the lead in Stanley Kubrick's next film." That is how I was cast. I never met Kubrick until I did the film, and that was the result of him having screened several films that I had already done. I won a Golden Globe award for *David and Lisa*, so he screened that, I was told. I did a war film called *The Thin Red Line* with Jack Warden, based on a story by James Jones, who had written *From Here to Eternity*, and Kubrick had seen that. He also screened some outtakes from *Bunny Lake Is Missing*. He was also obviously looking at film of a lot of people, but whatever he saw in those two films, and the outtakes, caused him to cast me.

Q: What was it like to work with Kubrick?

Dullea: It does not get better, not in film anyway. He was supportive. He was a sweet, quiet, intense man, with a wonderful sense of humor. He was a genius, you could tell that. He was a renaissance man, a true renaissance man. He was so knowledgeable about things having nothing to do with film, beyond his own field.

Q: How did Kubrick create, for you, and Gary Lockwood, the feeling of isolation, as the film successfully captured that?

Dullea: I do not think it was anything that we did. It was what he surrounded us with. It was the story. It was the fact that there were no other human beings in our scenes. It was the fact that the script was written in such a way. If you noticed, Gary and I hardly ever communicated. We had been there for I do not remember how long already, and there was an extraordinarily long journey that we had yet to take. Who knows, I do not remember now how long the whole journey was supposed to take. However, long enough that everyone else was in suspended animation, in hibernation. The only time that Gary and I really addressed each other, literally, was when things started going wrong, when HAL reads our lips. However, other than that, we hardly spoke, if you remember, we were very silent with each other. It was a pass-the-salt type of relationship. Gary was alone sunbathing, talking to his parents. I was talking to HAL, drawing pictures, all in utter silence with each other. That was all the way it was constructed around us.

Q: When you again played Dave Bowman in *2010*, all those years later, how did it feel to recreate that role?

Dullea: What was most astounding was walking on those sets that they recreated. They recreated them from scratch; there were no blueprints available from the production of *2001*, so they had to work backwards. They projected still frames of the film, then they got engineers with calipers, and did spatial measurements, and worked backwards, and made their own blueprints, and that is how they built the sets. It was like going back to a town you've grown up in, you hadn't been there since you were a kid, but it is still the same with the same town square, the same church on the corner, the town hall over there, the gazebo in the middle of the square, but there is not a soul on the street; otherwise it was all the same. You did not know a soul, which is what it felt like. Nevertheless, I did have the voice of HAL [Douglas Rain] to work with, which I had not had on *2001*. All we had back then was the assistant director feeding lines. Back in the early days, the AD fed us the lines; all of Douglas Rain's dialogue was overdubbed later on in postproduction.

Q: Does *2001* contain one of your best acting performances in a film?

Dullea: It is probably the greatest film that I have been in. It is not a showy role, although I'm very pleased with my performance in it. From an actor's point of view, there are other films that I have been in, like *David and Lisa*, which is one that I am particularly proud of in terms of performance, and there being challenges.

Q: What can you tell me about *De Sade*?

Dullea: That was initially a pleasant experience. I loved working with John Huston, and the director, Cy Endfield, who did *Zulu*. Endfield was a blacklisted director from the McCarthy era. Before being blacklisted, he had been a prominent Hollywood director, but when he resurrected his career, he returned with films like *The Sands of the Kalahari* and *Zulu*. I loved working with him, but he became very ill during the shoot and, two-thirds of the way into the film, had to be replaced by Roger Corman. Corman finished the film, so therefore, there was no real style to the movie, and Endfield never got to finish his own director's cut. I did not think it was a very good film. The best film work I've done, although I really consider myself a theater actor, the best film work I've done includes *Hoodlum Priest* with Don Murray, which was my first film. I was very proud of that, and it got very good reviews, and *David and Lisa*. I am not embarrassed like many other people about some other films. I like my performance in a film called *Madame X* with Lana Turner. I do not think it is a great film. It is a Ross Hunter film, but other than that, I certainly was not embarrassed by my work in it. *Paperback Hero* is a film that I did with Elizabeth Ashley that I liked.

Dullea as he appeared in *De Sade* (1969) (American International Pictures/CCC Film/Trans Continental).

Q: You seem to have appeared in quite a few films that have cult followings.

Dullea: I was recently surprised what a following there is for *Black Christmas*. I just can't believe it. It was kind of an uneventful film. I had a cameo role—at least, from my point of view, I thought I did. I think I completed that role in a week, and I became the red herring in the film. I do not really have any experiential knowledge of working on that film. I barely remember the experience. I was very proud of *The Fox* with Sandy Dennis. *2010* was a nice experience. I have done twenty-three feature films. It would take me a long time to remember them all.

Q: In the theater, what are some of your most favorite roles?

Dullea: I have done things in regional theater, which you would not know about, that I am equally proud of. On Broadway, it would have been *Butterflies Are Free* and *Cat on a Hot Tin Roof* with Elizabeth Ashley and Fred Gwynne. It is considered by those who have seen many theatrical revivals of the play, to be among the best, since the original Broadway production, possibly the best revival that has ever been done. I have done a production of *The Seagull* at a regional theatre in North Carolina. I have done like one hundred plays, so it is hard to recall them all. There was a play I did Off-Broadway, a one-man play called *The Other Side of Paradise*, which was about F. Scott Fitzgerald. I was maybe as proud of that as anything I have ever done in the theater.

Credits: 1960: *Mrs. Miniver* (television) [Germany]; *Westinghouse Desilu Playhouse: Cry Ruin* (1960) (television); 1961: *Alcoa Premiere: People Need People* (10/10/61) (television); *The Eleventh Hour: Cry a Little for Mary Too* (11/28/61) (television); *The Hallmark Hall of Fame: Give Us Barabbas!* (03/24/61) (television); *Hoodlum Priest*; *The Naked City: Murder Is a Face I Know* (01/04/61) (television); *Play of the Week: All Summer Long* (05/01/61) (television); *The United States Steel Hour: The Big Splash* (02/08/61), *The Golden Thirty* (08/09/61) (television); 1962: *Alcoa Premiere: Ordeal in Darkness* (11/15/62), *The Tiger* (03/20/62) (television); *Cain's Hundred: A Creature Lurks in Ambush* (04/17/62) (television); *Checkmate: A Very Rough Sketch* (01/24/62) (television); *David and Lisa*; *The Dupont Show of the Week: The Outpost* (09/16/62) (television); *Kraft Mystery Theater: Cry Ruin* (08/15/62) (television); *The United States Steel Hour: Far from the Shade Tree* (01/10/62) (television); 1963: *Alcoa Premiere: The Broken Year* (04/04/63) (television); *Bonanza: Elegy for a Hangman* (01/20/63) (television); *Empire: Stopover on the Way to the Moon* (01/01/63) (television); *Going My Way: One Small Unhappy Family* (02/13/63) (television); *The Naked City: The Apple Falls Not Far from the Tree* (01/23/63) (television); *The United States Steel Hour: The Young Avengers* (01/09/63) (television); 1964: *Mail Order Bride*; *Le Ore Nude* (a.k.a. *The Naked Hours*) [Italy]; *Pale Horse, Pale Rider* (television) [Great Britain]; *The Thin Red Line*; 1965: *Bunny Lake Is Missing* [Great Britain]; *Twelve O'Clock High: To Heinie—with Love* (02/05/65) (television); 1966: *Madame X*; 1967: *The Fox* (a.k.a. *D.H. Lawrence's The Fox*); 1968: *2001: A Space Odyssey* [Great Britain–U.S.]; 1969: *De Sade* [U.S.–West Germany]; 1970: *Black Water Gold* (television); 1971: *Montserrat* (television); 1972: *Il Diavolo Nel Cervello* (a.k.a. *The Devil in the Brain*) [Italy-France]; *McMillan and Wife: Blues for Sally M* (10/22/72) (television); *Pope Joan* (a.k.a. *The Devil's Imposter*) [Great Britain]; 1973: *Paperback Hero*; *Starlost* (television) [Canada]; 1974: *Black Christmas* (a.k.a. *Silent Night, Evil Night* a.k.a. *Stranger in the House*) [Canada]; *Paul and Michelle* [France–Great Britain]; *Starlost* (television) [Canada]; 1975: *Switch: The James Caan Con* (09/09/75) (television); 1976: *Law and Order* (television) [Great Britain]; 1977: *Full Circle* (a.k.a. *The Haunting of Julia*) [Canada–Great Britain]; *Mannikin* (short film); *Three Dangerous Ladies*; *Welcome to Blood City* (a.k.a. *Blood City*); 1978: *Because He's My Friend* (a.k.a. *Love Under Pressure*) (television) [Australia]; *Leopard in the Snow* [Great Britain–Canada]; 1979: *The Legend of the Golden Gun* (television); 1980: *Brave New World* (television); *The Hostage Tower* (a.k.a. *Alistair MacLean's The Hostage Tower*) (television); *The Starlost: The Beginning* (television), *The Starlost: The Alien Oro* (television), *The Starlost: Deception* (television) [Canada]; 1981: *No Place to Hide* (television); 1983: *BrainWaves*; *Loving Friends and Perfect Couples* (television) [Canada-U.S.]; 1984: *Blind Date* (a.k.a. *Deadly Seduction*); *The Next One* (a.k.a. *O Taxidiotis Tou Chronou*) [Greece-U.S.]; *2010* (a.k.a. *2010: The Year We Make Contact*); 1986: *The Guiding Light* (television); 1989: *Murder, She Wrote: Test of Wills* (11/26/89) (television); 1992: *Oh, What a Night* [Canada-U.S.]; 2000: *The Audrey Hepburn Story* (television); *The Divine Inspiration* (short film) [France]; *Sladke Sanje* (uncredited) [Slovenia]; *Songs in Ordinary Time* (television); 2001: *Law & Order: Hubris* (01/10/01) (television); *Witchblade: Convergence* (08/14/01) (television); 2002: *Ed: Nice Guys Finish Last* (02/06/02) (television); *Law & Order: Special Victims Unit: Justice* (04/05/02) (television); *3 Days of Rain*; 2003: *Alien Hunter* [U.S.-Bulgaria]; 2006: *The Good Shepherd*; *The Day My Towers Fell*; *A Lonely Sky*; 2007: *The Accidental Husband*; *Fortune*.

Sid Haig

Sid Haig was born Sidney Eddie Mosesian on July 14, 1939, in Fresno, California. An early interest in performing led him to take part in a children's Christmas show, and the rest is history. During his high school years, Sid finally got his chance to perform in a real show. The head of the school's drama department had been an actress on Broadway, and invited an old musical comedy friend of hers to come see her senior class play, which featured Sid in a major role. This person told the young student that he should seek his fortunes with the bright lights, and point his career path towards acting.

In addition to his feverish desire to act, Sid always loved music, and he found time to be the drummer for the band The T-Birds, who had a regional California hit with the single *Full House*. Two years later, in 1959, he enrolled in the Pasadena Playhouse, training ground for such esteemed actors as Robert Preston, Robert Young, and Gene Hackman. His first professional acting role was in a short UCLA student film directed by Jack Hill. (The short was titled *The Host*; it was recently unearthed and issued as an extra on the special edition DVD of *Spider Baby*.) Of course, the early horror comedy-cult favorite *Spider Baby* has grown in stature from an oddball diamond-in-the-rough to become one of the most revered, strange and surrealistic films in the entire horror genre.

Many genre film fans also know Haig as a familiar villainous face in a number of exploitation films produced by Roger Corman in the late sixties and early seventies. Bald, lanky and 6' 4", he was often cast as the bad guy in low-budget films. He is fondly remembered for being a villain in a number of Pam Grier classics of the seventies (*Coffy, Black Mama, White Mama, The Big Doll House,* and *Foxy Brown*), and reunited with her on-screen in Quentin Tarantino's *Pulp Fiction* (portraying a judge!).

After taking time off from the big screen for much of the nineties, Haig was an integral member of the cast of musician–director Rob Zombie's *House of 1000 Corpses* (2003). With his performance in this film as the decadently insane killer Captain Spaulding (who is often seen dressed as a clown), Haig managed to make himself an in-demand actor for a whole new generation of exploitation movie fans. Zombie's *House of 1000 Corpses* sequel *The Devil's Rejects* will definitely give most genre fans the jitters as it harkens back to the darker, low-budget, spook house thrill-ride horror films of the seventies. In fact, with its atmosphere of dread, it is not unlike the original *Texas Chainsaw Massacre*.

Haig has been around for a long time as an actor (he is also a licensed, certified hypnotherapist, among other things) and he keeps playing bad guys; but as he ages, he plays them with a nastier edge than he ever exhibited on-screen before. A lot of people may not even realize that Haig has also had an interesting career as a director, helming over fifty

The face of villainy: Sid Haig appears menacing in this scene from 1974's *Savage Sisters* (American International Pictures).

commercials for the Wang computer corporation (for distribution to television and cable), directed second unit on *The Big Bird Cage* (among other films), and has helmed over thirty stage plays in regional theater. Besides making the convention circuit in recent years, he is working on both an autobiography and, in collaboration with a psychologist, a book about hypnotherapy treatments.

Q: What made you interested in becoming an actor?

Sid Haig: I started when I was about seven years old, when I was a dancer in a play. When I was very young I always wanted to perform, and I remember playing in a school production of *The Wizard of Oz*. I always kept involved in all of the arts all during my scholastic years, and when I decided to finally get serious about it all, I went to Pasadena to fine-tune my craft at an acting college. And the rest is history.

Q: You are most fondly remembered for playing villains, and for essaying these roles often with the director Jack Hill. What can you tell us about your working relationship with him?

Haig: Working with Jack Hill has always been great. It has always been a generous and comfortable working relationship. He trusts me as an actor, and I trust him as a director. We are also good friends, so it helps to trust your friends both in and out of the business.

Q: Do you think that some of your best performances in '70s films may have been unjustly ignored by film critics because of the violence contained in them?

Haig: Being a success nowadays is a very funny thing. When many of those movies first came out, in the seventies, most mainstream critics trashed them. Today, a good many of them have cult followings, and those cult following groups include some very talented filmmakers who have grown up on those movies, and understand them for what they were and are... entertainment. Same thing happened with Rob Zombie's *House of 1000 Corpses*, which I co-starred in. When that movie first came out the mainstream critics hated it. Now, some of those same critics revere it.

Q: How does it feel to have filmmakers like Quentin Tarantino, who has given you small roles in some of his recent movies, come to you and say that he really appreciates your work?

Haig: I enjoy the fact that people enjoy my work. What else can I say? I enjoy my own performances for the most part, although it is tough to pick a favorite role of mine. I enjoy many of the movies I have made, even when I was stuck in typecasting hell. I would say at the top of the list would have to be *Spider Baby*. And I enjoyed working on *Swashbuckler*, the pirate movie that starred Robert Shaw, I think primarily because I got to use my fencing skills on that movie. I guess the movie roles I am [most] fond of, are the ones that gave me the most joy, and that I got paid for!

Q: *Spider Baby* has an unusual cult around it.

Haig: Sometimes people stop me in the street and mention that movie. However, I will tell you, since being in Rob Zombie's *House of 1000 Corpses* and *The Devil's Rejects*, it has changed; now I have a completely new audience. It became very apparent when I appeared at film conventions like *Chiller Theatre*. People who may not know me from many of those villainous roles of the seventies, now know me from those [Zombie] films, and it is rewarding. With every year, *Spider Baby*'s fame grows, and it gains a whole new audience. However, because of *House of 1000 Corpses* and *The Devil's Rejects*, I have a bunch of new fans, an entirely new audience.

Q: Before your current spate of activity, you seemed to have been semi-retired for a few years. Then you showed up (and reunited with Pam Grier) in Tarantino's *Jackie Brown*.

Haig: I was originally offered the role of Marcellus Wallace in Tarantino's *Pulp Fiction*, but it did not work out, so I guess the timing was right for *Jackie Brown*.

Q: What can you tell me about the production of the Rob Zombie–directed films?

Haig: They, especially the second one, *Devil's Rejects*, are much more realistic, scary movies. They feel, especially the second one again, like a little bit of *The Wild Bunch*, actually. I have described the second film several times as *House of 1000 Corpses* meets *The Wild Bunch* at Jeffrey Dahmer's home. It is just more of the fantastic adventures of "Captain Spaulding" and company. There is a whole list of interesting performers in this movie. There's Bill Moseley, Sherri Moon, who is married to Rob Zombie, Deborah Van Valkenburgh, Ginger Lynn Allen, Danny Trejo, Michael Berryman, Ken Foree, Matt McGrory, P.J. Soles, Leslie Easterbrook, Diamond Dallas Page, William Forsythe, Tyler Mane, Priscilla Barnes, Steve Railsback... and, oh yeah, Mary Woronov. It's quite, quite a movie. The horror genre fans will love it.

Q: You have appeared in numerous television series over the years—*Batman, Charlie's Angels, Star Trek, Gunsmoke, Mission: Impossible*, and others too numerous to mention. Do you have any favorite roles?

Haig: No, I really do not, and to be honest, television is not something I am that anxious to get back into... unless it is a series.

Q: So, what does Sid Haig do when he is not onscreen being a psychopathic villain?

Haig: I work with ceramics. I am interested in horticulture, specifically Bonsais. I enjoy music, and I like watching blues bands especially. However, as for the psychopathic villain roles that I play... within every one of my roles is a bit of the real Sid Haig, because everything eventually comes from within me, from the inside. Maybe I am a scary person deep inside, or I know how to fine-tune little bits of myself, to make myself seem much more intense than I am, or as some people envision me. I'm also working on writing a book, so if I ever manage to finish it, it will all be there, perhaps.

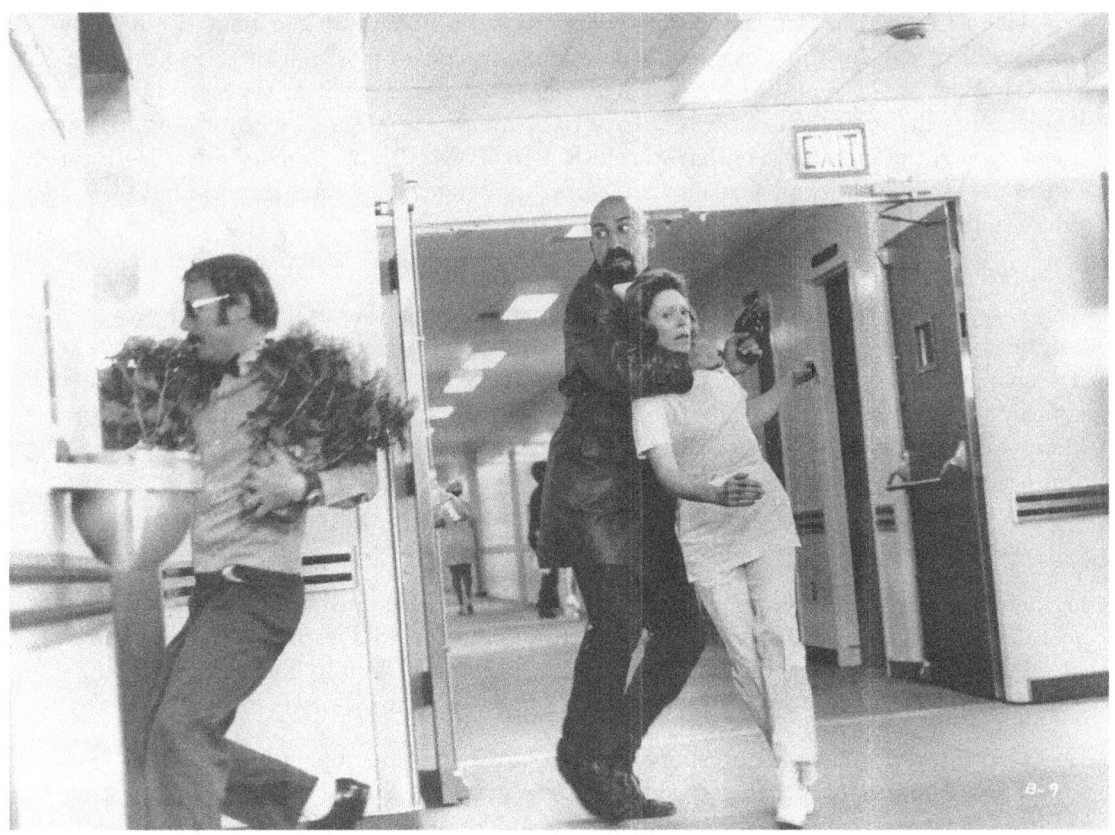

A different kind of urban villainy, Sid Haig (in black leather, other actors unidentified) on the run from police in Peter Hyams' *Busting* (1973) (Chartoff-Winkler Productions/United Artists).

Credits: 1960: *The Host* (short film); 1962: *The Firebrand*; 1965: *Beach Ball* (uncredited); 1966: *Batman: The Spell of Tut* (09/28/66) (television); *Batman: Tut's Case Is Shut* (09/29/66) (television); *Blood Bath* (a.k.a. *Track of the Vampire*); *Gunsmoke: Stage Stop* (11/26/66) (television); *The Iron Horse: Town Full of Fear* (12/05/66) (television); *Laredo: The Last of the Caesars—Absolutely* (12/02/66) (television); *Mission: Impossible: Fakeout* (12/03/66) (television); 1967: *Get Smart: That Old Gang of Mine* (12/02/67) (television); *It's a Bikini World*; *The Man from U.N.C.L.E.: The When in Rome Affair* (03/17/67) (television); *Mission: Impossible: The Slave: Part 1* (10/08/67) (television); *Mission: Impossible: The Slave: Part 2* (10/15/67) (television); *Point Blank*; *Star Trek: The Return of the Archons* (02/09/67) (television); 1968: *Daniel Boone: The Scrimshaw Ivory Coast* (01/04/68) (television); *The Flying Nun: The Return of Father Lundigan* (10/17/68) (television); *The Hell with Heroes*; *Mission: Impossible: Trial By Fury* (03/10/68), *The Diplomat* (12/01/68) (television); *Spider Baby* (a.k.a. *Spider Baby, or the Maddest Story Ever Told*); 1969: *Che!*; *Get Smart: Shock It to Me* (03/01/69) (television); *Gunsmoke: MacGraw* (12/08/69), *A Man Called "Smith"* (10/27/69), *Time of the Jackals* (01/13/69) (television); *Here's Lucy: Lucy and the Great Airport Chase* (02/03/69) (television); *Mission: Impossible: Commandante* (11/02/69), *Doomsday* (02/16/69) (television); *The Winner*; 1970: *C.C. and Company* (a.k.a. *Chrome Hearts*); *Get Smart: Moonlighting Becomes You* (01/02/70) (television); *Here Come the Brides: Break the Bank of Tacoma* (01/16/70) (television); *Mannix: Déjà vu* (12/12/70) (television); *Mission: Impossible: The*

Choice (03/22/70), *Decoy* (11/07/70) (television); 1971: *Alias Smith and Jones: Pilot* (01/15/71), *The Day They Hanged Kid Curry* (09/16/71), *Return to Devil's Hole* (02/25/71) (television); *The Big Doll House* [U.S.-Philippines]; *Diamonds Are Forever* [Great Britain–U.S.]; *THX 1138*; 1972: *The Big Bird Cage* [Philippines-U.S.]; *Black Mama, White Mama* [U.S.-Philippines]; *O'Hara, U.S. Treasury: Operation: XW-1* (01/07/72) (television); 1973: *Beyond Atlantis* [U.S.-Philippines]; *Coffy*; *Emperor of the North Pole*; *Wonder Women* (a.k.a. *Deadly but Beautiful*); 1974: *The Don Is Dead*; *Busting*; *Foxy Brown*; *Police Story: Cop in the Middle* (01/29/74) (television); *The Rockford Files: Caledonia—It's Worth a Fortune* (12/06/74) (television); *Savage Sisters* [U.S.-Philippines]; 1975: *Emergency: Smoke Eater* (01/11/75) (television); *The No Mercy Man*; *Who Is the Black Dahlia?* (television); *The Woman Hunt* [U.S.-Philippines]; 1976: *Electra Woman and Dyna Girl: Ali Baba: Part 1* (10/23/76), *Ali Baba: Part 2* (10/30/76) (television); *The Return of the World's Greatest Detective* (television); *Swashbuckler*; 1978: *Charlie's Angels: Diamond in the Rough* (01/18/78) (television); *Evening in Byzantium* (television); *Fantasy Island: The Sheikh/The Homecoming* (09/16/78) (television); *Jason of Star Command* (television); *Police Woman: Blind Terror* (01/04/78) (television); *Tarzan and the Super 7* (television); 1979: *Death Car on the Freeway* (television); 1980: *Buck Rogers in the 25th Century: Flight of the War Witch* (03/27/80) (television); *Hart to Hart: Murder, Murder on the Wall* (11/11/80) (television); *Loose Shoes*; 1981: *Buck Rogers in the 25th Century: Time of the Hawk* (01/15/81) (television); *Chu Chu and the Philly Flash*; *The Fall Guy: Colt's Angels* (12/02/81) (television); *Fantasy Island: My Late Lover/Sanctuary* (01/03/81) (television); *Galaxy of Terror* (a.k.a. *Mindwarp: An Infinity of Terror*); *Underground Aces*; 1982: *The Aftermath*; *Bret Maverick: The Eight Swords of Dyrus and Other Illusions of Grandeur* (03/23/82) (television); *The Dukes of Hazzard: Miz Tisdale on the Lam* (01/29/82) (television); *The Fall Guy: Bail and Bond* (10/27/82) (television); *40 Days of Musa Dagh*; *T.J. Hooker: Hooker's War* (04/03/82) (television); 1983: *The A-Team: Black Day at Bad Rock* (02/22/83) (television); *Automan* (pilot) (12/15/83) (television); 1984: *The Fall Guy: Undersea Odyssey* (03/21/84) (television); 1985: *Amazing Stories: Remote Control Man* (12/08/85) (television); *The Fall Guy: Reel Trouble* (04/10/85) (television); *MacGyver: Thief of Budapest* (10/13/85) (television); *Misfits of Science: Fumble on the One* (12/06/85) (television); *Scarecrow and Mrs. King: Ship of Spies* (01/07/85) (television); *Wildside: Don't Keep the Home Fires Burning* (04/11/85) (television); 1986: *MacGyver: To Be a Man* (02/16/86) (television); 1987: *Commando Squad*; 1988: *Goddess of Love* (television); *Werewolf: King of the Road* (02/07/88) (television); 1989: *Just the Ten of Us: St. Augie's Blues: Part 1* (11/30/89), *St. Augie's Blues: Part 2* (12/01/89) (television); *Warlords*; *Wizards of the Lost Kingdom II*; 1990: *The Forbidden Dance* (a.k.a. *Lambada, the Forbidden Dance*); *Genuine Risk*; *Just the Ten of Us: Comedy Tonight* (01/04/90) (television); 1992: *Boris and Natasha*; 1997: *Jackie Brown*; 2000: *E! Mysteries and Scandals: Lon Chaney Sr. and Jr.* (11/09/00) (television); 2003: *House of 1000 Corpses*; 2004: *Kill Bill Vol. 2*; *Unconventional* (documentary); 2005: *The Devil's Rejects* [U.S.-Germany]; *From Spiders to Switchblades* (video supplement); *Horror Business* (documentary); 2006: *House of the Dead 2: Dead Aim*; *Little Big Top*; *The Night of the Living Dead 3D*; 2007: *Brotherhood of Blood*; *Dead Man's Hand*; *Razor*; *Wittenberg*.

Tippi Hedren

Tippi Hedren was born Nathalie Hedren on January 19, 1931 in New Ulm, Minnesota. In 1957, she gave birth to a daughter who later became known as the actress, Melanie Griffith. Tippi Hedren was discovered while appearing on a television commercial, and was thrust into the Hollywood limelight when Alfred Hitchcock and Universal Pictures signed her to play the leading role of Melanie Daniels in *The Birds* (1963). The nail-biting ecological suspense thriller pitting man (and woman) against nature became a horror movie staple over the years, and continues to win acclaim for its literate script, taut ensemble acting, and ferocious bird attacks upon the cast members. In an interview with the *Soho Weekly News* in 1979 she stated, "When I barged into the bird-ridden attic to face the impending hordes of the title, I said to Hitch, 'Why would I do a thing like that?' He said, 'Because I told you to.'" Due to the success of the film, Hitchcock presented a miniature doll of Hedren to her daughter Melanie, but caused a brief commotion, as the doll was presented within a wooden box. Young Melanie could not handle the effigy of her mother in what appeared to be a coffin.

Variety noted of her performance in *The Birds* (March 27, 1963), "Aside from the birds, the film belongs to Miss Hedren, who makes an auspicious screen bow. She virtually has to carry the picture alone for the first forty-five minute stretch, prior to the advent of the first wave of organized attackers from the sky. Miss Hedren has a star quality and Hitchcock has provided her with a potent vehicle to launch her career."

Hedren then starred as Marnie Edgar (alongside Sean Connery) in Hitchcock's *Marnie* (1964). A psychological thriller, *Marnie* brought Hedren more good notices, but the adult themes of the movie made it under-appreciated at the time; it has grown to be viewed as one of the best of his films with the passing years. Of her performance in this film, *Variety* remarked (in their June 16, 1964 review), "Hedren ... returns in a particularly demanding role. Miss Hedren, undertaking a role originally offered Princess Grace Kelly of Monaco for a resumption of her screen career, lends credence to a part never sympathetic. It's a difficult assignment which she performs satisfactorily."

Hedren suddenly disappeared from the big screen for a couple of years. Charles Chaplin's last film, *A Countess from Hong Kong* (1967) brought her back to the cinema in a supporting role, but it was two films, shot in Africa at the turn of that decade, which introduced Hedren to the wonder and the plight of African lions. In an attempt to raise awareness for wildlife, she then spent nearly eleven years bringing *Roar* (1981) to the screen. A very personal and heartfelt film about lions in the wild, the movie was released abroad; *Variety* called it a "passionate plea for the preservation of African wildlife." It was before,

Tippi Hedren, circa 1964.

during, and after the production of *Roar* that Hedren created the Shambala preserve in Los Angeles, and later the Roar Foundation, which enables her to continue her work in the care and preservation of lions and tigers.

Hedren has also appeared in such television genre fare as *The Bionic Woman* (1976), *Alfred Hitchcock Presents* (1985), *Dream On* (1994), and a sequel/remake of *The Birds*, *The Birds 2: Land's End* (1994). She has also been seen on the big screen in *The Harrad Experiment* (1973), *Pacific Heights* (1990), and *I Woke Up Early the Day I Died* (1999), which was produced from a screenplay by the late tyro genre director Ed Wood. Hedren has received awards for her roles in the short films *Mulligans!* (1997) and *Tea with Grandma* (2001);

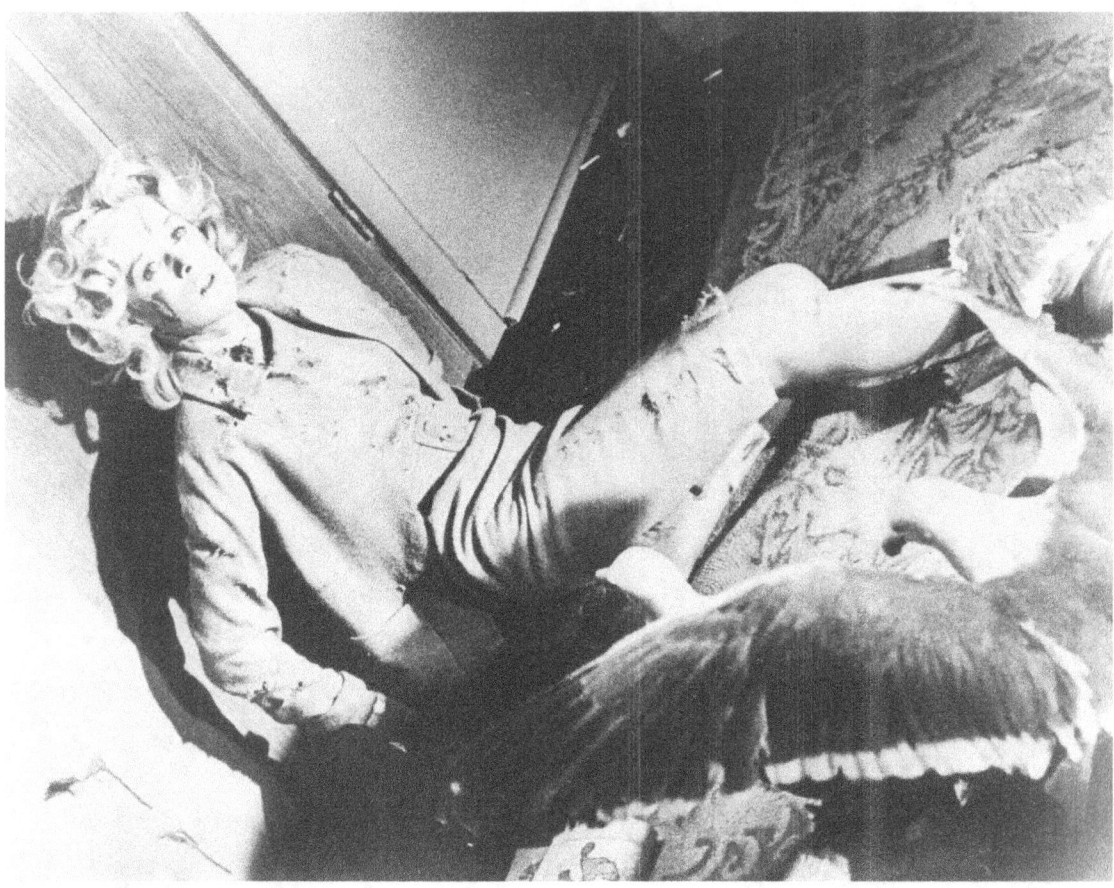

Hedren has had just about enough as evidenced in this scene that takes place near the climax of Alfred Hitchcock's *The Birds* (1963) (Alfred Hitchcock Productions/Universal Pictures).

among her more recent latest roles is an appearance in the genre film *Diamond Zero* (2003). Her continuing animal activism still brings her major media attention: In April 2002, she was scheduled to confront Washington, D.C. lawmakers, to argue the need for restrictions on the domestic breeding of exotic animals.

Q: Can you recall what made you want to become first a model, and then an actress?

Tippi Hedren: Actually, all of it was handed to me, sort of, on a silver platter. One day, I stepped off a streetcar on my way home from school; this was when I was around fourteen years old. A woman handed me her card and said, "Would you ask your mother to bring you down to Donaldson's department store, where I would like to have you model in our Saturday morning fashion shows?" Therefore, we did that. That really is what started everything. All of my life prior to that time, I had wanted to be an ice skater. I worked so hard too, with the figure skating. My parents did not have enough money to send me to classes so I would go and watch my friends when they took their classes. There were lakes all over Minneapolis where I grew up, so I would practice out there. Then I had to have an operation on my foot, so I could not skate for the rest of the year, because in those days they did not get you up right immediately after an operation and say, "Go, live your life." The following year, I had to have another operation, and so my skating career rather went by the boards. I then really did truly take up modeling seriously, and I continued that when we moved to California. Then of course, New York beckoned. I was with the Eileen Ford modeling agency for ten years or something like that. I appeared in a number of commercials, and one of them was airing on the *Today* show and Hitchcock saw it, and he decided to find out who the girl was, and where she was located, and that's how that happened.

Q: And that commercial was for a milk product, I believe?

Hedren: It was a pet milk product. Hitchcock then had me interviewed by a man at Universal studios. That was on a Friday the 13th of October. He asked if I would leave my photo book over the weekend, which I did. On the following Monday morning I went to pick it up and I was introduced to another executive at Universal, and then another one, and another one. All this time, nobody would tell me who this producer or director was. I was becoming very curious. On the following Tuesday morning I had to go to MCA, which at that time was the main agency for Universal; it had not yet become the enormous conglomerate that it has become today. I was asked to meet with an agent there, and he said that Alfred Hitchcock wanted to sign me to a contract, and if I agreed to the terms of the contract, then we would go and meet him. Therefore, we did. We went over to meet with him, I walked into the office, and he stood there looking very pleased with himself. We discussed almost anything but acting or films. We talked about travel and foods, and wines, and all kinds of different things. Following that, I was introduced to Edith Head, and all the different members of the crew who worked with Hitchcock. It was really pretty amazing. I was under the impression that I would be appearing in one of the television shows that he did every week. Then, they decided to do a screen test. I think it was certainly the largest screen test at the time, certainly the most expensive and most elaborate of all of Hollywood. We performed scenes from *To Catch a Thief* and *Notorious* and *Rebecca*. They were three entirely different roles with major women characters. It took three days to do it. There was a full crew involved in it, a full color crew. Hitchcock had even flown Martin Balsam (also in Hitchcock's *Psycho*) in to be my leading man.

It was an amazing time, I must say. In addition, after the screen test was completed, Hitchcock had invited me to Chasen's, for dinner. Chasen's was, in those days if you were a working actor, the place to be seen, and if you were not a working actor and wanted a Hollywood career, it was, for some, the place to be discovered. All along, during this time, I knew that they were working on *The Birds*, that they were in pre-production on that film. So anyway, I went to dinner with the Hitchcocks, and [Universal executive] Lew Wasserman was with us. Hitchcock had placed a beautifully wrapped package in front of me, and I opened it. It contained a very beautiful gold and sea pearl pin of three birds in flight, and he said, "We want you to play Melanie Daniels in *The Birds*." I have to tell you, I almost burst into tears. It was such an exciting time. It was such a great honor. It was just amazing. Hitchcock was sitting there looking very pleased with himself, and that started the whole thing.

Q: What was it like to be in your first starring role in a film?

Hedren: The feeling was just so powerful. It was powerful and it was frightening at the same time to be given that kind of responsibility.

Q: Was Hitchcock an exacting, or demanding person to work for?

Hedren: He was absolutely fabulous. He was not only my director, he was my drama coach. Had he not given me the assurance and security that I was able to do this role, I do not think I would have been able to do it.

Q: According to press clippings dating from the time that the movie was released, you had said in interviews something about a scene where you were in a wired area and that actual birds were thrown at you.

Hedren: Oh, yes. That was when I go up to the upstairs bedroom. They had told me that they were going to use mechanical birds for that.

Q: And they did not?

Hedren: No and they had no intentions of doing that. We started that scene on a Monday morning and I walked onto the set and into my dressing room, and the assistant director came in. He could not look at me. He looked at the floors, at the ceiling, towards the walls. I said, "What's the matter with you?" He said, "Uh, the mechanical birds don't work. We have to use real ones." I just blanched white, because by that time, I had seen many of the bird trainers with their thick leather gauntlets, and we had all been pecked. It was very frightening to be thinking of doing this scene without mechanical birds. I walked onto the set and there was a cage built around the door that I come in, and all these birds were already in boxes, in huge cartons, and so there had been a great deal of effort put into this. This was not a spur-of-the-moment thought that the mechanical birds were not going to work. Therefore, all along, they had intended that they were going to use real birds. I had no time to think any more about it than that, so for a week, they hurled birds at me. It was not a fun time.

Q: What do you have to say about *The Birds 2: Land's End*?

Hedren: Oh, it is absolutely horrible. It embarrasses me horribly.

Q: In retrospect, *Marnie* has become known as one of the great psychological thrillers, but it was sort of under-appreciated by the majority of critics at the time of its release. In recollection, what do you think of this role?

Hedren: I thought the role was absolutely one of the best in Hollywood. It was a film that was way before its time. In the sixties, people were not thinking about what happened to you as a child, what the effects on your adult life can be. Up until that time, if anything terrible happened to you as a child, it was somewhat hushed, and nobody talked about it. It was not until much later, in fact, not been until quite *recently* that psychological traumas have been dealt with, and in a proper way. That is, of course, what the story of *Marnie* was about. Every actress in Hollywood wanted that role, and I felt very, very fortunate. Actually, Hitchcock had purchased the rights to film the book, *Marnie*, for Grace Kelly. At the time that I heard about that, I thought, "Isn't that bizarre, that Grace would even consider doing this film?"—and not only Grace, but also, "What would the whole principality of Monaco think?" How could a princess play a compulsive thief as well as a frigid woman who screamed every time a man came near her? [The character] was absolutely brilliant in the way she carried out these robberies. Of course, that is what happened. The people and the Prince of Monaco said, "No, we would not want our princess do this movie."

Q: At the time of the release of *The Birds* and during the pre-production of *Marnie*, you were being called the next Grace Kelly in the press of the day. Did this put any pressure on you?

Hedren: Not at all. I feel very sure of myself. Being associated with someone else was not at all a terrible thing. And not only that, I was being associated with a very, very fine, wonderful actress. Therefore, I had no complaints about that.

Q: Charles Chaplin's *A Countess from Hong Kong*, in which you co-starred opposite Marlon Brando and Sophia Loren—do you recall how you got that role?

Hedren: I had just gotten out of my contract with Hitchcock. Charlie Chaplin called and asked if I wanted to be in this film, which was his last. So of course, I said, "Yes, would you please send me a script?" However, they did not send any scripts out, because Charlie did not want anyone reading it, and reporting it to the press or whatever. Therefore, Marlon and I both accepted the film without reading the script. We were just told over the phone what the characters were like, what the relationships to the people were like, all of that, as much as they could tell us, verbally. Of course I thought, how could I not accept this wonderful role, what a gift it was, and Marlon felt the same way. When I got to England, I went right from the airport to the set, because I was so excited about meeting everyone. It was joyous getting to know everybody. I talked to everyone, and I said, "May I have a script?" and they handed me the script and everybody left the stage. I had been told that I was going to play the part of Martha, Marlon Brando's wife, and that he was playing the ambassador, that our relationship was in very, very bad straits, and that I would come in, oh, halfway through the script. Therefore, I sat down with the script, and I was paging through it and looking for Martha. I got halfway through and there was no Martha, and I got three-quarters of the way through and then appears Martha. Instead of being all the way through the remainder, she is in four scenes. I was a little bit upset about the whole thing, I mentioned this to Charlie, and he said, "Why don't you come and have dinner with Oona and me?" Prior to that, when Marlon arrived in London and read the script, he promptly got the flu. He was very upset about the script. Therefore, I went to have dinner with Oona and Charlie, and during dinner I said, "Charlie, why didn't you just tell me this was a cameo? I would have done this film anyway." Every actor in the world was asking if they could do this film, to just do a walk-on, without even being paid for it. When I said, "Why didn't you just tell me that it was a cameo?" he said, "I didn't think you would come," which was very sweet. He was a very clever man.

Q: With Hitchcock, didn't you have a seven-year contract?

Hedren: I did, but eventually he became a very controlling person, and made my life so difficult. I had finally had to get out of it.

Q: Were you always interested in animal rights?

Hedren: I have always been interested in animals. I love them, and I wanted to learn more about them. They have always been a very, very important part of me, of my existence. Of course, I have this Shambala Preserve. I have been involved with these animals since 1970. We bought the place in 1972, and it became a preserve in 1985. We did a movie titled *Roar*, which was incredible. You will never see a picture like this dealing with animals, ever again.

Q: About *Roar*, why did you set out to make your own film?

Hedren: When I first did the two films that were shot in Africa, during the times that I was there, it was incredible to see the animals running free. Africa is so big, just an incredible continent. During that time, people who lived there were saying, "You should have been here fifteen years ago, twenty years ago. The animals were so much more plentiful." Because of encroaching civilization, sport hunting, and poaching, the number of animals was decreasing at a rapid rate, and environmentalists were saying that if we did not do something right now to save the animals, by the year 2000, they would be gone. A great deal of awareness is going out all over the world about saving the animals. My then-husband [Noel Marshall] and I decided to do a movie about the animals in the wild after seeing a house that had been abandoned by a game warden in Mozambique, because it flooded during the rainy seasons, and subsequently been taken over by lions. It was an amazing thing to see: The lions were sitting in the windows, they were going in and out of the doors, they were sitting on the verandas, they were on the top of the Portuguese house, and they were in the front of the house. The big-maned lions, the lionesses, the rowdy young cubs, everybody was there. It grew to be the largest pride in all of Africa. It was such a unique thing to see and we thought, for a movie, let us use the great cats as our stars. It worked very well because they fascinate almost everyone for one reason or another. They either think that they are magnificent or should be worshipped, from afar. Some people may be scared to death of them, and that is probably smart. They may want to hug them and cuddle them and tickle their tummies, but it is not a good idea. So, anyway we were going to originally use Hollywood-acting animals, and have a nine-month shoot. But as soon as the trainers read the script about the house with the lions living in it, and working with thirty, maybe forty cats, they laughed at it and said it cannot be done because of instinctual dictates to fight. They suggested that we get our own animals to do the movie, introduce them very carefully, and do it that way. Well, it opened a whole new can of peas. The first one was a rescue, and from then on, we became a very important facility in taking in these animals that needed a home. Because of all kinds of different things including accidents where all of us were hurt by the lions at one time or another, we would run out of money, we had a terrible flood that destroyed us for a full year... the film took five years to complete. It was finally released all over the world but not the United States, because the United States distributors wanted the lion's share of the profits, and we thought it ought to go to the beautiful animals that made the movie. We are still trying to get a distributor, and I think that we will. The film holds up beautifully... and unfortunately, nothing has changed. The animals are still being poached, they are still losing their lands, it's a terrible thing. The film still holds up very, very well.

Q: Is that the purpose of the Roar Foundation? To raise awareness?

Hedren: The Roar Foundation is the financial support arm for the Shambala preserve. After our movie was over, it was unconscionable to see the animals go any place else. There are not that many places that can take them and zoos cannot handle this great number of lions and tigers. We said we would become a foundation so that we can take in donations so that we can keep the cats here, and that is what we did.

Q: How many lions and tigers do you have?

Hedren: At one point, we had one hundred forty, but now we maintain a population of sixty. Prior to that, we had taken in large numbers of animals, like eight or ten animals at a time, and they could live together. Now we have three prides, one of four, one of three, and other lions that live together. The tigers have to live alone because of their instinctual dictates, because they are actually loners in the wild, and that goes on, even in captivity. We maintain about fifty-eight to sixty animals all the time.

Q: Where do they come from?

Hedren: They are born in the United States. They are bred to be sold as pets, and unfortunately, they are not a very good pet, they are very, very dangerous animals. After they have hurt somebody, people do realize that this animal is unmanageable and that they have to find a home for it. That is where sanctuaries like Shambala come in. It is extremely costly. We keep the animals in very, very big areas. In fact, sometimes you cannot even find them; the areas are so big that they can hide. We are here to give them a good life and one much better than what they came from. Their mental and emotional health is just as important as their physical health, so we move them around so they do not get bored, we spend our lives trying to give them a good life, and there is no breeding, no buying, no selling, and no trading, which is how our sanctuary is defined.

Hedren as she appeared in The *Harrad Experiment* (1973) (Cinema Arts Productions Inc./Cinerama Releasing Corporation).

Q: You recently received a Best Actress award, for the short film *Tea with Grandma*, from the New York International Independent Film and Video Festival. What was it like to receive this accolade?

Hedren: It was absolutely wonderful. I was thrilled, and much honored.

Q: You seem to be working more regularly as an actress than in the past. Is there any particular reason for this activity?

Hedren: I have absolutely no idea, but I am enjoying it and I am having great fun with it. I must say that I have more fun with my acting career than I used to. I do not take it quite so seriously. It's just fun.

Q: Of the recent films that you have appeared in, including the cult favorites *Pacific Heights* and *I Woke Up Early the Day I Died*, are there any personal favorites?

Hedren: *I Woke Up Early the Day I Died* was an incredible film. I must say I really loved that film. It was a unique kind of film to do also, because of the fact that it had no dialogue in it. It was very, very different. I am starting a film, which is going to be very interesting. I read the script and said, "I've got to do this, I've got to do this." It is such an off-the-wall idea. The title is *Diamond Zero*. It involves a machine that makes it possible to make diamonds from men who have been cremated. Because we are carbon after we are gone, this machine will make diamonds out of the remains. Of course, my character is extremely diabolical and is quite a scary woman. About three weeks ago, I was watching *The Today Show*, and would you believe that they have come up with a machine that does this? It's in Germany, and on the *Today Show*, they had a family who was going to do this to the father. The father was terminally ill but still alive, and sitting on the couch was the mother, the father, and the son. This son had brought this idea to his mother. They asked the whole family how they felt about this procedure, and the wife thought it was a wonderful idea, that she would have something like this to cherish her husband, a diamond that she could wear. The father was okay with it, and the son thought it was a really great idea. Then, they brought out the man who invented this machine. He was talking about how wonderful it was that people could have something that they could really wear. To have close to them all the time, rather than all those objects up in the attic, and he explained how the device works, and that it takes about sixteen weeks before the diamond is produced, and the cost could be up to twenty thousand dollars. I tell you, I just sat there with my mouth open watching this on television. Can you imagine all of the people looking at the urn on their fireplace thinking, "Hmmm... I could have a diamond here."

I will tell you something: People come up to me and they say that they have appreciated my work. I appreciate their love and devotion. It is always very heartwarming to know that there are people out there who really care about your work. There is a tremendous amount that goes into being an actor. I think the fans appreciate that.

Credits: 1950: *The Pretty Girl* (uncredited); 1963: *The Birds* (a.k.a. *Alfred Hitchcock's The Birds*); 1964: *Marnie*; 1965: *Bob Hope Presents the Chrysler Theatre: Bob Hope Christmas Variety Special* (television) (12/22/65); *Kraft Suspense Theatre: The Trains of Silence* (06/10/65) (television); *Run for Your Life: Someone Who Makes Me Feel Beautiful* (09/27/65) (television); 1967: *A Countess from Hong Kong* [Great Britain–U.S.]; 1968: *Tiger by the Tail*; *The Man and the Albatross* [France]; 1970: *The Courtship of Eddie's Father: Free Is a Four-Letter Word* (02/25/70) (television); *Santa's Harvest* (a.k.a. *Devil's Harvest*) [South Africa]; 1971: *The Courtship of Eddie's Father: A Little Get-Together for Cissy* (01/06/71) (television); 1973: *Docteur Caraibes* (television) [France]; *The Harrad Experiment*; *Mr. Kingstreet's War* [South Africa]; 1976: *Alla Donde Muere El Viento* (a.k.a. *Where the Wind Dies*) [Argentina]; *The Bionic Woman: Claws* (02/25/76) (television); 1981: *Roar*; 1982: *Foxfire Light*; 1983: *Hart to Hart: Hunted Harts* (01/04/83) (television); 1984: *Tales from the Darkside: Mookie and Pookie* (11/04/84) (television); *Terror in the Aisles* (video); 1985: *Alfred Hitchcock Presents: Man from the South* (television); *Hitchcock: Il Brividio Del Genius* (television) [Italy]; *Our Time* (08/03/85) (television); 1988: *Hotel: Double Take* (01/02/88) (television); 1989: *Deadly Spygames*; 1990: *The Bold and the Beautiful* (television); *Pacific Heights*; *Return to Green Acres* (television); 1991: *The Bold and the Beautiful* (television); *In the Cold of the Night*; *In the Heat of the Night: Liar's Poker* (10/29/91) (television); *Shadow of a Doubt* (television); 1992: *The Bold and the Beautiful* (television); *Through the Eyes of a Killer* (a.k.a. *The Master Builder*) (television); 1993: *The Bold and the Beautiful* (television); *Murder, She Wrote: Bloodlines* (11/09/93) (television); *Perry Mason: The Case of the Skin-Deep Scandal* (television); 1994: *The Birds II: Land's End* (television); *Dream On: I Never Promised You Charoses, Martin* (09/07/94) (television); *Teresa's Tattoo*; *Treacherous Beauties* (television) [Canada]; 1995: *Dream On: She Won't Do It, But Her Sister Will* (10/04/95) (television); 1996: *Citizen Ruth*; *Dream On: Finale with a Vengeance* (03/27/96), *Second Time Around* (01/24/96), *The Way We War* (02/14/96) (television); 1997: *The Guardian: Pilot* (03/18/97) (television); *Mulligans!* (short film); *Sean Connery, an Intimate Portrait* (television); 1998: *Arli$$:*

Stanley Babson—Win, Place or Show (08/02/98) (television); *Chicago Hope: Psychodrama* (01/21/98) (television); *Batman: Gotham Knights: Mean Season* (04/25/98) (animated) (television) (voice only); *Break Up*; *Expose* [Sweden-U.S.]; *I Woke Up Early the Day I Died* (a.k.a. *Ed Wood's I Woke Up Early the Day I Died*); *Invasion America* (animated) (television) [voice only]; 1999: *A & E Biography: Sophia Loren—Actress Italian Style* (television); *Bull: A Beautiful Lie* (television); *The Darklings* (television); *Hitchcock: Shadow of a Genius* (a.k.a. *Dial H for Hitchcock: The Genius Behind the Showman*) (video supplement); *Nature: Extraordinary Cats* (television); *Replacing Dad* (television); *Reputations: Alfred Hitchcock* (television) [Great Britain]; *The Storytellers*; 2000: *All About 'The Birds'* (video supplement); *Hollywood Off-Ramp: Simple Simon* (06/05/00) (television) [Canada-U.S.]; *Internet Love* (television) [Germany]; *Intimate Portrait: Betty White* (television); *Life with Big Cats* (television); *Mind Rage* (a.k.a. *Mind Lies*); *Providence: The Thanksgiving Story: Part 1, Part 2* (11/24/00), *The Unsinkable Sydney Hansen* (11/17/00) (television); *The Hand Behind the Mouse: The Ub Iwerks Story* (video supplement); *The Trouble with Marnie* (video supplement); 2001: *AFI's 100 Years, 100 Thrills: America's Most Heart-Pounding Movies* (television); *Hitchcock: Alfred the Great* (a.k.a. *Biography: Hitchcock—Alfred the Great*) (television); *Ice Cream Sundae* (short film) [Luxembourg]; *Tea with Grandma* (short film); 2002: *Hollywood Legend* (television); *Leute Heute* (02/04/02) (television) [Germany]; *Screen Tests of the Stars* (television); 2003: *Dark Wolf*; *IceMaker*; *Julie and Jack*; *Rose's Garden*; *Searching for Haizmann*; *This Morning* (05/12/03) (television); 2004: *Hollywood Legenden* (television) [Germany]; *I Heart Huckabees* (a.k.a. *I Love Huckabees*) [U.S.-Germany]; *Raising Genius*; *Return to Babylon*; 2005: *Cinema Mil* (09/24/05) (television) [Spain]; *Corazon de...* (10/12/05) (television) [Spain]; *Strike the Tent*; 2006: *Rodeo Girl*; 2007: *Diamond Zero*; *Her Morbid Desire*.

Gloria Hendry

Gloria Hendry was born on March 3, 1949, in Jacksonville, Florida. She moved with her family to Jersey City, New Jersey during her early scholastic years, and then settled in Newark. One of her first jobs was as a secretary for the New York office of the NAACP. When she became infatuated with acting, she began to take acting, dancing, and singing

Gloria Hendry and her huge gun battle villains in the Philippines-lensed action movie, *Savage Sisters* (1974) (American International Pictures).

lessons, leading to a stint as a Bunny in a Playboy Club in New York. During this time, she also began to model.

Hendry was discovered at the Playboy Club and offered a small role in the film *For the Love of Ivy* with Sidney Poitier and Abbey Lincoln. For her role in the film, she wore a Bunny-type costume. Soon afterwards, she landed many parts in television commercials; by the early seventies, she had appeared in approximately thirty of them. Other small roles in the films *The Landlord* starring Beau Bridges and *Across 110th Street* with Anthony Quinn, and Yaphet Kotto followed.

She was the lead actress (alongside popular black male star Fred Williamson) in the gritty urban action film *Black Caesar* and its follow-up *Hell Up in Harlem,* and co-starred with martial artist–actor Jim Kelly in *Black Belt Jones*. Quickly garnering positive notices as a no-nonsense actress with an abundance of beauty, charm, and wit, she graduated to battling *The Man* alongside another former pro athlete, Jim Brown, in *Slaughter's Big Rip-Off,* and worked in the Philippines (with co-star Cheri Caffaro of Ginger series fame) on the equally gritty *Savage Sisters*.

Because of her involvement in urban action films, Hendry was brought to the attention of the producers of the popular James Bond films and signed to play the role of Rosie Carver in the first Roger Moore Bond film, *Live and Let Die* (1973). In a 1973 interview with the *New York Amsterdam News*, Hendry recalled how she was selected for the part of the first (and until Halle Berry's turn in the twentieth Bond film *Die Another Day* [2003] the only) African-American woman to both share the bed and the battles of the British super secret agent: "It all began when my agent called me from New York. I was in Hollywood at the time, and he insisted that I come over for a screen test. At first I hesitated. I actually did not have the bread just to fly over for a test, but he kept insisting, and so I gave up, and went, saw producer Harry Saltzman. Before I knew what happened they sent me off to New Orleans to meet director Guy Hamilton. I liked him immediately and I like him even better now after having worked with him...."

Remarking in the same interview about her first scene with Roger Moore, which took place beneath the Eden waterfalls in Ocho Rios, Jamaica, "It was one of the most beautiful places I've ever seen. It really turned me on for a love scene with James Bond."

Not all her scenes in the film were so deliriously wonderful for the actress. "I was hiding in the fish hole of this fishing boat, a cruiser, and it was rocking down there, and smelled of fish so badly, I suddenly got very sick. One of the crew members suggested I take a dip in the cold water, and I would feel better fast. I climbed over the side of the boat, holding on to a rope, and just as I was all the way in the water I see these funny fins: Sharks! I have never been cured so fast in my life! And out of that water I went!"

The film also found Hendry shooting automatic weapons and dodging bullets. United Artists promoted her appearance in the film in some urban city markets by touting her as Mrs. James Bond. The advertising gamble fizzled quickly, most likely due to a combination of racial tensions in some areas, as well as the fact that Hendry's character dies, a victim of Bond's nemesis Mr. Big (Yaphet Kotto); Bond's paramour in the remainder of the film was played by screen newcomer Jane Seymour.

The Hendry films *Black Belt Jones* and *Savage Sisters* followed. *Variety* said of her *Black Belt Jones* performance (in a review dated January 30, 1974), "[She is] equally adept at physical jousting as providing a good romantic interest." When changing societal mores meant less mainstream audiences attending exploitation-oriented films, the market for such features began to dry up. The action movie *Bare Knuckles* attempted to keep her in the same kind of action roles as before. However, urban action films, especially those labeled with the Blaxploitation moniker, were vanishing as quickly as the audiences who were now clamoring for higher budgeted adventure, horror, and science fiction fare like *Jaws*, *Raiders of the Lost Ark*, *Superman* and *Star Wars*.

Hendry has resumed her career as a singer, model, and stage actress, with occasional television and film appearances. Nowadays, she is working on her autobiography; has completed a music CD featuring her singing; and has appeared in a one-woman show about Billie Holiday and produced the theatrical production, *The Paul Robeson Story*. She has also appeared in *Black Kissinger*, a film reuniting her with Fred Wiliamson, her *Black Caesar* co-star. To most of her fans, she will always be remembered as *Live and Let Die*'s Rosie Carver, the first African-American leading lady in a James Bond film.

Q: In *Savage Sisters*, *Black Belt Jones*, and *Live and Let Die* you played very strong characters. I'm sure that in some urban areas, you became a role model for women, particularly young minority women, and they might have even looked up to you as a heroine. Were you aware of that at the time?

Gloria Hendry: Well, no, I was not aware of that while I was working, only afterwards. I did not have to work at making myself athletic, I'm a naturally athletic person, I play tennis, basketball, volleyball, I lift weights, I love horseback riding, skiing, I do all of these sports. One of the reasons that I was chosen for these particular roles, like the one in *Black Belt Jones*, is because I had the athletic body. For that particular film, I was trained by Chuck Norris' stunt team to get me ready for the start of principal photography. The one thing that I was aware of while performing in these movies, was my part in the script, being a female, but not being the victim, but being the tough woman. I felt at the time that I was in a wholly different type of role, empowered, and empowering. I feel that now I can look back and see it all for what it truly was, and is. However, during the time, whatever came my way, I made the best of it. I am not proud of everything I did, of every role I played. Nevertheless, I know that my persona was affecting, where people saw me in a certain way, or as a certain type. Someone like Pam Grier and I should have done a movie together. It would have featured two strong women characters. I still think that it would be a good idea; it is a good time for it. Did you know that Pam Grier and I were supposed to appear in a movie together, years ago, but it never was made? We were supposed to play roller skaters, on opposing sides. We were about to begin pre-production, but then the whole thing fell through at the last minute. I met Pam again, some years later, when she was working on *Jackie Brown*, and she said, "We've got to do a movie together." Therefore, whoever is listening, I think it would be a very good marriage for both of us. Really, I think it would go over very well.

Q: How did you get the role of Rosie Carver in *Live and Let Die*?

Hendry: My manager called me from New York. I am a New Yorker, but I had gone out to California and I was working on *Black Caesar*. At the end of *Black Caesar*, I got a phone call from my manager. He asked me to come back to New York for an audition. I said, "No thanks. I'm okay here, I've got a movie coming out, and I just finished *Black Caesar*." He said, "Look, Gloria, they want to see you for this movie." I was just numbed out. I said, "Well, are they flying me in?" and he said, "No." Well, I did fly in and I put on my best outfit and I went to see Harry Saltzman. I walked in through the door, I sat down and he said, "Madam, how soon can you fly?" and I said, "This evening." And off I went. They put me onto the next flight and they sent me out to meet with Guy Hamilton and Roger Moore in New Orleans. I was on the plane, first class, going to New Orleans, and Roger and Guy Hamilton met me when I got off the plane. We talked about the role but there was no script reading or anything like that. They asked me to stay overnight and I said, "No, I have to go back to New York." I flew back to New York, and then California. A week later, my manager called me and said I got the part.

Q: So you did not have to read the script or audition for this role at all?

Hendry: No, as far as I knew they saw my credits, and maybe even saw me in a few parts, and that was all good enough. I guess I fit the type... I got lucky. Should I say it? I got lucky.

Q: How did you find working with Roger Moore in *Live and Let Die*?

Hendry: Wonderful. I have never experienced such a kind, creative person. I did not, and I *do* not know Roger personally, but it was a wonderful environment that he created, because when you are one-to-one with your acting partner, there is nothing else. Regarding our onscreen relationship, he wanted everything to work, and so did I. He was a very giving person. I felt very relaxed working with him, and he helped to make the atmosphere on the set very relaxed as well.

Q: I find this interesting because it was also *his* first Bond film.

Hendry: He always seemed very relaxed to me. In fact, there was a time where he shared his autographs with me. People would come up to him and ask for his autograph... he was very popular for years because he was on that television show, *The Saint*. Anyway, people would ask him for his autograph and he would then give me the pad and pen as well to sign. We often shared the same limousine, and he made sure that I got to the set on time. He was just wonderful to be with, and to work with.

Q: You must have seen some of the Sean Connery James Bond films before you appeared in this movie. What did you think of Roger Moore's performances as Bond, compared to Connery's?

Hendry: First, I could not compare because before making this film, he had not been Bond at all. When we first met, he was just getting ready to go through the motions of doing the film. I mean, everybody would love to act with Sean Connery, there is nobody that could replace him, he started Bond, and he will always be Bond in the minds of many, many people. Without him, there would be no Bond series today. Roger just carried on the line of the Bonds, his own way, and he did it well.

Q: Did you travel to England to shoot the interiors?

Hendry: Yes. In fact, most of the interiors were shot in London, at Pinewood Studios.

Q: Can you recall if any of the exteriors were done in Jamaica?

Hendry: All of the exterior material, including the scenes featuring us walking across the alligators at the alligator farm, were filmed in Jamaica. Up in the hills; I believe we even passed Ian Fleming's home on our way to a location while on a boat ride. Yes, it was pointed out to me that one of the locations was Ocho Rios, Goldeneye, and Ian Fleming's home for many years.

Q: Do you recall if the love scenes between you and Moore caused some controversy while you were shooting? Apparently, in some countries where the film was distributed, they became controversial and, it is rumored, had to be snipped by local censors.

The first African-American sex symbol in a James Bond film, Hendry paved the way in 1973's *Live and Let Die* with Roger Moore (Danjaq Productions/Eon Productions/United Artists/MGM).

Hendry: Did it cause that much of a ruckus? I was not aware of that kind of large ripple effect. Because of the love scene, and because of the roles that we were playing during those love scenes, we were never thinking one way or the other about who was who or anything like that. We were playing the roles as one human being to another, and as I was lying on top of him doing the scene, it worked beautifully. It was also a closed set. I'll tell you a story, I have just remembered this, and it's funny because I had forgotten it for so many years, but there was a time when I had eaten a lot of garlic the night before we were to shoot a scene. The next day I'm bending over Roger and he said, "You didn't!" and I said, "Yeah, I did, I had garlic last night." He said, "You're lucky, I'm married to an Italian woman." And as I was kissing him, we were not going through a turmoil of feelings about kissing one another, we were having fun.

Q: I saw this film when it first came out in 1973 and I had no problem with it whatsoever. I felt the fact that the character of Bond was with a woman of color also emboldened the film somewhat, and that the scenes between you and Moore were much better than the stagnant, uncomfortable romantic ones between him and Jane Seymour. But maybe in some states, somewhere, someone did not like the interracial scenes. I have been in contact with people who claimed that indeed there were cuts made to the film because of it. Was this anything that you were aware of?

Hendry: That there were cuts because of the love scene? Yes, in fact, I did become

Hendry shows who's in charge in this scene from *Savage Sisters* (1974) (American International Pictures).

aware of this, but after the fact, *much* later, after the mad rush of the publicity was all over. Actually, my name was pulled in various places where the film was exhibited. My name was no longer being mentioned in the same breath as the movie where advertising was concerned. As opposed to how it was in the beginning when I saw my picture on the covers of different magazines about me being Mrs. Bond, which I was. However, after the storm of the immediate publicity blew over, all of a sudden, you did not see me anymore, you did not hear about me anymore, regarding this film. Suddenly, after the initial premieres, I was not invited to anything, or being made aware of anything connected with the film. All of a sudden, it is a Bond movie where even if you rented the video, it is as if I did not exist. I did not exist, and there were cuts in the movie—*that* I learned later on. I was surprised. It hurt; it hurt in a major way. The point of whoever had that kind of control angered me. I was very disappointed. How dare they, how dare they. This is something creative, how dare they. As I am talking about it now ... I can tell how, creatively, it affected me.

Q: Do you have any recollections of other scenes in that film?

Hendry: Another very amusing story is about when I was flipped over when I first meet Bond in his room. Of course, my wig was not supposed to have fallen off. I do not remember clearly but I think that there was a length of something that was caught onto the wig, and my wig fell off, and that was embarrassing and hysterical at the same time. I felt that it would be funny to let people know how I really felt about that.

Q: Do you recall shooting anything that did not end up in the finished version?

Hendry: Not right now. Not off the top of my head, sorry. It has been so long ago. All I recall is that death scene where I am running on a hill where someone has shot me. The director told me that I was supposed to go down at this point, and I wound up lying in this pit of ants. It was an anthill!

Q: What is your single most outstanding memory of working on *Live and Let Die*?

Hendry: Oh, the grand time that I had. The feeling that I had about being part of such a wonderful production. The grandiosity of it all, the love, the cheer. The single most outstanding memory at this stage of my life is to remember that. If I had to do it all over again, I would gladly do it. If they wanted me there for six months again, I would be there for six months.

Q: As an audience member and as a viewer, have you seen the subsequent Bond films?

Hendry: Before I did *Live and Let Die*, I had seen a lot of them including *Dr. No*, *Goldfinger*, *Diamonds Are Forever*, and *From Russia with Love*. After that, I saw *The Spy Who Loved Me* and *A View to a Kill*, and the first one that Timothy Dalton did. *The Living Daylights*. However, I particularly liked both *Dr. No*, and *Goldfinger*—those two always stand out in my mind.

Q: Of your main credits through the seventies, which included *The Landlord*, *Across 110th Street*, *Slaughter's Big Rip-Off*, the two films you did with Fred Williamson, *Live and Let Die*, *Black Belt Jones* and *Savage Sisters*, which contain your favorite roles?

Hendry: I liked doing *Black Caesar*, because it had a nice story line. I also like *Live and Let Die* and *Black Belt Jones*.

Q: Those are three good films, and three of your best films I believe. There was a period where you had not worked in films for some time...

Hendry: I had not done a feature until 1995. Jeff Burr came along and wanted me to work with him in *Pumpkinhead II*. I had never done a horror film before. It was a scary experience, but also very refreshing.

Q: You have completed a film called *South Bureau Homicide* that I do not know much about.

Hendry: It was shot a couple of years ago. It is a short film about a real-life situation where a student in a school had been killed by a bullet from blocks away—a stray bullet from a gang war. I played a principal.

Q: What can Gloria Hendry's fans expect from her in the future?

Hendry: I am going to be in a movie with Fred Williamson, a takeoff on the James Bond films called *Black Kissinger*. I had taken a turn at directing for the stage, which is something that I always wanted to do, and I am singing professionally too. I am a jazz singer, I have been singing over the years. I love performing. I have been in a one-woman show called *The Waiting Room*, in which I played Billie Holiday. And I am working on my autobiography. I would like to call the book *Gloria*.

Credits: 1968: *For the Love of Ivy*; 1970: *The Landlord*; 1972: *Across 110th Street*; 1973: *Black Caesar*; *Hell Up in Harlem*; *Live and Let Die* [Great Britain–U.S.]; *Love, American Style: Love and the Flunky* (10/19/73) (television); *Slaughter's Big Rip-Off*; 1974: *Black Belt Jones*; *Savage Sisters* [U.S.-Philippines]; 1977: *Bare Knuckles*; 1981: *The Brady Brides: Cool Hand Phil* (04/10/81) (television); 1984: *Emerald Point N.A.S.: The Assignment* (01/09/84) (television); 1987: *Falcon Crest: Opening Moves* (10/02/87) (television); 1988: *Doin' Time on Planet Earth*; 1990: *Hunter: The Incident* (10/24/90) (television); 1991: *Seeds of Tragedy* (television); 1994: *Pumpkinhead II: Blood Wings* (a.k.a. *Pumpkinhead II*); 1996: *South Bureau Homicide* (short); 1998: *Lookin' Italian* (a.k.a. *Showdown*); 1999: *Inside 'Live and Let Die'* (video supplement); 2000: *Superfly: Ron O'Neal Story: The E! True Hollywood Story* (television); 2002: *Baadasssss Cinema* (video) [U.S.–Great Britain]; 2005: *Seven Swans*; 2007: *Black Kissinger* [Canada-Jamaica-U.S.].

Richard Herd

Richard Herd was born on September 26, 1932, in Boston, Massachusetts. Like many of the male actors interviewed for this project, he has an impressive list of stage, television, and feature film credits, beginning his acting career while still a student, at age sixteen. An audition for a small theater troupe made up of students, and a role in a local radio production of *A Tale of Two Cities* led Herd to a life as a character actor in a variety of roles. He has played coaches, quite a number of businessmen, army generals, alien leaders, union leaders, etc. His career has run the gamut from a likable older relative, to a reptilian leader of an alien race seeking to enslave all of humanity. He is equally at home with comedy, as seen in his *Seinfeld* portrayal of Mr. Wilhelm, the Yankees baseball team boss of Jason Alexander. Other television addicts might recall him as the authoritarian figure in many programs featuring police officials. He co-starred as Police Captain Sheridan for three seasons of the popular show *T.J. Hooker*, starring William Shatner.

Despite years of honing his craft on the theatrical stage, Herd firmly believes that one of his best roles was that of Captain Galaxy in an episode of the dramatic science fiction show *Quantum Leap*. In an early–'90s *Big Reel* interview by Charles P. Mitchell, Herd fondly recalled it as "the warmest, most real, and vulnerable role I was ever given the opportunity to play." He also enjoys playing the villain, a role he has essayed countless times. He told *Drama-Logue* magazine in March 1989, "When you play a heavy, you never think of him as a heavy; you just think of him as a person doing whatever in life he has to do."

An accomplished artist who enjoys painting and writing, Herd continues to appear in film and television roles. He has taken his *Cecil B. DeMille—A One-Man Show* on the road numerous times, and continues to resurrect the well-received biographical evening of anecdotes and revealing stories. Of course, Herd will be forever associated with his role as the alien leader John, the green-skinned, human-eating lizard leader from outer space, in the *V* miniseries. "It has become like *Star Trek*... [it's] been replayed on the Sci-Fi Channel and is on video and DVD. There has always been a huge interest in me from fans of that show. People are still fascinated, after all these years, by *V*."

Q: How did you get your start in the acting profession?

Richard Herd: I met a group of actors who were going to Boston University, Harvard, and Emerson Colleges. They were involved with a radio show, and had rented a rehearsal room at Boston English, the High School. The [radio] show, *Fiction Fair*, was broadcast on Saturday mornings, out of Quincy, Massachusetts. They had heard me sing, because I sang with the [high school] band, and they said that there was a part for me in [a radio production of] *A Tale of Two Cities*. They were doing a radio version of the play, and would I like to audition for it. I said yes immediately. I auditioned and got the job and ended up doing a whole year of radio. There was another group called the Boston Catholic Theatre. They, too, had heard that I sang. At some point, some years before, Walter Kerr had written a musical called *Sing Out, Sweet Land*, and someone from the Boston Catholic Theatre suggested that I audition for a role in that production. I went in, auditioned, and got the part. I also performed in Passion Plays with the Boston Catholic Theatre, and we would tour all over New England with them, playing at colleges, universities, and high schools. I started working with various theater companies in Boston before I got my Equity card. For the Boston Summer Theatre, I walked in one day and I did an audition, and they put me on as an apprentice. They had a place in Framingham, Massachusetts. I also was a stagehand. We would build the sets, drive them to Boston, and then set them up. I would perform in the productions as well. Lee Falk, who created the comic strips *Mandrake the Magician*, and *The Phantom*, and Al Capp who created the comic strip *Abner Li'l* co-owned the Summer Theater in Boston. Many big name stars came through there, people such as Claude Rains, Ben Gazzara, Ossie Davis, Ruby Dee, Eileen Heckart and Veronica Lake. Two years later, I worked with Veronica Lake as an assistant stage manager in *I Am a Camera*, the show that *Cabaret* is based on. I liked her, and I thought she did a hell of a job as an actress in *I Am a Camera*. Alexis Smith, Victor Jory, Eva Marie Saint, they also came through the Boston Summer Theatre.

Eventually I began taking the train to New York, which at the time they called the Night Owl because you would ride all night long, and get into New York in the morning. I would take the train to New York to catch Broadway shows. I could not afford the full-price tickets, so I would get standing room. I saw the original productions of *Guys and Dolls*, *Paint Your Wagon*, *A View from the Bridge*, shows like that. I found a hotel room for $2 a night and, I'll tell you, this hotel—it was like every *film noir* you ever saw or heard of. Right outside my hotel room window was a neon sign that flashed **RIO HOTEL, RIO HOTEL**, into my room.

When I got to New York, I felt prepared. I was armed with my union card from the Boston Summer Theatre. I auditioned for Claire Tree Major's children's theater troupe. A day or two later I learned that I had been cast in three roles in her production of *Penrod*. Her theatre company was located in Pleasantville, New York. We performed everywhere, all over the place, as far south as Mississippi. We played grade schools and high schools. I was in Buffalo just before Christmas and my mother, who was tracking the show, contacted me and said that Uncle Sam needed my services for the Korean War. During basic training, I was hit in my bad knee with a rifle butt, and my knee flared up. I came out of the service with an honorable discharge. I then went to Maine, where I worked in the theater. I returned to New York and got a role, Off-Broadway, in *Hobson's Choice*. Then I ran into Robert Ludlum, who is known primarily as an author today, but back then he was a really good actor. Bob and I went out to the Army Signal Corps in Long Island, where they made all these Army training films. He auditioned for films about World War I, and I auditioned to play roles set in World War II. We said our dialogue directly into the camera; there was not much time for rehearsing beforehand. They paid us $60 a day. I had an Eisenhower jacket on, it came to just around the belt buckle line, one's midriff, and the battle streamers were flowing—I looked quite impressive. A few months later, they called me and said we had to do it again, because the Pentagon said that there were creases in my jacket, can you imagine? Because there were creases in my jacket in this training film, someone deigned that we had to re-shoot this training film. However, that was okay by me, as I got to be paid again. Anyway, Bob Ludlum had always wanted to be a producer, and he opened up the North Jersey Playhouse in New Jersey. Ludlum called me and cast me in the plays *The Seven-Year Itch and Light up the Sky*. The Playhouse on the Mall in Paramus, New Jersey was where I performed in *The Andersonville Trial*. That's around the time that Bob started writing his first novel, and a month later Bob had a deal, and it was published.

Around that time, I was called for my very first part in a commercial. I didn't know what the hell commercials were at the time... I always thought that they were using pretty people, but then they started using real people, and I got my very first commercial role. I was in a cigarette commercial for the Newport brand, where I didn't even have to smoke! Back in those days, actors used to love commercials, because they supported your acting habit. I got a call from a casting agent who was casting smaller parts for films. She said, "Would you be interested in being a stand-in for David Niven? He's doing a film with Mitzi Gaynor and Patty Duke." I said, "I'll take it." It was two weeks worth of work.

Q: Was this film titled *The Happy Anniversary*?

Herd: Yes, I believe it was. I went in, and Johnny Quill, an old friend of mine, production assistant, said to me, "Make sure you say hello to the production manager," who was his mentor. Anyway, I went in, and I was standing there watching the rehearsal. I always had great respect for David Niven. When the rehearsal was over, Niven walked over to me, shook my hand and asked me my name. And he said, "If there's anything that I can do for you, anything that you need, you let me know, because this is the way that I started [as a stand-in]." It was a wonderful learning experience for me, coupled with being on-camera in the Army training films.

I later got a call from another casting director who said, "[Elia] Kazan is looking for background people for his film *Splendor in the Grass*." I said, "Is Mr. Kazan going to give me lines?" They said, "No, it's a background part." I said I wasn't interested. In retrospect, maybe I should have done it. Just to be around and to listen to what he had to say [as a filmmaker]. Many background people were actors I knew. I once got a call, "Jimmy Cagney's shooting a movie on the Brooklyn docks called *Never Steal Anything Small*." I thought, "Jimmy Cagney!" However, it was the middle of winter, and I would freeze on the Brooklyn docks. They said, "You'll get a box lunch, and twenty-three bucks a day." I said, "I'll do it." I froze my ass off, but I was around Jimmy Cagney, whom I got to be friends with later on.

Q: Did you do a lot of work as a background person?

Herd: Only about four or five films, but I was meeting people all the time. My friend Johnny Quill, who was also an actor, and me, we got a job at night selling Bibles, door to door. We sold Bibles in places in New York like Red Hook, Bed Stuy, Spanish Harlem, from 6 to 9 PM. We would go to apartments in neighborhoods that were all over the place, to the top of the roofs, and on down. I cannot tell you how hard this was, carrying these huge Bibles around, but I was making enough money to support myself and my acting career. Johnny finally got a gig as an assistant director, which was something else that he always wanted to do. He called me and he said to come in and audition for a part in "an Italian movie with Richard Conte." I got the part. The film was titled [in English] *My Brother Anastasia*. Alan Arthur Siedleman auditioned me for *Hercules in New York*, and I got that part. That was Arnold Schwarzenegger's first film. In my business, there are some people who, after you work for them and prove yourself, call you again. You do not have to go in and audition all over again. There are some people who recommend you for jobs, and the same is true for all the industry—theatre, television, and film. There are people who have been loyal to me like the director, Burt Kennedy, God bless him, he is gone now, but Burt always looked out for me. I did my first western for him, *Kate Bliss and the Tickertape Kid* with Tony Randall. People like that always looked out for me. However, some people do not look out for their fellow actors. They are so into themselves. Rod Steiger, who I worked with, told me, "One of the responsibilities of the star of the film, be he a man or a woman, is the morale of the company, to be supportive of his director, and to help his fellow actor." He told me, "It makes it a lot easier on the set, the actors work harder, and you get a better picture." You work with all kinds of directors, you work with directors who are just technicians, traffic cops, who don't know shit about actors, and don't know how to work with them. And then some of them are really into the camera. They know the camera, they know how to block for the camera, and they know how to shoot a script. It always surprises me when I find a director who can direct. I would imagine a director would say, "It surprises me when I find an actor who can act." Let me tell you, with the medium of film, you do not have to be a trained actor because, in the editing room, they can create the performance. In the theater, *onstage, that's* the master shot, and you got it or you do not. After I did *The China Syndrome*, I got a lot of attention. You do a part like that in a film; it carries you for five years of work. You do not have to audition, they give you work. After *The China Syndrome*, I said to myself "Yeah, now I'm ready. I'm ready for the next step, that next part." My agent said, "You're thinking logically. There's no A to B here, Dick, no A to B." The producers of *The China Syndrome* recommended me to the director of *Nine to Five*. I auditioned for the role that eventually went to Dabney Coleman. They even called me back a few times, and I kept saying to myself, "This is my next step, my next step...." *The China Syndrome* may have just been a fictional picture from a major studio, but then, not too long after its release, the Three Mile Island thing came along, and then *The China Syndrome* began making the Hollywood rounds, everyone wanted to see the picture after Three Mile Island happened. Everyone saw the picture, and everyone saw me in it. That is why I thought *Nine to Five* was my next step.

Well, for whatever the reason, I did not get to that next step right then, I did not get the part in *Nine to Five*. Then I worked in *F.I.S.T.* with Sylvester Stallone. It was one of the best parts in a film that I ever had, although I had to play that role down. I could have pulled the focus away from Stallone, but [director] Norman Jewison said to me [about the character], "That's not the kind of guy he is. This guy needs help, Dick. He has to go find somebody who can put a union together. You are a good guy, you're a strong guy, and you're a Teamster. If you play it with too much charisma, why the hell would I need Stallone here doing this part? I know it's hard for you to do, but I know you can do it." I loved that part. There were so many good actors in that film... Kevin Conway, Peter Boyle, Melinda Dillon. When it was done, many people thought that it was a wonderful picture. However, it went down the tubes when it was released. It crashed and burned with the critics, audiences. I believed at the time that that was the picture that was going to do it, make it, for a lot of us. It has become something of a cult film since.

Q: *T.J. Hooker* with William Shatner—how did you become involved with that show?
Herd: They offered me a role, and I did not want the part initially. I believed that I

Herd and *T.J. Hooker* co-stars Adrian Zmed, William Shatner, and Heather Locklear. (Photo courtesy Richard Herd)

reached the point in my career where I was doing bigger things, and I said, "To hell with this." I did not want to do a series and be overexposed, because I believed that I had a pretty decent film career. The Aaron Spelling people kept calling me, and calling me. It was a one-day guest shot playing Captain Dennis Sheridan in a scene set on a firing range, a big heavy-duty hard-ass argument with Shatner's character. Originally, the show was called *The Protectors*, and the original premise of the show was that [Shatner] had these six young rookies that he was training, and every once in a while, he'd take a couple of

The 1979 film *The China Syndrome* (IPC Films/Columbia Pictures) contained one of Richard Herd's most memorable roles. (Photo courtesy Richard Herd)

them out in the field. After my stint, I went back east. Later on, I got a call from the Spelling people saying that something was going on, that they were changing the show from the original intent to be about just a few rookies and their immediate commander; the producers now were interested in me playing Captain Sheridan. What did I know about series television back then? I took the job, and my agent made a sweet deal for me, with a commitment to the network for six episodes. However, they changed the whole concept of the show by getting rid of most of the young actors, although Adrian Zmed was still in the show. We went on the air, and the show did all right. The six episodes aired, and then they called and they picked up my contract for another thirteen episodes, and that is when Heather Locklear appeared on the show, playing my daughter. I adored her. My character had to have a sense of levity as well as a sense of command. However, as the show went on, I began to have less command.

Eventually, the roles reversed, Shatner's and mine. I noticed it in the writing, that the roles were reversing. Shatner's character was getting stronger, and my character was losing his authority, getting weaker, and more laughable. Finally, the producer said, "Dick, forget it. Put the money in the bank, and be happy." I said, "You're right." I was grateful, so I just did my work, and I put the money in the bank. The long and the short of it was that my role was becoming diminished. Whole scenes that I had would eventually end up in William's mouth. I will give you an example: There was a scene where my daughter, played by Heather, was shot, critically wounded. They wrote this five-page scene with Heather in the hospital, it was a wonderful scene, but then they completely re-wrote the scene and re-shot it. Two days later, guess who is sitting in the hospital with my little girl? T.J. Hooker, not Captain Sheridan. This went on and on, until it got to the point where they did not need me. What they did was, after a couple of years, they just dropped me.

Before I knew that they were going to drop me, we were ending a season, getting towards the end. It was a Friday night, we were finishing a take, and I knew we would be finishing the rest of the show on Monday, and we had this big party. I got home, and my agent called and said, "Dick, they're not picking up your contract." Therefore, it was expedient; the money they were paying me could be used elsewhere. That is the real world... that's real life. I call Hollywood bullshit and treachery anyway. Believe me, there is a lot of it going on out there. In Hollywood, they think what they do is right. I like it in New York, because in New York they tell you what they think, right to your face. It just happens to be a cold hard fact, and I have learned how to accept that. For *T.J. Hooker*, they got in authority figures of the week. Time went by, and they needed me again. Eventually, they did make a deal with me to return and appear in six more episodes, which I did. They got rid of Adrian Zmed, too, and replaced him with James Darren. I figured out what had happened because you always used to see Adrian and Bill going into the crime scenes together, as a team. Then, all of a sudden, Bill was like, "Wait here." That was the signal, that it was the end for Adrian on the show.

Q: What was your working relationship with Shatner like?

Herd: Well, I have to tell you, win, lose or draw he's a hard worker, although people have written many things about him, things like he is an enormously egotistical person and so on.

Q: Is it true that when you were offered the role of the alien leader in the series *V*, you were still involved in the *T.J. Hooker* series?

Herd: *V* happened during the same time as the *T.J. Hooker* series. There were a few overlapping days on *T.J. Hooker* and *V*, and the production coordinators arranged for me to work out a schedule. For example, one morning I would work on *T.J. Hooker*, and in the afternoon I would work on *V*. Then, the next morning I would be working on *V*, and in the afternoon *T.J. Hooker*. I was offered, and then they signed me to a series contract on *V*. I said, "Why are you offering me a series contract for *V: The Beginning*, the second season, when it says here in the [episode] I'm shooting now, two pages from the ending, that I get killed? It says here that Jane Badler blows me away... boom." They said, "Anything can happen in sci-fi. They want you back." Therefore, the show went on, and off the air, and then I got a call from the casting director who said, "We have you signed for a series contract." I said, "Yes, but I would like to be able to go audition for other things, other roles." She said, "We have you until such-and-such date." It was months and months and months away from the end of my contract... my agent could not send me out on a pilot because during this time I was signed to a series contract. I could go out for a guest shot, but he could not do anything better than that. They never did use me in the series [after Herd appeared in the miniseries], and they ended up tying me down for that entire time.

Q: On *V*, a lot of your footage consisted of sequences where you seem to be giving orders to others on a video screen, so you were actually on a blue- or green-screen special effects set, speaking directly to the camera. Are these scenes difficult to shoot?

Herd: They are, and I will tell you why. You have to know where the people are that you are talking to, that are not there. Specifically, if you are addressing something to certain people... what they would do is, they would give you marks. The blue mark is Tom; the red mark is Kate; this mark is Bruce, whatever. They would give you the levels too, where the eyes would be, and so on. I worked with a blue screen, where there is nothing there, and you have to imagine that there is something there. You have to conjure it up in your mind. You have to have a strong inner dialogue, a monologue; you have to be very present. Sometimes, it is difficult enough working with actors who show nothing in their eyes.

As the Alien leader John in the television miniseries *V* (Kenneth Johnson Productions/Warner Bros. Television), Richard Herd ushered in a new era of small screen villainy (photo courtesy Richard Herd).

Q: You are probably one of the few actors who appeared in all of the major prime time soap operas: *Dallas*, *Dynasty*, *Falcon Crest*, *Knots Landing*...

Herd: I've got to tell you, the wonderful thing about *T.J. Hooker* was meeting Aaron Spelling. He would use you any chance that he could in his series. He really was very kind to me. I always felt, and I continue to feel, that I always try to do the best job that I can. More importantly than that, I try not to complain, I try not to be a pain in the ass. It really bothers me working with actors who are always complaining, because they should be grateful that they are working. Sometimes I find myself telling them things like "Why did you take the job?" Every time I take a job, I take it because I am going to enjoy it.

Q: *SeaQuest DSV* was hyped as the next big science fiction hit for television, but it turned out to be a flop.

Herd: That was a disappointment. But I will tell you one thing, if I was called to work with Roy Scheider again, I would be there in a minute. He is one of the best actors I have ever worked with. He was the kind of person who tried to make the show better. He was a tough guy, but a tough guy in the right sense that he cares about the work, and he wanted it to be better. Everybody wanted that show to be a success, including all the *Star Trek* fans. The *Star Trek*, science fiction show type of fans were looking for a new science fiction show to latch onto. You do not know the opportunity that was presented to *SeaQuest*. There was no show on at that time that was even remotely like it. Today there are sci-fi shows all over the place. At that time, there was nothing besides *SeaQuest*, except for *Star Trek: The Next Generation*, really. They wanted it to be a success, and the people behind the scenes and everybody working on the show wanted it to be a huge success too. They had a huge response to the first couple of shows, then they had too many producers, too many people became involved, too many suggestions. I also believe that it wasn't set that far enough in the future either—it took place sometime around 2024. Still, the show had a fabulous cast. We had some good directors and we had some good guest stars... Shatner was a guest star, Topol was a guest, some wonderful people came on that show as guest stars. Then they paid for bigger names; we later had Charlton Heston on as a guest. However, the producers started to tinker with the show. What they did after the first year, was a terrible, terrible thing. They just about fired any actors involved over the age of forty-five. They dropped five actors, including myself, Royce Applegate, and a couple of others. They then replaced us with these nice kids; we used to refer to it as *Sea Hunk*. The show was moved to Florida, supposedly to save money on the sets and locations, and they ended up spending more money to put all those people up in houses, and whatever, and give them cars. However, they did not save any money. They brought me there to do a couple of more episodes in the second season.

Q: You were a regular on that show in the first season, and then...

Herd: I was a recurring character on that show. Here is how I got the role on *SeaQuest*... I had done what I consider my very best piece of work on television. I did a character called Captain Galaxy aka Moe Stein on an episode of *Quantum Leap* [*Future Boy October 6, 1957* (03/13/91)]. I did the last episode of *Quantum Leap* as well [*Mirror Image* (05/04/93)], reprising that character. *SeaQuest* came up, and Tommy Thompson who wrote *Future Boy* was one of the producers of that show. The pilot for *SeaQuest* was directed by Irvin Kershner, who had directed the second *Star Wars* film, *The Empire Strikes Back*. I had met Steven Spielberg [the executive producer of *SeaQuest*] when I was up for a role in the movie *1941*, but I lost that role to Robert Stack. I went in and auditioned for *SeaQuest*, and then Kershner had me back again, to be approved by Spielberg. I believe that it helped that Tommy Thompson was the fellow who worked on *Quantum Leap*.

Q: I read somewhere that you said you would want to do a horror movie and a western. I am surprised you have never appeared in a western.

Herd: I did, but I came late to the genre. When I came to Hollywood, all the westerns were pretty much already gone. However, I did actually get to appear in a western: Burt Kennedy cast me in *Kate Bliss and the Ticker-Tape Kid*, and I was just thrilled. Later on, Burt offered me another western, which I was unable to do. There was another western, where there was an audition that I went to, and the casting director came up to me, and said, "Can you ride?" and I said, "No." He said, "Oh my God, an honest actor." I said, "What do you mean?" He said, "Do you know how many actors come here for auditions, and then claim that they know how to ride a horse, and then get hurt on the first day?" I got a part, but not on a horse. I would also love to do a horror film. I am such a big fan of Vincent Price. I knew Vincent Price, and he said to me, "Dick, you've got to find a niche. I found a niche later in life with horror films, and you've got to find your niche."

People like Price, Peter Cushing, and Christopher Lee were all well-trained actors, and the things that they did were amazing. That is what I meant when I said that I wanted to do a horror film. I want to appear in a classic, classy horror film like the kind those people did. I do not want to do any slasher films, but I do want to be in a good, scary horror film and another western, a classic western.

Q: What was it like working with director Clint Eastwood *Midnight in the Garden of Good and Evil?*

Herd: It was one of the best experiences I ever had in my acting career. He is always pleasant and very relaxed on the set and whatever shots he had scheduled for the day, we always seemed to get the work done despite the relaxed atmosphere. There was no hustle, no bustle, and Clint never raised his voice. Everybody had a good time, and everybody was always prepared. My wife Patricia was in that picture with me, and she also acted in *Bird* for Eastwood. Clint Eastwood is quite a guy, quite a guy.

Q: What can you recall about the film *Trancers?*

Herd: Well, I really enjoyed working with Tim Thomerson. He was a great guy too. I worked with him later on an episode of *Midnight Caller.* He was a very funny person, a stand-up guy.

Q: He was a stand-up comedian, as well as an actor.

Herd: I had a really good time on that picture, and I thought that the money that they spent on that film looked really good on the big screen. It was a low-budget movie, but it looked good for the amount that they had to spend.

Q: You worked with Klaus Kinski in a film called *Schizoid.*

Herd: It was originally called *Murder by Mail*, or something like that. Klaus and I got along well. He had such a vast body of work. He was a classy actor. He was a little odd. He did not like people to touch him. He did not like people to get too close to him, like wardrobe people, people like that. He thought that they were getting into his aura, so to speak. Did you know that he spoke about six or seven languages, and would jet off around the world to work in films?

Q: Looking back over your career, besides *Quantum Leap* and *The China Syndrome*, are there any others that you are proud of?

Herd: I think my best piece of film work is in something that few people ever saw, *F.I.S.T.* I also enjoyed working with Norman Jewison on that film. I have no doubt that *F.I.S.T.* contains my best work on film. If I had played that character stronger, it would have diminished what Stallone was doing in the film. Intuitively, my character felt like he was supposed to be the leader of the union, but if he was supposed to be the leader of the union, why the hell would he need Stallone? That experience on *F.I.S.T.* was right up there with *The China Syndrome* as one of my favorite roles.

Q: Quite often, I come across actors who have made quite a career portraying heroes and villains. Which do you prefer?

Herd: When I performed onstage in Shakespeare's *Henry V*, there was a wonderful actress named Nancy Reardon working with me, and she said, "Richard, make sure you always play heroes, because you do them so well." I played Henry V, Daniel Boone, and all these heroic parts on stage, and I just loved those characters. In film, I would rather be a hammer than a nail. I do not want to be wallpaper on film, so I like the heavies, the villains, because there are more dimensions to them. There are more facets to their characters. They make things happen, their energy is vibrant. The villain ignites situations rather tan getting lost in the situation. When I was auditioning for *Blade Runner* for the role of the powerful figure [that Joe Turkel played in the movie], Ridley Scott said to me, "You're used to more power-driven roles, aren't you? You seem to want to be like the guy who makes things happen." I said, "I don't like to be passive." I like those types of parts, the roles that make things happen.

Credits: 1970: *Anastasia mio fratello ovvero il presunto capo dell'Anonima Assassini* (a.k.a. *My Brother Anastasia*); *Hercules in New York* (a.k.a. *Hercules Goes Bananas*); 1972: *Rivals*; 1973: *Pueblo* (a.k.a. *Pueblo Affair*); 1975: *The Rockford Files: Pastoria Prime Pick* (11/28/75) (television); 1976: *All the President's Men*; *Captains and Kings* (television); 1977: *The Feather and Father Gang: The Golden Fleece* (05/21/77) (television); *The Hunted Lady* (television); *Rafferty: Pilot* (09/05/77) (television); *The Streets of San Francisco: The Cannibals* (01/20/77) (television); 1978: *Dr. Scorpion* (television); *F.I.S.T.*; *Kate Bliss and the Ticker-Tape Kid* (television); *Terror Out of the Sky* (a.k.a. *Revenge of the Savage Bees*) (television); *Wolf Lake*; 1979: *The China Syndrome*; *Eight Is Enough: The Better Part of Valor* (02/21/79) (television); *Hart to Hart: Cop Out* (11/06/79) (television); *Ike* (television); *The Lazarus Syndrome: Malpractice* (10/02/79) (television); *The Onion Field*; *Marciano* (television); *Starsky and Hutch: Targets Without a Badge: Part 2* (03/11/79) (television); 1980: *Enola Gay: The Men, the Mission, the Atomic Bomb* (television); *Fighting Back* (a.k.a. *Fighting Back: The Story of Rocky Bleier*) (television); *M*A*S*H*: Back Pay* (03/10/80) (television); *Private Benjamin*; *Schizoid*; 1981: *Elvis and the Beauty Queen* (television); *The Greatest American Hero: The Greatest American Hero* (03/18/81) (television); *Hart to Hart: The Hartbreak Kid* (12/15/81) (television); *Lovely But Deadly*; *Strike Force: Kidnap* (11/20/81) (television); 1982: *Farrell for the People* (television); *Simon & Simon: Double Entry* (03/02/82) (television); *T.J. Hooker* (television); 1983: *Deal of the Century*; *The Powers of Matthew Star: Dead Man's Hand* (02/11/83) (television); *T.J. Hooker* (television) *V* (a.k.a. *V: The Original Mini Series*) (television); 1984: *Falcon Crest: Queen's Gambit* (01/13/84) (television); *Hardcastle and McCormick: Mr. Hardcastle Goes to Washington* (01/15/84) (television); *T.J. Hooker* (television); *V: The Final Battle* (television); 1985: *The A-Team: Waste 'Em!* (03/05/85) (television); *Hardcastle and McCormick: The Yankee Clipper* (10/07/85) (television); *Knight Rider: Knight Strike* (04/05/85) (television); *Matt Houston: The Beach Club Murders* (02/01/85) (television); *Simon & Simon: The Enchilada Express* (10/24/85) (television); *Summer Rental*; *T.J. Hooker* (television); *Trancers* (a.k.a. *Future Cop*); 1986: *Dynasty: The Cry* (04/16/86) (television); *Murder, She Wrote: Murder in the Electric Cathedral* (02/16/86) (television); *Scarecrow and Mrs. King: Photo Finish* (11/14/86) (television); *Simon & Simon: The Rookie* (11/06/86) (television); 1987: *Beauty and the Beast: A Children's Story* (12/04/87) (television); *Hill Street Blues: Norman Conquest* (02/10/87) (television); *Planes, Trains, & Automobiles*; *Rags to Riches: Foley Vs. Foley* (03/22/87) (television); 1988: *Favorite Son* (television); *My First Love* (television); *Simon & Simon: Ties That Bind* (03/03/88) (television); 1989: *Gleaming the Cube*; *The Golden Girls: The Impotence of Being Ernest* (02/04/89) (television); *Mancuso, F.B.I.: Little Saigon* (10/27/89) (television); *Matlock: The Captain* (01/10/89) (television); 1990: *The Big One: The Great Los Angeles Earthquake* (a.k.a. *The Great Los Angeles Earthquake*); *Camp Cucamonga* (a.k.a. *How I Spent My Summer*) (television); *China Beach: The Thanks of a Grateful Nation* (02/28/90) (television); *Corporate Affairs*; *Fall from Grace* (television): *Jake and the Fatman: God Bless the Child* (09/12/90) (television); *The Judas Pro-*

ject; *Midnight Caller: Protection* (television); *Nashville Beat* (television); *Seduction: Three Tales from the "Inner Sanctum"* (television); 1991: *Quantum Leap: Future Boy—October 6, 1957* (03/13/91) (television); *Tales from the Crypt: Deadline* (08/14/91) (television); 1992: *Majority Rule* (television); *Renegade: Mother Courage* (10/17/92) (television); 1993: *Dr. Quinn, Medicine Woman: Where the Heart Is: Part 1/Part 2* (11/20/93) (television); *Murder, She Wrote: The Petrified Florist* (02/21/93) (television); *Quantum Leap: Mirror Image—August 8, 1953* (05/04/93) (television); *SeaQuest DSV: The Devil's Window* (09/19/93) (television); *Star Trek: The Next Generation: Birthright: Part 1* (02/20/93), *Birthright: Part 2* (02/27/93) (television); 1994: *The Adventures of Brisco County Jr.: Bye Bly* (02/18/94), *High Treason: Part 2* (05/20/94) (television); *Cosmic Slop; The Gift of Love* (a.k.a. *Set for Life*) (television); *SeaQuest DSV: Better Than Martians* (01/02/94), *The Good Death* (05/15/94), *Greed for a Pirate's Dream* (01/16/94), *Hide and Seek* (02/27/94), *Higher Power* (05/22/94), *The Last Lap at Luxury* (03/20/94), *The Sincerest Form of Flattery* (11/13/94), *The Stinger* (02/20/94), *Whale Song* (02/06/94) (television); *Trekkies 2*; *Winnetka Road* (television); 1995: *ER: Men Plan, God Laughs* (02/27/95) (television); *Seinfeld: The Hot Tub* (10/19/95), *The Jimmy* (03/16/95), *The Wink* (10/12/95) (television); *The Secretary* (television); 1996: *A Case for Life* (television); *Grace Under Fire: Road to Nowhere* (11/06/96) (television); *Seinfeld: The Bottle Deposit* (05/02/96), *The Caddy* (01/25/96), *The Checks* (11/07/96), *The Fatigues* (10/31/96), *The Hot Tub* (10/19/96) (television); *Shattered Mind* (television); *Sgt. Bilko*; *Walker, Texas Ranger: Codename: Dragonfly* (11/02/96) (television); *Yesterday's Target*; 1997: *Dr. Quinn, Medicine Woman: Colleen's Paper* (02/08/97) (television); *Journey of the Heart* (television); *Midnight in the Garden of Good and Evil*; *Pacific Blue: Cop in a Box* (11/02/97) (television); *Seinfeld: The Millennium* (05/01/97), *The Nap* (04/10/97), *The Susie* (02/13/97) (television); 1998: *Buffy the Vampire Slayer: Killed by Death* (03/03/98) (television); *Caroline in the City: Caroline and the Big Night* (11/09/98) (television); *Diagnosis Murder: Write, She Murdered* (11/05/98) (television); *I Married a Monster* (television); *Johnny B. Goode* (unreleased); *Pacific Blue: With This Ring* (04/05/98) (television); *Seinfeld: The Finale: Part 2* (05/14/98) (television); *Snide and Prejudice*; 1999: *Star Trek: Voyager: Pathfinder* (12/01/99) (television); 2000: *Checkers*; *JAG: The Bridge at Kang So Ri* (02/29/00) (television); *Joseph: King of Dreams* (animated) (video) (voice only); *The Song of the Lark* (television); *Star Trek: Voyager: Inside Man* (11/08/00) (television); *Vic* (a.k.a. *Final Act*) (short film); 2001: *The Fugitive: Jenny* (02/16/01) (television); *Star Trek: Voyager: Author, Author* (04/18/01), *Endgame: Part 1/Part 2* (05/23/01) (television); 2002: *Family Law: Big Brother* (03/18/02) (television); 2003: *Everwood: Unhappy Holidays* (11/24/03) (television); 2004: *Everwood: Your Future Awaits* (05/03/04) (television); *NYPD Blue: My Dinner with Andy* (11/16/04) (television); *The O.C.: The Telenovela* (02/25/04) (television); 2005: *Confessions of a Pit Fighter*; 2006: *The Cabinet of Dr. Caligari*; *The Dog Days of Summer*; 2007: *Love's Unfolding Dream*; *TV Virus*; 2008: *InAlienable*.

David Hess

Born in September 1942, David Hess would become known to genre film audiences in the role of the psychopathic killer Krug in Wes Craven's film, *Last House on the Left*. What many people do not know, including genre film fans that might be very familiar with his work in this movie, is that Hess began his professional career as a songwriter in 1957. Using the pseudonym David Hill, Hess came up with the idea and recorded a song that Elvis Presley would later take straight up the charts: *All Shook Up*. Hess also composed songs for the late actor-singer Sal Mineo, the vocal group The Ames Brothers, and others. After *All Shook Up* became a major hit for Presley, Hess continued to write for him on and off throughout the remainder of the 1950s and the sixties. One of his compositions, *I Got Stung*, was covered by The Beatles. Hess also composed tunes for Andy Williams and Pat Boone, who had a Hess-penned hit single with the novelty song *Speedy Gonzalez*. Hess recorded two albums in the sixties for Kapp Records, and had a minor hit with the folk tune *Two Brothers*. In 1969, he became the head of A&R for Mercury Records in New York, scouting out local acts for possible inclusion in the Mercury records roster of talent. In New York, he also linked with classical music composer John Corigliano. Together, they created the Grammy-winning rock opera *The Naked Carmen*.

In 1972, Hess' career took off into a completely new trajectory when he starred in then-independent filmmaker Craven's *Last House on the Left*, for which he also composed the music. Genre film fans still recall the advertising tagline: "To avoid fainting, keep repeating it's only a movie... it's only a movie." The vicious thriller, which was like no American violent film ever made, took elements of the darker, negative aspects of the crazed late sixties at their most extreme, and mixed them with a Manson-like aura of death and destruction, delving into then-new and original cinematic territory with its horrific detailed crimes and their aftermath. In this infamous movie, two teenage girls journey to a large metropolis but are kidnapped, abused, raped, and murdered by a quartet of psychopaths. The violence-obsessed killers commit all of these deeds not far from the home of one of the victims, setting the film up for a tragic climax of Shakespearean proportions. In a 2002 online interview with the web site DVDHouseofhorror.com, Hess stated, "I started in high school productions. When I got to college, I continued to pursue the acting, but my essence has always been music. I pretty much lucked into the *Last House* role, as I originally wanted to do the music. I really was a last-minute choice for Krug. My sister's boyfriend at the time, Martin Kove, set the whole thing up. I had done some Off-Broadway work... and studied at the Actors Playhouse, and with Stella Adler, so I wasn't a complete novice, but as I said before, my real essence was music and remains so to this day."

The film's extreme tone, and Hess' powerful, seemingly uncontrolled performance made the film a cause celebre for many anti-violence groups of the time. Partly due to this, the movie suffered numerous cuts at the hands of scissors-happy movie censors. Soon after its initial release, there were so many mutilated versions of the film turning in circulation, that it took nearly thirty years for someone to track down a near-complete original cut of the film. When further acting roles did not come Hess' way in the wake of *Last House on the Left*, he accepted a position with Finger Records to work with the music label in Munich, Germany. While there, he eased back into the acting profession with a role in *The Swiss Conspiracy* (1975). This action-adventure film concerned a Swiss bank that calls in an American investigator (David Janssen), who soon uncovers a web of deceit and blackmail; Hess co-starred as the villainous Sando. He followed that role with a part in the internationally financed film *21 Hours at Munich*, a dramatization of a 1972 incident when Arab terrorists broke into the Olympic compound in Munich and murdered eleven Israeli athletes.

Hess returned to genre films to an unusual extent in 1978 with his appearance in the Italian thriller *Hitchhike* (a.k.a. *Autostop Rosso Sangue*) as a psychopathic hitchhiker who happens to grab a ride with Franco Nero and his wife, Corinne Clery. As the film progresses, the trio of characters enters into a downward spiraling miasma of violence and death. In 1979, he appeared in the all-star espionage adventure film, *Avalanche Express* alongside movie stars Lee Marvin, Robert Shaw, and television's *Mannix*, Michael Connors. Perhaps, his work in *Last House on the Left* and *Hitchhike* gained him the attention of maverick Italian director Ruggero Deodato, because the filmmaker cast Hess in *The House on the Edge of the Park* (a.k.a. *La Casa Sperduta Nel Parco*). In the role of Alex, a psychopathic mechanic, he rapes a woman in the park. Then, when a decadent couple pulls into his auto shop needing car repairs, they invite him and his mentally challenged friend to join them at a gathering in their home. Once there, the evil Alex amuses himself by tormenting, raping, and murdering the guests, not realizing the guests have an agenda of their own until they turn the tables on the interlopers.

In 1980 Hess was invited to direct his first feature film, a horror movie for the home video company Media Home Entertainment. Titled *To All a Good Night*, the film, about a group of teenagers at a party that find themselves being stalked by a maniacal killer in a Santa Claus costume, remains an unheralded gem among a glut of similar-themed, but inferior product in the early years of horror's video store reign.

In 1982, Hess had a featured role in Wes Craven's *Swamp Thing*, one of the earliest live action versions of a popular comic book anti-hero. The following year, he essayed the role of an Israeli military commander in the biofilm of Anwar Sadat, titled *Sadat*. He worked for Ruggero Deodato again in the Italian thriller *Body Count*, a distaff version of the stalk-and-slash movies made so popular by the *Friday the 13th* series and its ilk. In 1991, Hess appeared in the Italian western *Buck at the Edge of Heaven* and also composed the score for the movie, which was based on the stories of Jack London, and won the top prize for film and direction at the Italian Giffone Film Festival.

Hess also became involved in writing the English-language shooting scripts for German filmmakers Rainer Werner Fassbinder, Reinhardt Hauff, and Peter Schamoni. He collaborated with the latter as co-producer on the 1991 film *Max Ernst—Mein Vagabundieren—Meine Unruhe* (a.k.a. *Max Ernst—My Wanderings, My Unrest*), a documentary about the surrealist and visionary artist. He then spent two years working with Schamoni (also as a producer) on the film *Niki De Saint Phalle: Wer Ist Das Monster—Du Oder Ich?*, a documentary about painter-sculptor Niki De Saint Phalle, who began her career by shooting bags filled with paint hung over white canvas sheets, to create her distinctly original works. She also became famous for her sculptures of women.

In 1993, Hess acted in Enzo G. Castellari's *Jonathan Degli Orsi*, an adventure film starring Franco Nero that was screened in English as *Jonathan of the Bears*. In 1996 he appeared in the Italian television series *Noi Siamo Angeli*, directed by Ruggero Deodato and co-starring popular '60s–'70s western film star Bud Spencer (whose real name was Giancarlo Pedersoli) and former *Miami Vice* co-star Philip Michael Thomas. This series also featured other familiar genre veterans (and sometime villains) Michael Berryman and Richard Lynch in supporting roles.

In 2001, Hess co-starred in the independent psychological terror film *The Nutcracker*. Most recently, he has contributed to the music soundtrack of the 2003 independent horror film *Cabin Fever*, directed by Eli Roth, and has released two new CD recordings: *Caught Up in the Moment* and *Live and Unplugged in Hollywood, 2002*.

David Hess as he appeared in the role as the screen's ultimate bad guy in Wes Craven's *The Last House on the Left* (Lobster Enterprises/The Night Co./Sean S. Cunningham Films/Hallmark Releasing) (1972).

Q: You have said that *Last House on the Left* was a repertory effort. Nevertheless, your performance as Krug stood out and you became the lead villain, and then ultimately, the character that viewers recall most. Can you recall how you prepared for that role?

David Hess: It was really hard to prepare for that because there was so much improvisation that went on. The script itself became, after a while, useless. Therefore, we followed the outline of the script as well as we could and used it as a blueprint. You can prepare to some degree by looking at lines, and thinking about arcs in terms of where you can take your character, but the preparation usually takes place on the set and has to do with the leadership, and the producers, and how they set up the shooting schedules, etc. As I said, on this film there was more improvisation than there was a cast and crew following a set of rules, or even the script, as written.

Q: Were you aware, while you were making this film, what was happening with it, the intensity that was coming across via the performances, etc.?

Hess: Yes, and that added to the intensity.

Q: Did that make you uncomfortable as an actor?

Hess: No, it made it more real. I am not a person who gets uncomfortable very easily. If I can justify something by calling up an emotion from a real situation, that I had previously experienced then, it is not uncomfortable for me, because it is real. I do not want to be not real. That would be uncomfortable.

Q: After *Last House on the Left* came out there was a huge backlash against the cast members, and you in particular, some of it because of the violence in the picture, which was fairly graphic. Due to this, you took the blows, as an actor portraying a role, because people perceived you as the character you were portraying.

Hess: I was the role portraying an actor.

Q: How did you feel about the reaction to your character?

Hess: Terrible.

Q: Did you have a tough time getting work afterwards?

Hess: I did not get any work. I got no work at all. I lost an agent because of it, and I could not get an agent after that. God bless them, Steve [Minasian] and Phil [Scuderi], who ran Hallmark Releasing, gave Marc Sheffler [who played Junior in *Last House on the Left*] and me some money to go write a script. They paid for a six-week trip to Europe. We went skiing and wrote a script—that was their way of saying thank you, and I will never forget them for that. It was wonderful. We wrote a script called *Sugar Daddy*, which we subsequently lost. We could not find the script afterwards. All that remained is the name, *Sugar Daddy*. However, they wanted me to direct and star in it, and I would have, but something happened and it never got off the ground, and we lost the script. Minasian and Scuderi were loyal to us, and I will never forget them for that.

Q: I am curious about the original reactions in the media to the film, and how critics who reacted to your performance so strongly, had confused reality with fantasy. Do you think that there was some element of censorship involved with the generally unfavorable reactions to *Last House on the Left*? After all, it was produced by an independent company, directed by an independent filmmaker, and featured a cast of actors, mostly new to the big screen, and therefore chiefly unknown to cinema audiences.

Hess: All I know is that afterwards, I concentrated on my music. I composed music. Then somebody offered me a position with a record company in Germany. I packed up my apartment and put everything into storage, which to this day I have never recovered, and moved, with my dog, to Germany. I eventually returned to acting with roles in *The Swiss Conspiracy* (1975) and *21 Hours at Munich* (1976).

Q: How did you become involved with the Italian thriller *Autostop Rosso Sangue* in 1977?

Hess: It was an interesting role, wasn't it? I was attempting not to repeat myself. Work begets work. As for working in *Hitchhike*, well, Franco Nero was also in *21 Hours at Munich*, and we got to be friends because of it. I have to say this, in all humility: I have never heard anybody say that I was a bad actor. I have gotten recalls on things, that always gave me heart, and I was always secure in my work. I mean, many actors are booked five, six, ten years ahead. However, this never happened to me.

Q: Two years later, you appeared in *La Casa Sperduta Nel Parco* (1979) for Italian director Ruggero Deodato. During this period, when you essayed these psychopathic villain roles, did you believe that you might have problems playing a killer, after being associated with such a legendary bad guy in *Last House on the Left*?

Hess: No, because I think there are infinite versions of the villain that you can do. There are so many sources to tap, so much of your own personality to add. For me, the quintessential role is that of the bad guy. It is easy to play a good guy. I am playing a good guy right now, aren't I? I am really a good guy, in real life. Therefore, it is easy to play a bad guy.

Q: But were you aware of being typecast because of one movie?

Hess: There's always typecasting. That's a given.

Q: Few people may realize that you also composed the music for *Last House on the Left*, and I only recently learned that you had won four Grammy awards for composing music. Is that what you are doing in your spare time when you are not acting?

Hess: I am a composer. That is my first love. Acting is a wonderful adjunct. I have been blessed with many things, and with more than one kind of talent. I have been blessed with good looks. I have been blessed with being a good actor. I have been blessed with being intelligent. For me, music is the most important thing. Music is visceral, it strikes the ultimate chord. That is why my first love is music. I find it is the ultimate way of expressing yourself.

Q: *Body Count* (1986) was another Italian production for the filmmaker Ruggero Deodato, and it had an interesting cast of actors that included Mimsy Farmer and Charles Napier.

Hess: I remember very little about *Body Count*, other than the fact that we worked twelve to fifteen hours a day and that the makeup was God-awful. I looked like the Devil incarnate and it was laughable. I constantly had to play against my makeup. If you see touches of humor in my role, it is only because I had to add them, in order to pull this kind of character off. I did not think the film was a particularly good film. I tried to bring something to my character. I am not certain, but I think that my character was the part of a fallen angel, a man who has fallen from favor, not only from God, but himself, and wrongfully so. He is an outcast. That was a nice archetype to try to play... the good guy with the bad guy flavor.

Q: You worked in Russia on the Italian co-production *Jonathan of the Bears*, directed by Enzo G. Castellari, and starring Franco Nero.

Hess: I fell in love with Russia. I will tell you something regarding Franco Nero: He is an actor who I think has never been given his due. He is pissed off at me right now for some reason, which is okay; everybody gets pissed off at everybody else occasionally. However, other than the fact that he is very egocentric, and he is the quintessential hypochondriac, he is a wonderful guy. He has a real sense of what acting is all about, a real sense of the universe, a real sense of life, and he keeps putting his money back into the industry and making more films. For that, I love him. He really cares about his work and his art.

Q: Tell me about working on the Italian television series, *We're No Angels*.

Hess: *We're No Angels* was an Italian series with Bud Spencer and Phillip Michael Thomas, and I appeared in three episodes in the bad cop role. But, I played him as kind of a larger-than-life cop, as kind of a grandiose character. This series was a takeoff on

American actor Hess, movie villain, meets Brigitte Lahaie, French sex siren, in 2000. (Photograph: Louis Paul)

Extra Large. Extra Large was the detective character that Bud Spencer played in a series of films, and was very popular in Italy, and in other countries as well. I know that some episodes have even been dubbed into English for distribution over here in the U.S., but I do not think that any of them ever made much of an impression. The *We're No Angels* series was going to be released over here, incidentally; I do not know what happened. Possibly, some episodes may have appeared on cable television here in the United States.

Q: What do you see yourself doing acting-wise, in the future?

Hess: I have a project that I have wanted to make for a number of years now. It is based on a script that I wrote, called *Delusions*. I have been in the process of getting it off the ground. That is really a tough thing to do because you are always in a state of compromises. It is like solving a puzzle; you have to figure a way to compromise without compromising. The script is sold right now, and I think we can probably begin principal photography sometime in the not too distant future. I want to direct this. I really do. I have a real vision of the way this should go. *Delusions* is the story of four points of view of the same story, like *Rashomon*, but it goes even further than that, and it's a tribute to Akira Kurosawa, a tribute to the "idea" of illusion. We are all living in a kind of illusionary world, and why not take advantage of it?

The thing that strikes me as most relevant is that I have a fan base out there that, for years, I was not even aware of. I can cry sometimes when I think about it, because I think I probably neglected them, and not through any fault of my own, I had not known about them, and they have been waiting for another film from me. I think that if my roots are in making horror films, then the word horror has to be used in quotes and if you had to describe *Delusions* then you would have to describe it as an erotic thriller-horror, and that is what I want to do. I want to give something back to my fans. I am not a violent person, although I am physically imposing. Of course, I do not like to be imposed on as well. I know that I was a different person after making *Last House on the Left*, because of the nature of the violence. Having said that, I believe that making movies, going to the movies, is still one of the truest avenues of expression that we have for our kids, for the generations coming up. What better way is there that we can teach them that not all the world... humanity is based on violence?

Credits: 1970: *De La Part Des Copains* (a.k.a. *Cold Sweat*) [Italy-France-Belgium] (dubbed actor Michel Constantine's voice for English-language version); 1972: *Last House on the Left*; 1976: *Potato Fritz* (a.k.a. *Montana Trap*) [West Germany]; *Per Saldo Mord* (a.k.a. *The Swiss Conspiracy*) [U.S.–West Germany]; *21 Hours at Munich* (television); 1977: *Autostop Rosso Sangue* (a.k.a. *Hitch Hike* a.k.a. *Hitchhike: The Last House on the Left*) [Italy]; *Yung Chun Ta Hsiung* (a.k.a. *He's a Hero, He's a Legend* a.k.a. *The New Game of Death*) (dubbed voices for English-language version) [Hong Kong]; 1979: *Avalanche Express* [U.S.-Ireland]; 1980: *La Casa Sperduta Nel Parco* (a.k.a. *The House on the Edge of the Park*) [Italy]; 1981: *Jacqueline Susann's Valley of the Dolls* (television); 1982: *Swamp Thing*; 1983: *Knight Rider: Short Notice* (05/06/83) (television); *Manimal: Illusion* (10/14/83) (television); *Sadat* (television); *White Star* (a.k.a. *Let it Rock*) [West Germany]; 1985: *The Fall Guy: Reel Trouble* (04/10/85) (television); 1986: *The A-Team: Dishpan Man* (09/26/86) (television); *Armed and Dangerous*; *Let's Get Harry*; 1987: *Camping Del Terrore* (a.k.a. *Body Count*) [Italy-U.S.]; *Dynasty: The Test* (02/11/87) (television); *Surrender*; 1988: *14 Going On 30* (television); *Maybe Baby* (television); *To Heal a Nation* (television); 1989: Oceano (a.k.a. *Ocean*) (television) [Italy-Spain-Venezuela]; 1991: *Buck A Confini Del Cielo* (a.k.a. *Buck at the Edge of Heaven*) [Italy]; *Die Kaltenbach-Papiere* (a.k.a. *Fatal Assignment*) [Germany]; *Omicidio A Luci Blu* (a.k.a. *Homicide in Blue Light*) [Italy]; 1992: *Superboy: Threesome: Part 1* (02/09/92), *Threesome: Part 2* (02/16/92) (television); 1993: *Jonathan Degli Orsi* (a.k.a. *Jonathan of the Bears*) [Italy-Russia]; 1997: *No Siamo Angeli* (a.k.a. *We Are Angels* a.k.a. *We're No Angels*) (television) [Italy]; 2001: *Nutcracker* (a.k.a. *Nutcracker: An American Nightmare*); 2002: *It's Only a Movie: The Making of "Last House On the Left"* (video supplement); *Celluloid Crime of the Century* (video supplement); 2004: *The Absence of Light*; *Zombie Nation* (video); *Cabin Fever: Beneath the Skin* (video supplement); 2005: *Curse of the Beast*; *Zodiac Killer*; 2006: *Fallen Angels*.

Brion James

Brion James (1945–1999) was a character actor with a formidable presence both onscreen, and off. With his craggy, lived-in facial features, blonde hair and large 6'3" frame, he was easily recognized by most genre cinema and television fans, usually as the villain in a number of westerns, science fiction and horror films. It was villains which James excelled at when performing, and often he played them to the hilt.

Born in February 1945 in Redlands, California, Brion soon moved with his family to Beaumont, California, where his parents owned and operated a movie theater. Over the years, young Brion would spend many days and nights soaking up the imaginative world of the cinema. He enjoyed watching the movies, especially the westerns. James graduated from Beaumont High School in 1962 and then entered San Diego State University's Theater Arts program. Journeying to New York, he renewed a childhood friendship with fellow actor Tim Thomerson (of *Trancers* fame), and after serving in the Armed Forces together they lived under the same roof as assistants to the famed acting coach Stella Adler. After years toiling as a stand-up comedian and performing bit parts in New York small theater productions, James began to be noticed for his ability to inhabit the characters that he was assigned to portray. Important film roles soon followed. In his first year in Hollywood, James was recognized as an actor with that special something, who excelled in character parts. During that first year, he appeared in *Nickelodeon* (1976), *Blue Sunshine* (1976), and *Harry and Walter Go to New York* (1976).

In 1981, he began a working relationship with director Walter Hill that would turn into a friendship lasting several years, and which gave James some of the best roles of his career. In *Southern Comfort* (1981), his performance as a Cajun trapper gave the character equal amounts of pathos and menace. In *48 Hours* (1982), James would finally get a part equal to his talents: Kehoe, one of the main supporting roles in the Nick Nolte–Eddie Murphy film. He would return as this character in the belated, inferior sequel, *Another 48 Hours* (1990). But it was in *Blade Runner* (1982), the Ridley Scott film adaptation of the Phillip K. Dick science fiction novella *Do Androids Dream of Electric Sheep*, that James finally broke through the barrier of being a supporting player coloring the background, to a major supporting actor applying wide brushstrokes of characterization to parts that, otherwise, would have seemed small or inconsequential in the hands of lesser actors. In the role of Leon, the replicant who escaped from the Off World to find a (substantially longer) life cycle for himself and his companions on Earth, James' character, a villainous foe of Harrison Ford's heroic Blade Runner (a futuristic policeman), can be heard uttering several lines of dialogue that have become ingrained into the catchphrase-crazy subconscious that some science fiction fans thrive on. "I'll tell you about my mother!" and "Wake up... time to die!" are just two of Leon's phrases that have become synonymous with James' interpretation of this role. Despite *Blade Runner*'s dismal initial box-office performance, the film managed to gain an immeasurable reputation, and grew into one of the first cult classic films of the eighties. In time, it would be considered one of the ten greatest science fiction films ever made, and today is recognized by many cineastes as one of the best films ever made. In 1993 it was added to the National Film Preservation Board's National Film Registry.

James also became a recognizable fixture in a number of other films like *Enemy Mine* (1985), *Silverado* (1985), *Crimewave* (1985), *Steel Dawn* (1987), and *Cherry 2000* (1987). Although well-regarded by fellow actors, directors, and genre filmgoers, James was seldom singled-out for his work by critics, with one of the closest representations of a good review coming from a *Variety* review of the movie *Crimewave* May 22, 1985): "Best of all are Paul L. Smith and ratty Brion James as two exterminators who have expanded their field of victims from rodents to human beings."

In 1989, James was finally presented with a starring role in *The Horror Show*, an ill-fated attempt at a new horror film series franchise. As the supernatural serial killer Max Jenke, James elicited equal amounts of scares and sympathy from the audience. However, the film suffered from a confusing script and lackluster direction.

Over the course of the next few years, he would become an in-demand presence in some low-budget exercises in genre entertainment (*Nightmare at Noon* [1990], *Mutator* [1991], *American Strays* [1996]). And at the same time, he continued to appear in more mainstream films, in better roles (*Red Scorpion* [1989], *Tango and Cash* [1989], the aforementioned *Another 48 Hours*, and *Striking Distance* [1993]). Robert Altman gave James one of his most prestigious roles as a studio executive in his acclaimed 1992 film, *The Player*. James believed that this movie became a career turning point for him, leading to an even wider variety of roles. However, he was still in demand as a guest villain for a number of low-budget thrillers and science fiction films, many of which went straight to video.

In 1996, French director Luc Beeson (creator of the cult favorite movies *The Professional* [1994] and *La Femme Nikita* [1990]) signed James to appear in *The Fifth Element* as General Munro, the military advisor to the President of the Free World (played by retired professional wrestler, Tiny Lister), who assigns space jockey Bruce Willis to a special mission to save the universe. Once again, James' career was revitalized. Audiences appreciated its hip humor and wild visual effects all over the world, and made the film a substantial box-office hit in several countries. A larger-than-life icon on the big screen, James found time to act on the small screen as well. His appearances on television, while far from being voluminous, are noteworthy; some of his best small-screen roles were as a guest star or supporting actor on *CHiPs* (1977), *The Young Riders* (1989), and *M.A.N.T.I.S.* (1994). He had a recurring role on TV's *The Magnificent Seven* in 1998.

James made his first and last appearance at a genre film convention in May of 1999. At the *Chiller Theatre* Expo, he met with fans and well-wishers, many of whom he greeted with genuine warmth and honesty. I sat with James for over an hour, and the resulting interview is filled with truth, honesty, and some shocking admissions that, heretofore, I had not known about. As we were ending our conversation, he told me of upcoming projects, which included a role in a Merchant Ivory production to be shot in South Africa, and a possible major supporting role in another forthcoming Luc Beeson film. James also made it quite clear that he felt that the time was at hand for him to be taken more seriously as an actor, and that the best parts were now coming his way. However, the cinematic world lost an entertaining presence when Brion James died on August 7, 1999. James will be remembered, for he shocked and delighted innumerable audiences throughout the world. James' film roles were so numerous that movies that he had appeared in were still turning up for the first time as late as 2003.

Q: Is it true that you were influenced to become an actor because your father had owned a movie theater in Beaumont?

Brion James: Totally, absolutely, no question. I was watching movies in the theater in Beaumont since 1947, when I was two years old.

Q: I read that you had become an assistant to the famed acting teacher Stella Adler.

James: I was her servant and I cleaned her house in exchange for acting school.

Q: Servant?

James: Slave, cook, bartender, drove the car, cleaned the house. Tim Thomerson, his ex-wife and myself, three California kids. We were all slaves to Stella Adler in exchange for school, which was like, normally, $5000 a year.

Q: How did that come about?

James: When I got to New York City, Tim and his wife were servants for Stella, and when I came around, they became my best friends. We all did a lot of acid and pot in those days. I had just come to New York with 100 bucks. So once Stella busted us partying in the kitchen, and she said, "You're staying, aren't you," I said, "Yeah." She said, "So what can you do?" I said, "Well, I'm a good chef, I can do this, I can do that..." It was wild. Tim and his wife were middle-class kids from California, and Stella Adler was an aristocratic Russian-Jewish woman who took her class distinction seriously. I never knew anything about fucking class distinction until I lived with Stella. In addition, she taught very good acting classes. She taught us everything from learning about God on down, through her classes. Tim and his wife were crazy... they were always screaming and yelling and fighting, and Stella would go, "Please, darling I can't...." She and her husband were dressed as if they lived in the nineteenth century—her husband wore an ascot and everything. It was like the Oscar Wildes meet the Stanley Kowalskis. It was insane there, but it worked somehow. I was so lucky to be there. I met everybody there, I met Leonard Bernstein, I met everybody while I was in New York.

Q: Your first memorable cinematic appearances were in films like *Nickelodeon, Harry and Walter Go to New York, Blue Sunshine,* and *Kiss Meets the Phantom of the Park.* Of those early pictures, do you think that any of those roles, even though they were small, were the kind of roles that started getting you more attention from filmmakers?

James: Absolutely, work begets work.

Q: What do you recall about your role in director Walter Hill's *Southern Comfort*?

James: It was the hardest movie I ever made as far as being a physical part. It was cold and freezing in that swamp. Keith Carradine and the other guys, they all wore wetsuits under their clothes; I never wore one. I was miserable, but it worked for the part, it worked for the movie. I played a local Cajun trapper. It is the only accent I ever had to learn. I am a parrot. I can pick up an accent and just do it. That one I had to study and a real Cajun taught me how to do it. Therefore, I did this Cajun patois, sort of a form of

Brion James (far left) is the chief villain, a French-Canadian fur trapper, along with Fred Ward (center) and Powers Boothe (right), in Walter Hill's *Southern Comfort* (1981) (Cinema Group/EMI Films Ltd./ Phoenix/ 20th Century Fox Film Corporation).

bastardized French. It was a very different sound; it came out sounding like Southern black French.

Q: I have heard that Walter Hill was known as a taskmaster.

James: We called him The Emperor but, I will tell you, he is the most loyal guy in Hollywood. He hired me for that and for other films too. Walter Hill's one of the most loyal people in town. Not too many guys do that.

Q: Do you believe that the role of Leon in *Blade Runner* was responsible for getting you more exposure?

James: The role of Leon is what really launched my career, and now I am a cult figure, and have been so for eighteen years since that role. All these kids (that now are older and write, produce, and direct movies) have seen it, it's been well received after the fact, and it has been studied in almost every film school in the world. Therefore, it suits me that young directors study the film, and then want to work with me. For example, a director who was nineteen then, is now something like thirty-eight years old and says, "I want you in my movie." Therefore, I did the sci-fi thing into the nineties. Like I said, work begets work, and I do not fuck up, so I get more work. For the most part, as an actor, I am always better than the piece, than the movie I am appearing in. I am a character actor, so I do not take the hit if the movie is bad, the leading actors do. Therefore, I do not want to be the lead. He takes the hit, I don't. I did fifteen films last year, and I am still working.

Q: In the two *48 Hours* films it seems like there might have been more footage of your character, Kehoe, left on the cutting room floor.

James: The first one, no. In the second one, I was originally the third lead. I had ten scenes and they destroyed me [in the cutting room].

Q: Why was the footage cut from *Another 48 Hours*?

James: *Total Recall* came out a week before *Another 48 Hours* that summer, it made twenty-five million, became the number one movie in the country, and the studio panicked because they had invested a lot in the *48 Hours* franchise, but they felt that at well over two hours, that the movie might be too much. My stuff was in there until one week before the film opened; that is when they cut out twenty-five minutes out of that movie. It went from around 140 minutes to down around 95 minutes. They said, "Cut all the behavior, action, comedy..." I lost every major scene I had. That is the last time I ever cared about a movie because I went to the press screening, and it was like being kicked in the stomach, seeing what is not there. I *was* the third lead, and now I looked like a dress extra. All the stuff that they had in the set-up, stuff in the trailer, all those scenes were gone.

Q: I guess the way it *should* have been looked at is that you are an important character actor, you are very recognizable, and you are not in the movie unless there is a reason for you to be in the movie...

James: Exactly.

Q: Then all of a sudden... where are you?

James: Dress extra. That's around the time I realized that I could not care any more. I had to realize that I am a hired gun for these studios. I had to shut off the caring, because it chilled me. Therefore, I said I could not do this any more. Therefore, I fucking came into independent movies because now I am in control of my performance. That is the way I do it now.

Q: What do you remember about the Sam Raimi film *Crimewave*?

James: I was out of my mind on drugs. I got sober not too long after that.

Q: That was the film where you had the weasel-like voice.

James: I played one of the exterminators, the rat-man in that movie. I played the role like a rat, I moved a lot like a rat, and did something with my voice a little bit. I took over a lot of [co-star] Paul Smith's scenes—I guess you could say I stole scenes from him. They did not really like the way he did them, so they asked me and I said, "Okay." Therefore, I did the scenes with more verve, and I made them funnier.

Q: That was a very physical film for you.

James: Yes, very. Three months in Detroit, which was where we were, and it was not all fun. It is not called Murder City for no reason. I was really sick, I was doing a lot of drugs, but I told Sam Raimi, "Put me on, but don't say cut... let me go." He did, and I went and basically, I had the show all to myself. I stole it. It was around that time, prior to this movie, which came after *Blade Runner*, that they put me on a blacklist, because I would not be in the union. When I came up for *Crimewave* [the union] said, "You can't do the movie." [*Crimewave*'s producers] said, "We've got to have Brion James." The union said, "No, he's not working for us." Finally they [the *Crimewave* people] said, "Look, he's the only guy we want." The union said, "Fine, you can have him, but we're not paying our part." Therefore, the *Crimewave* producers wound up paying me for everything, since I

James as he appeared as the murderous humanoid killer Leon in Ridley Scott's *Blade Runner* **(1982) (The Blade Runner Partnership/The Ladd Company/Warner Bros.).**

was a non-union performer performing in the film. I worked for like ten weeks for twenty-five hundred dollars. You know, they say, "Don't make waves..." I learned my lesson.

Q: *The Horror Show*—wasn't that film designed for sequels?

James: Yes, they wanted me to be the next Freddy Krueger. I read the script, and I thought it was bad. Lance Henriksen came into the film and he saw it too [how bad the script was]. We spoke to each other about it and we both said, "I'll do it if you will." We told the producer Sean Cunningham that we liked it—we lied—and asked, "So, when are we doing it?" So we made the film as a parody of horror and science fiction. I made this guy [the villain] both intelligent and evil. In the script he was just a mindless slasher, there was nothing to it, he was evil for evil's sake. Therefore, I made the guy a person with a history: a child of seven molested by his mother, child of thirteen kills his parents. That way, the audience can see that the character of Max Jenke was not a regular child, and that's what fucked him up. I'll always show, and tell something, to the people, about the guy, how sick he was, and is. It was just fun, having fun playing a maniac. We had a lot of fun on that film, and it became a cult hit on video, but not one in the theaters.

Q: And not enough of a hit to generate a sequel.

James: No, thank God, because I do not want to do that kind of a role [again]. One time is enough.

Q: Any comments on the film *Red Heat*?

James: I told Walter Hill, "I'll do a walk-on for you, or a starring role, I don't care." He made me a film actor. When I first worked with him, he said, "Now you're a film actor in *Southern Comfort*," and it was one of the best roles I ever had. I told Walter, "I will do anything you want, just tell me." In *Red Heat*, I had one good scene. I played this guy like a white Negro. Snitch was his name. I processed the hair, wore these funky shoes, I made him like a real street kind of guy. Walter Hill, he loved it, loved what I did with that stuff.

Q: He gave you a lot of creative freedom?

James: Yes, because he knows I can bring the stuff in. Therefore, he gives it to me. I give him ideas, and he goes, "Great, do what you want." He knows I got it. He is a smart director, and in that role, I made that guy look good.

Q: Well, that is one of your specialties, isn't it?

James: I hold my own with all of these guys, the leading actors. I make them look better. I am a great nemesis. I am a con, I am an ex-junkie, so I know how to con people. I do it in a healthy way now; I do not do it in a self-serving way. Therefore, I can work myself into other things when I am doing a movie.

Q: Let's talk about *Tango and Cash* starring Sylvester Stallone and Kurt Russell...

James: In *Tango and Cash*, I had two scenes when I started the film. Andrei Konchalovsky [the original director] wanted to work with me for years, he worked for Cannon Films, but they could not afford to pay me, so I could not work for them. He wanted me to work with him on *Runaway Train*. Finally, I get to work with him, he calls me in, I meet Stallone and Russell, and they said, "Yeah, he's great." Originally, I just had two scenes with these guys, where they chase me around and I get beat up and that is it. So, I get there and I'm acting with Stallone, and I gave my character a Cockney accent just to add something different to it. I said to myself that I am in a movie with all of these people, how am I going to chew the scenery with all of these fuckers around? So, I created the Cockney accent, I just wasn't going to be just another hit man from Cleveland, and they all loved it, they played off of it, they got into it. Therefore, eventually Stallone started re-writing the script because the script was not really ready when we started filming, but [the stars] were there to go, so when you have to go, you go. Everyone else thought that the script was ready, but we knew otherwise, and when it was not, Stallone would fix it. The movie wound up being twenty million dollars over-budget, and I wound up being on the film for fourteen weeks. My part went from a few days of work, to a much bigger role. So, as the film was rewritten, I became the main bad person, and not Jack Palance.

Q: The director, Konchalovsky, lost that picture because of studio interference, didn't he?

James: He did a great job, but Sly Stallone was the one who got him fired. Sly is very protective about his work. He got his own DP [director of photography] in, and the film went twenty million dollars over-budget. So the studio had to justify it, and fired [Konchalovsky], saying it was the director's fault. It was not his fault. They did not have a finished script when they started shooting. I was even re-writing lines myself at the end of the day, repeatedly. They only had three weeks left, and they brought in Albert Magnoli. He did rock videos, and a Prince movie [*Purple Rain*]. They gave this person three-quarters of a million dollars to do three weeks. By the time he got there, I was like, "Don't talk to me, stay back. I knew this character for weeks; I know what I'm doing." It wound up being a great film, which eventually made a lot of money. I learned that it is reportedly one of the biggest pirated videos in the history of Russia. Warner Bros. was crazy not to market it properly, but that film was huge. Later on, I went to the Ukraine when I was shooting another film, and I was mobbed. I was in the Black Sea, and I had no idea that people even knew who I was.

Q: How did your role in *The Fifth Element* come about?

James: That person is a genius, the director.

Q: Luc Beeson?

James: Yes. He told me that since he was nineteen, he was studying movies that I was in, in film schools over in France. He said, "Come to England to be in my movie." However, he did not tell me anything about it. I went over, and I found myself in a locked room, where I read the script. I signed a contract saying that I would not tell anybody about the movie. When I looked at the script, I saw there was some comedy in it, which I was excited about. You know, stand-up comedy is where I pretty much started out. In addition, he knew every beat of that film. He wrote that story when he was sixteen years old. The first two weeks were tense, they did not know if it was going to work. He had a lot riding on his head, man. Nevertheless, it did well; it made about ninety million, so it was a big hit. After about two weeks, you would see the dailies and say, yeah, it looks okay, and then everybody relaxed. We had a great time. We laughed. Luc Beeson operates the camera too, he was his own cinematographer, which is why I wanted to work with him. He was on my wish list. To me, he makes perfect movies, *La Femme Nikita*, *The Professional*, perfect movies. I saw the long version of *The Professional*—have you seen that? He showed it to me, and I went "Wow." It was like a dream working with this guy. I very seldom give myself up entirely to a director. For him I said, "Do what you want." I trusted him, because I knew he knew what he was doing.

Q: What was your favorite movie role?

James: It is hard to say, but *Southern Comfort* was one of the best parts I ever got. Of

James (with helmeted actors, unidentified) terrorizes Dennis Quaid in the Wolfgang Peterson-directed science fiction fantasy film, *Enemy Mine* (1985) (Kings Road Entertainment/20th Century-Fox).

course Leon in *Blade Runner* was a great role. What I originally shot for the character of Leon you do not see. There was a lot of stuff...

Q: That was cut out of *Blade Runner*?

James: Yes, but there were scenes in other movies too that I admire my work in.

Q: What do you attribute your success to?

James: Hard work. You have to study, man. It is like any profession. I did eight years in theater. I studied for two years in school in New York with Stella Adler, the best teacher in the world. I studied under Nina Foch, and I did theater, I learned my craft. You have to learn how to build a character, there is a way to do it. Everything I ever did was different. I did many films and television shows, and you have never seen the same character twice from me. I think now, in my fifties, with Duvall, Finney, and Hackman, those people are getting up there in their sixties, it is my time. Moreover, I am making sure that I push myself into their slot. Therefore, my best work is coming.

Credits: 1974: *The Waltons: The Birthday* (12/19/74) (television); *1975*: *Gunsmoke: Manolo* (03/17/75) (television); *Hard Times* (a.k.a. *The Streetfighter*); *The Kansas City Massacre* (television); 1976: *Blue Sunshine*; *Bound for Glory*; *Harry and Walter Go to New York*; *Nickelodeon* [U.S.–Great Britain]; *Treasure of Matecumbe*; 1977: *The Rockford Files: The Battle of Canoga Park* (09/30/77) (television); *Roots* (television); 1978: *Chico and the Man: Waiting for Chongo* (television); *Corvette Summer*; *Flying High* (television); *The Incredible Hulk: Alice in Disco*

Land (11/03/78) (television); *KISS Meets the Phantom of the Park* (a.k.a. *KISS in Attack of the Phantom* a.k.a. *Attack of the Phantoms*) (television); *Mork & Mindy: Mork's Greatest Hits* (11/23/78) (television); 1979: *CHiPs: Drive, Lady, Drive: Part 1/Part 2* (11/10/79) (television); 1980: *Conquest of the Earth* (re-edited episodes of the television series *Galactica 1980*) (television); *Galactica 1980: Galactica Discovers Earth: Part 1* (01/27/80) (television); *The Jeffersons: The Arrival: Part 2* (02/10/80) (television); *Trouble in High Timber Country* (television); *Wholly Moses!*; 1981: *Benson: The Grass Ain't Greener* (11/13/81) (television); *CHiPs: Bomb Run* (11/15/81) (television); *Killing at Hell's Gate* (television); *The Postman Always Rings Twice* [U.S.–West Germany]; *Southern Comfort* [U.S.-Switzerland]; 1982: *The Ballad of Gregorio Cortez* (television); *Blade Runner*; *The Dukes of Hazzard: Big Daddy* (10/29/82) (television); *48 Hours*; *Hear No Evil* (television); *Little House on the Prairie: A Faraway Cry* (03/08/82) (television); *Quincy: Sleeping Dogs* (11/17/82) (television); 1983: *The A-Team: The Taxicab Wars* (11/01/83) (television); *Kenny Rogers as "The Gambler": The Adventure Continues* (television); 1984: *A Breed Apart*; *The Dukes of Hazzard: Cool Hands, Luke & Bo* (11/09/84) (television); *Silverado* (uncredited); 1985: *The A-Team: Lease with an Option to Die* (10/22/85) (television); *Amazing Stories: Mummy Daddy* (10/27/85) (television); *Crimewave* (a.k.a. *The XYZ Murders*); *Enemy Mine*; *The Fall Guy: King of the Stuntmen* (10/03/85) (television); *Flesh & Blood* [Netherlands-U.S.-Spain]; 1986: *Annihilator* (television); *Armed and Dangerous*; *Dynasty: The Trial: Part 1* (03/19/86), *The Trial: Part 2* (03/26/86) (television); *Sledge Hammer!: If I Had a Little Hammer* (11/29/86) (television); 1987: *Cherry 2000*; *Love Among Thieves* (television); *Matlock: The Author* (01/13/87) (television); *Steel Dawn*; 1988: *D.O.A.*; *Dead Man Walking* (video); *Desperado: The Outlaw Wars* (television); *Hunter: Renegade* (01/05/88) (television); *Miami Vice: Borrasca* (12/09/88) (television); *Nightmare at Noon* [Great Britain–U.S.]; *On My Honor* (short film); *Red Heat*; *Sledge Hammer!: Model Dearest* (01/07/88) (television); *The Wrong Guys*; 1989: *The Horror Show*; *Mutator*; *Red Scorpion* [South Africa–U.S.–Nambia]; *Tango & Cash*; 1990: *Another 48 Hours*; *Circles in a Forest* [South Africa]; *Enid Is Sleeping* (a.k.a. *Over My Dead Body*); *Mom*; *Street Asylum* (video); *The Young Riders: Fall from Grace* (01/04/90) (television); 1991: *Hunter: Under Suspicion* (01/16/91) (television); *Tales from the Crypt: Split Second* (08/07/91) (television); *Wishman*; 1992: *Batman* (animated): *The Joker's Wild* (11/19/92) (television) (voice only); *Overkill: The Aileen Wuornos Story*; *The Player*; *Ultimate Desires* (a.k.a. *Beyond the Silhouette*) (video) [Canada]; 1993: *Batman* (animated): *Robin's Reckoning: Part 1* (02/07/93) (television) (voice only); *Brain Smasher: A Love Story* (video); *Frogtown II* (a.k.a. *Hell Comes to Frogtown II*) (video); *Future Shock* (video); *Johnny Bago: Johnny Bago Free at Last* (06/25/93) (television); *Nemesis*; *Precious Victims* (television); *Renegade: Moody River* (04/26/93) (television); *Rio Diablo* (television); *Showdown*; *Striking Distance*; *Time Runner* (video) [Canada-U.S.]; 1994: *Art Deco Detective*; *Cabin Boy*; *The Companion* (television); *The Dark* [Canada]; *Highlander: The Cross of St. Antoine* (10/17/94) (television) [Canada-France]; *F.T.W.*; *Hong Kong '97*; *Knight Rider 2010* (television); *M.A.N.T.I.S.: First Steps* (08/26/94) (television); *Pterodactyl Woman from Beverly Hills* (video, also co-producer); *The Radioland Murders*; *Savage Land*; *Scanner Cop* (video); *Silk Stalkings: T.K.O.* (01/16/94) (television); *The Soft Kill*; *Spitfire* (uncredited); 1995: *Cyberjack* (a.k.a. *Virtual Assassin*) (video) [U.S.-Canada-Japan]; *Dominion* (video); *Evil Obsession* (video); *Malevolence*; *The Marshal: Kissing Cousins* (11/20/95) (television); *The Nature of the Beast*; *Sketch Artist II: Hands That See* (a.k.a. *Sketch Artist II*) (television); *Steel Frontier* (video); 1996: *American Strays* (video); *Assault on Dome 4* (television); *Billy Lone Bear*; *Bombshell*; *The Killing Jar*; *The Lazarus Man: Awakening: Part 1* (01/20/96) (television); *Marco Polo:*

Haparek Ha'aharon [Israel]; *Precious Find*; *Superman* (animated): *Feeding Time* (09/21/96) (television) (voice only); 1997: *Back in Business*; *Blade Runner* (video game) (voice only); *Deadly Ransom*; *The Fifth Element* [France]; *The Setting Son*; *Spawn* (a.k.a. *Todd McFarlane's Spawn*) (animated) (television) (voice only); *Snide and Prejudice*; *Superman* (animated): *Two's a Crowd* (02/15/97), *Double Dose* (09/22/97) (television) (voice only); *The Underground*; *Walker, Texas Ranger: Lucas: Part 1* (10/11/07), *Lucas: Part 2* (10/18/97) (television); 1998: *Black Sea 213*; *Border to Border*; *Brown's Requiem*; *Heist*; *In God's Hands*; *Jekyll Island*; *Joseph's Gift*; *Kai Rabe Gegen Die Vatikankiller* (a.k.a. *Kai Rabe Vs. the Vatican Killers*) [Germany]; *The Magnificent Seven: One Day Out West* (01/10/98) (television); *Men in White* (a.k.a. *National Lampoon's Men in White*) (television-video); *Millennium: Luminary* (01/23/98) (television); *A Place Called Truth*; *The Sentinel: Mirror Image* (02/11/98) (television); *The Thief & the Stripper* (a.k.a. *Strip 'n' Run*) (video); *Vengeance Unlimited: Justice* (10/22/98) (television); 1999: *Arthur's Quest*; *Diplomatic Siege*; *Dirt Merchant*; *Foolish* (uncredited); *The Hunter's Moon*; *The Magnificent Seven: The New Law* (01/08/99) (television) (uncredited); 2000: *The King Is Alive* (a.k.a. *Dogme 4—The King Is Alive*) [Sweden-Denmark-U.S.]; *The Operator*; 2001: *Farewell, My Love*; 2003: *Phoenix Point*.

Brigitte Lahaie

Brigitte Lahaie is known the world over as one of the most beautiful women to ever grace the celluloid screen in erotic films. While much of her film career has consisted of appearing in such fare, often produced in France, she had almost always turned in lifelike performances, smoldering with sensuality and lust, something that most of the cardboard-cutout erotic cinema actresses in other countries, particularly the United States, could not achieve, even when trying. Towards the middle of her career as an actress in adults-only films, she appeared in a small number of what are now considered powerful, influential, sexually-charged horror films, the majority of them directed by the French erotic horror pioneer Jean Rollin.

Lahaie was born Brigitte Van Meerhaeque on October 12, 1955, in Tourcoing, France. When she was 18, after spending much of her childhood reared in a middle class family, she moved to Paris. On February 6, 1976, she answered a classified advertisement that read "Models with large breasts required" and was selected out of dozens of young women for the coveted modeling "role," only to discover that in actuality it was an audition for a part in a hardcore pornographic film. This evidently did not bother her for she accepted the assignment, and began what is now considered one of the busiest careers in the business. She changed her family name to Lahaie (meaning brigade of the hedgerow bush) for her new profession, and the now-rechristened Brigitte Lahaie made dozens of these films.

Lahaie met the experimental filmmaker Jean Rollin while making her adult films and together, as star and director, they made a few adult films, and an equally small number of influential horror films, among them *Les Raisons De La Mort* (1978), *Fascination* (1979), *La Nuit Des Traquees* (1979), and *Les Deux Orphelines Vampires* (1997). Other non-pornographic roles were in films for Jess Franco, including the adult thriller *Je Brule De Partout* (1978), the action film *Dark Mission—Operacion Cocaina* (1987), and the horror tale *Les Predateurs De La Nuit* (1988), which updates Georges Franju's seminal thriller *Les Yeux Sans Visage* (1959) for a whole new audience.

She also co-starred with Alain Delon in the action film *Pour La Peau D'Un Flic* (1980), and appeared in the surreal art house hit *Diva* (1980), and could be seen in major roles in *Brigade Des Moeurs* (1984), *L'Executrice* (1985), and *Le Couteau Sous La Gorge* (1986). She even appeared briefly as a courtesan in Phillip Kaufman's *Henry and June* in 1990. In 1999, she briefly returned to pornography for the autobiographical video release *Tout Est Bien Qui Finit Bien* (1999), but had essentially retired from the film industry.

In 1987, Lahaie wrote her well-received autobiography *Moi La Scandaleuse* (I, the

Scandalous One), in which she talked candidly of her career in adult films, and expressed no regrets or shame about appearing in these films. She also hosted a radio talk show in 1992, and became an on-air dreams analyst for one season for another radio program. On television, she appeared as a singer in *La Plus Belle Nuit Du Cinema* (1989), and she even released the musical recording *Caresse Tendresse* in 1987. Besides *Moi La Scandaleuse*, she also wrote and published the following books: *Le Zodiaque Erotique* (1989), *La Femme Modele* (1990), *Les Sens De La Vie* (1994), and *Le Sexe Defendu* (1996). In 1995, she released the first of several CD-ROMs, *Brigitte Live,* an interactive guide to her career. Of late, Lahaie has returned to the silver screen in Jean Rollin's erotically charged, surrealistic vampire film *La Fiancée Du Dracula* (2002), and in the Gaelic thriller *Calvaire* (2004).

Q: Do you perceive the presence of a woman as an important presence in erotic and horror films? The primary audience for each genre are males, so do you think that the horror film, with or without eroticism, is less powerful or more powerful?

Brigitte Lahaie: I think there is a similarity between erotica and horror. The mixture of sex and death is always alluring and mysterious. I have thought a lot about this question... I think we are all afraid to die, or to see death as the next level. Therefore, when we think about sexual situations, it is also championing the triumph of life. I think that the power of sex, making men crazy, making them want me, etc., it is a power of life. Then again, all of my films, after the first half of my career, which primarily consisted of erotica, were to be strong without the idea of sex being used as a lure or a power. I believe that my position as a former star in the erotic cinema is an impressive one, and I understand the interest in that portion of my earlier career. I appreciate that people recognize me as an actress who is capable of making films where I use femininity as a power, rather than my sex.

Q: Did you enter the business as a model?

Lahaie: Well, not exactly as a model. I answered a newspaper advertisement, and my first job was in a pornographic movie, but no one could see my face then. I was a double for one of the lead actresses.

Q: A body double?

Lahaie: A body double. Afterwards, producers offered me roles in many pornographic films. I think I did not realize exactly what I was doing but I was a very shy, very inexperienced woman. It was for me like opening a door into a completely new world, opening all of my inhibitions. I really did not realize what I was doing. Afterwards, I understood the importance of what I was doing. It was over thirty years ago, and French society was not very open to sex.

Q: What was the name of this first film?

Lahaie: I do not remember. I think it was in 1976. I did many in 1976, then in 1977, in 1978...

Q: The first film in which you worked with Jean Rollin, which was not a hardcore production...

Lahaie: Yes it was, *Vibrations Sexuelles* in 1976.

Q: I am speaking of the first non–adults only feature film that you made. The film in which Jean Rollin directed you.

A luminous Brigitte Lahaie as she appears on an autographed postcard advertising her French radio and television program.

Lahaie: Yes, I understand what you are saying. You are referring to *La Raisons De La Morte*.

Q: This was the first non-pornographic film that you made. How did you feel about this transition, from what is essentially a visual format concerning titillation, to another, although related one, concerning horror. They both tap into primal desires, fears, etc.

Lahaie: For me it was the same. I was in front of the camera, and it was a very, very great pleasure. I did not think that I would ever become a real actress. At the time, I thought that it was like a big joke. It was a funny thing for me to become an actress. I did not realize that, maybe; I could be an actress after all and not just this sensual figure in erotic cinema.

Q: When you first worked with Jess Franco, I believe it was on the erotic thriller *Je Brule De Partout*. How did you come to meet him?

Lahaie: My first contact [on this film] with Jess was not very good. However, I was very, very wild back in those days, nearly thirty years ago. It was in Portugal where we met. I was very proud of the work that I had been doing on the film, and Jess did not really speak with me too much. During the production of this movie, I had only one idea, which was to come back home [to France]. Then, as we were nearing the end of the production, he told me that I would also be doing another movie for him, because we had finished the other one earlier than expected, and we had ten days more in Lisbon. I said, "No, it's not okay. I want to go home," and he was very, very furious with me. We stayed apart for a very long time. When he phoned me a long time afterwards, years later, I was very cautious about meeting him again. However, the second meeting was very, very good.

Q: Were there any erotic films in which you did some acting you were proud of? Was there any particular one that you liked?

Lahaie: No. I did many good movies. Some, you can forget; however, I think I did ten that I think are good.

Q: When *Fascination* came along in 1980, many people who admire your work, and many people who admire Jean Rollin's work, believed that you delivered such a great performance, almost as if this role was specifically written for you.

Lahaie: Yes, it is true that he had written this role for me. I did not think that it was going to do anything special for my career as an actress. Nevertheless, everything about this film was special. It was all like a dream. We were on a location, just outside of Paris, and the ambiance was special. I think I really believed that I could become a real actress after this film was finished.

Q: You also had a small role in an Alain Delon film, *Pour Le Peau D'Un Flic* (1981).

Lahaie: Alain Delon was the boyfriend of my best friend at the time. I had already met him outside of the film business. He offered me the small part in this film. I still see him around from time to time; I always try to keep in contact with people.

Q: *L'Executrice* (1986) was a completely different kind of role for you as the hero police officer.

Lahaie: I remember this film, but I do not recall it greatly. It was not terribly different from other films that I had made, except that I could now do action movies. I do recall that I played a strong woman in this film.

Lahaie wields a mean scythe in the Jean Rollin–directed horror film *Fascination* (1979) (Redemption/Image).

Q: In 1987, some years after you had stopped appearing in pornographic films, there was a videocassette [*L'Anthologie Du Plaisir*] which was essentially a compilation of some of your earlier erotic film roles. You introduced the clips.

Lahaie: It was an idea of my boyfriend at the time, Rene Chateau, an important film producer in France, to release this video. I think it is a good compilation but...

Q: But at that time you were not making these kinds of films any more. Did you feel that putting this tape out would affect your current career in any way?

Lahaie: I did not mind. I thought that we could have used better scenes, because it does not have momentum. I personally believe that some of the footage was just cut together in a haphazard fashion, and therefore, the sequences tend to become boring. There is no rhythm to the different scenes appearing in the way that they do.

Q: You returned to work with Jess Franco again in *Dark Mission* and in *Faceless*.

Lahaie: *Dark Mission* was a good experience. We had a lot of weapons and ammunition. It is great to shoot off automatic weapons. It was fun.

Q: In *Faceless*, you had this great role as the seducing villainess. It was a film that should have had a sequel featuring your character. What are your recollections about this film, and working with the cast?

Lahaie: Working with everyone in the cast was wonderful, but for one person: Helmut Berger. At first, he was difficult. He was like an animal, always trying to impress himself on me...

Q: He had an aggressive personality?

Lahaie: Yes, you could say that he was an aggressive person. However, afterwards, after two or three days when I did not accept his manners, we became very good friends. Caroline Munro was very special. You know, the first time I saw her, I thought she was very sweet, and she was.

Q: You appeared in Philip Kaufman's *Henry and June*, and then returned to work with Jean Rollin in *Deux Orphelines Vampires*.

Lahaie: In *Deux Orphelines Vampires* I had a very, very small part. I play a woman whom the girls ultimately kill. Then I appeared in two short films. You know, after my meeting with Philip Kaufman, I decided to do just what I wanted to do. I now have many occupations.

Q: You hosted a television program in France.

Lahaie: It was a talk show where people came to speak of their sexual and romantic problems.

Q: Did you have a live audience?

Lahaie: No. I think it is a problem when people come on to my show, and they have very difficult things to say. A live audience, I think, is a bad thing, because they react in different ways. I want to try to help people become comfortable with their sexuality. We do not have to ridicule people. We have to accept them. I am always pleased when the people who came on my show said to me afterwards that they felt comfortable enough to explain to me their problems. I felt like I had helped them in some way.

Q: What are your plans for the future?

Lahaie: I am writing a lot nowadays, and that is very important to me. I do not know what I want to do in the cinema, if anything any more. I do not want to be known as the sex goddess any more. To be called a beautiful woman is okay, but not a sex queen any more. It is difficult, because many people think still of me as this sexy woman, which I was in the seventies and eighties, but it creates problems. What I want to do, and what I could do, is compounded by people wanting me to still be this one thing, a sex goddess. I think that when the two come together, the formerly sexy woman, with the beautiful mature woman that I am, then I will act again.

Credits: 1976: *Jouissances* (a.k.a. *Belles D'Un Soir* a.k.a. *Supremes Jouissances* a.k.a. *Supreme Comings*) [France]; 1977: *Cathy, Fille Soumise* (a.k.a. *Cathy, Submissive Girl*) [France]; *Couples En Chaleur* (a.k.a. *Couples in Heat*) [France]; *Entrecuisses* (a.k.a. *Into the Bushes* a.k.a. *Possessions!*) [France]; *Exces Pornographiques* (a.k.a. *Perversion D'Une Jeune Marie* a.k.a. *Perversions of a Young Bride* a.k.a. *Pornographic Excess*) [France]; *La Face Cachee D'Hitler* (a.k.a. *Hitler's Hidden Face*) [France]; *Inonde Mon Ventre* (a.k.a. *Overflow onto My Belly*) [France]; *Je Suis Une Belle Salope* (a.k.a. *I Am a Beautiful Bitch*) [France]; *Jouir Jusqu'Au Delrie* (a.k.a. *Come...Until Delirium*) [France]; *La Mouillette* (a.k.a. *Honey Dripping*) [France]; *Nathalie, Rescapee de l'Enfer* (*Nathalie, Survivor from Hell*, *Nathalie Dans l'Enfer Nazi*) [France]; *Parties Fines* (a.k.a. *Indecenes 1930* a.k.a. *Education of the Baroness*) [France]; *Les Plaisiers Fous* (a.k.a. *The Mad Pleasures* a.k.a. *Wild Pleasures, Encore Plus, Even More*) [France]; *Sarabande Porno* (a.k.a. *Sexual Slaves on Catalog*) [France]; *Touchez Pas Aux Zizis* (a.k.a. *Don't Touch the Winnies*) [France]; *Vibrations Sexuelles* (a.k.a. *Sexual Vibrations*) [France]; 1978: *Blondes Humides* (a.k.a. *Viens J'Aime Ca* a.k.a. *Wet Blondes*) [France]; *Bordel SS* (a.k.a. *SS Bordello*) [France]; *Bouches Expertes* (a.k.a. *Expert Mouths*) [France]; *Chaleurs Intimes* (a.k.a. *Bourgeoisie Et Pute*) [France]; *Les Chattes* (a.k.a. *The Cats*) [France]; *Chaude Et Perverse Emilia* (a.k.a. *Hot and Perverse Emilia*) [France]; *La Clinque Des Fantasmes* (a.k.a. *The Clinic of Phantasmes* a.k.a. *Rx for Sex*) [France]; *Couple Cherche Esclave Sexuel* (a.k.a. *Couple Seeks Sex Slave* a.k.a. *Sexual Slave Wanted for Couple*) [France]; *Cuisses Infernales* [France-Canada]; *Enquetes 666* (a.k.a. *Investigation 666* a.k.a. *Call Girls De Luxe* a.k.a. *Luxurious Call Girls* a.k.a. *Paris Telephone 666* a.k.a. *Special Investigations for Perverse Couples*) [France]; *Etreintes* [France]; *Festival Erotique* (a.k.a. *J'aime Les Grosses Legumes* a.k.a. *I Love Big Vegetables*) [France]; *Les Grandes Jouisseuses* (a.k.a. *The Grand Sensualists* a.k.a. *Nuits Brulantes*) [France]; *Je Brule De Partout* (a.k.a. *I Am Burning All Over* a.k.a. *Rapt De Nymphettes*) [France-Portugal-Spain]; *Je Suis A Prendre* (a.k.a. *I Am Yours to Take* a.k.a. *Take Me, I'm Yours*) [France]; *Langues Cochonnes* (a.k.a. *Dirty Tongues*) [France]; *Ondes Brulantes* (a.k.a. *Burning Showers*) [France]; *Parties Tres Speciales* (a.k.a. *Very Special Parties*) [France]; *Porno Roulette* [France–West Germany]; *Prends-Moi De Force* (a.k.a. *Take Me, By Force*) [France]; *La Rabatteuse* (a.k.a. *The Female Pimp*) [France]; *Les Raisons De La Mort* (a.k.a. *The Grapes of Death* a.k.a. *Pesticide*) [France]; *Rentre C'Est Bon* (a.k.a. *Enter, It's Good*) [France]; *Soumission* (a.k.a. *Clarisse* a.k.a. *Submission*) [France]; *Tout Pour Jouir* (a.k.a. *Everything to Come* a.k.a. *La Vitrine Du Plaisir* a.k.a. *The Window of Pleasure*) [France-Canada]; *Viol* (a.k.a. *Rape*) [Switzerland–Canada–France–West Germany]; 1979: *Anna Cuisses Entrouvertes* (a.k.a. *Anna, Thighs Always Open*) [France]; *Auto-Stoppeuses En Chaleur* (a.k.a. *Hitchhikers in Heat* a.k.a. *Two At Once*) [France-Germany]; *Cette Malicieuse Martine* (a.k.a. *Martine, Venus der Wollust* a.k.a. *Martine, Venus of Lust* a.k.a. *Secretaires Sans Culottes*) [France–West Germany]; *Estivantes Pour Homme Seul* (a.k.a. *Visitors for a Single Man*) [France]; *Fascination* [France]; *Une Femme Special* (a.k.a. *A Very Special Woman*) [France]; *La Grande Mouille* (a.k.a. *The Big Orgy* a.k.a. *The Great Wetness* a.k.a. *Hunting Party in Sologne*) [France-Germany]; *L' Histoire Des 3 Petits Cochons* (a.k.a. *The Story of the 3 Little Pigs* a.k.a. *Trois Petits Cochons A Saint-Tropez* a.k.a. *Three Little Pigs in Saint-Tropez*) [France]; *I...Comme Icare* (a.k.a. *I, As in Icarus*) [France]; *Maitresses Pour Couple* (a.k.a. *All Purpose Sex* a.k.a. *A Mistress for a Couple*) [France]; *Parties Chaudes* (a.k.a. *Les Delices De L'Adultere* a.k.a. *The Delights of Adultery* a.k.a. *Hot Parties*) [France]; *Penetrations Mediteraneennes* (a.k.a. *Mediterranean Penetrations*) [France]; *Penetrez-Moi Par Le Petit Trou* (a.k.a. *Fuck Me, By the Small...*) [France]; *Le Retour Des Veuves* (a.k.a. *The Return of the Widows*) [France]; *Sechs Schwedinnen Im Pensionat* (a.k.a. *Six Swedes on a Campus* a.k.a. *Amorous Sis-*

ters) [Switzerland–France–West Germany]; *Secrets D'Adolescentes* (*Adolescent Secrets*) [France]; 1980: *Le Coup Du Parapluie* (a.k.a. *Umbrella Coup*) [French]; *Les Enfilees* (a.k.a. *Evenings of a Voyeur Couple*) [French]; *Gefangen Frauen* (a.k.a. *Island Women*) [Switzerland–West Germany]; *L'Heritiere* (a.k.a. *The Heiress*) [France]; *Le Journal Erotique D'Une Thailandaise* (a.k.a. *Carnet Intime D'Une Thailandaise* a.k.a. *Carnal Times in Thailand* a.k.a. *Emmanuelle 3*) [France–Thailand–Hong Kong]; *James Bande 00SEX No.2* [France]; *Julchen Und Jettchen, Die Verliebten Apothekerstochter* (a.k.a. *Come Play with Me 3*) [Switzerland]; *Laisse Ton Pere Au Vestiaire* (a.k.a. *Leave Your Father at the Cloakroom*) [France]; *Die Nichten Der Frau Oberst* (a.k.a. *Les Bourgeois De L'Amour* a.k.a. *Come Play with Me 2* a.k.a. *Secrets of a French Maid*) [Switzerland]; *La Nuit Des Traquees* (a.k.a. *The Night of the Hunted*) [France]; *Le Petites Ecoliers* (a.k.a. *The Little Schoolgirls* a.k.a. *French Lessons*); *Photos Scandale* (a.k.a. *Scandalous Photos*) [France]; *Sechs Schwedinen Von Tankstelle* (a.k.a. *Six Swedes at a Gas Station* a.k.a. *Six Swedes at a Pump* a.k.a. *Swedish Gas Pump Girls* a.k.a. *Swedish Erotic Sexations*) [Switzerland–France–West Germany]; *Le Segrete Esperienze Dio Luca E Fanny* [Italy-France]; *Te Marres Pas...C'Est Pour Rire!* (*Don't Laugh, It's a Joke*) [France]; 1981: *Antoine Et Julie* (television) [France]; *Diva* [France]; *Les Echapees* (a.k.a. *Les Paumees Du Petit Matin* a.k.a. *The Runaways*) [French]; *Parties Tres Speciales* [France]; *Paul Raymond's Erotica* [Great Britain]; *Pour La Peau D'Un Flic* (a.k.a. *For the Skin of a Cop* a.k.a. *For a Cop's Hide* a.k.a. *Whirlpool*); *Si Ma Gueule Vous Plait...* (a.k.a. *If You Like My Face*) [France]; 1982: *Les Brigades Vertes* (television); *Deux Gamines* (uncredited); *Electric Blue 5* [Great Britain]; *Nestor Burma, Detective De Choc* (a.k.a. *Nestor Burma, Shock Detective*) (uncredited) [France]; *N'Oublie Pas Ton Pere Au Vestaire...* [France]; *Professione P...Attrice* (documentary); 1983: *Education Anglaise* [France]; *Le Lavabo* (a.k.a. *The Toilet*) (television) (short film); 1984: *La France Interdite* (a.k.a. *Forbidden France* a.k.a. *French Prohibition*) (documentary) [France]; 1985: *Brigade Des Moeurs* (a.k.a. *Vice Squad*) [France]; *Joy Et Joan* (a.k.a. *Joy and Joan* a.k.a. *Joy 2*) [France–Great Britain]; 1984: *Cinematon* (documentary); 1986: *Le Couteau Sous La Gorge* (a.k.a. *Knife under the Throat*) [France]; *L'Executrice* (a.k.a. *The Female Executioner*) [France]; *Suivez Mon Regard* (a.k.a. *Follow My Gaze* a.k.a. *Follow My Eyes*) [France]; 1987: *L'Anthologie Du Plaisir* (video) [France]; *Le Diable Rose* (a.k.a. *The Pink Rose* a.k.a. *The Pink Devil*) [France-Germany]; *Johnny Monroe* (television) [France]; *On Se Calme Et on Boit Frait A Saint-Tropez* (a.k.a. *Let's Calm Down and Have a Cool Drink in Saint Tropez*) [France]; *Therese II: La Mission* (uncompleted?) [France]; 1988: *Dark Mission* (a.k.a. *Dark Mission* (*Operacion Cocaina*) a.k.a. *Dark Mission: Les Fleurs Du Mal* a.k.a. *Dark Mission: Flowers of Evil*) [France]; *Les Predateurs De La Nuit* (a.k.a. *Faceless*) [France]; 1989: *Derriere Lahaie* (television); *La Plus Belle Nuit Du Cinema* (television); *Le Triple Gagnant: Le Dernier Rendz-Vous Du President* (11/30/89) (television) [France]; 1990: *Henry & June* [U.S.-France]; 1992: *L'Abri* (a.k.a. *The Shelter*) (television) [France]; 1993: *Illusions Fatales* [Canada-France?]; *Turc A Toutes Heures* (television) [France]; 1995: *Electric Blue: Sex Model File #4* (video) (short film) [Great Britain]; 1996: *Un Siecle Du Plaisir—Voyage A Traver L'Histoire Du Hard* (documentary) (television); 1997: *Les Deux Orpheline Vampires* (a.k.a. *The Two Orphan Vampires*) [France]; 1999: *Tout Est Bien Qui Finit Bien* (a.k.a. *To All of You Girls...*) [France] (video); 2000: *La Dame Pippi* (short film) [France]; *Ma Sexualite De A a X* (documentary; also director) (video); 2001: *On Ne Peut Pas Plaire A Tout Le Monde* (10/26/01) (television) [France]; 2002: *La Fiancée De Dracula* (a.k.a. *The Bride of Dracula*) [France-U.S.]; 2004: *Calvaire* (a.k.a. *The Ordeal*) [France-Belgium-Luxembourg]; *Grand Journal De Canal+* (09/13/04) (television) [France]; *Nous Ne Sommes Pas Des Anges* (09/24/04) (television) [France]; *Questions Pour Un Cham-*

pion (03/02/04) (television) [France]; *Tout Le Monde En Parle* (09/18/04) (television) [France]; *20h10 Petantes* (10/29/04) (television) [France]; 2005: *On Ne Peut Pas Plair A Tout Le Monde* (04/24/05) (television) [France].

Ed Lauter

Ed Lauter was born on October 30, 1940 on Long Island, New York. A veteran of dozens of films and television shows of the seventies, eighties, and nineties, he is one character actor who has remained recognizable due to his seemingly never-changing physical appearance. In his heyday, moviegoers and television viewers could usually recognize Lauter as he portrayed a seemingly never-ending stream of thin, balding, sinister-looking villains. Although best remembered for his role as the ornery, sadistic Captain Knauer in the Robert Aldrich–directed Burt Reynolds hit *The Longest Yard* (1974), Lauter occasionally also essays sympathetic roles as well, but he seems most at home inhabiting the clothing of sinister gangsters, thieves, liars, and killers.

Lauter's mother, former actress-dancer Sally Lee, had performed in musical theatre shows in the 1920s, appearing in programs for impresarios David Belasco and Florenz Ziegfeld, and raised him in the family's small apartment in Long Beach, Long Island, New York. "She gave me great confidence in myself. How could you not have it, when your mom sits you down when you are like eight years old, and makes you believe in yourself? You have a great advantage when you are older and you go into a casting office and they do not pick you. You can shrug it off, 'cause you know you'll be back."

After completing his education, and a stint in the army, Lauter started out in the entertainment business as a stand-up comic. As a young comedian, he inhabited East Coast nightspots like the Café Wha?, the Champagne Gallery, the Improv, and the original Fat Black Pussycat Café in Greenwich Village. Said Lauter in an interview with the *New York Daily News* in February 1986, "Competition was fierce. You had to be good to survive." Eventually, Lauter found theater work via roles in Off-Broadway plays and in summer stock. His first role on television was as a heavy in the popular show *Mannix* in 1971. Throughout the seventies and eighties, he would continue this long streak, guest starring primarily as a villain in a succession of popular television programs including *Cannon* (1971), *The Streets of San Francisco* (1972), *Kojak* (1973), *The Rockford Files* (1974), *Baretta* (1975), and *Magnum P.I.* (1980). Subsequently, more varied work in *The X-Files* (1993), *Kung Fu: The Legend Continues* (1996), *C.S.I.: Crime Scene Investigation* (2002), and a recurring role on the popular medical show *ER*, as the chief of the local fire department, proved the versatility of this actor.

His first big screen appearance was as one of the Anglo gunslingers in the last of the *Magnificent Seven* sequels, 1972's *The Magnificent Seven Ride*. During the seventies, Lauter amassed a large number of screen credits with his ability to project a steel-like stare and a feral anger, making him a wanted man by Hollywood producers seeking an actor to fill

Eddie Albert (right) reddens with rage when Ed Lauter decides to not shoot Burt Reynolds at the climax of Robert Aldrich's *The Longest Yard* (1974) (Albert S. Ruddy Productions/Long Road Pictures/Paramount Pictures).

the role of a heavy. He was featured in such fare as *Hickey and Boggs* (1972), the western *Bad Company* (1972), *The Last American Hero* (1973), and others. Eventually, he saw a gradual change in the size of the parts given him. In the film *Lolly-Madonna XXX* (1973), he had a co-starring role as Hawk Feather, a cruel, overage country boy seeking redemption and a future outside of his rural life. Of his performance, journalist Alan Howard commented in the trade *The Hollywood Reporter*, "Ed Lauter [as] the son with fantasies of being a country-western star, moves from menace to sympathy with the ease of a genuinely talented actor."

Following his role in *Lolly-Madonna XXX* and perhaps due to it, Lauter got his major breakout part in *The Longest Yard*. In the 1974 film, Lauter is featured as Captain Knauer, the prison security chief who makes life hell for an ex-pro football player cum prisoner (Burt Reynolds) and his teammates, who are forced to battle guards in a series of increasingly dangerous and violent games, while working under the explicit orders of snide Warden Eddie Albert. For much of the film's running time, Lauter's character is despised by the audience (one might even suspect he is partly responsible for the death of a sympathetic character), but he shows signs of humanity. At the climax, just when you think he will pull out all the stops in villainy and shoot Reynolds in the back, he lowers his rifle and walks away despite the haranguing from an obviously disgruntled Eddie Albert. Lauter has allowed Reynolds to live, finally showing respect for the warrior.

One of Lauter's favorite parts was the character of Bud Delaney in the television film *The Last Hours Before Morning* (1975). As an ex-cop cum private investigator researching the death of a gambler, he gave a strong, boozy, blowsy performance in a telefilm that should have been the first episode of a television series. Additional high-profile roles in Alfred Hitchcock's *Family Plot* (1976), the Dino De Laurentiis *King Kong* (1976), and several films with action legend Charles Bronson (including *Breakheart Pass* [1975], *The White Buffalo* [1977], *Death Hunt* [1981], and *Death Wish 3* [1985]) kept Lauter in the public eye. Of his performance in *Family Plot*, *Variety* noted (on March 24, 1976), "There is a chilling turn by Ed Lauter as a lowlife henchman."

Recent credits include the comedy *Not Another Teen Movie* (2001), the award-winning *Seabiscuit* (2003), the direct-to-video *Starship Troopers 2: Hero of the Federation* (2004), and the 2005 remake of *The Longest Yard*, the latter reuniting Lauter with Burt Reynolds.

Q: How does it feel to be one of the most recognizable character actors working today?

Ed Lauter: Well, let me put it this way, it is a nice feeling just to be working. I remember reading something similar about Humphrey Bogart, and he said, "Always keep working." And that is just what it is that I live by. I am very appreciative just to keep working. My mom was an actress on Broadway, my cousin is Elaine Stritch, so I am just fortunate. I wanted to do this [act] since I was like eight years old, I am doing what I have always wanted to do, and yes, I feel very fortunate.

Q: Is it true that early in your career, you were a stand-up comic?

Lauter: I always knew I wanted to be an actor since I was a child. However, when I was in college, I liked comedy so I had a comedy act with a friend of mine and we were pretty funny. I said, "Larry, let's take it on the road" after college, and he said no. Now, he is a very good psychologist. So, I took myself on the road and won a talent show called No. 1 Fifth Avenue. I started working down in Greenwich Village. I worked with people like David Frye, Robert Klein, Gabe Kaplan, Richard Pryor, and people like that. I was at a ballgame and I was kind of cracking jokes with some people, and somebody said, "Hey, you're funny, how would you like to play Las Vegas?" I said, "*What?*" He said, "Yeah, I'm going to call this guy up about it. He's a friend of mine, and he knows you" and blah blah blah. And the next thing you know, I am playing Las Vegas at the Riviera, at the comedy room. I played two weeks there about five years ago.

Q: How does it feel to be immortalized in people's memories, primarily for that amazing performance in *The Longest Yard*?

Lauter: You know, I still have to pinch myself sometimes. I was once told that that movie was one of the most frequently played feature films on television. When we were making it, I knew we were having a lot of fun doing it. It is an honor to be recognized. I guess in a way it is another kind of payment, in a sense, from the public, to be recognized the way that I am. It signals to me that I have done a good job. It is nice to be somewhat immortalized, people stopping me on the street or yelling across an intersection at you, "Gameball!" and all that stuff.

Q: So you appreciate the reaction from the public?

Lauter: That is what we are here for. We are here for the people. Talking to Jimmy Stewart once, I said I remembered reading an interview with him where he told about

Lauter and fellow screen villain Bruce Dern in a scene from *Family Plot* (1976) (Universal Pictures).

how someone came up to him in the middle of a Nebraska field and said, "You know, you did a soliloquy about glow worms, and you were real good," and then walked away. Jimmy said, "See, now that's what it's all about. Getting to the people, touching the people." And that is what I do, and I have fun with it.

Q: I would guess that not too many audiences recall a 1976 television movie that you had the leading role in, *The Last Hours Before Morning*.

Lauter: That was a chance for me to play a lead. I was playing kind of an anti-hero, film noir, Bogart kind of a character, and I had a lot of fun with that. I even got to kiss the girl. When it came time for NBC to decide to make it a series or not; they had to make a decision between *Ellery Queen* and my show, and what did they take? *Ellery Queen*.

Q: You worked with Alfred Hitchcock on *Family Plot*. What do you recall about that film?

Lauter: Bruce Dern and I were rehearsing a scene with Hitchcock. I walked over to him and said, "Mr. Hitchcock what do you think of the scene?" He said, "Good, but I think it has a few too many dog's feet in it." I said, "Dog's feet? What do you mean?" He said, "Pauses." The guy drove me nuts... but he was the best. He wanted me to be in another film of his, and unfortunately, he passed away before he could make another movie.

Lauter in a quiet moment from the Alfred Hitchcock thriller, *Family Plot* (1976) (Universal Pictures).

He was great to work with. A Hitchcock script is so meticulously thought-out—I mean, you can take an amateur filmmaker and give him a Hitchcock script to make a movie, and it will turn out better than he intended. For Hitchcock, he used the script to make the movie because it says "...and then the camera pans down, it goes into the cigarette and then pulls back..."—it tells you exactly what to do.

Q: So, there was very little room for improvisation?

Lauter: Well, no. He let me improvise a little. If he thought it was okay, he would let you do it.

Q: Of the many television shows that you appeared in, including *Mannix* and *Murder, She Wrote*, were there any particular favorites?

Lauter: One of my favorites was a television movie called *The Migrants* [1974], about migrant farm workers, with Cloris Leachman, Ron Howard, Cindy Williams, and Sissy Spacek. It was such a poignant portrayal of these people by everybody involved. That year it was one of the highest rated movies for television. I also liked *The Jericho Mile* [1979] with Peter Strauss; working on that was a lot of fun. I had a recurring role on *ER*, and it might have developed into something like my own show, but tides turn. In this business, a phone call gets the part. You get a call, and someone, from out of nowhere, says you are going to play Peter Pan and that is what you do. Sure, I would love to do a series.

Q: What recent feature roles were you pleased with?

Lauter: I did a film in 2000 in Los Angeles called *Gentleman B*, a true story about a guy who robbed forty-seven banks in fourteen months. I played an older bank robber who teaches him how to rob a bank and get away with it. We got a wonderful review in *The Los Angeles Times*. In April of 2002, I had a guest-starring role on *CSI*, I had that continuing role of Fire Captain Danaker on *ER*, I have appeared on *JAG* and *NYPD Blue*... since *Gentleman B*. in 2000, I must have been in over thirty films. I appeared in *Thirteen Days* [2000] with Kevin Costner, *Seabiscuit* [2003] with Jeff Bridges, [the 2005] *The Longest Yard* with Adam Sandler and Chris Rock, and I'm back in westerns in *Seraphim Falls* [2006] with Pierce Brosnan and Liam Neeson. I am working harder than ever nowadays. You know what part I would really like to play? I would like to play a priest and do a story around that whole thing that was in the news [the molestation charges involving Catholic priests]. There are a lot of good parts in there, you know. I used to be an altar boy. John Candy was also an altar boy, and when I met him on the film *Wagons East*, which was unfortunately his last film, we used to trade our Latin prayers back and forth. I love playing heavies too—they are a lot of fun. I met somebody once who said, "You know what you are? You're a turn actor." I said, "What do you mean?" He said, "Well, the story goes along, and your character gets introduced, and the story takes a turn." I said, "I like that." So, I'm going to become a turn actor, it's my new moniker.

Credits: 1971: *Mannix: The Man Outside* (11/24/71) (television); 1972: *Bad Company*; *Cannon: A Flight of Hawks* (02/22/72) (television); *Dirty Little Billy*; *Hickey & Boggs*; *The Magnificent Seven Ride!*; *The New Centurions*; *Rage*; *The Streets of San Francisco: The Thirty-Year Pin* (09/23/72) (television); 1973: *Class of '63* (television); *Executive Action*; *The Last American Hero*; *Lolly-Madonna XXX*; *The Streets of San Francisco: A Trout in the Milk* (01/06/73) (television); 1974: *The Godchild* (television); *Kojak: Mojo* (03/27/74) (television); *The Longest Yard*; *The Midnight Man*; *The Migrants* (television); *The New Land: The Word Is Growth* (09/21/74) (television); *The Waltons: The Car* (03/14/74) (television); 1975: *Baretta: Woman in the Harbor* (01/31/75) (television); *Breakheart Pass*; *French Connection II*; *Kate McShane: Midnight Lady, Pretty Lady* (television); *Last Hours Before Morning* (television); *Satan's Triangle* (television); *A Shadow in the Streets* (television); 1976: *Family Plot*; *King Kong*; *Police Story: Odyssey of Death: Part 1* (01/09/76), *Odyssey of Death: Part 2* (01/16/76) (television); 1977: *Charlie's Angels: The Blue Angels* (05/04/77) (television); *The Chicken Chronicles*; *The Rockford Files: The Dog and Pony Show* (10/21/77) (television); *The White Buffalo*; 1978: *The Clone Master* (television); *Greatest Heroes of the Bible* (television); *How the West Was Won* (television); *Magic*; 1979: *B.J. and the Bear* (television); *The Boy Who Drank Too Much* (television); *The Jericho Mile* (television); *Love's Savage Fury* (television); *Undercover with the KKK* (a.k.a. *My Undercover Years with the KKK*) (television); 1980: *Alcatraz: The Whole Shocking Story* (television); *Guyana Tragedy: The Story of Jim Jones* (television); *Hawaii Five-O: The Golden Noose* (01/15/80) (television); *Loose Shoes* (a.k.a. *Coming Attractions*); 1981: *The Amateur*; *Death Hunt*; *Nero Wolfe: Blue Ribbon Hostage* (05/05/81), *Sweet Revenge* (06/02/81) (television); 1982: *In the Custody of Strangers* (television); *Rooster* (television); *Timerider: The Adventures of Lyle Swan*; 1983: *The A-Team: Black Day at Bad Rock* (02/22/83) (television); *The Big Score*; *Cujo*; *Hardcastle and McCormick: Rolling Thunder: Part 1/Rolling Thunder: Part 2* (09/18/83) (television); *Magnum, P.I.: Operation: Silent Night* (12/15/83) (television); *Manimal: Manimal* (pilot) (09/30/83) (television); *St. Elsewhere: Working* (04/05/83) (television); *Simon & Simon: What's in a Gnome?* (02/24/83) (television); 1984: *The A-Team: Deadly Maneuvers* (02/28/84) (television); *Automan: Murder, Take One* (03/19/84) (television); *The Cartier Affair* (television); *Crazy Like a Fox: Pilot* (12/30/84) (television); *Dead Wrong: The John Evans Story* (a.k.a. *Dead Wrong*) (television); *Eureka*; *Finders Keepers*; *Lassiter*; *Nickel Mountain*; *The Seduction of Gina* (television); *The Three Wishes of Billy Grier* (television); *The Yellow Rose: Land of the Free* (02/11/84) (television); 1985: *Death Wish 3*; *Girls Just Want to Have Fun*; *Real Genius*; 1986: *The Defiant Ones* (television); *Firefighter* (television); *The Last Days of Patton* (television); *Raw Deal*; *The Thanksgiving Promise* (television); *3:15*; *Youngblood*; *Yuri Nosenko, KGB* (television); 1987: *The Equalizer: A Place to Stay* (02/25/87) (television); *Murder, She Wrote: The Cemetery Vote* (04/05/87) (television); *Revenge of the Nerds II: Nerds in Paradise*; 1988: *The Equalizer: No Place Like Home* (03/16/88) (television); *Goodbye, Miss 4th of July* (television); 1989: *Booker: High Rise* (10/22/89) (television); *Born on the Fourth of July*; *Gleaming the Cube*; *Fat Man and Little Boy*; *Judgment*; *Tennessee Nights* (a.k.a. *Black Water*); 1990: *Father Dowling Mysteries: The Confidence Mystery* (03/15/90) (television); *Monsters: Malcolm* (12/23/90) (television); *My Blue Heaven*; 1991: *Golden Years* (a.k.a. *Stephen King's Golden Years*) (television); *The Rocketeer*; 1992: *Calendar Girl, Cop, Killer? The Bambi Bembenek Story* (television); *Renegade: Partners* (11/21/92) (television); *School Ties*; *Star Trek: The Next Generation: The First Duty* (03/28/92) (television); 1993: *Extreme Justice*; *Homicide: Life on the Street: And the Rockets' Dead Glare* (03/17/93) (television); *Poisoned by Love: The Kern County Murders* (a.k.a. *Murder So Sweet*) (television); *The Return of Ironside* (television); *True Romance*; *Under Investigation*; *The X-Files: Space* (11/12/93) (television); 1994: *Birdland: Plan B* (01/19/94) (television); *Highlander: Bless the Child* (02/14/94) (television); *Secret Sins of the Father* (television); *Trial by Jury*; *Wagons East*; 1995: *Digital Man*; *Girl in the Cadillac*; *Leaving Las Vegas*; *Ripple*; *The Tuskegee Airmen* (television); 1996: *Coyote Summer*; *Crash*; *For Which He Stands*; *Kung Fu: The Legend Continues: Circle of Light* (02/12/96) (television); *Mulholland Falls* (television); *Rattled* (television); *Raven Hawk* (television); *The Sweeper*; 1997: *Allie & Me*; *Mercenary* (television); *Top of the World*; *Under Wraps* (television); *Walker, Texas Ranger: Last of a Breed: Part 1* (11/01/97), *Last of a Breed: Part 2* (11/08/97) (television); 1998: *A Bright Shining Lie* (television); *A Dollar for the Dead* (television); *ER: Exodus* (02/26/98) (television); *Millennium: In Arcadia Ego* (04/03/98) (television); 1999: *ER: The Storm: Part 1* (02/11/99), *The Storm: Part 2* (02/18/99) (television); *The Magnificent Seven: Vendetta* (01/29/99) (television); *Night of Terror* (video); *Out in Fifty*; 2000: *Blast*; *Civility* (a.k.a. *Malicious Intent*) (video); *ER: Rescue Me* (11/23/00) (television); *Gentleman B.* (a.k.a. *The Gentleman Bandit*); *Law & Order: Entitled: Part 2* (02/18/00) (television); *Python*; *Thirteen Days*; 2001: *Charmed: The Good, the Bad, and the Cursed* (02/15/01) (television); *ER: Survival of the Fittest* (03/29/01), *Sailing Away* (04/26/01) (television); *Farewell, My Love*; *Knight Club*; *Not Another Teen Movie*; 2002: *ER: A River in Egypt* (01/17/02) (television); *CSI: Crime Scene Investigation: Cat's in the Cradle* (04/25/02); *Go for Broke*; 2003: *Nobody Knows Anything!*; *Seabiscuit*; 2004: *Art Heist*; *Grandpa's Place*; *The Librarians* (a.k.a. *Strike Force*) (video); *Starship Troopers 2: Hero of the Federation* (video); 2005: *The American Standards*; *The Longest Yard*; *Into the Fire*; *The Lost*; *NYPD Blue: Old Man Quiver* (02/01/05) (television); *Purple Heart*; 2006: *The Grasslands*; *Love Hollywood Style*; *Seraphim Falls*; *Something's Wrong in Kansas*; *Taken by Force*; *Talladega Nights: The Ballad of Ricky Bobby*; *Venice Underground*; 2007: *Camille* (2007); *A Modern Twain Story: The Prince and the Pauper* (2007); *The Number 23* (2007).

Christopher Lee

Christopher Lee was born in Belgravia, London, England on May 27, 1922. He attended Wellington College for three years, worked as an office clerk in various London shipping concerns, and eventually enlisted in the Royal Air Force during WWII. After his discharge, he struggled to become an actor, but because he was taller than most leading actors of the day, and because of his dark looks, traceable back to his exotic ancestry,* he was chiefly relegated to supporting roles.

After nearly a decade of such parts on stage, television and in films, he played the monster in the Hammer film production *The Curse of Frankenstein* (1957) and his star slowly began to rise. The film was a success worldwide and led to parts in similar productions, including the title role in Hammer Films' *Dracula* (1958). Lee appeared as the bloodsucker in various adaptations of the Bram Stoker classic, as well as seven Hammer sequels as Count Dracula, a scourge to heroes everywhere, but irresistible to the women who swoon, then deliver themselves to him. The actor began to become a little too associated with the role, and was frequently offered similar parts by a variety of filmmakers the world over.

Based on his appearances in the Hammer productions, Lee began to be quite well known as a horror film specialist, and appeared in hundreds of them, sometimes co-starring with personal friend Peter Cushing. However, worldwide acclaim came via the James Bond adventures *The Man with the Golden Gun* (1974), *The Three Musketeers* (1973) and *The Four Musketeers* (1974); in them he played villains, but ones colored with more varied strokes of his talents that were shown elsewhere.

Lee moved to America where his appearances were as varied as a heroic role in the film *Airport '77* (1977) and a hosting stint on the live television program *Saturday Night Live* in 1978. He worked for Steven Spielberg in the film *1941* (1979) and, in the eighties, appeared on the television program *Charlie's Angels* (1980), and sang and danced (while he was trying to rule the world) in *The Return of Captain Invincible* (1983). In the nineties, he appeared alongside Peter O'Toole and Omar Sharif in Alejandro Jodorowsky's surreal *The Rainbow Thief* (1990), and even ended up in the comedic *Police Academy: Mission to Moscow* in 1994. He returned to England and, after a brief hiatus, relaunched his career with a cameo role in Tim Burton's *Sleepy Hollow* (1999), a throwback of sorts to the Hammer films of the sixties. Lee has also appeared as the insidious Count Dooku in *Star Wars: Episode II—The Attack of the Clones* (2002) and *Star Wars: Episode III—Revenge of the Sith*

---

*Lee is descended from the Italian Carandinis, a noble family which included an ancestor who was the Papal Secretary of State during the time of Napoleon, and who refused to attend the coronation of the diminutive leader.

Veronica Carlson with Christopher Lee in his most recognizable screen persona, as Count Dracula, in the film *Dracula Has Risen from the Grave* (1968) (Hammer Films Productions/Warner Bros.).

(2005), and appeared in all three parts of Peter Jackson's epic *Lord of the Rings* trilogy: *The Fellowship of the Ring* (2002), *The Two Towers* (2002), and *The Return of the King* (2003). Lee worked with *Sleepy Hollow* director Tim Burton again in *Charlie and the Chocolate Factory* (2005) and as a voice actor in the animated film, *Tim Burton's Corpse Bride* (2005). Among his own personal favorite roles was the real-life East Indian diplomat Mohammed Ali Jinnah in the film *Jinnah* (1998).

I had known fellow author Tom Johnson for a number of years, having been introduced by Tom Weaver, a mutual friend. Tom Johnson and I are both British horror movie buffs and especially fans of Hammer Films. Having similar tastes, we also both enjoy the work of Lee and Peter Cushing.

In 1999, it was Tom who informed me that Lee had written an updated version of his autobiography and that a U.S. promotional tour for the book (*Christopher Lee: Tall, Dark and Gruesome* [Midnight Marquee Press, 1999]) was beginning; in fact, a book signing appearance at a Virgin Records Megastore in New York's Times Square was just a few hours away. The thought of finally meeting someone who gave me chills and thrills throughout most of my childhood and early teenaged years, made me pause for a moment. Then I also thought about the many stories that have circulated over the years. After all, there were rumors that Lee was inhospitable to his fans, was very critical of his genre work, and did not enjoy discussing much of it. Nor did he relish talking about his deep personal friendship and close working relationship with Peter Cushing; Cushing had succumbed to cancer in the summer of 1994 and those wounds were still too deep for Lee.

Thinking that, if nothing else, I would get a chance to thank the reportedly irritable actor for his contributions to my enjoyment of film, get an autograph, and perhaps a photo with him, my expectations were low. However, I was not prepared for the surreal hours that lay ahead. When I entered the Virgin Records Megastore about two hours prior to the scheduled start of the book signing event, I spotted Tom Johnson in a coffee shop on the lower level of the complex; he said he was getting Mr. Lee his lunch (at 6PM!) and that he had requested an egg salad sandwich but all that was available was something that he could not quite describe (although it looked suspiciously like a Mexican fajitas wrap). Tom said to me, "Would you like to come upstairs?" I said, "What's upstairs?" He said, "Mr. Lee is waiting in the staff office area." I said, "Sure, why not." And this chapter begins...

The manager in charge of the Virgin staff arrived to check on things, and Tom asked her if it was all right if I joined the entourage. She said "Sure." The food arrived, and we went over to the staff elevators. When the doors opened on the second floor, there was Christopher Lee speaking to a few Virgin staffers, looking sharp and larger-than-life, and... quite tall.

Passing through the Virgin staff and heading into the manager's office, I was introduced to Mr. Lee, who said, "I know all about you, I've heard a lot about you." After scowling at the fajita wrap, he said he could not eat this food. He did not know what it was, and after I listed the contents of a fajita wrap, he seemed even *more* put off by the food. He really wanted his egg salad sandwich, so Tom said he would get him one. I offered to go along but Lee said, "No, you stay, and we'll talk." So, there I was alone in a room with Christopher Lee. The man put me at ease almost immediately and seemed genuinely warm.

Christopher Lee: You know, I have made so many films over the years, but I really do not have anything in terms of memorabilia from a lot of the television work that I have done, especially in England. I would really love to have, say, stills from *Moby Dick*, which was a film that I did with Orson Welles for British television. (In it, I wore a wig with long hair, and I had sideburns. It was a very good role). There comes a time where as you get older, you realize that you would like to have some kind of memento, a record of work that you've done, and I only recently have started collecting such things. Some of it of course is for my daughter, for her financial future. *Moby Dick* is a film that I can find no trace of, not film or stills. I have checked all over, even the British Film Institute, but they seem to be the weakest when it comes to collecting such materials. I have even written to Orson Welles' partner but I have received no reply.

Q: Jess Franco completed Welles' *Don Quixote* with the assistance of this woman, Oja Kodar, who was the business and life partner of Welles in his later years, and maybe you could contact her through Jess Franco, to find some images from *Moby Dick*.

Lee: I am sure she must have an archive of Welles' material locked away in this house that she lives in; in fact, I have heard of such. You know, there are other films. In fact, a list has been compiled of such films where I have been unable to find any still or film record of my performances. Offhand I can recall *White Hunter, Sailor of Fortune, William Tell, The Scarlet Pimpernel*; all of these were made for British television. In some of them, I only appeared in one episode or in a small role, but I would love to see even a still from these. Did you know that I appeared in a television show made in Poland?

Q: No, I did not. What was this program called?

Lee: *Theater Macabre*. It was even dubbed into English. I believe it may have even been shown on American television. I was the narrator, and I would introduce each episode. I appeared in every single episode, although sometimes it was only in a small part. In one episode, I would be seen as a blind organ grinder with a monkey; in another, I could be seen as the man who would inhabit a chair of death, an electric chair.

Q: I had no idea that you even appeared in such a program, much less one for Polish television.

Lee: It is the same thing with posters. I could have had twenty copies of each Hammer poster if I wanted, but I was not interested at the time. The ones I am talking about are the early Hammer Dracula and Frankenstein films. Nowadays, those posters sell for £10,000. Today, if I had signed them, the price would increase. I am sorry I never really collected those things.

Q: Well, you were a busy person then.

Lee: I am still busy. I just completed a small role in *Sleepy Hollow*, which is coming out later this year. I really liked working with Tim Burton, who is editing the film now to prepare its release.

Q: I had no idea that you were even in this film and I recently saw the trailer...

Lee: It is a small part, maybe five minutes long, but I enjoyed the work. It was fun to work with Burton and Johnny Depp, who is a very good actor, he really is. He is capable of so many things.

[The egg salad sandwich arrived and I asked Mr. Lee if he would feel more comfortable eating in peace. He said, "No, nonsense. I want you to stay and talk with me." So, I stayed.]

Lee: I'll tell you a story: When I was working on one of the Fu Manchu movies, we were filming in Hong Kong, and there I was with the makeup applied, with the slanted eyes, and the long mustache, and someone came up to me, and said, "What is your name?" I answered, "Lee." They really thought that I was Chinese. That was a fun film to work on.

Q: Those are fun films, especially the ones directed by Jess Franco.

Lee: Ah yes, Jess Franco. He is a very, very good director. In fact, he is so good that no one can really see how good he can be because he is often limited by the confines of his producers.

Q: Like Harry Alan Towers?

Lee [*puts head in hands in mock horror*]: Harry Alan Towers, I will tell you something about Harry Alan Towers. We were shooting what I still consider to this day, to be the finest representation of Dracula on film, *Count Dracula*, as directed by Jess Franco, which was ultimately not a successful film. But, still, it's the only one that shows the character growing younger from older, and I put into the film some of Stoker's original lines to make it more authentic. Anyway, Harry Alan Towers was the producer, and he would keep rushing the film, saying, "Faster, faster, we must have it completed." Instead of using dolly tracks and different cameras, it was his idea to have Jess zoom in and out with the camera at a furious pace to exemplify the passage of time, and to help create a mood. It hurt the film, among other things. Still it was a good cast to work with—Klaus Kinski, Herbert Lom...

Q: Did you know that Franco is still working?

Lee: He is? What kind of films is he making now [*slightly sarcastic*]?

Q: Well, he has made six films in the past few years, although their budgets are minimal. In fact, he's made a Fu Manchu film starring himself as Fu Manchu, only he is calling his character Dr. Wong! [*Dr. Wong's Virtual Hell* would not be released on DVD until the summer of 2006.]

Lee: He *has*! [*laughter*]

The author and Lee in 1999.

Q: Yes, but in the dubbing he had to change Fu Manchu to Dr. Wong. It has something to do with Harry Alan Towers owning the name of Fu Manchu or something like that I believe.

Lee: Well, I always enjoyed working with Jess. Yes, we did a number of films together...

Q: Like *The Bloody Judge*?

Lee: Well, that was another film that was based on actual historical records, but the end product changed much from the intent.

Q: It is a very bloody and gory film. I think the best, most complete version out there may be the German-language one.

Lee: Regarding that

film, I really dislike when after I've left a project the producers step in and alter it with extra things like that, more gore, or sex and violence. It was really intended as a much different movie than the version that I signed on for.

Q: Speaking of German films, it was a real find for me to locate a German-language tape of one of the Edgar Wallace films that you appeared in where you are speaking in German with your own voice, not dubbed.

Lee: I made three Edgar Wallace films. We would shoot them all in two different versions. We would shoot the movie in English, then go back and shoot it all over again in German. Sometimes with the English-language version we would use an English director. There was *The Puzzle of the Red Orchids*, and *The Devil's Daffodil*...

Q: Yes, with Joachim Fuchsberger...

Lee: Where I played a Chinese agent named Ling!

Q: I also have seen the obscure film *The Devil's Agent*, which is a British-German co-production.

Lee: Yes, that one had a wonderful cast. Many of the actors in that film came from the theater. It was a good little film.

Q: Peter Van Eyck was good in it as well.

Lee: Well, now that he is dead, I can say that he was not a very nice man at all. [*Lee spots a book in my book bag*] What's that book you have there?

Q: It is a book I have written on Italian horror films; it is in German.

Lee: I see. May I look at it?

Q: Sure.

Lee [*noticing that the book cover features a still from a Dario Argento movie*]: Dario Argento... the man is insane!

Q: Really, why would you think so?

Lee: Well, not too long ago I was at a film festival and he came over to me. I knew who he was of course, but he embraced me warmly, and spoke highly of my work. He said that he wanted to shoot some footage of me reminiscing about my Italian heritage. My family is originally from royal Italian stock, and he wanted to shoot this over a period of a few hours. Therefore, I went off into the hills with him and his crew, and the man became a madman. I never before have heard such language. He was shouting and cursing at his crew the whole time, for even the simplest set-ups. It was only about three hours of work or so, but I made up my mind that if he ever approached me about appearing in one of his features that I would decline, and not be interested.

Q: I am sure that this would be something to see. A documentary directed by Argento narrated by yourself, about your family...

Lee: I have not really done horror in a long time, but working with him, sure felt like one. Do you know that it has been over thirty years since I was in a Dracula film, and not matter what, I will most likely go to my grave being remembered mostly for that one role. However, I continue to work on other things. I have made this film *Jinnah* in the Middle East. It was well received in the trades and at film festivals, but it has yet to play anywhere theatrically.

[At this point, word reaches Tom Johnson that the Virgin Megastore has sold out of all of the hardcover and softcover copies of Lee's book, in anticipation of his signing.]

Lee: This is terrible news. Now, people who have come from afar, will not be able to get this book. What are we going to do? This is not good. I will of course greet them, but if they have come for the book, we will not have any.

Q: Well, there is another Virgin Megastore down on 14th Street. Maybe they can put in a call and ship some copies over here quickly. But I have an idea: since they have DVDs and VHS tapes, they could offer them to you to sign since all of the books are gone.

Lee: What is a DVD?

Q: It looks like a compact disc, actually, with the original negative usually being the source material. In fact, *Dracula, Prince of Darkness* has recently appeared containing the audio commentary that you recorded for it.

Lee: Audio commentary?

Q: Yes, with you and the other members of the cast.

Lee: Oh yes, when we were all sitting around and watching the film, and saying, "This is where so and so fell into this and that..."

[The Virgin manager comes into the office.]

Lee: I have just had an idea. We could let people purchase videotapes and DVDs, and I will gladly sign them.

[Lee decides that he will meet and greet anyone who has come to see him, but the decision is made to sign no memorabilia other than the book and VHS-DVD items purchased at Virgin, this to keep the line moving briskly and talk at a minimum. Finally, the moment comes and the security guards usher Mr. Lee, Tom Johnson, the just-arrived Tom Weaver, and myself into the staff elevators. When Lee is spotted by the throngs on the basement level, he is greeted by the applause of hundreds of people who have lined up to meet Christopher Lee.]

As I get set to make my goodbyes, I find myself officially drafted as both entourage member and semi-official security. For the next two hours, hundreds of people are shepherded to the man that they came to meet. Occasionally, someone will come up and say, "Who is that guy?" The answer is usually "He played Dracula in six movies, he's a horror movie legend, he's Christopher Lee." Or, as one middle-aged man in the crowd exclaimed, "He's the guy who gave me nightmares throughout my childhood." Lee is all these things and more. My hour alone with him showed me that he is a warm, gentle soul happy to sit with a fan and just chat. Afterwards, upon reflection, I realize that I did not ask about the Hammer Films, Peter Cushing, or many of the other items someone like me would love to hear someone like Christopher Lee reminisce about. I may have chided myself for not being more prepared to ask questions, but I never thought that I would get an hour alone with a living legend.

Credits: 1948: *Corridor of Mirrors* [Great Britain]; *Hamlet* (uncredited) [Great Britain]; *My Brother's Keeper* (scenes deleted) [Great Britain]; *One Night with You* [Great Britain]; *Penny and the Pownall Case* (short film) [Great Britain]; *Saraband for Dead Lovers* (a.k.a. *Saraband*) (uncredited) [Great Britain]; *Scott of the Antarctic* [Great Britain]; *Song of*

Lee strikes terror into the heart from the DVD cover of *The Satanic Rites of Dracula* (1973) (Hammer Films Productions/Warner Bros.).

Tomorrow [Great Britain]; 1949: *Trottie True* (a.k.a. *The Gay Lady*) [Great Britain]; 1950: *Prelude to Fame* [Great Britain]; *They Were Not Divided* [Great Britain]; 1951: *Captain Horatio Hornblower* [U.S.–Great Britain]; *Valley of the Eagles*; 1952: *Babes in Baghdad* [Great Britain–Spain–U.S.]; *The Crimson Pirate* (uncredited); *Innocents in Paris* (uncredited) [Great Britain]; *Mr. Potts Goes to Moscow* (a.k.a. *Top Secret*) (uncredited) [Great Britain]; *Moulin Rouge* (uncredited) [Great Britain]; *Paul Temple Returns* (a.k.a. *Bombay Waterfront*) [Great Britain]; 1953: *Douglas Fairbanks, Jr. Presents: Destination Milan* (03/25/53), *The Death of Michael Turbin* (11/18/53) (television); *Les Vacances De Monsieur Hulot* (a.k.a. *Mr. Hulot's Holiday*) (dubbed voices in English-language version) (uncredited) [France]; 1954: *Colonel March of Scotland Yard: At Night All Cats Are Grey* (10/04/54) (television) [Great Britain]; *Destination Milan* [Great Britain]; *Douglas Fairbanks, Jr. Presents: The International Settlement* (03/31/54) (television); 1955: *The Cockleshell Heroes* [Great Britain]; *Crossroads* (short film) [Great Britain]; *The Dark Avenger* (a.k.a. *The Warriors*); *Douglas Fairbanks, Jr. Presents: Border Incident* (01/26/55), *The Immigrant* (12/12/55) (television); *Final Column* (short film) [Great Britain]; *Man in Demand* (short film) [Great Britain]; *Moby Dick Rehearsed* (television) [Great Britain]; *Police Dog* [Great Britain]; *Storm Over the Nile* [Great Britain]; *That Lady* [Spain–Great Britain]; *The Vise: The Final Column* (01/14/55), *Price of Vanity* (05/20/55) (television) [Great Britain]; 1956: T*he Adventures of Aggie: Cut Glass* (television) [Great Britain]; *Alias John Preston* [Great Britain]; *The Battle of the River Plate* (a.k.a. *Pursuit of the Graf Spree*) [Great Britain]; *Beyond Mombassa* [Great Britain]; *Port Afrique* [Great Britain]; *Private's Progress* [Great Britain]; *Sailor of Fortune: The Desert Hostages* (10/19/56), *Stranger in Danger* (11/23/56) (television) [Great Britain]; *The Scarlet Pimpernel: The Elusive Chauvelin* (03/16/56) (television) [Great Britain]; 1957: *Bitter Victory* (a.k.a. *Amere Victoire*) [Great Britain–France]; *Assignment Foreign Legion: As We Forgive* (03/02/57), *The Anaya* (12/24/57) (television) [Great Britain]; *The Curse of Frankenstein* [Great Britain]; *Errol Flynn Theater: Evil Thoughts, Fortunes of War, Love Token,* and *The Model* (television) [Great Britain]; *Fortune Is a Woman* (a.k.a. *She Played with Fire*) [Great Britain]; *The Gay Cavalier: The Lady's Dilemma* (07/26/57) (television) [Great Britain]; *Night Ambush* (a.k.a. *Ill Met by Moonlight*) [Great Britain]; *Stowaway Girl* (a.k.a. *Manuela*) [Great Britain]; *The Traitor* (a.k.a. *The Accursed*) [Great Britain]; *The Truth About Women* [Great Britain]; 1958: *A Tale of Two Cities* [Great Britain]; *Dracula* (a.k.a. *Horror of Dracula*) [Great Britain]; *The Battle of the V.1* (a.k.a. *Missile from Hell*) [Great Britain–U.S.]; *Ivanhoe: The German Knight* (02/16/58) (television) [Great Britain]; *O.S.S.: Operation Firefly* (01/13/58) (television) [U.S.–Great Britain]; *White Hunter: The Hungry Hell* (03/01/58) (television) [Great Britain]; 1959: *The Hound of the Baskervilles* [Great Britain]; *The Man Who Could Cheat Death* [Great Britain]; *The Mummy* [Great Britain]; *Tempi Duri Per I Vampiri* (a.k.a. *Hard Times for Vampires* a.k.a. *Hard Times for Dracula* a.k.a. *Uncle Was a Vampire*) [Italy-France]; *The Treasure of San Teresa* (a.k.a. *Hot Money Girl* a.k.a. *Long Distance*) [Great Britain–West Germany]; *William Tell: Manhunt* (02/02/59) (television) [Great Britain]; 1960: *Beat Girl* (a.k.a. *Wild for Kicks*) [Great Britain]; *The City of the Dead* (a.k.a. *Horror Hotel*) [Great Britain]; *Tales of the Vikings: The Bull* (television); *Too Hot to Handle* (a.k.a. *Playgirl After Dark*) [Great Britain]; *The Two Faces of Dr. Jekyll* (a.k.a. *The Two Faces of Dr. Jekyll* a.k.a. *House of Fright*) [Great Britain]; 1961: *Alcoa Presents: One Step Beyond: The Sorcerer* (05/23/61) (television); *Ercole Al Centro Della Terra* (a.k.a. *Hercules at the Center of the Earth* a.k.a. *Hercules in the Haunted World*) [Italy]; *Das Geheimnis Der Gelben Narzissen* (a.k.a. *The Devil's Daffodil* [West Germany–Great Britain]); *The Im Namen Des Teufels* (a.k.a. *The Devil's Agent*) [West Germany–Great

Britain–Ireland]; *Les Mains D'Orlac* (a.k.a. *Hands of Orlac* a.k.a. *Hands of a Stranger* a.k.a. *Hands of the Strangler*) [France–Great Britain]; *Taste of Fear* (a.k.a. *Scream of Fear*) [Great Britain]; *The Terror of the Tongs* [Great Britain]; 1962: *Corridors of Blood* [Great Britain]; *Lolita* (uncredited: television footage from *The Curse of Frankenstein*) [U.S.–Great Britain]; *The Pirates of Blood River* [Great Britain]; *Das Ratsel Der Roten Orchidee* (a.k.a. *The Puzzle of the Red Orchid* a.k.a. *The Secret of the Red Orchid*) [West Germany]; *Sherlock Holmes Und Das Halsband Des Todes* (a.k.a. *Sherlock Holmes and the Deadly Necklace*) [West Germany–France–Italy]; *Stranglehold* [Great Britain]; 1963: *La Cripta E L'Incubo* (a.k.a. *Crypt of Horror* a.k.a. *La Maldicion De Los Karnsteins* a.k.a. *Terror in the Crypt*) [Spain-Italy]; *La Frusta E Il Corpo* (a.k.a. *The Whip and the Body* a.k.a. *What!*) [Italy-France]; *Katarsis* (a.k.a. *Sfida Al Diavolo*) [Italy]; *La Vergine Di Norimberga* (a.k.a. *The Virgin of Nuremberg* a.k.a. *Horror Castle*) [Italy]; 1964: *Il Castello Dei Morti Vivi* (a.k.a. *Castle of the Living Dead*) [Italy-France]; *The Devil-Ship Pirates* [Great Britain]; *The Gorgon* [Great Britain]; 1965: *Dr. Terror's House of Horrors* [Great Britain]; *The Face of Fu Manchu* [Great Britain–West Germany]; *She* [Great Britain]; *The Skull* [Great Britain]; 1966: *The Alfred Hitchcock Hour: The Sign of Satan* (05/08/64) (television); *The Brides of Fu Manchu* [Great Britain–West Germany]; *Dracula, Prince of Darkness* [Great Britain]; *Rasputin—The Mad Monk* [Great Britain]; *Das Ratsel Des Silbernen Derieck* (a.k.a. *Circus of Fear* a.k.a. *Psycho-Circus*) [Great Britain–West Germany]; *Theatre of Death* (a.k.a. *Blood Fiend*) [Great Britain]; 1967: *The Avengers: Never, Never Say Die* (03/18/67) (television) [Great Britain]; *Night of the Big Heat* (a.k.a. *Island of the Burning Damned* a.k.a. *Island of the Burning Doomed*) [Great Britain]; *Die Pagode Zum Funfen Schrecken* (a.k.a. *Five Golden Dragons*) [Great Britain–Liechtenstein–West Germany–Hong Kong?]; *Die Rache Des Dr. Fu Man Chu* (a.k.a. *The Vengeance of Dr. Fu Manchu*) [Great Britain–Ireland–West Germany–Hong Kong]; *Die Schlangengrube Und Das Pendel* (a.k.a. *The Snake Pit and the Pendulum* a.k.a. *The Blood Demon* a.k.a. *Castle of the Walking Dead*) [West Germany]; *Victims of Terror* (a.k.a. *Victims of Vesuvius*) (narrator) (television) [Great Britain]; 1968: *The Curse of the Crimson Altar* (a.k.a. *The Curse of the Crimson Cult* a.k.a. *The Crimson Altar* a.k.a. *The Crimson Cult*) [Great Britain]; *The Devil Rides Out* (a.k.a. *The Devil's Bride*) [Great Britain]; *Dracula Has Risen from the Grave* [Great Britain]; *The Face of Eve* (a.k.a. *Eve*) [Spain–Great Britain–Liechtenstein–U.S.]; *Die Todeskuss Des Dr. Fu Man Chu* (a.k.a. *Fu Manchu and the Kiss of Death* a.k.a. *Kiss of Death* a.k.a. *Kiss and Kill* a.k.a. *Against All Odds* a.k.a. *The Blood of Fu Manchu*) [Spain–West Germany–Great Britain–U.S.]; 1969: *The Avengers: The Interrogators* (01/01/69) (television) [Great Britain]; *Die Folterkammer Des Dr. Fu Man Chu* (a.k.a. *The Castle of Fu Manchu* a.k.a. *Assignment Istanbul*) [West Germany–Italy–Spain–Great Britain–Liechtenstein]; *Light Entertainment Killers* (television) [Great Britain]; *The Magic Christian* [Great Britain]; *The Oblong Box* (a.k.a. *Edgar Allan Poe's The Oblong Box*) [Great Britain]; *Scream and Scream Again* [Great Britain]; 1970: *El Conde Dracula* (a.k.a. *Count Dracula*) [Spain–West Germany–Italy–Great Britain]; *Die Jungfrau Und Die Peitsche* (a.k.a. *Eugenie* a.k.a. *Eugenie...The Story of Her Journey Into Perversion* a.k.a. *De Sade '70* a.k.a. *Philosophy in the Boudoir*) [Spain–West Germany]; *The House That Dripped Blood* [Great Britain]; *Julius Caesar* [Great Britain]; *One More Time* (uncredited) [Great Britain]; *The Private Life of Sherlock Holmes* [Great Britain]; *The Scars of Dracula* [Great Britain]; *Taste the Blood of Dracula* [Great Britain]; *Il Trono Di Fucoco* (a.k.a. *Der Hexentoter Von Blackmoor* a.k.a. *The Bloody Judge* a.k.a. *The Night of the Blood Monster* a.k.a. *The Throne of the Blood Monster*) [Italy–Spain–West Germany]; *El Umbracle* (documentary) (television) [Spain]; *Vampir* (a.k.a. *Cuadecuc, Vampir*) (Documentary) (television) [Spain]; 1971: *Hannie Caulder* [Great

Britain]; *I, Monster* [Great Britain]; 1972: *Death Line* (a.k.a. *Raw Meat*) [Great Britain]; *Dracula A.D. 1972* [Great Britain]; *Nothing But the Night* (a.k.a. *The Devil's Undead* a.k.a. *The Resurrection Syndicate*) [Great Britain]; 1973: *The Creeping Flesh* [Great Britain]; *Dark Places* [Great Britain]; *Panico En El Transiberiano* (a.k.a. *Panic on the Trans-Siberian Express* a.k.a. *Horror Express*) [Spain–Great Britain]; *Poor Devil* (television); *The Three Musketeers* (a.k.a. *The Three Musketeers: The Queen's Diamonds*) [Great Britain–U.S.–Spain?–Panama?]; *The Wicker Man* [Great Britain]; 1974: *The Four Musketeers* (a.k.a. *The Four Musketeers: Milady's Revenge*) [Great Britain–U.S.–Spain?–Panama?]; *Great Mysteries: The Leather Funnel* (07/13/74) (television) [Great Britain]; *The Man with the Golden Gun*; *The Satanic Rites of Dracula* (a.k.a. *Count Dracula and His Vampire Bride*) [Great Britain]; *This Is Your Life: Christopher Lee* (04/03/74) (television) [Great Britain]; 1975: *Le Boucher, La Star Et L'Orpheline* (a.k.a. *The Butcher, the Star, and the Orphan*) [France]; *Diagnosis: Murder* [Great Britain]; *Vem Var Dracula?* (a.k.a. *In Search of Dracula*) (television) [Sweden–France–Great Britain]; 1976: *Albino* (a.k.a. *The Night of the Askari* a.k.a. *Whispering Death*) [West Germany–Great Britain–South Africa–Zimbabwe]; *Dracula Pere Et Fils* (a.k.a. *Dracula and Son*) [France]; *The Keeper* [Canada]; *Killer Force* (a.k.a. *The Diamond Mercenaries*) [Ireland–Switzerland–South Africa–U.S.]; *Space: 1999: Earthbound* (01/23/76) (television) [Great Britain–U.S.–Italy]; *To the Devil a Daughter* (a.k.a. *To the Devil...a Daughter*) [Great Britain–West Germany]; 1977: *Airport '77*; *End of the World*; *Meatcleaver Massacre* (a.k.a. *Evil Force* a.k.a. *The Hollywood Meatcleaver Massacre*); *Starship Invasions* [Canada]; 1978: *Caravans* [U.S.–Iran]; *Circle of Iron* (a.k.a. *The Silent Flute*); *How the West Was Won* (television); *The Pirate* (a.k.a. *Harold Robbins' The Pirate*); *Return from Witch Mountain*; *Saturday Night Live* (host) (television) (03/25/78); 1979: *An Arabian Adventure* [Great Britain]; *Bear Island* (a.k.a. *Alistair MacLean's Bear Island*) [Great Britain–Canada]; *Captain America II: Death Too Soon* (television); *Jaguar Lives!* [Great Britain–U.S.];*1941*; *Nutcracker Fantasy* (animated) [Japan]; *The Passage* [Great Britain]; 1980: *The American Movie Awards* (television); *Charlie's Angels: Angel in Hiding* (11/16/80) (television); *Once Upon a Spy* (television); *Serial*; 1981: *Desperate Moves* (a.k.a. *Steigler and Steigler*) [Italy]; *Evil Stalks This House* (a.k.a. *Tales of the Haunted*) (television) [U.S.–Canada]; *An Eye for an Eye*; *Goliath Awaits* (television); *Safari 3000*; *La Salamandra* (a.k.a. *The Salamander*) [Italy–U.S.–Great Britain]; 1982: *Charles & Diana: A Royal Love Story* (television) [U.S.–Great Britain]; *Das Letzte Einhorn* (a.k.a. *The Last Unicorn*) [U.S.–Great Britain–Japan–West Germany]; *Massarati and the Brain* (television); 1983: *House of the Long Shadows* [Great Britain]; *New Magic* (short film advertising Showscan special effects); *The Return of Captain Invincible* [Australia]; 1984: *Faerie Tale Theatre: The Boy Who Left Home to Find Out About the Shivers* (09/17/84) (television); *The Far Pavilions* (television) [Great Britain–Italy–U.S.–West Germany]; *The Rosebud Beach Hotel*; 1985: *Howling II: Stirba—Werewolf Bitch* (a.k.a. *Howling II: Your Sister Is a Werewolf*) [U.S.–Great Britain]; *Mask of Murder* [Canada-Sweden]; 1986: *The Disputation* (television) [Great Britain]; *The Girl* [Sweden–Great Britain]; *Un Metier Du Seigneur* (a.k.a. *Der Verrater*) [Italy–France–West Germany]; *Shaka Zulu* (television) [U.S.–Italy–Australia–South Africa–West Germany]; *Valhalla* (animated) (voice only) [Denmark]; 1987: *Jocks* (a.k.a. *Road Trip*); *Mio Min Mio* (a.k.a. *Mio in the Land of Faraway* a.k.a. *The Land of Faraway*) [Sweden–Soviet Union–Norway]; *Wetten, Dass...?: Wetten, Dass...? Aus Kiel* (10/31/87) (television) [West Germany]; 1988: *Dark Mission (Operacion Cocaina)* (a.k.a. *Dark Mission: Les Fleurs Du Mal* a.k.a. *Dark Mission: Flowers of Evil*) [Spain-France]; 1989: *Around the World in 80 Days* (television) [U.S.–Italy–West Germany–Yugoslavia]; *La Chute Des Aigles* (a.k.a. *The Fall of the Eagles*) [France-Belgium];

Murder Story [Netherlands–Great Britain]; *The Return of the Musketeers* [Great Britain–France–Spain]; *La Revolution Francaise* (a.k.a. *The French Revolution*) [France–Italy–West Germany–Canada–Great Britain]; 1990: *L'Avaro* (a.k.a. *The Miser*) [Italy-France-Spain]; *The Care of Time* (television) [Great Britain]; *Gremlins 2: The New Batch*; *Honeymoon Academy*; *The Rainbow Thief* [Great Britain]; *This Is Your Life: Peter Cushing* (02/21/90) (television) [Great Britain]; *Treasure Island* [Great Britain–U.S.]; 1991: *Curse III: Blood Sacrifice* [Great Britain–South Africa]; *Fear in the Dark* (television); *Incident at Victoria Falls* (a.k.a. *Sherlock Holmes and the Incident at Victoria Falls* a.k.a. *Sherlock Holmes: The Star of Africa*) (television) [Great Britain–Italy–Belgium–Luxembourg–France–U.S.]; *Wahre Wunder* (television) (host) [Germany]; 1992: *Double Vision* (television) [Canada–France–Great Britain–Germany]; *Jackpot* (a.k.a. *Cyber Eden*) [Italy-France]; *Kabuto* (a.k.a. *Shogun Warrior*) [Japan–U.S.–Great Britain]; *Sherlock Holmes and the Leading Lady* (television) [Great Britain–France–Italy–Belgium–Luxembourg–U.S.]; *The Young Indiana Jones Chronicles: Austria, March 1917* (09/21/92) (television); 1993: *Death Train* (a.k.a. *Alistair MacLean's Death Train* a.k.a. *Detonator*) (television) [U.S.–Great Britain]; 1994: *A Feast at Midnight* [Great Britain]; *Flesh and Blood: The Hammer Heritage of Horror* (television-video) (co-host) [U.S.–Great Britain]; *Funnyman* (a.k.a. *Funny Man*) [Great Britain]; *Ghosts* (video game) (voice) [Great Britain]; *Police Academy 7: Mission to Moscow*; *The Vampire Interviews* (video); 1995: *The Tomorrow People: The Ramses Connection: Part 1* (01/04/95), *The Ramses Connection: Part 2* (01/11/95), *The Ramses Connection: Part 3* (01/18/95), *The Ramses Connection: Part 4* (01/25/95), *The Ramses Connection: Part 5* (02/01/95) (television) [Great Britain]; 1996: *The Blue Heelers: Miss Mount Thomas* (11/19/96) (television) [Australia]; *A Century of Science Fiction* (video); *The Many Faces of Christopher Lee* (video) [Great Britain]; *Moses* (a.k.a. *The Bible: Moses*) (television) [U.S.–Czech Republic–Great Britain–France–Italy–Germany–Spain]; *100 Years of Horror* (video) (host); *100 Years of Horror: The Aristocrats of Evil* (video) (host); *100 Years of Horror: The Count and Company* (video) (host); *100 Years of Horror: The Double Demons* (video) (host); *100 Years of Horror: The Evil Unseeable* (video) (host); *100 Years of Horror: The Frankenstein Family* (video) (host); *100 Years of Horror: Freaks* (video) (host); *100 Years of Horror: Giants and Dinosaurs* (video) (host); *100 Years of Horror: Maniacs* (video) (host); *100 Years of Horror: The Monster Makers* (video) (host); *100 Years of Horror: Scream Queens* (video) (host); *100 Years of Horror: Sorcerers* (video) (host); *100 Years of Horror: The Walking Dead* (video) (host); *100 Years of Horror: Witchcraft and Demons* (video) (host); *La Sorellina E Il Principe Del Sogno* (a.k.a. *Prinzessin Alisea*) (television) [Italy-Germany]; *Soul Music* (animated) (television) [Great Britain]; *The Stupids* [U.S.–Great Britain]; *Welcome to the Discworld* (short film): pilot [Great Britain]; *The Wyrd Sisters* (animated) (voice only) (television) [Great Britain]; 1997: *A–Z of Horror* (a.k.a. *Clive Barker's A–Z of Horror*) (television); *The Blue Heelers: Gold* (04/29/97) (television) [Australia]; *Ivanhoe* (television) [Great Britain–U.S.]; *The New Adventures of Robin Hood: Robin and the Golden Arrow* (01/27/97), *A Race Against Death* (02/03/97), *The Legend of Olwyn* (02/24/97), *Nightmare of the Magic Castle* (04/07/97), *The Scepter* (10/11/97) (television) [France–U.S.–Netherlands–Great Britain]; *Strictly Supernatural* (host) (television); *The Odyssey* (a.k.a. *Odissea*) (television) [Turkey–Malta–Italy–Great Britain–Germany–Greece–U.S.]; 1998: *The Blue Heelers: All in the Family* (11/04/98) [Australia]; *Dare to Dream* (television) (documentary on the making of the film *Jinnah*) [Pakistan]; *The New Adventures of Robin Hood: The Auction* (12/13/98) [France–U.S.–Netherlands–Great Britain]; *Tale of the Mummy* (a.k.a. *Talos the Mummy*) [U.S.–Luxembourg–Great Britain]; 1999: *The Adventures of Young Indiana Jones: Adventures in the Secret Service* (video); *The*

Blue Heelers: Lies and Whispers (05/12/99) (television) [Australia]; *Jinnah* [Great Britain–Pakistan]; *The Rocky Interactive Horror Show* (video game) (narrator) [Great Britain?]; *Sleepy Hollow*; 2000: *Death of an Empire* (narrator) (television) [Ukraine]; *Ghost Stories for Christmas* (a.k.a. *Christopher Lee's Ghost Stories for Christmas*) [Great Britain]; *Gormenghast* (television) [Great Britain–Canada–U.S.]; *Ian Fleming: 007's Creator* (video supplement); *In the Beginning* (television); *Inside "The Man with the Golden Gun"* (video supplement); *Legends* (television) [Great Britain]; *Sleepy Hollow: Behind the Legend* (video supplement); *Turning Points*; 2001: *The Big Breakfast* (12/11/01) (television) [Great Britain]; *Burnt Offering: The Cult of the Wicker Man* (video supplement) [Great Britain]; *Conquest: Frontier Wars* (video game) (voice); *The Lord of the Rings: The Fellowship of the Ring* [U.S.–New Zealand]; *National Geographic: Beyond the Movie—The Lord of the Rings* (television); *Once Upon a Time in Europe* (television) [Spain]; *A Passage to Middle-Earth: The Making of "The Lord of the Rings"* (video supplement); *The Quest for the Ring* (television/video supplement); *R2D2: Beneath the Dome* (television/video supplement) (uncredited); *Les Redoutables: Confession* (television) [France]; *The Wicker Man Enigma* (video supplement); 2002: *Actor's Notebook: Christopher Lee* (video supplement); *Best Ever Bond* (television) [Great Britain]; *From Puppets to Pixels: Digital Characters in Episode II* (a.k.a. *From Puppets to Pixels: Digital Characters in Star Wars Episode II*) (video supplement); *The Heaven and Earth Show* (06/23/02) [Great Britain]; *James Bond: A BAFTA Tribute* (television) [Great Britain]; *Leute Heute* (05/27/02) (television) [Germany]; *The Lord of the Rings: The Two Towers* [U.S.–New Zealand–Germany]; *The Lord of the Rings: The Two Towers* (video game) (voice); *Star Wars: Episode II—Attack of the Clones*; *To the Devil...The Death of Hammer* (video supplement); 2003: *Breakfast* (11/11/03) (television) [Great Britain]; *Christopher Lee: A Life in Films* (television) [Great Britain]; *Dracula's Bram Stoker* (television) [Ireland]; *Freelancer* (video game) (voice) [Canada-U.S.]; *From Hollywood to Borehamwood* (television) [Great Britain]; *The Lord of the Rings: The Return of the King* [U.S.–New Zealand–Germany]; *The Lord of the Rings: The Return of the King* (video game) (voice); *The Making of a Legend* (video) (documentary) [Great Britain]; *National Geographic: Beyond the Movie—The Lord of the Rings: Return of the King* (television); *The 100 Greatest Movie Stars* (television) [Great Britain]; *Richard & Judy* (11/04/03) (television) [Great Britain]; *This Morning* (11/12/03) (television) [Great Britain]; 2004: *Everquest II* (video game) (voice); *Goldeneye: Rogue Agent* (video game) (voice); *Greasepaint and Gore: The Hammer Monsters of Phil Leakey* (television) [Great Britain]; *Greasepaint and Gore, Part 2: The Hammer Monsters of Roy Ashton* (television) [Great Britain]; *The Lord of the Rings: The Battle for Middle-Earth* (video game) (voice); *The Lord of the Rings: The Third Age* (video game) (voice); *Les Rivieres Pourpres II—Les Anges De L'Apocalypse* (a.k.a. *The Crimson Rivers 2—The Angels of the Apocalypse*) [France–Italy–Great Britain]; *The Ultimate Film* (television) [Great Britain]; 2005: *Charlie and the Chocolate Factory* [U.S.–Great Britain–Australia]; *Corpse Bride* (a.k.a. *Tim Burton's Corpse Bride*) [U.S.–Great Britain]; *Greyfriar's Bobby* [Great Britain]; *Star Wars: Feel the Force* (television) [Great Britain]; *Star Wars: Episode III—The Revenge of the Sith* [U.S.–Great Britain]; 2006: *The Last Unicorn* (animated) [South Africa–U.S.–Great Britain]; *Cowboys for Christ* (a.k.a. *May Day* a.k.a. *The Riding of the Laddie*) [Great Britain]; *Pope John Paul II* (television) [Italy-U.S.]; 2008: *The Heavy*.

Marrie Lee

Asian actress Marrie Lee was one of the original female action stars of the seventies, although for years, few outside of a small group of hardcore fans knew about her series of deliriously entertaining action movies about an attractive, martial arts–trained Interpol agent named Cleopatra Wong. Approached by Philippine producers to star in a film, Singapore native Lee, whose real name is actually Doris Young Siew Keen, saw her life change before her very own eyes as she was introduced to the world as an actress with a pseudonymous name to create some sort of false impression of a familial relation to the late actor Bruce Lee. The movies in which she starred as the lithe, heroic Cleopatra Wong, kicking, punching, and outwitting many a villain, are *They Call Her... Cleopatra Wong*, *The Devil's Three*, and *Dynamite Johnson: Bionic Boy*.

Although distributed theatrically worldwide when they were first produced, the Cleopatra Wong films began to achieve a certain kind of cult status notoriety with fans of unusual action movies from countries such as the U.S. and Europe. When interest in Hong Kong action films abated in the late eighties–early nineties, genre film fans who had nearly exhausted the Chinese cinematic genre discovered the wealth of Philippine-produced action movies that existed; resultantly, screenings of the Cleopatra Wong series elevated Marrie Lee to the ranks of a true cult film icon. The Cleopatra Wong titles also received videocassette distribution throughout the world in the early eighties through a variety of sources. Today, due to the demise of the videocassette format, collectors will be hard put to track down and locate any of these titles in used VHS bins, driving up the prices of such items on Internet auction sites like eBay.

The first and best film in the series, *They Call Her... Cleopatra Wong* featured Lee as an international Interpol agent assigned to crack a counterfeiting group, whose sole objective was to destabilize the currencies of Singapore, Malaysia, Indonesia, Thailand and the Philippines. It took a smart, sexy, and deadly woman to combat this European-led assault on these Asian countries. In the sequel, *The Devil's Three* (also popularly known as *The Devil's Angels*), an underworld kingpin's daughter is kidnapped by his own men. For help, he turns to his archenemy, Interpol agent Cleopatra Wong, who brings along a special team (including a heavyset female psychic, and a fey female impersonator). Although the comedy element is obviously apparent, there is still plenty of action. In the third (and most unusual) film of the series, Cleopatra Wong takes a backseat to real-life nine-year-old karate champion Johnson Yap. In *Dynamite Johnson: Bionic Boy*, Yap co-stars as Cleopatra's nephew. After he is outfitted with bionic legs, arms and ears, he joins Cleopatra on a mission to combat a neo–Nazi with plans for world domination. His uranium mine is guarded by a mechanical fire-breathing dragon, which also launches rockets from its eyes and machine gun bullets from its tail. Insane action cinema from the East rarely got better than this.

Lee soon stood tall alongside other familiar female action star heroines like Angela Mao-ying, Pam Grier, and Tamara Dobson, who portrayed the tall, thin martial arts fighting agent Cleopatra Jones, (the American namesake of the Cleopatra Wong character who appeared in two blaxploitation films in the seventies).

Lee was born Doris Young Siew Keen on November 25, 1959, in Singapore. Growing up in a home with an older brother and sister, Marrie never had to vie for familial attention, as she was the youngest child. After her parents passed away, Marrie, who had just completed high school, took several jobs to supplement her income. Then she was discovered by a movie producer who offered her the leading role in a film.

After her first taste of acting, Marrie responded to an advertisement for a local Singaporean woman to play the leading role in a film. She spent the next three years making film after film in the Philippines and then retired from acting in 1981. After her acting career ended, she formed and managed a dance troupe called The Devil's Angels (named for characters from one of her Cleopatra Wong films) for two years, and then married and raised a family.

Marrie returned to the fulltime use of her birth name, Doris Young, and then successfully entered the world of business accounting, finance, sales and marketing, and created her own business ventures. In recent years, attention to the Cleopatra Wong films has grown to the point where even the American filmmaker Quentin Tarantino managed a homage to the Cleopatra Wong films with his epic two-part *Kill Bill Volume 1* and *Kill Bill Volume 2* (2003, 2004); the similarities are obvious. In the *Kill Bill* films, Uma Thurman wears a striped tracksuit and motorcycle helmet, and uses a sword adroitly, just like Cleo Wong. Even some of Uma's character's basic fighting skills can be traced back to the Cleopatra Wong films. Tarantino admitted that the similarity was intentional in interviews conducted near the release of the *Kill Bill* films.

Now living in her native country, Marrie runs a successful health supplements wholesale business in Singapore, in relative anonymity. She graciously answered my questions about acting in the Philippine film industry, and most importantly, the Cleopatra Wong films. The Singapore Film Commission also recently honored her for her role in the Cleopatra Wong films, and for contributing to Singaporean cinema in general, as the Cleo Wong films were a co-production between the Philippines and Singapore. Suddenly, even in Singapore, younger film audiences interested in the country's cultural cinematic history are finding out about these films; and thanks to Quentin Tarantino, people everywhere else are attempting to track down and watch one of the inspirations for the *Kill Bill* films.

After Marrie and I corresponded via letters and emails for a number of years, in the Spring of 2006 I learned that, due to the renewed interest in the Cleopatra Wong films, Marrie has returned to the acting fold. Reuniting with the original producer of the Cleopatra Wong films, she will once again return to the screen in *The Vengeance of Cleopatra Wong*. Slated to be filmed in Singapore and the Philippines, the action film will co-star Australian martial artist and actor Gary Daniels (who appeared in a number of Hong Kong–produced films opposite Jackie Chan in the eighties). The film is slated to revolve around the death of the daughter of the retired Cleopatra Wong, who undergoes a startling transformation and seeks revenge. Marrie also co-produced the film (utilizing the

"D'Young Films International" banner name), from an unproduced script titled *Lady Executioner*, written by producer Bobby Suarez. Marrie may also appear in yet another action film, tentatively titled *Wandering Samurai* (alongside Franco Guerrero in the leading role), but the production of the new Cleopatra Wong film awaits and there are many genre film fans who are anxious to see it.

Here is what Marrie Lee a.k.a. Doris Young had to say about it all…

Q: Can you give some personal background information about yourself, and tell us how you first became involved in films?

Marrie Lee: I was born in Singapore on November 25, 1959, the third child of John and Mary Young. My full name is Doris Young Siew Keen. My dad was a contractor who built one of the neighborhood cinemas, and being familiar with the owners, he would bring us to the movies whenever there was a new film showing. Whether the film was good or bad, it just became a regular family outing. Those days, it was quite common for film distributors to bring in Hong Kong actors and

A luminescent Marrie Lee circa 1978. (Photo courtesy Marrie Lee)

actresses to promote the screening of their movies, and I got to meet many of them. I was probably four or five then. I have always wanted to be like them, and made acting one of my life's goals. When I was just out of high school, I was working in a restaurant as a receptionist, and a Hong Kong film producer spotted me. He offered me a small role in one of his movies that were filmed on location in Singapore. That was my first taste of acting. It was a small part, and I played a lady detective. I cannot even remember the name of the movie as it was filmed in Chinese, maybe something like *Showdown at the Equator*. I then got some other small parts in a couple of films too. A year later, I saw an advertisement looking for a local unknown to make the movie *Cleopatra Wong, Interpol Agent*, and I went for the interview. The producers were looking for a new face among the 300 or so hopefuls, and I guess I was lucky to clinch it. Maybe I was considered tall for an Asian, maybe it was because I could ride a motorbike, but I think most of all, the producers liked the fact that my face was photogenic. I was only seventeen, but could pass for a person in their early twenties, and had quite a serious face, which was suitable for a no-nonsense Interpol agent. I did not have any formal grading in martial arts, but my brother, who was a black belt karateka, trained me. The first thing the producers did when I arrived in the Philippines was to put me on a regular training schedule with a sixth degree black belter martial arts instructor who was also our martial arts director on the movie set. Throughout the three years I was there filming, he trained me continuously, but this fighting style was more adapted for the cinema.

Q: According to the credits for that first film, *They Call Her... Cleopatra Wong*, this was your first featured role in a film using the Marrie Lee name. Is this true and, if so, was the name imposed upon you by the producers of the film?

Lee: Yes, that is correct; my producers did not like the name Doris Young. They said it was not glamorous enough, and chose the name Marrie Lee. Marrie spelled with a double R so that it's not so common, and Lee because the only Chinese actor that made it big in the West at that time was Bruce Lee, probably hoping that the name, Lee, would rub off some of its fame onto me. I did have strangers walking up to me during the filming, exclaiming that they have watched all my brother's movies.

Q: What can you recall about the Philippine film industry in general during the time that these films were made?

Lee: At that time, many low-budget movies, quickies as they were called back then, were made. They were called Bakie, so-called for the Bakia crowd. Bakia is a localized Filipino term for the generally low-income, low-education majority. Action, and hot and steamy romance movies were the "in" thing back then, and I do not suppose that it has changed much since. Of course, technologically, and cinematically, the Philippine film industry was more advanced at that time than my birth country, Singapore, which did not even have a proper film industry. In Singapore, even television production was then, in its infancy. As far as the Philippine film industry was concerned, there were no proper guidelines with regards to safety. I don't remember the producers buying insurance for me while I working for them, and I did a lot of my own stunts, which gave me injuries I sustained up to this day. Glass used then for stunts, it was not the candy glass type used in Hollywood productions, but the shatterproof type; I still have a cut at the back of my knee when I had to jump through one such window back then.

I remember one old man who was the special effects person on one of the Cleopatra Wong films. He was very shy, and kept very much to himself. Well, the next movie with another company that he worked on after the first *Cleopatra Wong* film... I heard that he was blown up due to carelessness, with no insurance compensation for his family. Another thing that I remember was that our soundman was promoted to the production manager. He was an old man, past sixty years of age, and as the soundman, he was always sitting down, with his sound equipment. As a production manager, he had to go chasing after everybody, and run around. The last time I saw him, he was running after the cab I was in while we were filming a scene from *Dynamite Johnson: Bionic Boy* to make sure that I had a drink of water. The next thing, he was on the ground, foaming at the mouth. He died that same night. The doctors said that he died from heat stroke. The irony was that he was trying to make sure that I had something to drink. I cried for days afterwards. Oh

Was the world ready for the ultimate Asian heroine? *They Call Her...Cleopatra Wong* (1978) (BAS Film Productions Ltd.) (Original poster reproduction courtesy Marrie Lee).

gosh, as I start recollecting, some of the things I have encountered really made me so disillusioned with life. I tend to get a bit jaded, sorry.

Q: Were there more than the three Cleopatra Wong films that I know about?

Lee: We did shoot parts of a fourth movie called *The Vengeance of Cleopatra Wong*, but things did not work out between Bobby Suarez, the producer, and his Malaysian partners, and we had to abandon the project. We went on to shoot *The Devil's Three* instead. My contract ended, and I returned to Singapore. We could not agree on the terms of the new contract so I did not renew my contract with Bobby Suarez. The funny thing is, back then, all those years ago, we were supposed to shoot a movie entitled *The Vengeance of Cleopatra Wong*, which is the movie that we are going to shoot now, 26 years down the line.

Q: Are there any particular anecdotes that you would like to share about the making of these movies?

Lee: On *Dynamite Johnson*, Bobby Suarez, the director, was with the high-speed camera team, and had two assistant directors. One was in the helicopter, and the other on the ground level. Normally we have a rehearsal before rolling the cameras but in this case, since the special effects dragon was made to only explode once, Bobby decided to film it without a rehearsal. So after the explosion, and the take, Bobby made the thumbs-up signal to the assistant in the helicopter, who returned thumbs-up. The other assistant director, Pepito Diaz, gave the thumbs-*down* though. He thought it was a rehearsal, and did not roll the camera. Bobby had a fit. It was no laughing matter at that time but thinking back it was really comical to see Bobby throw down his cap and run down the ledge chasing after Pepito. We all thought that he would probably kill him if he caught him. Luckily, Pepito was a better runner, and they ended up running around in circles.

Q: Is it true that Bobby Suarez, the producer-director of these films, also took on a supporting acting role?

Lee: Bobby never showed his face on film if he could help it. He would not even let his photo be taken. He had this great big fear that if his face were shown in the tabloids, he would put himself and his family in risk of being kidnapped or come to possible harm. I did not blame him, though. At that time, there were some well-known show business personalities who were kidnapped for ransom. He directed most of these films himself, and I remember him doing a small role, as a pilot, in *Dynamite Johnson*, but with his face well covered. I remember him telling a story about how he came to Hong Kong many years before with just a small suitcase and a film to sell. He was so poor, he slept overnight in a railway station. Bobby is very charismatic. He had a vision, and he could convince people to see his vision and work for him. He could be a slave driver, but he can be nice and warm too.

Q: What other acting credits do you have?

Lee: The other movies I made, I consider so small, that they are not worth mentioning.

Q: Have you really retired from acting, and when did this happen?

Lee: I retired in 1980, when my contract with BAS Film Productions ended. I had an offer to make a television pilot in the U.S., supposedly the first episode of a series, if it was successful. The title was *Charlie Chan's No. 1 Daughter*. Everything was discussed and agreed upon, and I was supposed to go to Hawaii for the filming of the first episode, but that was when the industry's [actors. musicians, scriptwriters, etc.] strikes began in 1980–81, and you know what happened, right? The entire Hollywood industry was at a standstill. [By the time] it was resolved, I was already married, and my husband then did not want me to go.

Q: Are you aware that there is a cult of interest in these Cleopatra Wong films, especially in Australia and America?

Lee: No, I was not aware of this when you first contacted me in 2001. That was why I was very surprised that copies of my movies are still available. Today, I have learned that there exists great interest in my work of the past, and recognition for what I have done. Any performer will tell you, they will never be tired of an audience. Whether it was back in the seventies or now, recognition will always be just as welcome and appreciated.

Credits: 1978: *They Call Her Cleopatra Wong* (a.k.a. *Cleopatra Wong* a.k.a. *The Female Big Boss*) [Philippines-Singapore]; 1979: *The Devil's Three* (a.k.a. *The Devil's Three: The Karate Killers* a.k.a. *Pay or Die* a.k.a. *Mean Business*) [Philippines-Singapore]; 1980: *Dynamite Johnson* (a.k.a. *Dynamite Johnson: Bionic Boy*) [Hong Kong–Philippines–Singapore]; 2007: *The Vengeance of Cleopatra Wong*.

Valerie Leon

Valerie Leon was born on November 12, 1945, in London, England. The tall (5'11"), statuesque brunette became for a brief period, one of the most startling finds in British horror cinema with her performance in the Hammer film production, *Blood from the Mummy's Tomb* (1971). Leon had prior cinema, stage, and television experience, but her leading role in this movie, which was produced near the end of the cycle of successful genre pictures made by the notable, influential British film company, brought her immediate genre stardom.

She played the dual roles of Queen Tera, an Egyptian princess, and Margaret Fuchs, her reincarnated self born centuries later. Cinema audiences were struck by Leon's icy, cold, and tempestuous performance as the undead Egyptian goddess as well as her performance as a woman unable to come to terms with a hereditary horror that has turned her world inside out. Better yet was the seldom-equaled, erotically charged cinematic attention paid to the actress' voluptuous body. Surely, of all the Hammer actresses whose visage became synonymous with sex and blood, Valerie Leon was an actress that few moviegoers would forget.

Sadly, her career took a downward turn with appearances as nearly forgettable sex objects desired by many men in a number of British sex comedies of the early seventies. She appeared in at least six films in the then-popular *Carry On* series, but her roles onscreen ended up with her last few film roles relegated to those of the sensual mature woman in the romantic thrall of a younger leading man. She briefly appeared with Roger Moore in *The Spy Who Loved Me* (1977), Peter Sellers in *The Revenge of the Pink Panther* (1978), and Sean Connery in *Never Say Never Again* (1983); she is one of a select group of actresses who can lay claim to appearing in more than one James Bond film, although with different actors portraying the lead.

Q: Why did you go into the acting profession?

Valerie Leon: When I was a child, I was always what one might call stage-struck. I recall it all began when I was working at the Harrods department store in London as a fashion buyer in training. I was reading the trade magazine, *The Stage*, and I saw an advertisement for chorus singers who were wanted for a touring production of *The Belle of New York*. I played truant from what was going to be a very respectable job for this store, and went off for the audition, and got the part of a chorus singer. I chose to give up working at Harrods and launched, wholeheartedly, into a career in show business. Unfortunately, this musical show, which I thought was going to be a fantastic introduction into the world of show business, only lasted six weeks. When it folded, I ended up on the dole, without a job, and did not know what to do. I eventually went back to the theater, where I started. I got into the West End stage production of *Funny Girl* with Barbra Streisand. That was a great decision that I made, and working on *Funny Girl* onstage led to me getting an agent, and to subsequently getting roles in television shows like *The Avengers, The Baron, Randall and Hopkirk Deceased,* and *The Saint.* So, that sort of started me off.

Q: The movie, *Smashing Time* (1967), seems to be one of your first feature film appearances.
Leon: I do not recall that movie. Do you have that down in my credits?

Q: Yes. The film starred Rita Tushingham. Maybe you had a walk-on role or were an extra.
Leon: What happened was, I started out as an extra in the sixties, and I was always being picked out for a line or a few bits. Sometimes, they needed to fill the role of a very naughty-looking or very sexy girl in the background or in a party scene, or what have you. I think that if I were indeed in *Smashing Time,* that it might have been one of the movies where I had a very, very tiny role.

Q: You appeared in quite a number of the *Carry On* films.
Leon: In England, the *Carry On* films were very successful. I started off as one of the harem girls in *Carry On Up the Khyber,* and that was worth quite a few weeks of work, and then because I appeared in that film, I had to do a lot of publicity, an almost mini-tour of England, to promote the movie. I graduated to uttering two lines in *Carry on Camping,* showing Charlie Hawtrey how to "erect" his tent [*laughter*]. In *Carry on Again, Doctor,* I had a scene with Jim Dale where I was coming on really strong, and he was acting totally somewhat bemused. With each *Carry On* film I appeared in, I graduated to having more and more to do.

Q: You had a substantial role in *Carry On Up the Jungle.*
Leon: I was the leader of this Amazonian tribe of women. In *Carry on Matron,* I gave birth to triplets. In *Carry on Girls,* I started really plain, a bit frumpy. In that film, Bernard Bresslaw played my fiancée. Then Barbara Windsor helps to sort of create a beauty queen out of me. They were great fun to do, those movies. I also appeared in *Carry on Stuffing* in 1972, which was a Christmas television special that featured a lot of the *Carry On* alumni.

Q: We never got to see too many of those *Carry On* films here in the States, they were considered either too ribald or too British for American audiences. Was there a favorite *Carry On* role for you?
Leon: Yes, I think the one role I had in *Carry On Up the Jungle* was my favorite, although in *Carry On Girls,* there was a bigger part for me. I really enjoyed working on *Carry On Up the Jungle.*

Q: *Zeta One,* which is also known as *The Alien Factor,* has become a cult favorite everywhere.
Leon: I know!

Q: Do you recall anything about that film?
Leon: Yes, I do! I recall being freezing! We filmed it in the winter, primarily on outdoor locations, and I was dressed in a sort of very skimpy white skin suit.

Q: Like a jump suit?
Leon: Yes, all the strategic parts of my body were covered with ropes and things. I

Valerie Leon appears to be tangling with herself in this scene from the Hammer horror film, *Blood from the Mummy's Tomb* (1971) (Hammer Film Productions Ltd./EMI Films Ltd./American International Pictures).

think, actually, in one scene, I wore absolutely nothing except some sort of fabric or tape covering over my nipples. I was always very, very cold. That is one thing I remember more than anything else about that movie, that it was very cold when we filmed it. It is a very weird movie because it's sort of a sci-fi flick, and then it is almost sort of a soft porn movie, and then it is a sci-fi take-off of the James Bond films. It is a bit of everything, isn't it really?

Q: If I recall correctly, one of the versions of the movie opens with a strip poker scene between the male leads [Robin Hawdon as a low-rent Bond manqué named James Word] and a woman [Danish-born Hammer Films starlet Yutte Stensgaard]. In essence, this paved the way for the rest of the movie to go off into absolutely any zany direction at all. The sort of movie I would call cheesy fun.

Leon: I would agree with you there.

Q: Can you recall how you got the leading role in *Blood from the Mummy's Tomb?*

Leon: I auditioned for the role. I did a screen test, and there were a few of us who were chosen for the final count. I had met Sir James Carreras, who was head of Hammer; I did a bit of charity work for him around that period, but whether he put my name forward or not, I do not really know. Nevertheless, I did screen test for it, and won the part, but it did turn out to be a jinxed movie.

Promotional poster for Leon's *Blood from the Mummy's Tomb* (1971) (Hammer Film Productions Ltd./EMI Films Ltd./American International Pictures).

It was my first leading role. I was thrilled that the director was Seth Holt who had directed *Danger Route*. He was a very good director, very much respected, and I had worked with him previously, doing a walk-on part in a movie years previous, in France. I stood in for Julie Newmar or somebody. I think the film was called *Monsieur Lecoq*, and was produced by Carl Foreman. However, I do not think that that movie ever saw the light of day; I do not think it was ever finished, or *something* happened. But I remembered Seth from that experience, and he was directing *Blood from the Mummy's Tomb*. On my very first day of shooting on the movie, I had scenes with Peter Cushing, who played my father. We did an entire day of shooting, and he was lovely, very helpful, of course, as always— he was a gentleman. At the end of the day he heard that his wife was really, really sick, she was so sick that he had to leave the picture. The rest of the shoot had to be rearranged, and those scenes were very hastily rescheduled as they went on a search for another actor for the role. Andrew Keir replaced him.

Q: I have seen stills of Cushing and yourself from this one day of shooting. It appears that there was quite a bit of footage shot that day.

Leon: Absolutely. The whole business where my father gives me the ring for my twenty-first birthday was shot on that day. It was a very sad experience, but Andrew Keir took over, and he was helpful as well, so everything worked out fine... for a while. But then a week before completion of the film, Seth Holt had taken ill, and then he suddenly died. I was devastated. Michael Carreras, the son of Sir James, took over the filming. You know, these things were done on a really, really low budget, and therefore on a really, really tight filming schedule, and they really wanted to finish the film. Therefore, unbelievably, I was not allowed to go to the funeral of my own director because I was still shooting my scenes with the replacement director, Michael Carreras.

Q: What did you think of the completed film?

Leon: I know they had a lot of trouble editing it because when Seth had shot the film he had a certain vision for it in his mind. He was like that, known for keeping the editing of the movie within his own mind. We had many wonderful scenes, he shot for hours and hours, and a lot of the footage could not be used because although there was a script to be followed, Seth had deviated from it in such a way that he began to shape the film differently in his own mind. If you remember the movie, we had this one scene where I am walking, and my hair is flowing back. Seth had this sort of vision of the movie he wanted to make, a very visually striking, very different kind of film. When Michael came in to replace him, and had to direct the remainder of the film, it was quite difficult for him. We had to scrap a lot of already filmed footage and attempt to bridge the narrative gaps in the story and come out with a completed feature film. I believe it was released as a major feature film paired with *Dr. Jekyll and Sister Hyde*. Now, it has become a cult film. They show it again and again on television in Britain, and I get asked all over the world about the movie.

I think it is quite spooky. In fact, I gave a copy recently to my hairdresser, he's this rough kind of guy, and his wife said that he was clutching her the whole time he was watching the movie, he found it so spooky. However, I have not watched it recently myself.

Q: *Queen Kong*, which was considered a lost film for decades, was recently rediscovered and issued on DVD.

Leon: I remember filming in Shepperton Studios in England, and I remember playing a high priestess, and that it was quite fun to do. *Queen Kong* was an extraordinary film to work on. It's way, way out. So much so, I do not know what to make of it, it is just so strange. It did not get much of a release at all because of the Dino De Laurentiis version of *King Kong*, which was distributed at the same time. At the time, De Laurentiis and the studio that was handling the release of his *King Kong* [Paramount] made sure that no one would infringe on their copyrights or something like that. Anyway, someone recently handed me a poster calling it *Queen Gorilla*, it has been released in certain places under the title *Queen Gorilla*, so the producers of *Queen Kong* were attempting to get their film out there in some way.

Q: Robin Askwith was the male lead.

Leon: I had worked with Robin previously. Ruta Lenska was in it too. I think that the script was just very strange, very way out, and I do not know what people make of it. People remember it, and talk about it although, again, like *Zeta One*, like *Blood from the Mummy's Tomb*, it's something that psyched somebody's imagination, and fantasies, and it worked on enough people to cause the film to have some kind of cult status among aficionados of such things.

Q: You appeared in two James Bond films, *The Spy Who Loved Me* and *Never Say Never Again*, where you had a larger role.

Leon: Regarding *The Spy Who Loved Me*, I still can recall my interview with the producer, Cubby Broccoli. I remember going to the studio and saying, "I don't want to be killed off. I would love to be in the movie, but please don't kill me off." Therefore, I ended up as a hotel receptionist, who wasn't killed off, but it was quite a boring role. At least I got to be in the film. I was flown to the location with Richard Kiel and his wife. The minute that I arrived, I got shown to my hotel room, and I got bitten on the head, literally, by a mosquito, and my face swelled so badly. I was not needed for filming anytime soon, so I was holed up in my room wishing that the swelling would go down. Then Cubby Broccoli summoned me, saying, "Where is she? She should be down here" and so on. So, I had to get out for the filming. It was great. It was a tiny role, but people always remember it. It just surprised me how everyone just latched onto even the smallest supporting parts because you are still typed as being a Bond girl; whether you have a cameo role or if you are a leading lady, you are a Bond girl, which is really amazing.

That was in 1977. *Never Say Never Again* was in 1983. For that film, I had an audition at ten in the morning with the American producers, and I turned up in a maroon cat suit with a gold brocade sleeveless coat over it, and the producers said, "What kind of a look do you call that?" Anyway, I do not know if it was the outfit, but I got the part. It was chaotic on that set. Wardrobe never sorted me out. I flew out to the Bahamas, and I had to get my own bikinis and stuff when I was out there. It was great working with Sean Connery. It was the rogue Bond film. Warner Bros. made it; it was not a Cubby Broccoli film. Of course, that was the one where Sean's wife said, "*Never Say Never Again...*" because he did it.

Never Say Never Again was my last movie. I had a son and a daughter, both of whom I raised. I also formed a promotion company where I was promoting other people, other things, restaurants, arts-related events, etc. A French film director had offered me a role of recent, and last I heard, they are attempting to get the financing for it. I am not fully retired however; I have been doing television commercials. I do many interviews for television as well.

Q: How do you feel about people's interest in your work, the attention you still get?

Leon: My mother says, "I just don't understand it, Valerie" but I am terribly flattered. When I think back to when I did *Blood from the Mummy's Tomb*, it was in 1971, I never thought that thirty-something years hence that I would make appearances at trade fests, and at conventions, and meet people who tell me that they are my fans, or fans of my work, or appreciate my work. I am flattered. I had done an appearance at a film convention in the United States and I met someone who said that he drove for six hours just to come and meet me, to see me. I do not know what to say... it is extraordinary.

Valerie Leon as she appears today.

Credits: 1967: *The Baron: Countdown* (04/12/67) (television) [Great Britain]; *The Saint: To Kill a Saint* (02/24/67) (television) [Great Britain]; *Smashing Time* (uncredited) [Great Britain]; 1968: *The Avengers: Whoever Shot Poor George Oblique Stroke XR40?* (10/30/68) (television) [Great Britain]; *Carry On, Up the Khyber* (uncredited) [Great Britain]; *If There Weren't Any Blacks You'd Have to Invent them* (television) [Great Britain]; 1969: *Carry on Again Doctor* [Great Britain]; *Carry on Camping* [Great Britain]; *The Italian Job* (uncredited) [Great Britain–Italy?]; *A Promise of Bed* (a.k.a. *This, That and the Other!*) [Great Britain]; *Randall and Hopkirk (Deceased): That's How Murder Snowballs* (10/19/69) (television) [Great Britain]; *Zeta One* (a.k.a. *Alien Women* a.k.a. *The Love Factor*) [Great Britain]; 1970: *All the Way Up* [Great Britain]; *Carry On Up the Jungle* [Great Britain]; *The Man Who Had Power Over Women* [Great Britain]; *The Rise and Rise of Michael Rimmer* [Great Britain]; *Up Pompeii: The Senator and the Asp* (04/13/70) (television) [Great Britain]; 1971: *Blood from the Mummy's Tomb* [Great Britain]; *The Persuaders!: The Long Goodbye* (12/10/71) (television) [Great Britain]; 1972: *Carry On Christmas: Carry On Stuffing* (television) [Great Britain]; *Carry On Matron* [Great Britain]; 1973: *Carry On Girls* [Great Britain]; *Doctor in Charge: In Place of Strife* (11/03/73) (television) [Great Britain]; *No Sex Please: We're British* [Great Britain];

1974: *Can You Keep It Up for a Week?* [Great Britain]; 1975: *Space: 1999: Death's Other Dominion* (11/14/75) (television) [Great Britain–U.S.–Italy]; *The Ups and Downs of a Handyman* [Great Britain]; 1976: *The Goodies: It Might As Well Be String* (10/19/76) (television) [Great Britain]; *Queen Kong* [Great Britain–France–West Germany–Italy–Egypt?]; 1977: *That's Carry On* [Great Britain]; 1982: *The Spy Who Loved Me* [Great Britain–U.S.]; 1978: *The Revenge of the Pink Panther* [Great Britain–U.S.]; *The Wild Geese* [Great Britain–Switzerland]; 1982: *The Strangers: A Swift and Evil Rozzer* (09/15/82) (television) [Great Britain]; 1983: *Carry On Laughing's Christmas Classics* (television) [Great Britain]; *Never Say Never Again* [Great Britain–U.S.–West Germany]; 1998: *What's a Carry On?* (television) [Great Britain]; 2000: *I Love Seventies: I Love 1975* (08/26/00); *I Love a Seventies Christmas* (television) [Great Britain]; *Inside "The Spy Who Loved Me"* (video supplement) [Great Britain–U.S.].

Richard Lynch

Born in Brooklyn, New York, on February 12, 1940, Richard Lynch is a character actor who, because of his many roles in a wide variety of films, became one of those villains that everyone loved to hate. "Ever since *Scarecrow* with Al Pacino," says the actor, "it's been my luck, be it as it may, to be the in-house heavy." After years spent acting on the stage, the blonde, soft-spoken, and thoughtful actor with the strong, gaunt, slightly scarred facial features became known as a premier bad guy through numerous appearances in television programs the likes of *The Streets of San Francisco* and similar hard-edged police procedurals of the seventies.

However, before all of that, he was seen onscreen in the 1968 film *LSD: Trip to Where?* In a disturbing interview, the then-unknown actor detailed how, during a particularly bad acid trip in Central Park during the summer of 1967, he doused his body with gasoline and set himself on fire, inadvertently giving himself a scarred, partially disfigured face. Many plastic surgery operations rectified the damage to a degree. This same footage also appears in another documentary, *The Mindbenders: Scary Drug Education Films from the 60's: Volume One*.

Lynch performed on the live stage in a variety of parts. The role of Moon, a psychopathic hitman, in the on-the-edge action film *The Seven-Ups* (1973) brought him to the notice of movie audiences, and his work in films as diverse as *Scarecrow* (1973) and *The Ninth Configuration* (1980) displayed Lynch's craft, honed to perfection after a number of years on the stage on the East Coast. "I was very anxious to be part of [*The Ninth Configuration*], because I believed in it so much. It's very parapsychological, and deals with highly religious conceptual stuff. Most people aren't familiar with it, but it's a great little film."

Stardom of sorts seemed to come with the low-budget action fantasy *The Sword and the Sorcerer* (1982), where he played a villainous king. He was even awarded an acting prize by the Academy of Science Fiction, Fantasy, and Horror Films. "I've had a very strange career, because I've been all over the board. I have been lucky in that I have been able to move from stage to television to film and back and forth. I didn't realize that I'd started to move more and more towards genre films. People have made that point to me, and I guess I have."

Roles in Italian genre features (especially for *Cannibal Holocaust* director Ruggero Deodato) followed. Lynch brought movie villainy to new heights in the eighties in films such as Chuck Norris' *Invasion U.S.A.* (1985). *Variety* noted in an October 2 review "Film has a message: Americans are sitting ducks because they are soft and ignorant of the nature of their own freedom. That fanatic moral is voiced by arch heavy Richard Lynch, whose performance is so richly pernicious that he, and not Chuck Norris, is the lynchpin of the film. A picture like this needs a terrific crazy, and Lynch, with solid classical training, is the only excuse to see the film."

Bad Dreams (1988), a failed bid to recreate the success and aura of the *Nightmare on Elm Street* films, found Lynch starring as the villain. *Variety*'s April 6 review summed up what went wrong with this film: "Story concerns a young girl who survives a Jonestown-style suicide ritual (concerning fire) presided over by a cult leader (Richard Lynch). After 13 years in a coma she awakes (as Jennifer Rubin), and is put into a group therapy session. Lynch, overused as a villain, is cast in extremely poor taste whereby his heavily scarred (from a real-life accident) face and neck give way to Michele Burke's post-fire makeup effects."

Richard Lynch as he appeared in the film *Scarecrow* (1973) (Warner Bros.).

Nevertheless, he was an effective villain in this film, as well as in *Puppetmaster III: Toulon's Revenge* (1991) and others. Off screen he claims to be far from the villainous personas, he essays onscreen. "In real life, I'm reclusive. I do not have much interest in the publicity and hype about what I do. I just love my work."

But he stayed true to his acting craft by delivering fine character performances in movies as diverse as *The Forbidden Dance* (about the brief Lambada dance craze), *Eight Men Out*, and a recent film version of the classic *Crime and Punishment*, filmed in Moscow where the original story is situated. "I played a wealthy and rather dastardly Russian. The interesting thing about the novel *Crime and Punishment* is that it is applicable to what is taking place in Russia today [2001]. It is not a period piece. It's basically the same story: Raskolnikov, the young student, commits a murder; aggravated and influenced by social and political conditions, he slips into the rather negative philosophy of Nietzsche's Ubermensch, that he is a superior being, and laws can be broken by superior beings."

Lynch continues to portray character roles on film, but is weary of the villainous parts. "I'd like to play different parts, which I do when I go back on stage. On occasion, I do get the part of a protagonist, and I feel myself moving in that direction. However, people see you in a particular way, and most of the parts that are offered to me tend to be the antagonist. Still, I've been lucky to work, and I'm grateful."

Q: You started as an actor in the New York theater community in the sixties.

Richard Lynch: I started out in the Herbert Berghof studios, located in Greenwich Village, after my tour of duty in the Marine Corps. I performed in a lot of theater in those early years. I spent the better part of the first ten years of my career on the stage, and as a result, I got an opportunity to work in the film business. I made my film debut in *Scarecrow* opposite Al Pacino, which that year won the Golden Palm Award at the Cannes Film Festival. Later on, Pacino took me out to California with him, and I have not looked back.

Q: Of the theatrical work that you did in the sixties, is there anything that you fondly recall?

Lynch: Oh yes, a couple of really special memories I have is that in those days we had a really wonderful group of actors all working together, guys like Dustin Hoffman and others. There was a whole bunch of us who used to work through the Boston Theater Company. When things were somewhat quiet on the boards in New York, we would go up to Boston and work on our craft there in different plays. David Rabe's play *The Basic Training of Pavlo Hummel* was a big hit, we worked on that play for years, and that production holds a very special part of my memories as far as my stage work.

Q: One of the first times that I can recall that I saw you on television was in a *Streets of San Francisco* episode in 1972. The next year I saw you in a small but impressive part in *The Seven-Ups*. What can you recall about that film?

Lynch: *The Seven-Ups* was a very interesting film. It was directed by Phil D'Antoni, the person responsible for most of the car chases in action films made during that period. He worked on three films primarily, his trilogy you might say: *Bullitt*, *The French Connection* and *The Seven-Ups*. Then I understand he got out of the business. The car chase in that latter film is, of course, well remembered. I actually rode in that car that is featured onscreen in the high-speed chase scenes. I rode through most of it, because it was the only way that they could get the footage of me that they needed with the camera mounted on the outside of the door. I had a wonderful stuntman by the name of Bill Hickman who did the driving. I think he did the driving in *The French Connection* as well. It was a frightening experience, man. Sitting in the front seat of that car, at those high speeds, going through the streets of New York City, then on major expressways, it was scary.

Q: Were there any accidents or near accidents?

Lynch: There were many close calls when you work on a picture like that with those kinds of real effects in it. In particular, I recall the amazing scene where at the climax of the car chase, Roy Scheider's car goes and slams hard into the truck, under the semi; a stuntman did the real crash. I was there that day, it was filmed up near the Saw Mill River Parkway [north of New York City], and it was a five-camera coverage shoot. Everybody stood by, and the driver really plowed into that damn thing. It was one of the longest moments I can recall. Nobody moved. We waited, and then everybody started rushing to the car. He got a little hurt, the stuntman, he was a little damaged, he got a lot of glass damage. But for the most part, stuntmen know what they are doing.

Q: In *God Told Me To*, the Larry Cohen film, you had a very interesting part.

Lynch: All I can recall about that film is that we shot in a secret mint underneath that is located beneath the streets of New York City. It was located somewhere in midtown Manhattan, a treasury mint storage facility that very few people know of, way down on the bottom level. I do recall that I had a lot of fun with Larry as a writer and director, but it is a movie that I have to review again just to remind myself what went down.

Q: I recall how positive the reviews were for the television film *The Vampire*. Is it true that the program was originally intended to become a series, but the network botched it?

Lynch: It was one of Steven Bochco's early pilots. He is responsible for *NYPD Blue* and *Hill Street Blues* and shows like that. What happened was that the television film got great notices but for some reason we just did not get the [kind of] ratings that these network guys look at, and instead of giving it a chance, they just washed it. That happens quite often. It was a great show but they did not have the nerve to go with it.

Q: But they were intending it to be a series?

Lynch: Yes, they were intending it to be a series. Actually, Jason Miller and I approached another production outfit, and another network, to see if we could get three other two-hour movies made, but it did not work out.

Q: The independent production *The Sword and the Sorcerer* was a breakthrough film for you in some ways. It seemed to come out of nowhere and it became a sleeper hit. Do you think that your performance as the villainous King Titus Cromwell may have been partly responsible for you getting larger roles in the films that followed?

Lynch: On *The Sword and the Sorcerer*, I am going to give all the credit to the director, Albert Pyun. He is a very creative writer. It's one of his earliest movies, and he was very inventive what he did with film. It was a difficult film to make, by the way; a person was killed on that picture. There were many difficulties working on it. Films run in cycles and that was the year that they came out with *Excalibur*, and then there were a whole lot of movies that were just like it. Brandon Chase, one of the producers on *The Sword and the Sorcerer*, decided to make this little movie, and they made a large profit on it. It was the number one top-grossing independent film worldwide that year. My work stood out, and I won a Saturn award from the Academy of Science Fiction, Fantasy and Horror.

Q: Is there anything else that you recall about the production of that film?

Lynch: The death of Jack Tyree, who was a wonderful stuntman. God, man, that is a heavy thing to remember, but I remember the day it happened. He jumped off a cliff and missed his airbags. It is a dangerous job, stunt work. I will never forget that, it was a very sad event. The other thing was the heat. We shot a lot of it in Riverside, California, and in those costumes, it was boiling.

Q: Some would say that *Invasion U.S.A.* was the movie that brought you to villainy stardom, as the character of Rostov.

Lynch: Well, I think that the film that really opened the door for me was *Scarecrow* with Pacino and Hackman. That was the picture that gave me a career as far as film is concerned. I spent years on the stage, and I would have been just as happy staying on the stage, which I do go back to all the time. *Invasion U.S.A.* was a big picture at that time, and it was a good part for me, and I believe I worked well in it. It was an early Chuck Norris film; he was a terrific guy, and it was an action movie that worked. There are other parts that I have done just as well, if not better. It's just that I was stuck doing the villains.

Q: How was it to work the Italian genre filmmaker Ruggero Deodato?

Lynch: He is a wonderful, wonderful director. He's also a good friend, a personal friend; I've done four films with Ruggero, and possibly I will do a fifth. I have more fun working with the Italians than anybody else. The Italian filmmakers are very different from the Hollywood breed, they are very loyal, they hire you back, you become like a member of the family, and there is nothing more comfortable than to work on a set like that. Deodato is not a cold filmmaker, he is a terrific director, and he should get more recognition.

Q: Is there one recent film role that you have especially enjoyed?

Lynch: Actually, there is a movie that I did called *Eastside*. Filmmakers have often typecast me as the villain, as the heavy; I have been fortunate to work, and again, I am very lucky to have had a full career out of it. But there are other sides to my personality, and I get to show that in *Eastside*. I played a character called Gabriel; the name makes it sound like some kind of a metaphor for an angel, but he's not. My character turns a young boy around from a potential life of crime, and street gangs, and sets him on the straight and narrow. I feel good about that role.

Q: You also made *Crime and Punishment*, a film that has gone unreleased.

Lynch: It was a terrific film. We had a great opportunity to update the story; how can you go wrong with Dostoevsky, and a classic like *Crime and Punishment*? It's kind of an updated, modern-day version of *Crime and Punishment*, but it also has all of the political atmosphere that was present in Russia, right after the collapse of the government around 2000. When we shot this film in Moscow, there seemed to be the same conditions that were around in the classical era when Dostoevsky wrote the original story. It has a great cast, including John Hurt, Vanessa Redgrave, and Margot Kidder. Unfortunately, because of some legal matters which I am not very clear on, the film was more or less seized in a bankruptcy lien, and it is being held hostage to satisfy the investors. But it'll eventually come out, we will just have to wait for it because if it's going to have to produce any money to pay back these investors, they'll release it and put it out in the market.

Q: What can you tell me about your production company, Fusion Films?

Lynch: Fusion Films is a little company that I created to start to produce films myself. I want to take advantage of my exposure, of my thirty-something years in the profession. I have a modest audience out there, I have good exposure in the foreign markets in Europe, the Middle East, and in Asia, and I am going to start to produce myself. I'm a creative guy, I've got my own ideas about film, and I want to see what I can do with them. That's what Fusion Films is all about.

Credits: 1968: *LSD: Trip to Where?*; 196?: *The Mindbenders: Scary Drug Educational Films from the 60's Volume 1*; 1973: *Scarecrow*; *The Seven-Ups*; 1974: *Open Season* [Spain–Switzerland–Great Britain–U.S.–Argentina]; 1975: *The Happy Hooker*; *Starsky and Hutch: Pilot* (04/30/75); 1976: *Baretta: They Don't Make 'Em Like They Used To* (10/20/76); *Bronk: Target: Unknown* (02/08/76); *God Told Me To* (a.k.a. *Demon*); *The Premonition*; *Serpico: Prime Evil* (11/19/76); 1977: *The Baron*; *Dog and Cat* (television); *Good Against Evil* (television); *Police Woman: Solitaire* (02/22/77); *Roger & Harry: The Mitera Target* (television); *The Streets of San Francisco: Time Out* (06/16/77); *Stunts* (a.k.a. *Who Is Killing the Stuntmen?*); 1978: *Battlestar Gallactica: Gun on Ice Planet Zero: Part 1* (10/22/78), *Gun on Ice Planet Zero: Part 2* (10/29/78); *The Bionic Woman: Out of Body* (03/04/78); *Deathsport*; *Starsky and Hutch: Quadromania* (05/10/78); 1979: *Barnaby Jones: Nightmare in Hawaii: Part1/Part 2*

Lynch (with unidentified actor) as movie villainy personified in this scene from the Chuck Norris action film, *Invasion USA* (1985) (Cannon Films).

(09/27/79); *Buck Rogers in the 25th Century: Vegas in Space* (10/04/79); *Charlie's Angels: Angels on the Street* (11/07/79); *Delta Fox*; *A Man Called Sloane: Masquerade of Terror* (10/13/79); *Starsky and Hutch: Starsky vs. Hutch* (05/08/79); *Vampire* (television); *Vega$: Kill Dan Tanna!* (01/24/79); 1980: *Alcatraz: The Whole Shocking Story* (television); *Conquest of the Earth* (compilation of *Galactica 1980* episodes) (television); *The Formula* [U.S.–West Germany]; *Galactica 1980: Galactica Discovers Earth: Part 1* (01/27/80), *Galactica Discovers Earth: Part 2* (02/03/80), *Galactica Discovers Earth: Part 3* (02/10/80); *The Ninth Configuration* (a.k.a. *Twinkle, Twinkle, Killer Kane*); *Steel*; 1981: *Sizzle* (television); *Vega$: Dead Ringer* (04/29/81); 1982: *Bring 'Em Back Alive: Escape from Kampoon* (11/30/82); *McClain's Law: The Sign of the Beast: Part 1* (01/22/82), *The Sign of the Beast: Part 2* (01/29/82); *The Phoenix* (television); *The Sword and the Sorcerer*; 1983: *The Last Ninja* (television); *Manimal: Illusion* (10/14/83); *Partners in Crime: Double Jeopardy*; *T.J. Hooker: Carnal Express* (10/08/83); *White Water Rebels* (television); 1984: *The A-Team: Hot Styles* (12/11/84); *Automan: Renegade Run* (03/05/84); *Blue Thunder: Second Thunder* (01/06/84); *Cover Up: Murder in Malibu* (12/01/84); *The Fall Guy: Stranger Than Fiction* (09/26/84), *The Winner* (12/19/84); *Masquerade: Flashpoint*; *Matt Houston: Apostle of Death* (10/19/84); *Treasure: In Search of the Golden Horse* (narrator) (voice); 1985: *Airwolf: The Horn of Plenty* (09/28/85); *Inferno in Diretta* (a.k.a. *Amazon: Savage Adventure* a.k.a. *Cut and Run*) [Italy]; *Invasion U.S.A.*; *MacGruder and Loud: Odds Favor Death*; *Riptide: Curse of the Mary Aberdeen* (01/29/85); *Savage Dawn*; *Scarecrow and Mrs. King: You Only Die Twice* (04/01/85); 1986: *The Last Precinct: Never Cross a Vampire*; 1987: *The Barbarians* (a.k.a. *I, Barbari* a.k.a. *The*

Barbarians and Co.) [Italy-U.S.]; *The Law and Harry McGraw: Mr. Chapman, I Presume?* (10/13/87); *Nightforce*; *Once a Hero: The Return of Lazarus* (10/03/87); *Werewolf: Nightmare at the Braine Hotel* (11/08/87); 1988: *Bad Dreams*; *Chopper Wars* (narrator); 1989: *The Heat* (television); *High Stakes*; *Hunter: The Legion: Part 1* (11/11/89), *The Legion: Part 2* (11/18/89); *Little Nikita* (a.k.a. *The Sleepers*); 1990: *Aftershock*; *The Forbidden Dance* (a.k.a. *Lambada, the Forbidden Dance*); *High Performance: Invasion Force*; *Juggernaut*; *Kojak: Flowers for Matty* (television); *Lockdown*; *One Man Force* (video); *Return to Justice*; *Super Force: Sins of the Father: Part 1, Part 2*; *True Blue: Hickory, Dickory, Dock* (01/12/90); 1991: *Alligator II: The Mutation*; *Dark Justice: I Hate Mondays* (05/31/91); *Puppet Master III: Toulon's Revenge*;

Richard Lynch. [Photo courtesy Richard Lynch]

1992: *Jake and the Fatman: Where or When?: Part 1* (09/18/92), *Where or When?: Part 2* (09/25/92); *The Last Hero*; *Maximum Force*; *Merlin* [Great Britain]; *Murder, She Wrote: To the Last Will I Grapple with Thee* (03/15/92); *Trancers II* (a.k.a. *Future Cop II* a.k.a. *The Return of Jack Deth*); 1993: *Double Threat*; *The Hat Squad: The Liquidator* (06/23/93); *Inside Edge*; *Showdown*; *Star Trek: The Next Generation: Gambit: Part 1* (10/09/93), *Gambit: Part 2* (10/16/93); 1994: *Cyborg 3: The Recycler* (video); *Death Match* (video); *Loving Deadly*; *Murder, She Wrote: Amsterdam Kill* (10/02/94); *Necronomicon* (a.k.a. *Necronomicon: Book of the Dead*) [U.S.-Canada]; *Phantom 2040* (animated) (television) (voice only); *Roughcut* (video); *Scanner Cop* (video) [Canada-U.S.]; *Thunder in Paradise: Blast Off* (11/06/94); 1995: *Baywatch: Deep Trouble* (05/01/95); *Destination Vegas*; *Dragon Fury*; *Highlander: Blind Faith* (02/13/95); *Midnight Confessions*; *Takedown*; *Terminal Virus* (television); 1996: *Diamond Run*; *The Garbage Man*; *Terrified*; *Vendetta*; *Warrior of Justice* (a.k.a. *Invitation to Die*); *Werewolf* (a.k.a. *Arizona Werewolf*); 1997: *Divine Lovers* [India-U.S.]; *Ground Rules*; *Noi Siamo Angeli* (a.k.a. *We Are Angels* a.k.a. *We're No Angels*) (television) [Italy]; *Total Force* [Canada-U.S.]; *Under Oath* (a.k.a. *Blood Money*); 1998: *Armstrong*; *Breaking the Silence*; *Love and War II*; *Mike Hammer, Private Eye: Dead Men Talk* (05/31/98); *Shattered Illusions*; 1999: *Acapulco H.E.A.T.: Code Name: The Stolen Leg* (05/22/99); *Air America: Old Gold* (01/23/99); *Battlestar Galactica: The Second Coming* (fan-produced film; remains unreleased outside of conventions); *Eastside*; *Enemy Action*; *Lone Tiger* (a.k.a. *Tiger Mask*) [U.S.-

Japan]; *Strike Zone*; *Sotto Il Cielo Dell'Africa* (a.k.a. *Thinking About Africa*) (television) [Italy-Germany]; 2001: *Ancient Warriors*; *Ankle Bracelet*; *Death Game*; *The Friggin' Mafia Movie* (video); *The Hunted: Star Power*; *The Joe Spinell Story* (video); *The Korean War* (television) [China-U.S.-Canada]; *Reflex Action* (video); 2002: *Crime and Punishment* [U.S.-Poland-Russia]; *Outta' Time*; *Six Feet Under: I'll Take You* (05/19/02); *Uncut and Run* (video supplement); 2003: *Charmed: The Day the Magic Died* (02/16/03); *Corpses Are Forever*; *The Curse of the Forty-Niners* (a.k.a. *Miner's Massacre*); *Fabulous Shiksa in Distress* (uncredited); *Final Combat*; *First Watch*; *The Mummy's Kiss*; *Puppet Master: The Legacy* (video); 2005: *The Great War of Magellan* (short film); *Mil Mascaras Vs the Aztec Mummy*; 2006: *Roney's Point*; 2007: *Halloween*.

Charles Napier

Charles Napier was born on April 12, 1936, in Mt. Union, near Scottsville, Kentucky. With interests in photography and painting, he became a sergeant in the U.S. military's 511th Airborne Infantry division. After the completion of his military service, Napier moved through a variety of positions, including one as a teacher, which he often returned to. In 1964, the acting bug bit him and he performed in a number of local community theater productions (at one point he even played Iago in *Othello*!). At the Old Globe Theater's Shakespeare Festival in San Diego, California, he performed in a variety of minor roles before finally heading out to Hollywood.

Napier's first memorable appearance on television was in an early 1967 episode of *Mannix*, followed by a featured role on *Star Trek* (as Adam in the 1969 episode *Way of Eden*). Afterwards, he decided to see the country via the road, and took on a position as a photographer and journalist for the trucking magazine *Overdrive*.

During this period, Napier became friendly with another former military man, an army personnel photographer named Russ Meyer. Meyer, who had been experimenting with mature-themed subject matters for his movies, cast Napier in *Cherry, Harry and Raquel* (1969), *Beyond the Val-*

A promotional movie photo depicting Charles Napier (as the hero for a change) in *Hornsby and Rodriguez* (1992) (Reteitalia/Trinidad Films).

ley of the Dolls (1970), *The Seven Minutes* (1971), and *Supervixens* (1977). In time, Napier became Meyer's (some say misogynistic) male muse, the brutish, square-jawed comic book everyman who becomes an insatiable object of masculinity to women everywhere in Meyer's fantasy world where extremely well-endowed women supplicate themselves at the feet of he-men like Napier.

Napier also appeared on the television programs *Mission: Impossible* (in unrelated guest starring roles in episodes in 1968, 1971, and 1972), *The Rockford Files* (1977), *Starsky and Hutch* (unrelated guest starring roles in episodes in 1975 and 1978), and others, plus co-starring roles in two short-lived western series, *Oregon Trail* (1977) and *The Outlaws* (1986), both with Rod Taylor. These acting parts paved the way for appearances in more mainstream films (often helmed by directors who were fans of his work, and who recalled him in the Russ Meyer movies) all are in the credits list.

Q: How does it feel to be one of the most recognizable actors in Hollywood?

Charles Napier: It's what I do for a living. I like to meet the people, the fans, because they are the ones who made you.

Q: Is it true that, after performing in community theater productions, you became a journalist-photographer for a magazine for truckers, enabling you to see the country at the same time?

Napier: I was in a movie called *Moonfire* with Richard Egan and Sonny Liston, and it was about trucking. Afterwards, I took a three-year hiatus and became a photographer and then a writer for *Overdrive*, the trucking magazine. It was a great three years traveling all over the United States. I went wherever the trucks were going, and I learned a lot more about life in general than you can anywhere else.

Q: How did you get involved with Russ Meyer?

Napier: As I recall, I had a girlfriend or a friend, I can't remember if she was a girlfriend or a friend, probably both. And she had an interview with Russ Meyer. I didn't know who he was, and she said that he made X-rated flicks. Back in those days, that meant like that was almost like pornographic, but not so. I went along with her, and met Russ, and he wound up using me in his movie, and not her.

Q: What was it like, appearing in those early Meyer films?

Napier: It was kind of strange because in those days most of them played...

Q: Specialty theatres?

Napier: Yeah, especially in places like New York, in Los Angeles, in Chicago, wherever. But, when we made *Cherry, Harry and Raquel*, United Artists picked us up for distribution. So there I am in two thousand theaters across the country with my butt hanging out. It never hurt my career though, appearing in these kinds of movies, it actually helped it. You have to remember that I have been doing this for over thirty-five years. Therefore, the people who were young, or growing up during the peak of the Russ Meyer films, became directors like John Landis, and Jonathan Demme, and Ben Stiller. All those guys who were kids who grew up to be directors and whatever, they wound up working with me. Even Alfred Hitchcock, who is said to have seen *Supervixens*, and enjoyed it, helped to put me on a contract with Universal Studios.

Q: Of the films that you did with Meyer, were there any particular favorites?

Napier: No, because they all seemed the same. They were all hard to do—it was brutally hard work. You have to understand that I have been in the army, I was in the 11th Airborne Division, and working for Russ Meyer, it was like going through three basic trainings because you go out into the desert with a camera and sound and that was it. You did all the stunts yourself, all the driving, all the fighting, and stayed out in the desert until the movie was made. Then we came out and were allowed to return home.

Q: You also worked quite a bit with Jonathan Demme.

Napier: As I can recall, Jonathan Demme told me that he was once in the Philippines and saw me in one of those Russ Meyer movies and said, "One day I'd like to work with that guy." I had been working for him for eighteen years doing walk-ons, whatever, and then the character of the judge in *Philadelphia* was written expressly for me. I was then mostly cut out of the picture. In this business, if you are in a big movie with somebody who has been nominated for an Academy Award, or even won one, then you lose screen time to him or her. That's the way it is.

Q: You worked in Europe for Antonio Margheriti and Umberto Lenzi and others.

Napier: Antonio Margheriti would probably be my favorite European director, and second would probably be Umberto Lenzi. My favorite European-made film was *Hornsby and Rodriquez*. We shot that in Italy and the Dominican Republic. I always enjoyed working with the Italians very much. They always treated me very good, so it was generally a good experience. We worked pretty hard but, like I always say, after Russ Meyer, everything else is easy.

Q: Do you have a particular approach to acting, or does it just come naturally to you?

Napier: When we were kids, we played cowboys and Indians, gangsters, whatever. If you remember that, you didn't have to stop and think about getting into character. I think actors have very childish minds, or are more *uninhibited*, let's put it that way. And you're just able to do that, to inhabit another role, without too much of an awareness of making a fool out of yourself by doing this or doing that, or being this and being that. Or, maybe some of us actors, and even non-actors... maybe we don't even have a real self so it's easy. Basically, that's it. When you were a kid, you didn't think about it. You just played this part, you played that part. Some children who grow up to be adults are able to do that, some aren't, and I can't really [explain acting] in any other way except that. In addition, what you look like counts towards what they will cast you for, your voice quality, your speech pattern, your accent or whatever, all that stuff is included. In my particular case it broke down into one, two, three, four, I look like a truck driver. When I was younger, I was playing bad guys. Now that I'm older I'm playing judges, I'm playing a lot of army military officers, and I've sort of become that kind of token character in Hollywood. Sometimes, somebody throws me into their film just to say that they have me in their film, but that's okay too.

Q: What are your favorite film roles?

Napier: I judge films by the amount of fun I have had working on them, like *The Blues Brothers*. John Belushi was great fun. *Rambo II*, because of the location, Acapulco, for two months. As far as the roles, I just go and do them, really. If I ever get a chance to do comedy, I will. That is more fun than anything else is, and all bad guys are really funny guys. I like those kinds of movies, I would like the chance to be funnier on the screen, and I would like to think I am funny in real life too. To be an actor in a straight, non-comedic role in a heavy drama is okay but it is much more fun to do comedy if somebody gives you a chance.

Q: What have you been working in recent years?

Napier: I do a lot of voiceovers for commercials, I do a lot for General Motors. And I do a lot of cartoon voices for a variety of television programs. I guest star on *The Simpsons* on occasion, I was a regular on the animated television series version of *Men in Black*, and I have done voices for *Rugrats* and *The Critic*.

Q: So, at least, if no one has ever seen your face, which is a very recognizable one, you will at least always be remembered by the people who hear that voice.

Napier: Let's hope so.

The author and perennial movie villain Charles Napier in 2002.

Credits: 1968: *Mission: Impossible: The Play* (12/08/68) (television); 1969: *The Hanging of Jake Ellis*; *Hogan's Heroes: The Missing Klink* (01/04/69) (television); *The House Near the Prado* (a.k.a. *Diary of a Madam*); *Star Trek: The Way to Eden* (02/21/69) (television); 1970: *Beyond the Valley of the Dolls*; *Cherry, Harry & Raquel*; *Love and Kisses*; 1971: *Mission: Impossible: Run for the Money* (12/11/71) (television); *The Seven Minutes*; 1972: *Mission: Impossible: Cocaine* (10/21/72) (television); *Moonfire*; 1975: *Baretta: Double Image* (10/15/75) (television); *Kojak: My Brother, My Enemy* (09/21/75) (television); *The Rockford Files: Two Into 5.56 Won't Go* (11/21/75) (television); *Starsky and Hutch: Texas Longhorn* (09/17/75) (television); *The Streets of San Francisco: No Place to Hide* (09/25/75) (television); *Supervixens* (a.k.a. *Russ Meyer's Supervixens* a.k.a. *Vixens*); 1976: *Alien Attack* (television) (uncredited); *Baa Baa Black Sheep: Best Three Out of Five* (09/23/76), *Flying Misfits: Part 1/Part 2* (television); 1977: *Handle with Care* (a.k.a. *Citizen's Band*); *The Oregon Trail* (television); *Ransom for Alice* (television); *The Rockford Files: New Life, Old Dragons* (02/25/77) (television); *Thunder and Lightning* (a.k.a. *Thunder on the Highway*); 1978: *Big Bob Johnson and His Fantastic Speed Circus* (television); *Starsky and Hutch: Satan's Witches* (02/28/78) (television); 1979: *B.J. and the Bear: Pogo Lil* (10/20/79), *Gasohol* (11/24/79) (television); *The Incredible Hulk: The Slam* (10/19/79) (television); *Last Embrace*; 1980: *B.J. and the Bear: Siege* (01/19/80) (television); *The Blues Brothers*; *Gridlock* (a.k.a. *The Great American Traffic Jam*) (television); *Melvin and Howard*; 1981: *B.J. and the Bear: Snow White and the Seven Lady Truckers Part 1/Part 2* (01/13/81) (television); *The Dukes of Hazzard: Bye, Bye, Boss* (03/13/81) (television); *The Incredible Hulk: Triangle* (11/13/81) (television); 1982: *The Blue and the Gray* (television); *CHiPs: Something Special* (11/21/82) (television); *Dallas: Where There's a Will...* (10/08/82) (television); *Knight Rider: The Movie* (television); *Knight Rider: Knight of the Phoenix Part 1/Part 2* (09/26/82) (television); *Simon & Simon: Mike & Pat* (10/14/82) (television); 1983: *The A-Team: Labor Pains* (11/08/83) (television); *China Lake*; *The Dukes of Hazzard: Targets: Daisy and Lulu* (11/18/83) (television); *Gun Shy: Pardon Me Boy, Is That the Quake City Choo Choo?* (03/22/83) (television); *Tales of the Gold Monkey: High Stakes*

Lady (01/26/83) (television);*Wacko*; 1984: *The A-Team* (television); *The Cartier Affair* (television); *In Search of the Golden Sky*; *Night Court: Hi Honey, I'm Home* (05/31/84) (television); *The Outlaws* (television); *Swing Shift*; *Whiz Kids: May I Take Your Order Please* (06/02/84) (television); 1985: *The A-Team* (television); *Rambo: First Blood Part II*; *Street Hawk: Hot Target* (03/01/85) (television); 1986: *Instant Justice* (a.k.a. *Marine Issue*); *Kidnapped*; *Married to the Mob*; *Murder, She Wrote: Death Stalks the Big Top: Part 1* (09/28/86), *Death Stalks the Big Top: Part 2* (10/05/86) (television); *Outlaws* (television); *Something Wild*; *War and Remembrance* (television); 1987: *Camping Del Terrore* (a.k.a. *Body Count*) [Italy-U.S.]; *Deep Space*; *The Night Stalker*; 1988: *The Incredible Hulk Returns* (television); 1989: *Alien Degli Abissi* (a.k.a. *Alien from the Deep*) [Italy]; *Hit List*; *One Man Force*; *Paradise: A Gather of Guns* (09/10/89) (television); 1990: *Cop Target* (a.k.a. *Obiettivo Polziotto*) [Italy-U.S.]; *Dragonfight*; *Ernest Goes to Jail*; *Future Zone* (a.k.a. *Future Force 2*) (video); *The Grifters*; *Maniac Cop 2*; *Miami Blues*; *Sulle Tracce Del Condor* (a.k.a. *Condor* a.k.a. *After the Condor*) [Italy]; *l'Ultima Partita* (a.k.a. *The Opponent* a.k.a. *The Last Match*) [Italy-U.S.]; 1991: *Indio 2—La Rivolta* (a.k.a. *Indio 2—The Revolt*) [Italy]; *Killer Instinct*; *L.A. Law: The Beverly Hills Hangers* (03/14/91) (television); *Lonely Hearts*; *The Silence of the Lambs*; 1992: *Center of the Web*; *Eyes of the Beholder*; *Hornsby E Rodriguez—Sfida Criminale* (a.k.a. *Mean Tricks*) [Italy]; *Soldier's Fortune* (a.k.a. *Soldier of Fortune*); *Treacherous Crossing* (television); 1993: *Body Bags* (a.k.a. *John Carpenter Presents "Body Bags"* a.k.a. *John Carpenter Presents "Mind Games"*) (television); *Body Shot* (video); *Frogtown II* (a.k.a. *Hell Comes to Frogtown* a.k.a. *Return to Frogtown*) (video); *Loaded Weapon 1* (a.k.a. *National Lampoon's Loaded Weapon*); *Philadelphia*; *Renegade: Fighting Cage: Part 1* (05/10/93), *Fighting Cage: Part 2* (05/17/93), *Windy City Blues* (11/15/93) (television); *Skeeter* (video); 1994: *Coach: Head Like a Wheel* (05/17/94) (television); *The Critic* (television) (voice only); *Jailbreakers* (television); *Raw Justice* (a.k.a. *Skip-Tracer*); *Savage Land*; *Silent Fury* (video); *Silk Degrees* (a.k.a. *Target Witness*); *To Die, to Sleep*; 1995: *Ballistic* (a.k.a. *Fist of Justice*); *The Critic* (television) (voice only); *Fatal Choice*; *Hard Justice* (video); *Hudson Street: Guess Who's Coming to Dinner?* (11/07/95) (television); *Jury Duty*; *Max Is Missing* (television); *Murder, She Wrote: The Dream Team* (03/19/95) (television); *Lois & Clark: The New Adventures of Superman: Target Jimmy Olsen* (04/02/95) (television); *Star Trek: Deep Space Nine: Little Green Men* (11/13/95) (television); *3 Ninjas Knuckle Up*; 1996: *Alien Species*; *Billy Lone Bear*; *The Cable Guy*; *Expert Witness*; *Felony*; *Original Gangstas*; *Pacific Blue: Genuine Heroes* (10/20/96) (television); *The Real Adventures of Jonny Quest* (animated): *Without a Trace* (12/30/96) (voice only) (television); *Ripper Man*; *Spycraft: The Great Game* (video game) (voice only); 1997: *Austin Powers: International Man of Mystery* [U.S.-Germany]; *George & Leo: The Housekeeper* (11/10/97) (television); *Hollywood Rated "R"* (a.k.a. *Les Deniers Du Culte*) (French television); *Macon County Jail*; *Men in Black: The Series* (animated) (voice only); *No Small Ways*; *Riot*; *Steel*; *Superman* (animated): *The Promethean* (voice only) (09/12/97) (television); 1998: *Armstrong*; *Beloved* (uncredited); *Breaking the Silence*; *Centurion Force*; *Fatal Pursuit*; *Party of Five: Here and Now* (01/28/98) (television); *Second Chance*; *The Thief & the Stripper* (a.k.a. *Strip 'n Run*) (video); 1999: *Austin Powers: The Spy Who Shagged Me*; *The Big Tease* [Great Britain–U.S.]; *Cypress Edge*; *Los Gringos* (short film); *The Hunter's Moon*; *The Magician* (animated) (voice only) [France-U.S.]; *Pirates of the Plain*; *Walker, Texas Ranger: Fight or Die* (11/09/99) (television); 2000: *Buzz Lightyear of Star Command* (animated): *Haunted Moon* (Voice only) (11/10/00) (television); *God, the Devil and Bob:* (animated): *Bob Gets Involved, Bob's Father, The Devil's Birthday* (03/28/00), *In the Beginning* (03/09/00) (voice only) (television); *Down 'n Dirty*; *The Frozen Inferno* (video); *Never Look*

Back; *The Nutty Professor II: The Klumps*; *Roswell: Summer of '47* (10/23/00) (television); *Superman* (animated): *Legacy: Part 1* (02/05/00), *Legacy: Part 2* (02/12/00) (voice only) (television); *Very Mean Men*; 2001: *Diagnosis Murder: Sins of the Father: Part 1* (02/09/01), *Sins of the Father: Part 2* (02/09/01) (television); *Extreme Honor*; *Forgive Me Father*; *The Practice: Awakenings* (02/18/01), *Gideon's Crossover* (03/11/01) (television); *Return to Castle Wolfenstein* (a.k.a. *Return to Castle Wolfenstein: Operation Resurrection* a.k.a. *Return to Castle Wolfenstein: Tides of War*) (video game) (voice only); *The Simpsons* (animated): *Pokey Mom* (01/14/01) (Voice only) (television); 2002: *Son of the Beach: Three Days of the Condom* (06/09/02) (television); *Spirit: Stallion of the Cimarron* (animated) (voice only); *We Get to Win This Time* (video); 2003: *Dr. Phil: Fifteen Minutes of Fame* (05/23/03) (television); *The Mummy: The Animated Series* (animated): *Like Father, Like Son* (03/08/03) (voice only) (television); *The Simpsons* (animated): *The Fat and the Furriest* (11/30/03) (voice only) (television); *Trash: Pilot*; 2004: *DinoCroc*; *Justice League* (animated): *Fearful Symmetry* (09/04/04) (voice only) (television); *The Simpsons* (animated): *The Wandering Juvie* (03/28/04) (voice only) (television); 2005: *The 4400: Wake-Up Call* (06/05/05) (television); *The Lords of Dogtown* [U.S.-Germany]; *The Manchurian Candidate*; *The Simpsons* (animated): *The Seven-Beer Snitch* (04/03/05) (voice only) (television); *Suits on the Loose*; 2006: *Annapolis*; 2007: *Your Name Here*; 2008: *One-Eyed Monster*, *Pearblossom*; *Two: Thirteen*.

Linnea Quigley

Born Linnea Barbara Quigley on May 27, 1958, in Davenport, Iowa. Linnea Quigley later moved to California, where she was encouraged to model, and act by friends. Today, she is considered one of the horror industry's most beloved scream queens, and has appeared numerous times in genre publications the likes of *Fangoria*. Quigley first appeared in minor roles in low-budget thrillers like *Stone Cold Dead* (1979), and *Psycho from Texas* (1981), and gained notoriety, acclaim, and notice from critics and fans alike for her startling turn as a sexy zombie in *Return of the Living Dead* in 1985.

The genre turns out many very low-budget straight-to-video features that often attempt to capitalize on the fan base of aging B-movie actresses; Quigley differs little from her fellow starlets.

Linnea Quigley poses for fans at a film convention.

However, it was in her many roles in genre films of the eighties that bolstered her rep as a performer in demand; at one time, she was the reigning Scream Queen (a moniker attributed to a small number of actresses that also included Brinke Stevens and Michelle Bauer, a personal friend and co-star of Quigley's). Linnea Quigley has also tirelessly worked for animal rights either on her own or in tandem with PETA (People for the Ethical Treatment of Animals). In her 1995 autobiography *I'm Screaming as Fast as I Can*, she related stories about her more than twenty-five years in genre films. With appearances in more than eighty motion pictures to her credit, she still reigns as one of the great Queens of the B Movies.

Q: You are one of the original actresses to receive the celebrated title of Scream Queen. What are your feelings about this?

Linnea Quigley: I really love it because it is something that I did not set out to do in my life or when I started acting. But it happened anyway, and it is a really good surprise when it does happen. I am proud to be called a Scream Queen.

Q: How do you feel about the adulation that you receive in print and on the Internet?

Quigley: I am amazed. It sort of doesn't compute when people tell me that I have such a following. I don't understand it, but I am really honored by it, and it probably would not have happened if I had not done these roles and been a Scream Queen. If I had done what I set out do in life, it probably would not have happened. Therefore, to me, that is like a real honor.

Q: I read in an old issue of *Femme Fatales* magazine that you preferred to be referred to as the Queen of the Scream Queens. Was that because you started out earlier than other actresses or was that because you had the most film credits at the time?

Quigley: Before me, there really were not any other people announcing that they were Scream Queens. It wasn't something that people wanted to be or anything like that. Then a lot, a lot, a lot of girls wanted to jump on the bandwagon. They literally did not have any credits to speak of, or might have posed in a magazine or two, scantily clad or in nude layouts, and all of a sudden, they have this title of Scream Queen. I think that is why I probably referred to myself as the Queen of the Scream Queens: because I do have a body of work in the genre, and because I do have more credits that many of these other actresses.

Q: What are some of your favorite films?

Quigley: *Return of the Living Dead*, *Savage Streets* and *Hollywood Chainsaw Hookers*... I liked working on that one. *Death Mask*, and of course, *Mari-Cookie and the Killer Tarantula*, which was for the director, Jess Franco.

Q: In the mid to late eighties, it was mentioned in *Variety* that you were the busiest actress in show business. Do you think that was an accurate claim?

Quigley: Yes, I think it was. At that time, I was performing with no limits, acting like crazy. I was not making as much as some other actors and actresses, but I was going nuts appearing in so many roles in so many films, albeit ones with low, low budgets. But they were still roles, and I was acting.

Q: Is that why around 1992, you considered retiring from the business?

Quigley: Yes, it was. I think I was very tired of it all. I had just gone on and gone on and gone on, and at that point, I was beginning to act in films that required me to wear a lot of prosthetic appliances, which was due to my character usually being killed in films. I really hate prosthetics on my face, and so I think that it came to the point where it was something I started to hate to do, and I really didn't want to do that anymore, wear prosthetics.

Q: Let's talk about some of the more mainstream films you appeared in over the years. You have had small roles in *Innocent Blood*, the *Nightmare on Elm Street* movies, and *Pumpkinhead II*, as well as lower-budgeted features like *Night of the Demons*. What comments can you give about how Hollywood-based productions work as opposed to the smaller budgeted films?

Quigley: On the higher budgeted films, it always seemed like there was much more

Quigley is flanked by two of her scariest fans.

pressure. It was like, "Oh my God, I have to live up to their standards. Are they looking at me as a B-movie queen or as an actress, a plain old actress?" It was kind of like being a freshman going to high school, kind of like, "Oh, boy, here I go...." It is also strange that, in the lower budgeted films, where I was known as a Scream Queen, I was a sort of mini-star, and not in the major Hollywood productions. It was somewhat scary.

Q: I have read that you once read for a role in Quentin Tarantino's *Reservoir Dogs*, but that the part was cut out before cameras rolled.

Quigley: Yes, he and a friend of mine had written *Natural Born Killers*, and there was a role in that film that was written with me in mind, but I did not get the role. Therefore, they had me read for *Reservoir Dogs* for a part as a female cop, and the role was totally cut out of the film before production started.

Q: You worked with actress Michelle Bauer a number of times in low-budget horror films, and the two of you were the only American actresses in Jess Franco's film *Mari-Cookie and the Killer Tarantula*, filmed on location in Spain.

Quigley: It was fun because Michelle, who I think is an excellent actress, is also the nicest person. We had a lot of fun on that film. It was great to be with her over there in Spain. Kevin Collins, one of the producers of the film, contacted me and mentioned that Jess Franco wanted to work with me and Michelle. We both thought, "Well, yes, okay we'll do it."

Q: Were you aware of Jess Franco before working with him as a director?

Quigley: I knew of his work, but I had never met him before. He is a great director. He really cares about his work, as opposed to many other directors. He makes sure you know your lines, he really cares, and he is inspirational. Who knows what the film has done for me career-wise? Very little probably, but I go into every film with that same idea of, "Who knows?" Lina Romay was also a nice, sweet woman. She was really cool. Both she and Jess are sweet people.

Q: You worked with Franco again in the film *Blind Target*.

Quigley: I played a reporter who gets too close to a political candidate, who may be the target of an assassination attempt.

Q: I'll just throw out titles and get a reaction from you, and it does not have to be in many words. *Fatal Frames*, the Italian production?

Actress, activist, and scream queen Linnea Quigley.

Quigley: That was a very cool film to work on, and I had to go back twice to film my role. It was cool working with David Warbeck and Donald Pleasence, and the way it was filmed, it was gorgeous, it was filmed beautifully. Although, in actuality, it rather scares me to think that three people died during the making of that film, partly because the film was in production for so long. Two of them were very ill, even while filming their scenes.

Q: *Jack O'Lantern*?

Quigley: Working on that one was really a blast because I love the director, and I love Florida.

Q: *The Black Room*?

Quigley: I made that one a long time ago, it was back when I really didn't know what the hell I was doing, although in retrospect, I guess it is really a very intense film that I hear has a cult following of sorts.

Q: *The Guyver?*

Quigley: Making that movie was fun, because I got to work with people who made me laugh like crazy.

Q: *Savage Streets?*

Quigley: That was a film that I did with Linda Blair, who was great to work with. However, my scenes involved being raped. My character was not allowed to have any lines. It was a very hard film to make.

Q: *Mari-Cookie and the Killer Tarantula?*

Quigley: It was interesting to see how films were made in Spain, and to see how Jess Franco works. There was certainly more nudity on the set than I have ever seen in any American film that I had ever been involved with. I played the young mother of this one girl. I find her in this place where they have these live sex shows, and I play a repressed woman, and in some strange way, what they do in this place turns me on, but also it's nothing that I would ever do in real life. Like my character wants to let her hair down, but is afraid to. It is a very interesting role. Franco is a director who always has new ideas for his actors. I like some of his films, some of them are better than others. I have not seen all of them yet, but one I do like was *The Bare-Breasted Countess.*

Q: You hosted a short-lived series on horror on the E! channel, interviewed other actresses for magazines like *Femme Fatales*, wrote your autobiography, and even produced two films [*Murder Weapon* and *The Girl I Want*]. What are your plans for the future?

Quigley: I take everything one day at a time because I think that there is no way that you can plan anything.

Credits: 1978: *Auditions*; *Deathsport* (uncredited); 1979: *Fairy Tales*; *Stone Cold Dead* (uncredited) [Canada]; *Summer Camp*; 1981: *Don't Go Near the Park*; *Graduation Day*; *Nice Dreams* (a.k.a. *Cheech & Chong's Nice Dreams*); 1982: *Psycho from Texas*; 1983: *Get Crazy* (uncredited); *Kidnapped Girls Agency*; *Nudes in Limbo* (uncredited) [Canada-U.S.]; *Playboy Video Magazine, Vol. 6* (video); *Simon & Simon: The Bare Facts* (11/17/83) (television); *Still Smokin'* (a.k.a. *Cheech & Chong's Still Smokin'*) [U.S.-Netherlands]; *Young Warriors* (a.k.a. *The Graduates of Malibu High*); 1984: *The Black Room*; *Fatal Games* (a.k.a. *Killing Touch*); *Savage Streets*; *Silent Night, Deadly Night*; 1985: *The Return of the Living Dead*; 1986: *Avenged*; *Beverly Hills Girls*; *Sweethearts*; 1987: *Creepozoids*; *Drive-In Madness* (a.k.a. *Screen Scaries*) (video); *Nightmare Sisters* (a.k.a. *Sorority Succubus Sisters*); *Silent Night, Deadly Night Part 2*; *Treasure of the Moon Goddess* [U.S.-Mexico]; 1988: *Dead Heat* (uncredited); *Hollywood Chainsaw Hookers*; *Night of the Demons*; *A Nightmare on Elm Street 4: The Dream Master*; *Sorority Babes in the Slimeball Bowl-O-Rama* (a.k.a. *The Imp*); *Vice Academy*; 1989: *Assault of the Party Nerds*; *American Rampage*; *Blood Nasty*; *Deadly Embrace*; *Dr. Alien* (a.k.a. *I Was a Teenage Sex Maniac* a.k.a. *I Was a Teenage Sex Mutant*); *Sexbomb*; *This Is Horror* (television); *Witchtrap*; 1990: *Diggin' Up Business*; *Linnea Quigley's Horror Workout* (video); *Murder Weapon*; *Robot Ninja*; *Vice Academy Part 2*; 1991: *The Guyver*; *Scream Queen Hot Tub Party* (video); *Shock Cinema Vol. 4* (video); *Virgin High*; 1992: *Blood Church*; *Innocent Blood*; 1993: *Beach Babes from Beyond* (video); *Future Shock* (footage from *Return of the Living Dead*) (video); *The Girl I Want*; 1994: *Pumpkinhead II: Blood Wings* (a.k.a. *Pumpkin-

head II) (video); *Vampire Hunter* (video); 1995: *Assault of the Party Nerds 2: The Heavy Petting Detective* (a.k.a. *Assault of the Party Nerds 2*) (video); *Burial of the Rats* (a.k.a. *Bram Stoker's Burial of the Rats* a.k.a. *Roger Corman Presents Burial of the Rats*) (video) [U.S.-Russia]; *Jack-O*; *Scream Queen Private Party* (video); *Stripteaser* (uncredited); 1996: *Fatal Frames* (a.k.a. *Fotogrammi Mortali*) [Italy]; *100 Years of Horror: The Scream Queens* (video); *100 Years of Horror: The Walking Dead* (video); *100 Years of Horror: Witchcraft and Demons* (video); *Sex Symbol Dynasty: Women Behind the Dynasty* (video); *Sick-o-pathics* (video) [Italy]; 1997: *Bimbo Movie Bash* (video); *Hollywood Cops*; *Whispers from a Shallow Grave*; 1998: *Boogie Boy* (video); *Curse of the Lesbian Love Goddess* (video); *Death Mask* (video); *Girls of the "B" Movies* (video); *Mari-Cookie and the Killer Tarantula* (a.k.a. *8 Legs to Love You*) (video) [U.S.-Spain]; *Moving Targets*; 1999: *Animals* (video); *The Killer Eye* (uncredited); *Kolobos* (video); *Play It to the Bone* (uncredited); *Sex Files: Pleasureville* (video); 2000: *Blind Target* (a.k.a. *Obietivo A Ciegas*) (video) [U.S.-Spain]; *Prophecy 3: The Ascent* (a.k.a. *God's Army*); 2001: *Horrorvision* (video); *Kannibal* (video) [Great Britain]; *The Monster Man* (video); *Venice Beach* (video); 2002: *Antena Criminal: Making a Jess Franco Movie* (video); *Each Time I Kill* (video) (unreleased?); *Scream Queen* (video); 2003: *Charlie and Sadie* (a.k.a. *Miss Maniac*) (video); *Corpses Are Forever* (video); *Zombiegeddon* (video); 2004: *Frost* (video) [U.S.-Switzerland]; *My Demon Nights* (a.k.a. *My Demon Nights with Linnea Quigley*) (video); *The Rockville Slayer*; *Spicy Sister Slumber Party* (video); *Super Hero Central* (video); *Super Secret Movie: Rules: Slashers* (television); 2005: *Hoodoo for Voodoo*; *It Came from Trafalgar*; *Lost Girls*; *Wolfsbayne*; 2006: *Dust to Dust*; *RiffRaff*; *Spring Break Massacre* (video); 2007: *Each Time I Kill*; *Strangers Online*.

Steve Railsback

Steven Railsback was born November 16, 1948, in Dallas, Texas. Primarily known for his intense characterizations in a number of high-profile genre films, his first role on the silver screen was in director Elia Kazan's 1972 film *The Visitors*. The seldom-screened feature about Vietnam veterans brought Railsback favorable critical notices, but he did not get his moment in the spotlight until his powerful portrayal of Charles Manson in the superior 1976 television miniseries *Helter Skelter*. So realistic was Railsback's portrayal of Manson that it disturbed audiences and critics alike, and it took him four years to find another role equal to his chameleonic talents. In Richard Rush's *The Stunt Man* (1980), Railsback played a Vietnam veteran, on the run from something mysterious, cajoled into becoming the stunt man on an epic film about WWI. A megalomaniacal director named Eli Cross (Peter O'Toole, in a great performance) demands that Railsback's character do more and more dangerous stunts. At times, the film mixes great farce with intellectual wit. Railsback was nominated for a Golden Globe award for Best Supporting Actor for this role.

The next year, he was seen in the controversial Australian science fiction thriller *Escape 2000* for director Brian Trenchard-Smith. Set some time after a holocaust, survivors are herded into prison camps whose politicized leaders hunt them for sport. Railsback co-stars as Paul, who maintains his humanity and seeks a way out of the futuristic death camps in this weird hybrid of the *Mad Max* films.

Railsback bounced back into leading roles in major Hollywood product with the feature film *Torchlight* (1984). However, his too-real portrayal of a successful man, who with his wife (Pamela Sue Martin) spirals downwards into the hell of cocaine abuse, made the film hard to watch. He also gave one of the greatest performances of his career in *Lifeforce* (1985) as an American astronaut who encounters a beautiful space vampire (the statuesque French actress Mathilda May). Tobe Hooper's bizarrely cast (Patrick Stewart and Chris Jagger, Mick's brother, as vampires) movie was a paean to the Nigel Kneale–penned British *Quatermass* films of the 1950s, mixed with small sections of the original source novel, author Colin Wilson's book *Space Vampires*. Studio interference and massive cuts reduced the already crazed film to nearly two hours of incoherent science fiction–horror fun with a Playmate-like nude vampire running around a destroyed London.

Railsback's higher profile roles dwindled a bit with brief surges like the violent actioner *The Survivalist*, directed by music mogul Sig Shore; the thriller *Distortions*, directed by Armand Mastroianni; and the oddly titled *Blue Monkey*, directed by William Fruet, about a lab experiment gone awry, and a huge insect creature terrorizing a small town. True to genre film conventions, Railsback stars in the latter as the first doubting, then heroic police officer–hero.

He gave a brave, powerful performance as a Vietnam POW in James Keach's HBO telefilm *The Forgotten* (1989) and appeared as a villain in a failed, splashy, sexy, somewhat incoherent science fiction vehicle for Pamela Anderson, *Barb Wire* (1996).

In 2000, Railsback landed a starring role in the low-budget action film *Termination Man*, as an unstoppable secret agent–type battling Russian terrorists. Possibly, it was this role that reminded filmmakers that Railsback was still around, because his next film (which he also co-produced), *In the Light of the Moon* contained a harrowing impersonation of serial killer Ed Gein. Produced in 2000, the film languished on the shelves until its brief theatrical release in 2002, and then became a cable mainstay and a popular DVD rental. As the film unspools at a slow and deliberate pace, we slowly watch the unhinged mind of the rural small-town killer at work.

Steve Railsback as the beleaguered astronaut in love with a space vampire in Tobe Hooper's epic horror–science fiction film, *Lifeforce* (1985) (Cannon Group/Easedram Limited/Golan-Globus Productions Ltd./Tristar Pictures).

Railsback seems back on track with several projects awaiting release, including *Barstow*, his second effort as a director. His first film as a director, 1994's *The Spy Within* starred Theresa Russell (*Crimes of Passion, Bad Timing*) as a beautiful spy who trades secrets for sex, and Scott Glenn as a reclusive explosives expert with a tragic past; it was well received by both audiences, and critics. Fans and critics also hailed him for his performance as Duane Barry in two episodes of the television series *The X-Files*. Railsback is married, has a son and a daughter and currently resides in Los Angeles. During my interview I came to the realization that he had rarely been interviewed, making our conversation seem even more intriguing, and rather special.

Q: What made you want to become an actor?

Steve Railsback: Since I was a child, I always wanted to be an actor. I recall that during my scholastic years I played the cousin of the prince in a production of *Cinderella* at the local college, and that was really it for me. I never acted again in Texas, but I knew I was going to go to New York to become an actor.

Q: You just knew that that was going to happen, that you were going to be an actor at a young age?

Railsback: I just knew that that was what I was going to do. I don't know how to explain it. I have known it all my life... it's somewhat strange. Nobody in my family was into acting, it is just something that I felt I was going to do and I have been doing it now for over thirty-five years.

Q: Let us cut right to the big question: *Helter Skelter*. How did you get that role?

Railsback: I was performing in a play on Broadway, and it was about ready to close. My agent called me and he said, "There are some people interested in talking to you about this *Helter Skelter* role." I had already worked on a film for Elia Kazan, I had one of the leading roles in his picture *The Visitors* which really opened doors for me, so it wasn't like I was an unknown in Hollywood. So I said to my agent, "Fine." For some reason, I just knew I was going to get that part in *Helter Skelter*, and I don't really know why. I drove across country, and auditioned for it, and the role was mine.

Q: Was it a tough film to make?

Railsback: Yeah, I guess. There was a lot to do. I did a lot of research for that part. I read the books by Ed Sanders and the attorney on the case, Vincent Bugliosi. The producers gave me audio tapes of Manson speaking, talking, and I would listen to them all the time, I do not really know why, because they were full of contradictions. I did as much research as I could, and then, for the rest, I used my imagination a lot. The great thing about playing Manson was you could do just about anything, and it's okay. The thing was, I had to play the characterization as written. It was pretty strict as far as the script went. For example, when we had scenes in the courtroom, everything was taken from the original court transcripts. So every if, and, or but, whatever, was [verbatim].

Q: You were amazing in that film. Your performance was truly incredible.

Railsback: Thank you.

Q: But, do you think that because you *were* so good, that you became typecast? Did playing Charles Manson hurt your career a little bit?

Railsback: You know what? It did for a while, but not for very long. There was a time I was offered every killer role in town after I played Manson. It did not matter if it was a movie role or on television, whatever. I turned them all down. I knew if I did them I would have a chicken ranch, but I would not have a career in two years. Thank God, things happened for me... roles in movies like *The Stunt Man*, *From Here to Eternity* on television, and things like that. However, there was a year or so after *Helter Skelter*, where I did not work because I turned everything down because I did not want to be typecast. I did not want to be caught up in what they wanted me to be caught up in. That is the way they do things in Hollywood. They pigeonhole you, or they try to.

Q: What can you tell me about working on *The Stunt Man*?

Railsback: It was one of the greatest experiences I have ever had in my life. Peter O'Toole was brilliant. However, the real brilliance behind that film was Richard Rush, who wrote and directed it. He was a phenomenal human being, and one of the most creative people I have ever been around in my life.

Q: It's a very deep, almost impenetrable film, with so many layers. Was that a challenge for you as an actor, knowing that there were different versions of realities all going on, and that Richard Rush was figuring it out as the film was being shot?

Railsback: It was all in his head. It was so multi-layered, you can imagine reading the script how it could be very difficult. You know, I always remembered what O'Toole said about Richard Rush. It was for an interview in the *L.A. Times*, he said, "I've worked for two directors in my career. David Lean and Richard Rush." I believe that is the greatest compliment somebody can get, and that is what Peter said about Richard. The man was something else. It was all in his head, and as tired as you were or whatever, you worked. Like, for example, I got one working day off in the four and a half months it took to film *The Stunt Man*. Peter, and I, and everybody else, you could not wait to get to the set every day, because you knew that something creative and exciting was going to happen. It was that man, Richard Rush, who made you feel that.

On the run from just about everything: Railsback in a scene from Richard Rush's *The Stunt Man* (1980) (Simon Productions/20th Century Fox).

Q: It seemed like a very energetic role for you as well.

Railsback: It was, it was. As I said, I worked on that for four and a half months of my life, a time which I will likely never forget.

Q: What can you recall abut the production of the film *Escape 2000*, otherwise known as *Turkey Shoot*? The film does have a bit of a cult following?

Railsback: Yes, it has a cult following, and I am surprised. I can say some things but I might be sued. There were some crooked things going on with that film, and I think I am going to get myself in trouble here, so I am not going to talk about that film.

Q: Can I ask you about director Tobe Hooper's film, *Lifeforce*?

Railsback: I loved it. I had a great time. I had never done a special effects picture with blue screen and green screen effects before. I had never done a film on that scale either—it took six months to shoot. I learned a lot, because you have marks—even when you are flying around on wires and stuff like that, you have marks. If you miss that mark by so much, it becomes a blurred image. It is so tedious, especially the spacewalk work. It took so long to make. You might get one shot a day. However, I had a lot of fun. I have never done a film like that before or since, so I had a ball, I really did. Tobe Hooper has been a friend of mine for many, many, many years. Therefore, we always have a good time together.

Q: What did you think of Mathilda May, your co-star in the film?

Railsback: I thought she was terrific. She was twenty years old, and beautiful.

Q: How did you manage to work yourself into a fever pitch for *Lifeforce*? In that film, your role has you always on the edge because you want to be possessed by the space vampire girl.

Railsback: I know what you are talking about. I had to work myself up to have my character want to be possessed by her, and at the time, I was trying to save the world. I don't know... I was just using my imagination. It wasn't so much a fever pitch that I was working myself up to, as there was a conflict in the guy that I played. He was being pulled towards her, and he was trying to pull away from her. He was trying to save the world, and he was trying to be with her at the same time. It is kind of like life, I guess [laughs].

Q: What did you think of the production company, Cannon Films, cutting the film for its theatrical release?

Railsback: It was not a very good decision. I do not think that the theatrical version was as good as the director's cut. I thought the longer British version of the film was great, and the director's cut was great. What they released in America and everywhere else was a shorter, different cut. I thought the version they released in North America ended up seeming too busy. It has now been released uncut on DVD in America.

Q: There is an unusual genre film that I want to ask about, *Blue Monkey*. Any remembrances about that odd little movie about a giant insect monster?

Railsback: It *was* an odd little movie. I had fun making that, I really did. It did not come out as I necessarily wanted it to, but I never go into anything for the money. That is something I have never done. I've turned down a lot of things, I wish to God I hadn't, and I've taken things sometimes I wish I hadn't. I always go into something like it is going to be a winner. I always give a movie 100 percent, 115 percent. It had some good things in it, *Blue Monkey*.

Q: What can you recall about appearing in *Barb Wire*?

Railsback: That was an interesting experience. I have had some interesting experiences in my life as an actor. I have had some great experiences too, by the way. Pamela Anderson was at a time in her life where if she decided to show up on the set, she decided to show up on the set. If she decided that she did not want to show up, she did not, and if she decided she wanted to go home, she did. You cannot get anything done like that. It was fine with me, the picture went over schedule, it went on three months longer than it was supposed to, and I was paid. It was a weird thing. You would go to the set, and they would say, "Pamela decided not to come in today." I would go "okay, fine, I'm going home too." I do not think I will say any more about that film.

Q: What can you recall about working on the film about the real-life serial killer Ed Gein?

Railsback: It [*In the Light of the Moon*] was a great experience. I loved that film. It was originally offered to me as a slasher movie. I was not interested in doing a slasher movie. Then I became an executive producer on the film, and said, "I'm interested in doing this, if we do it as a character study," and that is what we did. There is not a lot of blood in it, really. I really believe it is one of the best performances I have ever given. I am very proud of that film, very much.

Q: It must have been interesting to play opposite Carrie Snodgrass as your mother when in reality you two are about the same age.

Railsback: I had known Carrie for so long, about twenty-five years. It was great working with her. She was a wonderful actress. She's much older than I am. No, I'm kidding [laughs]. No. I prepared for that for almost three months. I had that character down so much, that I could have taken that character, put him in a bar in Paris, and done things with him. I just knew him really well, inside and out. I read all five books that have been written about Ed Gein. I read psychiatric books that I got from UCLA psychiatry students about all the different mental illnesses. He was a schizophrenic, and I read all about the different types of schizophrenia, and the various characteristics of schizophrenia. I researched this person so much because it was a character study that I wanted to do. I wanted to find every color, every thing that made him what he was, and find out who he was. As an actor, as a person, I am very proud of the work that I did in that film. I accomplished the work that I wanted to do as an actor, and you cannot say that about everything.

Q: You have done a number of guest starring roles in television programs...

Railsback: I have only done about ten programs I think in all my over thirty-five years of acting. I do them for friends usually. However, I have appeared in many movies of the week, and a few miniseries.

Q: What about theater work?

Railsback: I have done about twenty-five plays. I have done Off-Off Broadway, Off Broadway, and I have done Broadway. I did *The Skin of Our Teeth* on Broadway in 1975; I loved working in that. I also appeared in a version of *The Cherry Orchard* that Arthur Penn directed at Lincoln Center. I love the stage because there is an intimacy; there is that audience right there before you, and every night, that makes things happen. When it all works, between you, and the audience, you float right off that stage.

Q: What films have you been working on, or have in production?

Railsback: I made a movie called *Slash* in 2002, I star in it. I have two films coming out. One is called *The Box* with James Russo, Brad Dourif, Michael Rooker, and Theresa Russell. I have a picture called *Neo Ned* [made in 2005] coming out soon, and I plan to direct another picture soon. It will be called *Barstow*. It is a crazy film I have planned; I want to have Jason Priestley and Joe Pantoliano co-starring in it. It is about these three characters that live in trailer parks, and it is a slice-of-life drama with a twist. It will be a very dark, dark film.

Credits: 1972: *The Visitors*; 1974: *Cockfighter* (a.k.a. *Born to Kill*); 1976: *Charlie Ciringo* (television); 1976: *Helter Skelter* (a.k.a. *Massacre in Hollywood*) (television); 1978: *Angela* [Canada-U.S.-Italy]; 1979: *From Here to Eternity* (television); 1980: *The Stunt Man*; 1982: *Deadly Games* (a.k.a. *The Eliminator*); *Turkey Shoot* (a.k.a. *Blood Camp Thatcher* a.k.a. *Escape 2000*) [Australia]; *Trick or Treats*; 1983: *The Golden Seal*; *Veliki Transport* (a.k.a. *Heroes*) [Yugoslavia]; 1985: *The Hitchhiker: Petty Thieves* (01/15/85); *Lifeforce* (a.k.a. *Space Vampires*) [Great Britain]; *Torchlight*; 1986: *Armed and Dangerous*; *Spearfield's Daughter* (television); *The Twilight Zone: Dead Run* (02/21/86); 1987: *Blue Monkey* (a.k.a. *Green Monkey*) (video) [Canada-U.S.]; *Distortions* (video); *Scenes from the Goldmine*; *The Survivalists*; *The Wind* (video); 1988: *Deadly Intent* (video); 1989: *The Assassin*; *The Forgotten* (television); 1990: *La Cruz De Iberia* [Spain]; *Good Cops, Bad Cops* (television); 1991: *Alligator II: The Mutation*; *Scissors*; *The Young Riders: The Peacemakers* (01/19/91); 1992: *Forever*; *Sunstroke*;

1993: *Aftershock* (a.k.a. *Quake*) (video); *Bonds of Love* (television); *Calendar Girl*; *Final Mission* (video); *In the Line of Fire* (uncredited); *Nukie* [South Africa]; *Private Wars*; *Save Me*; 1994: *Separated by Murder* (television); *The X-Files: Duane Barry* (10/14/94), *Ascension* (10/21/94); *Walker, Texas Ranger: The Guardians* (10/07/95); 1996: *Barb Wire*; 1997: *Pressure Point*; *Stranger in the House*; *Street Corner Justice*; *Vanishing Point* (television); *The Visitor* (television); 1998: *Disturbing Behavior* [Australia-U.S.]; 1999: *Made Men*; *Me and Will*; 2000: *Charmed: Give Me a Sign* (02/24/00); *In the Light of the Moon* (a.k.a. *By the Light of the Moon* a.k.a. *Ed Gein*); *Say Goodnight, Michael* (short film); *The Sinister Saga of Making "The Stunt Man"* (video supplement); *Termination Man* (video); 2001: *The Practice: Killing Time* (09/30/01); *Storytelling*; *Zigs* (a.k.a. *Double Down*) (video); 2002: *Family Law: Children of a Lesser Dad* (02/25/02); *Slash*; 2003: *The Box*; *The Hitcher II: I've Been Waiting* (video) (uncredited); 2004: *The Handler: Give Daddy Some Sugar* (01/30/04); *Unconventional*; 2005: *The Devil's Rejects* (uncredited); *The In Between*; *King of the Lost World*; *Kojak: All Bets Off: Part 2* (05/22/05); *Neo Ned*; *Supernatural: Pilot* (09/20/05); 2007: *Plaguers*; *Ready or Not*.

Tura Satana

Tura Satana was born Tura Luna Pascual Yamaguchi on July 10, 1935, in Hokkaido, Japan. Her family moved to the U.S. during her early teenage years. As she stated in an autobiographical sketch that appeared on an earlier version of her website www.turasatana.com, "I was raised in an Italian, Jewish, Polish neighborhood known as the Mafia section of town in the west side of Chicago. We were sent there after we were relocated from the Mazanor relocation camp in California.... In the neighborhood that we were sent to, the feelings towards Orientals was extremely distasteful. I used to have to fight my way to and from school against a team of girls. There were at least five of them, and sometimes more...." However, an even greater tragedy struck at an early age: "Just before I was ten years old ... I was raped by five guys, all Caucasian. They left me in an alley when they were finished with me, and I had to crawl home from there.... When they were finally brought to trial for what they had done, one [guy's] father paid off the judge, and I was sent to reform school. The reason for that was that [it was decided in court that] I had 'tempted' those boys to do what they did to me...."

But, as Satana related in an interview with *Village Voice* columnist Michael Musto in April 1996, she took her revenge. "It took me twelve years to get even with them, but I got them all. One speaks in a very high voice now. I took him, and hung him up by his balls, and they fell off. Another, I just kept taking pieces of skin off with my nails. Another, I kicked in the face, and in the crotch. Moreover, another, I told, 'You left me in a pile of broken glass, and you made me crawl home!' I got to work on him, and he's still a vegetable."

Satana began her career in entertainment as a stripper. What is unusual is that she began her exotic dancer career when she was only thirteen, incorporating humor and sensual beauty into an art form. On the Internet Movie Database website, she is quoted: "When I was dancing burlesque, it was an art, it was considered to be a classy art, and I always thought it was elegant and required talent. I got out of it when it started to become raunchy, and lost the art."

Newspaper clippings in the New York Public Library for the Performing Arts Billy Rose Theatre Collection file on Satana mention her headlining a burlesque revue coming to Newark, New Jersey in 1956. In addition, a *Variety* article (dated March 1959) has a headline that stated "New Lounge in Dallas Bowing with Japanese Sexotic Satana."

She is known for her cinematic ascension to cult icon status via appearances in low-budget movies like Russ Meyer's *Faster, Pussycat! Kill! Kill!* (1966) and the Ted V. Mikels films, *The Astro-Zombies* (1967) and *The Doll Squad* (1973).

In her prime, the dark-eyed, jet-black-haired beauty had an exotic appeal; accentuated by an extraordinarily pronounced bust-line* and the sultry combination of her American Indian (Apache), Irish, and Japanese heritages. Her first film role, in Billy Wilder's *Irma La Douce* (1963), led to her appearance in the legendary *Faster, Pussycat! Kill! Kill!* The movie became a *cause celebre* at the time with Satana and her female companions seen as three deadly women that no man would want to meet. The trio (including the equally alluring and buxotic Lori Williams and Haji) were voluptuous vixens who would beat, terrorize, and murder—but also find time to titillate their (mostly male) captive. This was B-movie entertainment at its height. Satana was immediately elevated to a cult status as Varla, the leader of the bad girls. She flipped, karate-chopped, and killed men and women. *Variety* stated (in a February 9, 1966, review), "Story concerns a trio of bosomy swingers led by Tura Satana, her female lover Haji, and ambiSEXtrous (sic) Lori Williams.... Miss Satana has a mystic Oriental face that could be developed for better offbeat roles."

Satana also appeared on the television shows *Burke's Law*, *The Man from U.N.C.L.E.* and its sister show, *The Girl from U.N.C.L.E.*, and also appeared (uncredited) in the James Coburn spy movie spoof, *Our Man Flint* and the Dean Martin comedy *Who's Been Sleeping in My Bed?* (1963). At the time of our interview, her last major film role had been in a 1973 movie in which she co-starred with a bevy of gorgeous women. Since its release, Ted V. Mikels *The Doll Squad* has become a film that genre aficionados claim partly inspired the Aaron Spelling *Charlie's Angels* television show of the seventies. In *The Doll Squad*, Satana and others (including star Francine York) assemble to defeat a corrupt villain in league with a superpower from a foreign country. While the low-budget movie was bereft of Hollywood production values, it was far and away better than the previous Mikels film that Satana had appeared (*The Astro-Zombies*), where she essayed the role of Satana, a sultry and dangerous enemy agent. In that low-budgeter, the head of a group of villains working for a foreign power turns American lawmen into robots.

For years afterward, Satana had declined to be involved with the movie business for a variety of reasons. At one point, she worked as a nurse at a hospital, and was even rumored to have been shot by a patient. She was seriously injured in an automobile accident, resulting in two years of surgery and eight years of therapy, and worked security as a personal bodyguard and private investigator in Reno, Nevada. Satana planned a comeback back in 2000, and she still hopes that her fans will eventually get the opportunity to see her on the big screen once again. In 2002, she returned to the small screen via the video-only release of *Mark of the Astro-Zombies* for Ted V. Mikels. More recently, she appeared in the film *Please Sign It Love* (2004–05), which reunited her with *Faster, Pussycat! Kill! Kill!* co-stars Haji and Lori Williams, not to mention sixties B-movie and pin-up queens Kitten Natividad, Cynthia Myers, Theresa Ganzel, and Francine York. Now, what about the long-promised sequel or follow-up to *Faster, Pussycat! Kill! Kill!*?

Q: How did your entertainment career begin?

Tura Satana: I started dancing at the age of thirteen. I became a professional dancer at the age of fifteen. If the owners of the clubs I had worked in ever knew that I was only fifteen, I think that they would have had a heart attack. I started out as an interpretative dancer, but I was offered more money if I took my clothes off, so I did.

---

*At the time of her exotic dancing career, she proudly displayed a 36D bust. In 1998, she told the magazine Celebrity Sleuth that "currently I'm about a 40FF!"

Tura Satana prepares to steal the movie in this very rare on-the-set photo from Billy Wilder's *Irma La Douce* (1963) (Phalanx Production/The Mirisch Corporation/ MGM).

Tura Satana strikes an amazing pose in Russ Meyer's *Faster! Pussycat! Kill! Kill!* (1965) (Eve Productions Inc./RM Films).

Q: What can you tell me about working in Billy Wilder's *Irma La Douce*, the film that contained your earliest screen role?

Satana: I was working at the Pink Pussycat nightclub in West Hollywood. Wilder and his wife came in. His wife was the one who told him that he had finally found his Suzette Wong. After that, we were great friends. He always loved my professionalism.

Q: How did you become involved with Russ Meyer and the production of *Faster, Pussycat! Kill! Kill!*?

Satana: Russ Meyer approached me about *Faster, Pussycat! Kill! Kill!* while I was working on *Irma La Douce*. I came in for the interview in my costume of the bridesmaid from the church in *Irma*. It was hard to be tough and bitchy while I was wearing pink and flowers.

Q: How did you manage to convey so much anger, and take it to a new level on the screen, something that at that time had not been attempted before on film?

Satana: I took a lot of my anger that had been stored inside of me for many years, and let it loose. I helped to create the persona of Varla, and helped to make her someone that many women would love to be like.

Q: What can you recall about your appearance on television programs of the sixties?

Satana: In *The Man from U.N.C.L.E.* I was in the episode *The Finny Foot Affair*, and one of the guest stars was a very young Kurt Russell. I played a female spy and the heavy in that show. On *The Girl from U.N.C.L.E.* I was in *The Moulin Ruse Affair*, and I played Rabbit, the leader of the female guards in the house of a sinister villain Dr. Toulouse, played by Shelley Berman.

Q: What about *Our Man Flint*, with James Coburn?

Satana: I played both of the dancers in the nightclub where Flint finds a Bond clone, and they stage a fight.

Q: The 1973 film *The Doll Squad* was your last for many years.

Satana: I suggested to Ted Mikels that he hire Francine York for the [*Doll Squad* lead], since he wanted a more notable name than mine to be starring with Michael Ansara. We had a lot of fun doing the film with the gals that we had. All of the ladies were professional actresses, and we had our friendly little power plays, but they were all great to work with. I remember inviting Aaron Spelling to the screening of *The Doll Squad*. He thoroughly enjoyed seeing it. Shortly thereafter came *Charlie's Angels*, so one can draw their own conclusion.

Q: In retrospect, what do you think of the adulation that you have received and continue to receive?

Satana: I had a great deal of fun doing the films and the television shows and I was quite pleased to be able to associate with the caliber of stars that I did work with. I have been asked on several occasions to revive my career. I had been retired for many years because my husband did not care for show business in general. Since he passed away in October of 2000, I have received numerous offers to resume my career as an actress, and have three film projects pending. I even helped write one of them. [In that film] I will play the headmistress of a school of female assassins. The role I will play is very similar to my role in *Faster, Pussycat! Kill! Kill!* However, in a more subtle way. I hope that all of my fans enjoy it as much as I will enjoy making it.

Credits: 1963: *Irma La Douce*; *Who's Been Sleeping in My Bed?* (uncredited); 1964: *Burke's Law: Who Killed the Paper Dragon?* (03/20/64) (television); *The Man from U.N.C.L.E.: The Finny Foot Affair* (11/24/64) (television); 1965: *Faster, Pussycat! Kill! Kill!*; 1966: *Our Man Flint* (uncredited); 1967: *The Girl from U.N.C.L.E.: The Moulin Ruse Affair* (01/17/67) (television); 1969: *The Astro-Zombies* (a.k.a. *Space Zombies*); 1974: *The Doll Squad*; 1988–1989: *The Incredibly Strange Film Show: Russ Meyer, Ted V. Mikels* (television) [Great Britain]; 2002: *Mark of the Astro Zombies*; 2002: *Cleavage* (television); 2005: *Go, Pussycat, Go!* (video); *Please Sign It Love* (video); 2007: *Sugar Boxx*.

John Saxon

The very recognizable character actor John Saxon was born Carmine Orrico on August 5, 1936, in Brooklyn, New York. According to his New Utrecht High School yearbook in 1953, "Ricky's ambition is to become an actor. He likes dressing well, physical culture, and girls. We're sure he'll be a great success on the stage, or in the movies."

Saxon became interested in acting as a teenager and began attending dramatic school in Manhattan. After a photograph from a summer modeling job came to the attention of a Hollywood agent, Saxon became one of the young stock contract players at Universal Studios; weeks later, he arrived in Los Angeles ready for his new career. When interviewed by *Photoplay* magazine in the early sixties, he was very eloquent about his road to Hollywood: "I was raised in a New York neighborhood that wasn't too bad. Oh, it wasn't exactly Park Avenue, and yet it wasn't the Lower East Side either. I had to learn to take care of myself, and I managed to settle my share of problems my way. I fought, sure, but who doesn't, unless he's totally at peace with himself. I remember the ribbing I took from kids in the neighborhood, for example, when I posed for some dramatic illustrations in a magazine. I was supposed to look like a roughed-up teenager in the pictures. Well, I didn't exactly ignore that razzing when it got out of hand. It was those pictures that drew me to the attention of, and got me my contract at Universal."

After several screen tests, he received a co-starring role alongside Esther Williams in the 1956 drama *The Unguarded Moment*. Afterwards followed a series of leading man roles in *Rock Pretty Baby*, *Summer Love*, and *The Restless Years*. By 1958, Saxon was a highly publicized teenage heartthrob in movie magazines across the United States. According to a statement that he made to *Movie Life* magazine in the early sixties, "My biggest fight has always been to find myself. Most young kids have that difficulty. For a long time, I did not know where I was going. In the East, I floundered around. In Hollywood, I was told I had to be either a rebel or a sucker. But I think the only thing that matters is to be a real human being."

In 1961, after leaving Universal, he journeyed to Italy and played a number of roles, including one in horror genre director Mario Bava's *The Girl Who Knew Too Much* (a.k.a. *The Evil Eye*) (1962), then returned to Los Angeles. He told *Drama-logue* magazine in 1987, "Italian cinema was eclipsing Hollywood for a brief period. I had luck there but that's not to say it was good luck. I looked too Italian for them. They wanted to attract American actors who looked strictly American."

In 1965, he played a Mexican bandit opposite Marlon Brando in the highly regarded, violent western *The Appaloosa*. *Variety*, in its September 14, 1966, review, stated, "John Saxon handles himself well in the bandit role." Winning good notices and much attention for this portrayal, he landed another studio contract with Universal and appeared in some of the earliest feature-length films made expressly for television, such as *The Doomsday Flight* and *Winchester '73*. He also had a recurring role on the television series *The Bold Ones*.

In 1973, Saxon co-starred in *Enter the Dragon* with Bruce Lee and Jim Kelly. As Roper, a karate-kicking anti-hero running from the mob, he co-starred alongside the man (Lee) who made martial arts popular worldwide. As he explained to *Drama-logue*, there was a reason why he did not start showing up in *Enter the Dragon* clones after the commercial success of the movie: "Many people thought I missed my calling by not doing a series of karate pictures but again, I didn't see myself that way. At 38 I didn't want to mold myself into the larger than life hero who saves the free world once a year from the newest invading horde." In its August 22, 1973, review of *Enter the Dragon*, *Variety* stated, "Saxon ... is surprisingly adept in his action scenes, which include rugged battles as [Bruce] Lee's brother in the arts."

John Saxon and co-star Leticia Roman in a staged shot from the set of Mario Bava's *The Evil Eye* (1963) (Galatea Film/ Coronet s.r.l.).

In the years since *Enter the Dragon*, Saxon has been busy with numerous character-driven roles in many popular genre films, including numerous Italian crime films such as *I Kiss the Hand* (1973). He had prime roles in the Clint Eastwood western *Joe Kidd* (1972), the ingenious slasher thriller *Black Christmas* (1974), David Cronenberg's early biker film *Fast Company* (1978), *The Electric Horseman* (1979) alongside Robert Redford and Jane Fonda, the science fiction *Magnificent Seven* remake produced by Roger Corman titled *Battle Beyond the Stars* (1979), the apocalyptic black comedy *Wrong Is Right* (1981), and Dario Argento's thriller *Tenebrae* (1982). He received a major career resurrection with his heroic role in *A Nightmare on Elm Street* (1984).

Saxon also bravely states the truth about how Hollywood looks upon veteran actors: "Let's face it. The people in positions of casting are not film historians. We are talking over forty years of film work here but they may see me in one recent role, and deduce that is the thing I do from that one part. I was five years into my career before I got a character role with a blend of Portuguese, Greek, and Irish. You'd think that would've opened all doors from then on but that wasn't the case."

Q: What do you believe you owe your longevity as an actor to?

John Saxon: My family has some longevity in their background; maybe that has something to do with it. Another thing is time. When I started in the mid-fifties, I believe there wasn't much saturation for an actor as far as roles that he was seen in, and consequently there was a sense of duration to one's career. For example, in foreign countries that I have visited like South America, Argentina, even in some places in Europe, the older stars are treated with great veneration and respect, a sense of recognition. In America, we have a quick turnover society. We are very competitive, we do more of everything, consequently there are more new arrivals, and the new arrivals naturally push out the older people. My career probably has some of its strength in the fact that I have changed. I started as a kind of boy-next-door, which was foreign to me, coming from Brooklyn. At the time, I thought, "This is a role I've got to really practice on." Then, I began to do character roles, and as a result, I think, of being raised in Manhattan and in Brooklyn, I was aware of this sense of ethnic identities that surrounded all of us. Growing up, we knew the humor of other groups and their mannerisms and so on. I've played Jews, Arabs, Italians, of which I have a background myself, I've done Irish, even British, I've done Scandinavian, I've played all different kinds of roles. I think that helped because I kept moving around. Then I moved around geographically too. I went to Europe on occasion and would work there and come back to the United States. That's probably some of the reasons.

Q: Is it true that a modeling stint in your youth brought you to the attention of Universal?

Saxon: Yes, but it was not exactly modeling in the sense of fashion modeling or anything like that. What was going on in the early fifties when I was doing this was, there were magazines like *Modern Romance*, *True Romance*, and *True Stories*, which had stories illustrated by photographs. Therefore, I posed for whatever the story was; "Joe was crazy" or something like that. In fact, in the pictures that came to the attention of people, I played a Puerto Rican gang kid from the Bronx or some place, who was shot in a gang war and was lying by a trash can bleeding. It was a very attractive and sympathetic color portrait. People saw that and said, "Hey, look at this kid!" Therefore, it drew some attention and then I went to the West Coast, auditioned, and became a Universal contract player.

Q: Do you think that Universal tried to initially build you up to teenage audiences as a new young attractive rebel for the teen market?

Saxon: Yes, because that what was going on then. It was in a sense, a weak effort to rather make me their James Dean. However, I was not a James Dean type either.

Q: How did you come to star in *The Girl Who Knew Too Much* for the acclaimed Italian director Mario Bava, and what can you recall about that film?

Saxon: Actually, the first time I went to Italy was in 1958; after having worked in Paris, I wanted to go visit Italy. I wanted to see what the country of my parents was like and so on. Then in 1962, my contract had ended with Universal and I got an offer to do a film in Italy. I thought, "Hey, this is great." I went there and I didn't know what the hell to expect, or what it was really all about. I did not know who Mario Bava was. It was a hell of a different experience and a lot of fun. It was working in Italy in the sixties, that *La Dolce Vita* period. There was the recuperation after the war. People were beginning to feel good again, be outgoing and expansive again. It was a time to feel alive, it was fun, it was cheap to live, it was like a playground, and so was working on films. They did not have the production mentality of America yet, where if you finished at 4 PM you began the next day's work. In Italy, if you finished work at 4 PM, everybody went home.

Q: The English-language version of that Bava film changes some dialogue and plays some scenes more as a comedy whereas the original Italian version plays it a little more serious. Were you aware of this at the time?

Saxon: Not quite. It was an attempt to bridge what the term in Italy for these kinds of films is known as, that's sort of like funny, and not necessarily comic, but it's got a tone of...

Q: A little like a black comedy?

Saxon: No, the darkness was there already, but it was tongue-in-cheek, as it were, about itself. Bava, as a person, was a little bit like that. He wasn't quite superstitious. He believed [that] you didn't do this, you didn't do that... you didn't go under a ladder. You avoided whatever it was in the superstitions. He believed that and it was part of his personality, and yet I guess he was trying a hybrid.

Q: Other unusual roles followed including *Queen of Blood*.

Saxon: That film was really put together by a Corman. Not Roger, his brother, Gene. They had bought a Czech sci-fi film, for nothing probably, and part of it had to do with outer space and people were in outer space costumes and you could not see their faces. Around [this footage] they built a story with Americans. We did it very quick. I think we shot it about seven or eight days because a portion of the film was already done. Dennis Hopper was in it, and Dennis was trying very hard to keep a straight face throughout. It was a quick deal.

Q: What about *Night Caller from Outer Space*, the British film. It's a bit unusual for the period, being a very dark film with adult themes.

Saxon: I don't know if I have ever seen it. It was kind of fun also working in England at that time. In London, I went to the theater every night after work, whenever I could. It was an interesting experience too.

Q: Co-starring in *The Appaloosa* gave you some of your finest critical notices as an actor.

Saxon: There is a very funny Hollywood story about how I got the role. I had done another film in about 1959 for Allied Artists, a Jeff Chandler film where I played a young Mexican tough guy or something like that. My agent knew that I could play that kind of part, but when he approached the powers-that-be at [Universal], they laughed at the idea. They said, "What are you talking about? This has got to be a Mexican bandit who is the antagonist to Marlon Brando, forget it." They would not see me. Just prior to this thing, I happened to have done a play about the Cuban revolution, so I had a big handlebar mustache. My agent knew somebody, the secretary that was assigned to the director. She said, "I'll let him sit in the waiting room, but that's about as much as I can do." So, I'm sitting there and the director came out of his office, talking to somebody, and he glanced over his shoulder and he did a double take and he said, "See, now that's the kind of guy I'm looking for." They decided to test me, and I tested for that part, and was probably the most

Saxon (center) is pictured with co-stars Jim Kelly and Bruce Lee in *Enter the Dragon* (1973) (Concord Productions Inc./Sequoia Productions/Warner Bros.). The film made Lee a household name in the seventies; he died shortly after the film was produced and before it was released in the United States.

favorable because I got the role, and afterwards the powers-that-be at Universal said, "Okay, so you can play a Mexican bandit, what else can you play?" That's Hollywood.

Q: *Enter the Dragon* was a successful film. How do you feel about the fan reception towards that film now, over thirty years later?

Saxon: It's somewhat amazing. I had a feeling when I did that that the time was right for something involving the martial arts. I felt very, very different in the years before that. I thought, "No, no, this is private stuff, it's got nothing to do with entertainment." With *Enter the Dragon* I thought that the time was right, because I began seeing Dojos all over the city; in every mall they were springing up. The martial arts were becoming a kind of international phenomena, so I said to myself, "This is probably going to work out." However, I never thought that it was going to be something that people would come to me about over thirty years later and speak about it as a kind of a change of their lifestyle. But, it's understandable because Bruce Lee represented many, many things, like the little guy in *Jack, the Giant Killer*; he was also very ethnic. Being Chinese, I suppose many other people who were not in the dominant or superior group could identify with him, whether they were Chicano, black and so on, and certainly the Asians too. So it served a big, big market. It was a moment where a kind of hero like Jack, the Giant Killer could knock down big people. It has endured.

Q: Was *Planet Earth* originally designed as a pilot for a television series?

Saxon: The interesting thing about it was that, before we began, Gene Roddenberry, who had written the script, asked to talk to me and have lunch. He told me of his anxieties, which I did not understand quite at the time. He said, "What troubles me is the humor." I said, "How can that trouble you? That's the best thing in the film, that it's funny." But the powers-that-be at ABC at that time (this was before *Star Wars* and all that), they assumed that sci-fi had to be something somewhat serious, and felt that humor and sci-fi didn't go together. They were dead wrong because that's the kind of thing that made *Star Wars* successful. It had that live kind of thing where the creatures were funny and all of that was touched on in *Planet Earth*. All these years later, over thirty years later, *Planet Earth* has survived; it was a big seller in video stores and most people remember it very well and fondly because it was funny as well as being an action-adventure film.

Q: Of all the police crime melodramas that you have made in Italy, *I Kiss the Hand* is one of the better films.

Saxon: *Baciamo Le Mani*, which was done in Sicily in 1972 or 1973. That was somewhat interesting there too. I played sort of a new generation Mafioso who didn't go along with all the ideas of all the rhetoric about honor and fierceness and aggressiveness, and that was happening there for real at the time.

Q: Do you have a favorite of the crime melodramas that you did in Italy?

Saxon: There was another one that I did with Tomas Milian [*Il Cinico, l'Infame, il Violento* a.k.a. *The Cynic, the Rat, and the Fist* (1976)] that I thought was very good. It was somewhat interesting. In it, I played an American Mafioso who was visiting Italy.

Q: You worked with Antonio Margheriti on *Invasion of the Flesh Hunters* and Dario Argento in *Tenebrae*. What do you recall about those films?

Saxon: I have worked with Antonio since on other things. *Invasion of the Flesh Hunters*—the version of the script that I originally got [felt] was really kind of interesting. It was not a direct translation from the Italian, so it was sparse in a way. However, what I thought was interesting was that here they were talking about war like a disease, a virus that transmits itself from one person to another, and so on. When I spoke to Antonio at first, I said, "Gee, I like the script" and he said, "I don't." I said, "What, you don't? Why?" He really didn't quite tell me, and I didn't realize how graphic it was intended to be until I got into a scene where we were supposed to be sort of cannibalistic and they brought in some meat, and I said, "So, where does this meat come from?" I asked the question. It was supposed to be from the body of somebody, who had been chewed up, including the suggestion that it was his testicles, or something. I said, "You'll find me in my hotel, and if you don't like this, you'll find somebody else to finish that role." I never did that scene, and I was really depressed when I finally realized what was going on, what kind of movie I really was working on.

Q: And *Tenebrae*?

Saxon: Well, I only played a small role, what I considered pretty much nothing more than a cameo. Argento was kind of a strange, nervous character that I got to know only a little bit. He seemed to like me, admire me; he was calling me *maestro* because I had done a couple of things in scenes that were subtle, that he liked. However, I did not know much about his films; I had not seen much of them. Later, I began to be more acquainted through some of these sci-fi festivals and so on about what a following these people have.

Q: What can you recall about the Italian-Russian co-production *Jonathan of the Bears*, directed by Enzo Girolami?

Saxon: I had already known Enzo; I did a western with him in Spain in 1968. I do not know much about this film having not seen the completed version, so I cannot comment on it. However, it was filmed in Russia, and the most interesting thing I can say about it is, something about the background, about the way in which it was made. It was filmed at a Russian army base. There were shooting ranges just a few hundred yards away, grenade launchers. We, the actors, visited the military establishment, the commandos and captains and so on who let us shoot AK-47s and grenade launchers and so on. What an experience that was. That was something that I will remember for some time.

As a strong but distraught small town sheriff, Saxon has to save teenage coeds from a maniacal killer in the cult favorite *Black Christmas* (1974) (August Films/Canadian Film Development Corporation (CFDC)/Famous Players/Film Funding Ltd. of Canada/Vision IV/Warner Bros.).

Q: What can you tell me about *Death House*, a film that you directed?

Saxon: I saw it as an opportunity to direct something. I was very enthusiastic. I came on at the very last minute when another director did not want to do it. They were ready to shoot in a day or two. I said I needed some more time. I re-wrote the script, I hired friends to come on who were never intended to be in the cast and so on. I worked like a son of a gun, and the producer got so excited that he wanted to add more and more and more and more material and eventually the film got worse and worse and worse and I had no control over it. It was kind of a discouraging experience.

Q: Tell me about the *Nightmare on Elm Street* films, especially the last one [*Wes Craven's New Nightmare*] where you played the same character that you did in the first and third film, as well as yourself.

Saxon: I think my character in the last film was kind of like an approximation of who I am, or what I am in relation to what I seem to be. I seem to be an older friend to the girl who played my daughter, like an uncle, or even a father figure, and that was suggested. I think it worked out pretty well. I think the film was interesting. I think it was kind of a primer, like a whole basis for the mythology and horror.

As far as fans coming to meet me today, I find it very encouraging. They are very respectful, very courteous, very knowledgeable, and it has been very encouraging that people really remember and are touched by things that I have done.

Credits: 1954: *It Should Happen to You* (uncredited); *A Star Is Born* (uncredited); 1955: *Medic: Walk with Lions* (09/12/55) (television); *Running Wild* (a.k.a. *The Girl in the Cage*); 1956: *Rock, Pretty Baby; The Unguarded Moment* (a.k.a. *The Gentle Web*); 1958: *Summer Love; This Happy Feeling; The Reluctant Debutante; The Restless Years;* 1959: *The Big Fisherman; Cry Tough;* 1960: *Portrait in Black; The Plunderers; The Unforgiven;* 1961: *The Dick Powell Show: The Time to Die* (01/09/61) (television); *General Electric Theater: Cat in the Cradle* (10/01/61) (television); *Posse from Hell;* 1962: *Agostino: La Perdita Dell' Innocenza* [Italy]; *Mr., Hobbs Takes a Vacation; War Hunt; La Ragazza Che Sapeva Troppo* (a.k.a. *The Girl Who Knew Too Much* a.k.a. *The Evil Eye*) [Italy]; 1963: *Burke's Law: Who Killed Cable Roberts?* (10/04/63) (television); *The Cardinal;* 1964: *Bob Hope Presents the Chrysler Theatre: Echo of Evil* (06/05/64) (television); *Burke's Law: Who Killed the Horne of Plenty?* (10/07/64) (television); *Sette Contro La Morte* (a.k.a. *The Cavern*) [Italy–West Germany–U.S.]; 1965: *Gunsmoke: Dry Road to Nowhere* (04/03/65), *The Avengers* (12/18/65) (television); *The Night Caller* (a.k.a. *Blood Beast from Outer Space* a.k.a. *Night Caller from Outer Space*) [Great Britain]; *The Ravagers* [U.S.-Philippines]; 1966: *The Appaloosa; Bob Hope Presents the Chrysler Theatre: After the Lion, Jackals* (01/26/66) (television); *Dr. Kildare: The Art of Taking a Powder* (03/14/66), *Read the Book and Then See the Picture* (03/15/66) (television); *The Doomsday Flight* (television); *Gunsmoke: The Whispering Tree* (11/12/66) (television); *Queen of Blood* (a.k.a. *Planet of Blood* a.k.a. *Planet of Terror* a.k.a. *Planet of Vampires*); *Winchester '73* (television); 1967: *Bonanza: Black Friday* (01/22/67), *The Conquistadors* (10/01/67) (television); *Cimarron Strip: Journey to a Hanging* (09/07/67) (television); *Garrison's Gorillas: 20 Gallons to Kill* (11/14/67) (television); *Gunsmoke: The Pillagers* (11/06/67) (television); *Ironside: An Inside Job* (10/19/67) (television); *The Time Tunnel: Attack of the Barbarians* (03/10/67) (television); *The Virginian: The Modoc Kid* (02/01/67) (television); 1968: *I Tre Che Sconvolsero Il West—Vado, Vedo E Sparo* (a.k.a. *I Came, I Saw, I Shot*) [Spain-Italy]; *For Singles Only; Istanbul Express* (television); *It Takes a Thief: A Thief Is a Thief* (01/09/68) (television); *The Name of the Game: Collector's Edition* (10/11/68) (television); *The Virginian: Vision of Blindness* (10/09/68) (television); 1969: *The Bold Ones: The New Doctors* (television); *Bonanza: My Friend, My Enemy* (01/12/69) (television); *Death of a Gunfighter* (television); 1970: *The Bold Ones: The New Doctors* (television); *Company of Killers* (television); *The Intruders* (television); *Ironside: Ransom* (02/19/70) (television); 1971: *The Bold Ones: The New Doctors* (television); *The Virginian: The Regimental Line* (03/03/71) (television); 1972: *Banyon: The Clay Clarinet* (10/27/72) (television); *The Bold Ones: The New Doctors* (television) (television); *Joe Kidd; Kung Fu: King of the Mountain* (10/24/72) (television); *Night Gallery: I'll Never Leave You—Ever* (02/16/72) (television); *The Sixth Sense: Lady, Lady, Take My Life* (01/29/72) (television); 1973: *Baciamo Le Mani* (a.k.a. *Kiss My Hand* a.k.a. *I Kiss the Hand*) [Italy]; *Crossfire* (television); *Enter the Dragon* (a.k.a. *Long Zheng Hu Dou*) [U.S.–Hong Kong]; *Mr. Kingstreet's War* [South Africa]; *Snatched* (television); *Mitchell; Police Story: Death on Credit* (11/27/73) (television); *The Rookies: Cauldron* (11/27/73) (television); *Strange New World* (television); *The Streets of San Francisco: A Collection of Eagles* (02/01/73) (television); 1974: *Banacek: The Vanishing Chalice* (01/15/74) (television); *Black Christmas* (a.k.a. *Silent Night, Evil Night* a.k.a. *Stranger in the House*) [Canada]; *Can Ellen Be Saved?* (television); *Linda* (television); *The Mary Tyler Moore Show: Menage-a-Phyllis* (11/02/74) (television); *Planet Earth* (television); *The Six Million Dollar Man: Day of the Robot* (02/08/74) (television); 1975: *Gunsmoke: The Squaw* (01/06/75) (television); *Metralleta "Stein"* (a.k.a. *Blind Vendetta* a.k.a. *Fight to the Death* a.k.a. *The Stein Machinegun*) [Italy-Spain]; *Petrocelli: Mark of Cain* (09/17/75) (television); 1976: *Italia A*

Mano Armata (a.k.a. *A Special Cop in Action*) [Italy]; *La Legge Violenta Della Squadra Anticrimine* (a.k.a. *Cross Shot*) [Italy]; *Una Magnum Per Tony Saitta* (a.k.a. *A Special Magnum for Tony Saitta* a.k.a. *Blazing Magnums* a.k.a. *Shadows in an Empty Room* a.k.a. *Strange Shadows in an Empty Room*) [Italy-Canada-Panama]; *Mark Colpisce Ancora* (a.k.a. *Mark Strikes Again* a.k.a. *The .44 Specialist*) [Italy]; *Napoli Violenta* (a.k.a. *Violent Naples* a.k.a. *Violent Protection*) [Italy-France]; *Once an Eagle* (television); *The Rockford Files: A Portrait of Elizabeth* (01/23/76) (television); *The Six Million Dollar Man: The Return of Bigfoot: Part 1* (09/19/76) (television); *The Bionic Woman: The Return of Bigfoot: Part 2* (09/22/76) (television); *Starsky and Hutch: The Vampire* (10/30/76) (television); *The Swiss Conspiracy*; *Wonder Woman: The Feminine Mystique: Part 1* (11/06/76), *The Feminine Mystique: Part 2* (11/08/76) (television); 1977: *Il Cinico, L'Infame, Il Violento* (a.k.a. *The Cynic, the Rat & the Fist*) [Italy]; *The Fantastic Journey: Dream of Conquest* (03/10/77) (television); *Harold Robbins' 79 Park Avenue* (a.k.a. *'79 Park Avenue*) (television); *Quincy: Sullied Be They Name* (12/09/77) (television); *Moonshine County Express* (a.k.a. *Shine*); *Raid on Entebbe* (television); *Westside Medical: Intensive Care* (04/15/77) (television); 1978: *The Bees* [Mexico-U.S.]; *Fantasy Island: Escape/Cinderella Girls* (01/28/78) (television); *The Greatest Heroes of the Bible* (television); *The Immigrants* (television); *Shalimar* (a.k.a. *The Deadly Thief* a.k.a. *The Raiders of the Sacred Stone*) [India-U.S.]; 1979: *The Electric Horseman*; *Fantasy Island: The Victim/The Mermaid* (12/01/79) (television); *Fast Company* [Canadian]; *The Glove*; 1980: *Apocalypse Domani* (a.k.a. *Apocalypse Cannibal* a.k.a. *Cannibal Apocalypse* a.k.a. *Invasion of the Fleshunters*) [Italy-Spain]; *Battle Beyond the Stars* [U.S.-Japan]; *Beyond Evil*; *Running Scared* (a.k.a. *Back in the U.S.A.*); *Vega$: Aloha, You're Dead: Part 1, Aloha, You're Dead: Part 2* (11/05/80) (television); 1981: *Blood Beach*; *Falcon Crest* (television); *Fantasy Island: Chorus Girl/Surrogate Father* (02/21/81), *Cyrano/The Magician* (10/24/81) (television); *Golden Gate* (television); 1982: *Assassino Al Cimitero Etrusco* (a.k.a. *Assassin in the Etruscan Cemetery* a.k.a. *Murder in the Etruscan Cemetery* a.k.a. *A Scorpion with Two Tails*) [Italy-France]; *Desire* [Philippines-U.S.]; *Una Donna Dietro La Porta* [Italy]; *Dynasty* (television); *Falcon Crest* (television); *Rooster* (television); *Tenebre* (a.k.a. *Tenebrae* a.k.a. *Unsane*) [Italy]; *Wrong Is Right*; 1983: *The A-Team: Children of Jamestown* (01/30/83) (television); *The Big Score*; *Dynasty* (television); *Hardcastle and McCormick: Rolling Thunder: Part 1, Rolling Thunder: Part 2* (09/18/83) (television); *Prisoners of the Lost Universe* (television) [Great Britain]; *Savage in the Orient* (television); *Scarecrow and Mrs. King: The First Time* (10/03/83), *Saved By the Bells* (11/28/83) (television); 1984: *Dynasty* (television); *Fantasy Island: Surrogate Mother/Ideal Woman* (05/19/84) (television); *Finder of Lost Loves: White Lies* (10/20/84) (television); *Magnum, P.I.: Jororo Farewell* (01/05/84) (television); *Masquerade: The French Connection* (03/30/84) (television); *Murder, She Wrote: Hooray for Homicide* (10/28/84); *A Nightmare on Elm Street*; *Solomon Northup's Odyssey* (a.k.a. *Half-Slave, Half-Free*) (television); 1985: *The A-Team: Moving Targets* (02/12/85) (television); *Another World* (television); *Brothers-in-Law* (television); *Fever Pitch*; *Half Nelson: Diplomatic Immunity* (04/12/85) (television); 1986: *Another World* (television); *Falcon Crest* (television); *Vendetta Dal Futuro* (a.k.a. *Hands of Steel*) [Italy]; 1987: *Alfred Hitchcock Presents: The Specialty of the House* (03/21/87) (television); *Death House* (director) (a.k.a. *Zombie Death House*); *Falcon Crest* (television); *Hotel: Fallen Angel* (12/05/87) (television); *House Made of Dawn*; *A Nightmare on Elm Street 3: Dream Warriors*; 1988: *Falcon Crest* (television); *Murder, She Wrote: A Very Good Year for Murder* (02/28/88) (television); *Nightmare Beach* (a.k.a. *Welcome to Spring Break*) [Italy-U.S.]; 1989: *Criminal Act*; *Crossing the Line*; *My Mom's a Werewolf*; *The Ray Bradbury Theater: The Wonderful Death of Dudley Stone* (08/18/89) (television);

1990: *Aftershock*; *The Arrival*; *The Best of the Martial Arts Films* (a.k.a. *The Deadliest Art: The Best of the Martial Arts Films*) (video); *Blood Salvage*; *Final Alliance* [U.S.–South Africa]; *The Last Samurai*; *Monsters: The Waiting Game* (12/09/90) (television); 1991: *Blackmail* (television); *In the Heat of the Night: Liar's Poker* (10/29/91); *Matlock: The Parents* (01/15/91) (television); *Maximum Force* (video); *Monsters: The Waiting Room* (01/13/91) (television); *Payoff* (television); 1992: *Animal Instincts* (video); *Hellmaster* (video); 1993: *The Baby Doll Murders* (video); *Lucky Luke* (television) [Italy]; *No Escape, No Return*; *Jonathan Degli Orsi* (a.k.a. *Jonathan of the Bears*) [Italy-Russia]; 1994: *Beverly Hills Cop III*; *Killing Obsession*; *Melrose Place: Dr. Jekyll Saves His Hide* (11/07/94), *And Justice for None* (11/14/94), *Sex, Drugs, and Rockin' the Cradle* (12/12/94) (television); *Murder, She Wrote: Proof in the Pudding* (01/09/94) (television); *New Nightmare* (a.k.a. *Wes Craven's New Nightmare*); 1995: *The Killers Within* (video); *Liz: The Elizabeth Taylor Story* (television); *Melrose Place: They Shoot Mothers, Don't They* (01/16/95) (television); *Nonstop Pyramid Action*; 1996: *Frame-Up II: The Cover-Up* (a.k.a. *Deadly Conspiracy*); *From Dusk Till Dawn*; *Kung Fu: The Legend Continues: Escape* (10/07/96) (television); 1997: *Lancelot: Guardian of Time*; 1998: *Criminal Minds* (a.k.a. *Bottom Feeders*) (video); *Joseph's Gift*; *The Party Crashers* (video); *The Path of the Dragon* (video supplement); *Unseen Hollywood* (television); 1999: *Welcome to Primetime* (video); 2000: *Mario Bava: Maestro of the Macabre* (television-video); 2001: *Final Payback*; *Living in Fear*; *Night Class*; 2002: *Art of Darkness: A Night Gallery Retrospective* (television); *Outta' Time* (a.k.a. *The Courier*); 2003: *Blood and Steel: Making "Enter the Dragon"* (video supplement); *From Grasshopper to Caine: The Making of "Kung Fu"* (video supplement); *The Road Home* (a.k.a. *The Pitcher and the Pin-Up*) (video); *The Tao of Caine: Production and Beyond* (video supplement to *Kung Fu* DVD release); 2004: *Edgar G. Ulmer—The Man Off-screen* (video); 2005: *CSI: Crime Scene Investigation: Grave Danger: Part 1* (05/19/05) (television); *Genghis Khan* [Italy-China-Kirghizstan-Mongolia-Uzbekistan]; 2006: *The Craving Heart*; *Masters of Horror: Pelts* episode (television); *Stanley's Girlfriend*; *Trapped Ashes*; 2007: *God's Ears*; *The Mercy Men*.

Madeline Smith

Madeline Smith was born August 2, 1949 in Hartfield, Sussex, England. The doe-eyed, dark-haired British actress is notable for appearing in a number of film and television roles that highlighted her sensual beauty. She entered the entertainment industry purely by chance when she was working at her father's antiques shop. Just next door was a concert hall that attracted many famous bands and celebrities, and one day in 1967 she was approached by film producers and began her career as an actress. Although she was often been cast as the sexy girl in a number of ribald British comedies of the early seventies, she is most remembered for her roles in horror films produced by Hammer Films. A small role in *Taste the Blood of Dracula* (1970) led to a co-starring one (alongside Ingrid Pitt) as Emma, one of two female lovers who happen to be stricken with vampirism in *The Vampire Lovers* (1970), and a leading role, as Sarah, in *Frankenstein and the Monster from Hell* (1974). A frequent guest on many British comedy series of the seventies, she also appeared in the adventure-themed television shows *Jason King* (featuring Peter Wyngarde) and *The Persuaders* (starring Tony Curtis and Roger Moore) (both 1971). In terms of popularity and recognizeability, she is probably best known to audiences the world over for her too-brief role as the shapely Miss Caruso, the beautiful young Italian agent who sleeps with James Bond (Roger Moore) in the opening of *Live and Let Die* (1973); her incandescent blue dress' zipper meets its match in Bond's magnetic wrist watch. Nowadays, Madeline Smith primarily appears on the stage, her first love.

Q: Can you recall how you were cast in the film *The Vampire Lovers*?

Madeline Smith: I had already been in a Hammer film. In a small way, but a very enjoyable way, I was in *Taste the Blood of Dracula*. I think the producers quite liked me, because within what seemed to be like five minutes they cast me, without me having to audition, for *The Vampire Lovers*. What Hammer productions always did, and did very, very cleverly, I thought, was to cast a lot of heavy, good solid actors alongside relative unknowns. The veteran actors were always there for a lot of the key scenes. For example, I was in *Frankenstein and the Monster from Hell*, and a wonderful character actor played my father in it, my brutish father. I cannot remember his name now, but he was really famous. He was a real stalwart type of the British theater. What I am trying to say that in a large way, I think that helped to give Hammer films part of their quality. They were very, very carefully cast.

Q: *The Vampire Lovers* was certainly an opulent-looking film and it contained, for the period, quite a bit of nudity, making it controversial. Was the nudity a concern for you as an actress with a leading role in this film?

Smith: It wasn't so much the nudity, but the lesbian angle of the story. It's something about which one still does not speak freely, even after all these years later. What had happened, and I don't know why really, but that film had something to do with an attempted turnaround of the failing fortunes of Hammer at that time. I think they were attempting to give their films an injection of life. Sir James Carreras, the head of Hammer Films, was still very much alive at the time, he was the boss. I think it was his idea, this new direction. I think they thought that I had a sufficiently innocent face to play the victim. My answer to your question really is I did not actually mind it, particularly, the nudity. I do not think I was quite so innocent, and so young. Frankly, when I was cast I did not really know what was at stake, but in the end, I believe it was all done very tastefully, and the film had a wonderful director, Roy Ward Baker, who was always very gentle with me. The producers were very pleasant. It was like a little family really, working at Hammer Films.

The voluptuous Madeline Smith poses in this publicity photo from *Live and Let Die* (1973) (Danjaq Productions/Eon Productions/United Artists/MGM).

Q: You have appeared in a number of television shows in England, in numerous roles, and two of the shows, *The Persuaders* and *Jason King*, have cult followings.

Smith: *The Persuaders*, it was fantastic for me to be working on that show because when I was younger, I had fancied Tony Curtis, and then suddenly, there I was, working with him, which was wonderful. What a gentleman he was too, what a lovely guy. Roger Moore obviously liked me, because, I feel, as a result of appearing on *The Persuaders*, he suggested me for the small role in the Bond film *Live and Let Die*, and there we were

Madeline Smith shares a tender moment with Ingrid Pitt in this scene from the sensuous vampire film, *The Vampire Lovers* (1970) (American International Pictures/Hammer Film Productions Ltd.).

together again. However, working in *The Persuaders* was a super experience, particularly with my heartthrob Tony Curtis! You also asked me about *Jason King* with Peter Wyngarde. Peter Wyngarde took quite a shine to me. He was a very, very shy chap, and we became friends. He used me, in the nicest possible way, as his escort, to a number of openings, and closings, and first nights, and things like that, for quite a long time. In fact, I am even surprised we lost touch; he was quite a mate. Very, very shy, very, very nice, but a real gentleman. Oh, something has just come back to me, and this was hilarious. On the very first day of my role on *Jason King*, we had to get into a snuggle. I said, "Oh hello, you are Peter Wyngarde." He said, "Oh hello, you must be Madeline Smith," then the scene called for us to cuddle, cuddle, kiss, kiss, like we've known each other for ten years. That was quite funny to me.

Q: Two more films I would like to ask about are the sexy comedies *Up Pompeii* and *Carry on Matron*.

Smith: I'm surprised you even know about *Carry on Matron*! *Carry on Matron* was just one of the nicest things I ever did, ever. That was a family, working on the *Carry On* movies; everybody wanted to break into them. Peter Rogers, who produced most, if not all of them, I think he's Sir Peter Rogers now, I'm not quite sure, is still very much alive and well, and he's still got his offices there at Pinewood Studios. I had half a day on that film, *Carry on Matron*. In addition, the cast and crew worked like mercury, they were so quick. They got the script, they gave you the script. You got on, and did it, your role, and that was it. There was no messing about, or, as we say in England, no farting about. The love from the director, the cast members, between the cast members, and everyone on the set was palpable. I was really sad when it was all over, and even sadder when I was offered a part, a much bigger role, in another one, and I had to turn it down.

Q: Which one was that?

Smith: I do not remember. I think it might have been *Carry on Girls*. Whichever followed *Carry on Matron* was the one where I was offered a larger role [the role went to Valerie Leon, another interview subject in this book]. It broke my heart. Those were the days where I was actually shoving work away. Sometimes, I was actually offered three or four jobs together at one time, but I was already committed to one role. Actually, now that I think of it, I committed myself to some stupid movie promotional tour, and because of that, I had to miss the *Carry On* role after *Carry on Matron*.

Q: What about the film, *Up Pompeii*, with Frankie Howerd?

Smith: Bliss. *Up Pompeii* was your typical British comedy film of the period. It was set up by an old-time production company. To audition, I had to go to a little street in Chelsea, to a gorgeous twee little house, to meet the producer, and he gave me the role on the spot. There I was cast in the role of Erotica. I can't remember if that was the first time that ever I worked with Frankie Howerd, but I recall that I worked with him on many occasions, the last one being a play—that would have been around the time when Frankie Howerd was almost dying, around 1984. If you think that I did *Up Pompeii* with him in 1972, and was still working with him in 1984, one will suppose that we must have got on pretty well.

Q: Another comedic film that you appeared in during that period was *Percy's Progress*.

Smith: I have to be absolutely honest with you, I cannot remember a great deal about it, except that Leigh Lawson and I got on really well, and he asked me out. I think I was already hitched to someone else, but he asked me out just the same. He was an absolute dish. Later on, I had the enormous pleasure of working with him again in something that may have been seen in the States, an Agatha Christie adaptation called *Why Didn't They Ask Evans?* with Francesca Annis playing the sleuth. Leigh and I portrayed two murderers. That was great fun, because normally, I have been cast as innocent victims and such, and here I was at last playing a sort of demonic creature.

Q: It must have been something for him to ask you out, because on the set of *Percy's Progress* there were so many actresses...

Smith: You are absolutely right, voluptuous, and everything, but no, no, no. Leigh and I really hit it off. He was an absolutely delightful young man, who I think today is still very happily with Twiggy.

Q: You mentioned earlier how you got the role in *Live and Let Die*, but what can you recall about working on that film?

Smith: Well, I did have to audition. Even though Roger Moore suggested me for the role, the heavy production mob still had to okay me, and I believe that there were a number of other candidates. At that very time, I had just been cast to work with Sir Alec Guinness, to be in a play called *Habeas Corpus*. Moreover, dear old Roger Moore said to

Smith and Shane Briant (left) tend to wounded Dr. Frankenstein (Peter Cushing, center) in *Frankenstein and the Monster from Hell* (1974) (Paramount Pictures/Hammer Film Productions Ltd.).

me, "That's your real job, that's your real job. This is just a little three-day wonder. Get that tucked under your belt, and then you could go and do a real job." And, isn't it funny? All these years later, and nobody remembers a thing about *Habeas Corpus*, and everybody remembers the Bond movie. Who could have known at the time? The Bond films have actually gained massively in popularity since then. In those days, it was considered wonderful to do the Bond movies, wonderful. I was over the moon. Now, to be in a Bond film, you almost have to kill to do it.

Q: Concerning *Frankenstein and the Monster from Hell*, what was it like to work with Peter Cushing, David Prowse, and Shane Briant?

Smith: Shane was an absolute darling. He has disappeared from the scene and gone off to Australia, to carry on with his acting career. Dave Prowse was a lovely, lovely person. I had already known him because he was in *Up Pompeii*, and if you listen to the audio commentary track on the DVD of *Frankenstein and the Monster from Hell*, you will hear myself and Dave Prowse chatting, and reminiscing, about those days. He is a super chap. Peter Cushing of course was a dedicated man. What I mostly remember about dear Peter was that he did not eat anything. All he did was drink black coffee, and go about his business in an incredibly dedicated way. He was a lovely man, a gentle creature. He hardly ever raised his voice above a whisper, and I did not see much of him. I had nothing to say, my role in the film was that of a mute, so we had no scenes to rehearse, Peter and me. However, I do remember him and Shane Briant going off into little huddles together to get their scenes together absolutely right, for they did have dialogue. Peter would be writing little meticulous notes about the scene, and he and Shane would be discussing the scenes, rehearsing them and rehearsing them. That is why Peter Cushing is so renowned, famed, and loved, for his utter dedication to his craft.

Q: You have performed in the theater often, and I am sure done a lot of work that many of us are not even aware of. So, including everything you have done, in theater, television, and film, what portion of your work are you most proud of?

Smith: The most demanding, and perhaps slightly worrying role, and nobody in America will even know what I'm talking about, was a little four-hander play that I did called *The Canary Sometimes Sings*, written by Frederic Lonsdale, who is a sort of Noël Coward character, but more complex, with the most wonderful dialogue. I was cast as this wicked little beast called Elba. I really carried the play, and for me to go out on tour with that, and get nice reviews, was certainly easily, for me, the most satisfying job that I ever did. But perhaps the most enjoyable was a role on *The Two Ronnies*, a British comedy television show that I think has been shown on American television on occasion. I did a little spoof of a classic serial in the first show that they ever did. Ronnie Corbett and Ronnie Barker were the hosts and writers of the show. Ronnie Barker wrote the little spoof of a television serial called *Hampton Wick*, where I played the heroine. It was a wonderful little gig, and done just like a real classic serial. For me, aged around twenty-two, to be the heroine on this well-written show was just the most enjoyable thing. It was just amazing, just amazing. That was the most enjoyable role that I can remember.

Credits: 1967: *The Mini-Affair* (a.k.a. *The Mini-Mob*) [Great Britain]; 1969: *Some Like It Sexy* (a.k.a. *Come Back Peter*) [Great Britain]; 1970: *The Adventures of Don Quick: The Love Reflector* (11/20/70) (television) [Great Britain]; *His and Hers: Neighbors* (television) [Great Britain]; *Pussycat, Pussycat, I Love You* [Great Britain–U.S.]; *Tam Lin* (a.k.a. *The Ballad of Tam Lin* a.k.a. *The Devil's Widow*) [Great Britain]; *Taste the Blood of Dracula* [Great Britain]; *The Vampire Lovers* [Great Britain]; 1971: *Jason King: All That Glitters: Part 1* (12/08/71), *All That Glitters: Part 2* (12/15/71) (television) [Great Britain]; *The Persuaders: The Long Goodbye* (12/10/71) (television) [Great Britain]; *Doctor at Large: You Make Me Feel So Young* (03/14/71), *Doctor Dish* (03/21/71), *Modernizing Major* (03/28/71), *Congratulations—It's a Toad!* (04/04/71), *Change Your Partners* (04/11/71) (television) [Great Britain]; *The Magnificent Seven Deadly Sins* [Great Britain]; *The Mind of Mr. J.G. Reeder: Willing Victim* (television) [Great Britain]; *Mr. Forbush and the Penguin* (television) [Great Britain]; *Up Pompeii* [Great Britain]; 1972: *The Amazing Mr. Blunden* [Great Britain]; *Carry On Matron* [Great Britain]; *Clochemerle* (television) [Great Britain]; *Madly in Love* (television) [Great Britain]; *Up the Front* [Great Britain]; 1973: *Casanova '73* (television) [Great Britain]; *Live and Let Die* [Great Britain–U.S.]; *The Love Ban* (a.k.a. *Anyone for Sex?* a.k.a. *It's a 2' 6" above the Ground World*) [Great Britain]; *Ohh La La* (television) [Great Britain]; *Take Me High* (a.k.a. *Hot Property*) [Great Britain]; *Theater of Blood* [Great Britain]; 1974: *Frankenstein and the Monster from Hell* [Great Britain]; *Percy's Progress* (a.k.a. *It's Not the Size That Counts*) [Great Britain]; *Steptoe and Son: Back in Fashion* (09/04/74) (television) [Great Britain]; 1975: *Galileo* [Great Britain]; 1976: *The Bawdy Adventures of Tom Jones* [Great Britain]; *The 1936 to Didcott* (television) [Great Britain]; *Fern, the Red*

Deer [Great Britain]; *The Howerd Confessions* (09/16/76) (television) [Great Britain]; 1977: *The Black Knight: Romance: The Black Night* (television) [Great Britain]; 1978: *All Creatures Great and Small: Pride of Possession* (11/11/78) (television) [Great Britain]; 1980: *Why Don't They Ask Evans?* (television) [Great Britain]; 1981: *The Bagthorpe Saga* (television) [Great Britain]; *Blankety Blank* (09/03/81) (television) [Great Britain]; *Eureka!* (television) [Great Britain]; 1983: *All Creatures Great and Small: 1983 Christmas Special* (television) [Great Britain]; *The Steam Video Company* (television) [Great Britain]; 1984: *The Passionate Pilgrim* [Great Britain]; 2000: *Dark Knight: Dragon Singer* (09/09/00) (television) [Great Britain].

William Smith

Tall, broad-shouldered, and sporting a muscular frame, William Smith, the actor that genre movie fans love to hate, has a seemingly endless list of villainous celluloid credits. He has been called a brute, scary, a villain, a wild man with the sandpaper wisp of a voice, and in one case (in *Cinefantastique* magazine, September 1981), "the best, most crazed, absolutely stone-cold-over-the-edge villain in the business." Along with Don Stroud, and to a lesser extent Ed Lauter and Charles Napier, Smith remains one of the few character actors who has made a lucrative career out of playing villains, and in Smith's case, he trumps them all because he has been acting for well over fifty years.

William Smith was born on March 24, 1934 in Columbia, Missouri, and claims that he is a direct descendant of the legendary Western figures Kit Carson and Daniel Boone. As a child he appeared in many films, often as an extra. He joined the Armed Services, was in the Air Force during the Korean War, and received the Purple Heart for bravery. His fluency in five languages (English, French, German, Russian, and Serbo-Croatian) enabled him to land a teaching position within a top security agency within the armed forces. Smith also studied at the University of Munich and Syracuse University, and graduated cum laude from UCLA, where he taught French and Russian. While working towards his doctorate in foreign language studies, he was dissatisfied with teaching; instead he went under contract to MGM, beginning a long career of movie villainy. The brawny, rough–appearing, and muscular actor has appeared in well over three hundred feature films and television programs in a career that started in 1942 with one of his earliest roles in the Universal horror film *The Ghost of Frankenstein*.

In a number of counterculture exploitation films in the early seventies, Smith rode his own motorcycle and played rough characters. *Variety* gave him good to above-average notices for his performances in these films. For *Run, Angel, Run* (reviewed April 23, 1969), they stated, "William Smith, as Angel, is fine when the physical part of his role is expressed visually...." For *C.C. & Company* (reviewed October 21, 1970): "...Smith is impressive as the motorcyclists' guru; he's a big and handsome young guy who knows how to project." Finally, for *The Losers* (reviewed April 23, 1969) they stated, in what most certainly came to be the ultimate way to sum up his performances in these films, "William Smith as the leader of the cyclists is all muscle and wonderfully photogenic. The girls won't care whether he's acting or not." Smith also rode horseback in western garb in numerous television westerns, including the series *Wagon Train, The Virginian, The Guns of Will Sonnett*, and *Gunsmoke*.

Despite the hard-living roles he essayed in biker films and westerns, most grindhouse

William Smith, baddest of all the movie biker villains, pictured in a scene from *Run, Angel, Run* (1969) (Fanfare Films Inc.).

audiences recall Smith at his zenith (the '70s) from a plethora of gritty action films. His fists were often huge and flying into the faces of adversaries in films like *Darker than Amber* (1970) with Rod Taylor. *Darker than Amber* also has the distinction of featuring Smith and Taylor in one of the most grueling and realistic-looking fight scenes ever captured on film.

Variety, in its obviously unenthusiastic review of the film (August 19, 1970), called it "[a] gamy, gory private eye programmer starring Rod Taylor as John D. McDonald's Travis McGhee character. The very liberal doses of brutality and violence are obvious exploitation devices." *Variety* failed to single out the fabulously overwrought proto-testosterone performances from the leading male cast members and the incredibly vicious fight between Taylor's Travis McGee and Smith's character.

Smith was also a prominent villain in Blaxploitation films like *Hammer* (1972) (which featured ex–gridiron star and then-current and future box-office idol Fred Williamson), *Sweet Jesus, Preacher Man* (1973), *Black Samson* (1974), and *Boss Nigger* (1975). Of his portrayal of an amoral hitman in *Hammer*, *Variety* stated, "William Smith takes on the white syndicate enforcer chores with convincing gusto."

He also got to essay the role of the hero, or anti-hero, something he often did not get the chance to do, in films like *Scorchy* (1976) and *Seven* (1979). *Variety*'s October 3, 1979, review of *Seven* commented, "Smith, who attracted quite a femme following in the *Rich Man, Poor Man* vidseries as Falconetti, breezes through the role with laidback assurance."

Smith also studied martial arts, particularly kung fu and kenpo, with martial artist–

actor and stuntman Ed Parker; he even screen-tested for the television pilot of *Kung Fu* in the role of Kwai Chang Caine, wearing prosthetic eyepieces to make him appear Chinese. It is rumored that the ABC television network was interested in the actor for the leading role, but ultimately he was deemed too muscular and possibly menacing for the part; the role went to David Carradine instead. According to another unsubstantiated rumor, martial artist–actor Bruce Lee offered Smith a co-starring role in the film *Enter the Dragon*, but because another film Smith was working on at the time went over-schedule, John Saxon was given the role of Roper instead.

Smith has cultivated a persona as the ultimate cinematic man's man and movie villain perennial for over thirty years. A fitness fan in his prime, he is in possession of a Lifetime Achievement Award from the Academy of Bodybuilding and Fitness, and is a Guinness World record-holder for reverse curling his own body weight. Other notable fitness titles held include: Air Force Light-Heavyweight Champion. He played semi-pro football for the Wiesbaden Flyers in Germany, had a 31–1 record as an amateur boxer, and was an amateur downhill skier. He is an honorary member of the Stuntmen's Association of Motion Pictures.

Despite years of movie villainy, Smith is also remembered for appearing in the humorous role of Adonis, in the very last episode of the sixties pop art television program *Batman*. In the 1968 episode, *Minerva, Mayhem and Millionaires*, Smith co-starred with former celebrity glamour girl Zsa Zsa Gabor. In 1979–80, he was a series regular in *Hawaii Five-O*. Many fans also recall his knock-down, drag-out, seemingly endless fight with Clint Eastwood in *Any Which Way You Can* (1980). We get to see a more humanistic side of Smith in *Conan the Barbarian* (1982), where, as the blacksmith father to the young Conan, he was able to create his own dialogue.

Q: Is there someone that you always wanted to work with, and for one reason or another, never got the chance?

William Smith: I started working as an extra in 1942, and for that, I got a little brown envelope with eleven dimes in it. That is how I started in the movies. I always wanted to work with Henry Fonda; he was one of my favorite actors of all time, and I would have loved to work with him. I got to work with Yul Brynner. I got to work with Rod Taylor. I got to work with a whole bunch of good people. The only person I never got along with was Jack Lord.

Q: Why?

Smith: He was not a nice man. They had filmed eleven years of *Hawaii Five-O*, and I had come on to the show as a supporting lead for the twelfth year since James MacArthur had quit, reportedly because Jack Lord had never given him a dressing room. Did you know that Jack Lord made him change his clothes in the prop truck? That is the story. Anyway, James MacArthur quit and I went over to Hawaii and I filmed on the last year of the show. Jack Lord is the only actor in my over sixty-five years in this business that I could not get along with. He was just not a nice person. At the end of each month, he would have a luau, a celebration, and he would have one room for the Hawaiians who were really Samoans, and another for the white people. He separated us, and you are talking about people who are not only members of your own cast and crew, but people who are supposedly your friends. All of our Teamsters were Samoans, and all the Samoans that we had on the set in the cast were tough guys, man. I once said to a Teamster captain, "Why do you put up with this racist crap, man?" and he said, "I don't want to step on my wallet."

Q: According to your credits, you started out in movies as a child actor, and appeared in *The Ghost of Frankenstein*.

Smith: It was the first time that Lon Chaney Jr. ever played Frankenstein. There were three or four of us kids and we were kicking this ball around, and when they began shooting, the Monster came up behind us and roared. It scared us. I'll tell you something though, Lon Chaney Jr. was such a sweet guy; he was a nice person, and I got paid for that part too, so it turned out to be a pretty good deal. I was paid for seventeen hours of work. I received a little brown bag with eleven dimes in it, just as I said.

Q: Is it true that you were a teacher before resuming your acting career in the fifties?

Smith: Yes, I taught at UCLA. I taught Russian language studies. Some of my students were professors, but most of them were males between the ages of seventeen and twenty-two. I speak, among other languages, Russian, German, French and a little bit of English [*laughter*], and I actually worked for the NSA as a Russian interrogator and a Russian Intercept Operator.

Q: *High School Confidential!*—what do you remember about that film?

Smith: I had one line in that film, and my scene was with Mamie Van Doren. In fact, I was under contract with MGM and I wasn't supposed to be doing that little part. I had one line with her in a car outside the high school.

Q: You appeared in many television shows over the years, possibly too many for you to remember. But if you can, could you recall some favorite television roles?

Smith: There was one *Gunsmoke* episode called *The Hostage*, and there was a *Simon & Simon* episode that I liked.

Q: You were also a semi-recurring character on the television series *Daniel Boone*. You played a character named Amos.

Smith: That was a nice show too. Actually, the one television show that I appeared on that was a really good show that nobody ever recalls was a show called *The Asphalt Jungle* that ran in 1958. Jack Warden, Arch Johnson and I were all in it together, and Vince Edwards was in it too, as a doctor. The series was a television version of the movie. Anyway, it was during the very last show, because it was not very successful, that I said to Vince Edwards, "What are you doing after this?" and he said, "I don't know, I just did this stupid pilot as a doctor." It was a show called *Ben Casey*. At that time, we were on Channel 7, and it was a neophyte channel. Bing Crosby owned it, and he had just produced the pilot for the medical program *Ben Casey* and they kicked us off the air and put *Ben Casey* on in our slot, which was a shame. Vince Edwards got to keep on working, however.

Q: You also appeared in an episode of *Batman*.

Smith: That was a triumph of sorts because Zsa Zsa Gabor could never hit her marks. I was playing a big muscle-bound guy who was in this massage parlor. I would try to grab her hands so that she would hit her mark, and she would say, "Stop." Finally, the director said, "Miss Gabor, would you let William hold your hand so that you can hit your mark?" She said, "If he touches me again, I'm leaving." And she left.

Q: You made eleven biker movies. Which one was your favorite?

Smith: *Run Angel Run*, and I also had a lot of fun working on *C.C. and Company*, because Joe Namath was great to work with and so was Ann-Margret. *Run, Angel, Run*

Smith (left) and Greg Mullavy join former pro-football player Joe Namath (sitting) in the biker film *C.C. and Company* (1970) (AVCO Embassy Pictures/Namanco Productions/Rogallan Productions).

was the first one of those movies that I did. In addition, I liked working on *The Losers* a lot too.

Q: What was Joe Namath like to work with?

Smith: He was terrific. You know, he was never allowed to ride a motorcycle onscreen or even off the set because in those days he was still playing football. Therefore, every time they put him on a motorcycle, they put the camera on a truck, and attached the motorcycle to it and dragged it around.

Q: With all of the biker films that you made, you must have had some dealings with the Hell's Angels.

Smith: I did not have any problems with them, and I will tell you why. I had tattoos put on my head by a Hell's Angel biker for a film that I did. The best place to get a tattoo is on your head. If you do not like it, just grow your hair back. If you want to show it, you shave it. However, it took seven hours to do. I have a rose, a falcon's claw and an evil eye. When you get a tattoo on your head, there is no meat or sinew; it just goes right into your skull. When they finally finished work on it, the man who had done it said, "Man, you are unique. You know, one of these days they are going to bury you up on this hill. There's going to be a big rainstorm and it's going to wash your body down into the river. You will be the only man down there with a falcon's claw, an evil eye and a rose. You are unique." I said to myself [*incredulously*], "This is the guy who did the tattoo on my head?" When you work with the Angels during the day, they are fine. However, when they go out at night, if you are not an Angel, you should not hang out with them, really. I knew that. Nevertheless, two or three actors who ignored this really got hurt badly because they tried to party with them. Once they get a little drunk, or doped up or whatever they do, if you are not a real Angel, then you are an enemy, and they will hurt you. I did four or five movies with them and I never had any problems with them on the set. They liked me because I could really ride a Harley.

Q: What can you tell me about the film *Darker than Amber* that you made with Rod Taylor?

Smith: Best fight scene that I've ever done.

Q: Rod Taylor really hit you during that scene, didn't he?

Smith: He broke three of my ribs in the closet.

Q: Didn't the director, Robert Clouse, try to stop the fight?

Smith: No, Rod Taylor broke three of my ribs, and I broke his nose. I never let him know it but it hurt like hell. Rod is a tough guy. It's the best fight scene I ever worked on.

Q: I read somewhere that it has been rated as one of the best fight scenes ever recorded on film.

Smith: We jumped up on top of Ahna Capri in bed, who my character had just killed in the picture. I did not mean to, but I had to bust Rod's nose, because my ribs hurt so much. That was the most fun I had in the whole movie. Rod and I also worked together in the movie *The Deadly Trackers*, and on the set he had some problems with Richard Harris. Richard Harris didn't like my name so he usually referred to me by a derogatory remark. The two of them got into it a couple of times. Rod Taylor is a very tough guy, and Richard Harris, when he has a few drinks, wanted to fight. Rod Taylor beat him up so bad one night that they couldn't shoot for four days. I finished my bit. I had about seven or eight minutes of footage at the beginning of the film, I played a guy called Schoolboy. I only worked on the movie for nine days. However, the producers paid me to stay on the set for three weeks afterwards, after my scenes were all done and finished, just to keep them both from beating the hell out of each other. I found out the first night I went out with them together that they would start singing national folk songs when they would start drinking. Richard Harris would start singing, "When Roddie McCarthy starts marching down...," ... an Irish folk tune. And Rod would start singing *Waltzing Matilda*. Then, they would get mad at each other. I said, "You guys are embarrassing your countries because you can't sing, you can't carry a tune, and you don't even know the words, man." However, they would sing these songs, and when they would sing songs, they would not fight. It was when they would stop singing these silly songs that they would get into fights because of national pride or whatever. That's all I ever did for three weeks, and I got paid for it. It's the gospel truth. I'll tell you something else about Rod Taylor. In the town where we shot, if he saw somebody giving us a bad time, Rod would walk right up to that guy and say, "You'll leave Mr. Smith alone, or I'm gonna fuckin' dust you." That was a real compliment.

Q: You were physically pumped-up in *Darker than Amber*.

Smith: I had eighteen-inch arms.

Q: The movie *Hammer* starring Fred Williamson—do you recall how you got a role in that film?

Smith: Well, my agent got me the part, probably because of my tough-guy image.

Q: Did you get along well with the movie's leading man, Fred Williamson?

Smith: Oh yes. I'll tell you, when we shot my first scene, Fred came up to me and said, "They call me... The Hammer...." I couldn't stop cracking up. It was the way that he said it. Then, I worked on two similar films, *Boss Nigger* and *Sweet Jesus Preacher Man*.

Q: I have met many people who chiefly remember you for the low budget vampire thriller *Grave of the Vampire*. It is such an unusual movie.

Smith: It was so low-budget that it was made in eleven days for something like twenty-five thousand dollars. I had an interesting part. Michael Pataki played my father and when the movie began, he raped my mother in a grave. Because of this, I was born the son of a vampire. I was supposed to drink blood from my mother's breast when I was a baby, but I could not. It was an interesting part because I played a college student and Pataki played the vampire masquerading as a teacher, and all I wanted was revenge, two vampires going at it.

Q: Tell me about one particular scene in the film *The Ultimate Warrior*: the vicious fight between your character and Yul Brynner's character.

Smith: Yeah, where I dropped down into this chute after I cut his arm off. They had about three hundred trained rats that they dropped on top of me. They were all used previously in the film *Willard*. But they were very nice guys, the rats, they really were. They even walked on my eyes, and didn't hurt my eyes. The character that I played had a red beard and a mustache and they put some Karo syrup and peanut butter on my face to attract the rodents. Then this little rat came down and started eating the stuff, and while we were shooting, my mouth was wide open. They were photographing it all at about eighty frames, in slow motion.

Q: *Fast Company* was a David Cronenberg film, and one of the few movies that he did that was not horror-oriented.

Smith: That is right, and I thought that that was a nice movie. I remember that it was very cold in Canada while we were filming. John Saxon was in it too. Around that time, I also worked in a film in Canada called *Blood and Guts* [1978]. It was about professional wrestling. I found out that there are more professional wrestlers in Canada than in any other place in the world.

Q: What can you recall about working with Clint Eastwood?

Smith: Clint Eastwood is one of the most professional guys I ever worked with. The big fight scene that we had in *Any Which Way You Can* has to be one of the longest two-man fights ever done on film without doubles. We shot it in Jackson, Wyoming, which is about eight thousand feet high in altitude and I was smoking so hard at that time. We shot it in a day and a quarter. Clint really knows how to run a company and he treats everybody really well.

Q: What can you tell me about your role in director John Milius' production of *Conan the Barbarian*?

Smith: I was on that set for thirteen weeks, but I was only on screen for seven minutes. I do recall that I beat Arnold Schwarzenegger in arm wrestling and I never worked

Smith as an intense hero in the film *Seven* (1979) (American International Pictures/International Video Entertainment (IVE)/Triunfo/VPS Film-Entertainment GmbH).

with him again. I recall that the very first day he came to the set he spoke very little English. I speak German and he speaks Austrian, and he came directly from the gym, having worked out with a friend of his and I beat him at arm wrestling. And as he walked out my front door, he turned around and said, in German, "I will be a movie star" and he was and is, and now so much more! The one thing about Schwarzenegger that I will never forget is that nobody could double him, be his stunt double, because of the physical shape that he was in. He did all his own stunts. He worked twelve hours a day, and then he walked two miles. Then he would work out for two hours. In *Conan*, I just had one speech, to the young Conan, and John Milius kept saying to me, "I want something about steel and fire and strength." He came to me one day and said, "We're gonna shoot that monologue of yours now." I said, "What monologue?" He said, "The one I've been telling you about." In addition, there was no monologue scheduled or even in the script, so, the monologue that I did in *Conan* was off the top of my head. "Not man, not woman, not beast can you trust. This, can you trust... the sword." I did the same thing in *Red Dawn*. I wrote the whole Russian speech in that.

Q: Tell me about that.

Smith: John Milius said, "Bill, I want you to tell us why the Russians are having a hard time getting ahead with their invasion of the United States." So, I did this whole long thing, this scene. We had four cameras running, and it was like a four-page monologue We filmed and printed it and that evening I went to John and I said to him, "There's one thing I have to say to you, and I hope you don't get upset, but what I really said in that speech was that the real reason that the Russians are invading here is because of the film business, and because the bullshit directors are gay, and they don't deal with it well." Milius said, "Did you really say that?" I said, "Yes, John." But I told him the next morning that I didn't really say that because I knew he was going to shoot the whole thing over again.

Q: What do you recall about Francis Ford Coppola's *Rumblefish*?

Smith: I had a small role in that film and I was only on screen for about twelve minutes. I was down in Tulsa, Oklahoma where we were shooting that movie for thirteen weeks. I keep getting jobs like that, where I'm hired for an image or a certain look or whatever, and I'm hired to be down on the set nearly the entire shoot, and I am getting paid, but when it's all said and done, I end up on the screen with very little screen time. I would really like to have more lines but as long as they pay me, who really cares? On this film, there was a scene where Mickey Rourke tried to throw me off a bridge but I rammed him up against a cement wall and got his attention. He didn't try to throw me off anything else. However, I must admit something about Mickey, and I was very proud of this. The last scene that we had together, he was looking at this fish in the tank. He wasn't getting it right and Francis Coppola was not happy with what he was doing. I just took Mickey aside and I said, "You don't care about anything but these fish. When you go around the tank, just look at them. Don't care about Matt Dillon or me, or anybody else in the scene. Just make love to these fish, to the Rumblefish." He did, and Francis Coppola said, "That's a print." But, that incident made me feel really good. Mickey grabbed me, hugged me, and said he appreciated what I had done for him. I have never seen him again, thank God. Coppola never came on the set. He had a motor home that he called the Silver Fish. He filmed, edited, shot everything from that motor home. He had people on the set, camera crew, etc., but he himself, he was rarely, physically, on the set.

Q: Who was the best director you ever worked with?

Smith: Robert Clouse on *Darker than Amber*. I also liked working for Leo Penn, and Robert Aldrich, on *Twilight's Last Gleaming* was terrific too.

Q: Of all of your film appearances in the last few years, and you seem to be still working quite often, are there any roles that stand out in your memory?

Smith: I liked working on *The Mean Season* a lot.

Q: And you appeared in a *Nash Bridges* episode in recent years.

Smith: Yes, I played a Russian gangster. I got to speak Russian again, this time onscreen. I had not done that in a film in years.

Q: I know that you have written poetry. Do you have any plans to retire from acting and become a full-time writer, and possibly even write your autobiography?

Smith: No, I just want to keep on acting and writing poems. As for my autobiography, absolutely not. I don't think anybody would be interested in reading that.

Q: What would you like your epitaph to read when your name is listed in a book on the great character actors?

Smith: Keep your legs crossed and your mouth shut!

Credits: 1942: *The Changing World* (uncredited); *The Ghost of Frankenstein* (uncredited); 1943: *The Song of Bernadette* (uncredited); 1944: *Going My Way* (uncredited); 1944: *Meet Me in St. Louis* (uncredited); 1945: *A Tree Grows in Brooklyn* (uncredited); 1946: *Gilda* (uncredited); 1947: *I Wonder Who's Kissing Her Now?* (uncredited); 1948: *The Boy with Green Hair* (uncredited); 1951: *Saturday's Hero* (uncredited); 1954: *Kraft Television Theatre: Edie and the Princess* (07/28/54) (television); 1958: *The Ed Wynn Show: Nature Knows Best* (10/16/58) (television); *High School Confidential!* (a.k.a. *Young Hellions*); *Strange Awakening* (a.k.a. *Female Fiends*) (uncredited stunt double for Lex Barker); 1959: *Ask Any Girl* (uncredited); *The Gazebo* (uncredited); *Girls Town* (uncredited); *The Mating Game*; *Never So Few* (uncredited); 1960: *Mr. Lucky: The Gladiators* (03/05/60) (television); *The Lawbreakers* (uncredited); 1961: *The Asphalt Jungle* (television); *Atlantis, the Lost Continent*; *Go Naked in the World* (uncredited); 1962: *Zero One* (television); 1963: *Combat: Anatomy of a Patrol* (11/26/63) (television); *The Farmer's Daughter: I Am the Most Beautiful* (12/04/63) (television); *Stoney Burke: Point of Entry* (03/04/63) (television); *The Virginian: A Killer in Town* (10/09/63) (television); 1964: *The Alfred Hitchcock Hour: The McGregor Affair* (11/23/64) (television); *Broadside* (10/11/64) (television); *Combat: The Eyes of the Hunter* (01/21/64) (television); *Kraft Suspense Theatre: My Enemy, This Town* (02/06/64) (television); *Mail Order Bride*; *Perry Mason: The Case of the Frightened Fisherman* (02/27/64) (television); *Tom, Dick and Mary: Bad Day at Bristol Court* (10/05/64) (television); *The Virginian: Rope of Lies* (03/25/64), *Dark Destiny* (04/29/64) (television); *Wagon Train: The Bob Stuart Story* (09/20/64), *The Richard Bloodgood Story* (11/29/64) (television); 1965: *Laredo* (television); *36 Hours* (uncredited); *The Virginian: Timberland* (03/10/65), *We've Lost a Train* (04/21/65) (television); 1966: *Laredo* (television); 1967: *Custer: Death Hunt* (11/22/67) (television); *Daniel Boone: A Matter of Blood* (12/28/67) (television); *The Guns of Will Sonnett: The Favor* (11/10/67) (television); *Laredo* (television); 1968: *The Banditos*; *Batman: Minerva, Mayhem and Millionaires* (04/14/68) (television); *Daniel Boone: Flag of Truce* (11/21/68) (television); *The Guns of Will Sonnett: End of the Rope* (01/12/68), *The Fearless Man* (12/13/68) (television); *I Dream of Jeannie: Operation: First Couple on the Moon* (03/19/68) (television); *The Second Hundred Years: Dude Hand Luke* (02/21/68) (television); *Texas Rangers and Us*; *Three Guns for Texas*; *The Virginian: Silver Image* (09/25/68) (television); 1969: *Backtrack!*; *Daniel Boone: A Very Small Rifle* (09/18/69), *Hannah Comes Home* (12/25/69) (television); *Death Valley Days: The Restless Man* (01/02/69), *The Understanding* (01/28/69) (television); *Felony Squad: Blind Terror* (01/09/69) (television); *Here Come the Brides: Wives for Wakendo* (01/22/69) (television); *Ironside: Poole's Paradise* (10/02/69) (television); *Lassie: What Price Valor? Part 1* (01/12/69), *What Price Valor? Part 2* (01/19/69) (television); *The Mod Squad: Never Give the Fuzz an Even Break* (12/23/69) (television); *The Over-the-Hill Gang* (television); *Run, Angel, Run*; 1970: *Angels Die Hard*; *C.C. and Company*; *Crowhaven Farm* (television); *Daniel Boone: The Landlords* (03/05/70) (television); *Darker than Amber*; *Death Valley Days: The Contract* (04/18/70), *The Dragon of Gold Hill* (01/24/70) (television); *The Losers* (a.k.a. *Nam's Angels*); *The Most Deadly Game: Model for Murder* (12/19/70) (television); 1971: *Bearcats! The Return of Esteban* (12/23/71) (television); *Chrome and Hot Leather*; *Dan August: The Meal Ticket* (03/18/71) (television); *Julia: The Gender Trap* (03/16/71) (television); *Longstreet: The Shape of Nightmares* (10/28/71) (television); *Mission: Impossible: A Ghost Story* (02/27/71), *Encounter* (10/30/71) (television); *The Mod Squad: We Spy* (03/16/71), *The Loser* (11/30/71) (television); *Runaway, Runaway*; *Summertree*; 1972: *Alias Smith and Jones: What Happened at the XST?* (10/28/72) (television); *Colombo: The Greenhouse Jungle* (television); *Gunsmoke: Hostage!* (12/11/72) (television); *Hammer*; *The Manhunter* (television); *Mission: Impossible: Movie* (12/11/72) (television); *Piranha, Piranha* [U.S.-Venezuela]; *The Thing with Two Heads*; 1973: *The Deadly Trackers*; *The Fuzz Brothers*; *Gentle Savage* (a.k.a. *Camper John*); *Grave of the Vampire*; *Invasion of the Bee Girls*; *Ironside: Downhill All the Way* (11/08/73) (television); *Kung Fu: The Chalice* (10/11/73) (television); *The Last American Hero* (a.k.a. *Hard Driver*); *Search: The Twenty-four Carat Hit* (01/24/73) (television); *Sweet Jesus Preacher Man*; *A Taste of Hell* [U.S.-Philippines]; 1974: *Black Samson*; *Kolchak: The Night Stalker: The Energy Eater* (12/13/74) (television); *Planet of the Apes: The Gladiators* (09/20/74) (television); *Police Woman* (a.k.a. *The Insiders*); *The Rockford Files: Backlash of the Hunter* (03/27/74) (television); *The Six Million Dollar Man: Survival of the Fittest* (01/25/74) (television); *The Streets of San Francisco: Commitment Fittest* (01/03/74) (television); 1975: *Another Day at the Races*; *Boss Nigger*; *Bronk: Wheel of Death* (09/28/75) (television); *Death Among Friends* (television); *Dr. Minx*; *Gunsmoke: Hard Labor* (02/24/75) (television); *Movin' On: Prosperity Number One* (11/18/75) (television); *Police Story: Breaking Point* (12/12/75) (television); *S.W.A.T.: Time Bomb* (10/04/75) (television); *The Swinging Barmaids*; *The Ultimate Warrior* (a.k.a. *The Last Warrior*); 1976: *Barnaby Jones: Hostage* (01/15/76) (television); *Bert D'Angelo—Superstar: A Concerned Citizen* (04/03/76) (television); *The Blue Knight: Mariachi* (02/11/76) (television); *City of Angels: A Lonely Way to Die* (03/02/76) (television); *Crackle of Death* (television); *Hollywood Man*; *Police Woman: Brain Wash* (11/16/76) (television); *Rich Man, Poor Man* (television); *Rich Man, Poor Man—Book II* (television); *Scorchy*; 1977: *Logan's Run: Half Life* (10/31/77) (television); *The Oregon Trail: Evan's Vendetta* (television); *Twilight's Last Gleaming* [U.S.–West Germany]; 1978: *Blackjack*; *Blood & Guts*; *The Eddie Capra Mysteries: Murder Plays a Dead Hand* (11/17/78) (television); *Fantasy Island: The Funny Girl/Butch and Sundance* (03/18/78) (television); 1979: *Fast Company* [Canada]; *The Frisco Kid*; *Hawaii Five-O* (television); *Lion in the Streets*; *The Rebels* (television); *Vega$: Demand and Supply* (02/14/79) (television); *Seven*; 1980: *Any Which Way You Can*; *Buck Rogers in the 25th Century: Buck's Duel to the Death* (03/20/80) (television); *CHiPs: Satan's Angels* (12/14/80) (television), *E.M.T.* (01/19/80) (television); *Hagan: Jeopardy* (04/10/80) (television); *Hawaii Five-O* (television); *Trapper John, M.D.: Short Odds* (03/09/80) (television); *Wild Times* (television); 1981: *B.J. and the Bear: The Fast and the Furious: Part 1* (01/20/81), *The Fast and the Furious: Part 2* (01/27/81) (television); *The Cop Killers*; *The Dukes of Hazzard: Ten Million Dollar Sheriff* (11/20/81) (television); *Fantasy Island: The Lady and the Monster/The Last Cowboy* (01/27/81) (television); 1982: *Code Red: Revenge* (02/07/82), *Trial By Fire* (02/28/82) (television); *Conan the Barbarian*; *The Fall Guy: Licence to Kill: Part 1* (01/13/82), *Licence to Kill: Part 2* (01/20/82) (television); *Matt Houston: Who*

Would Kill Ramona? (10/31/82) (television); *Tales of the Apple Dumpling Gang* (television);1983: *The A–Team: Pros and Cons* (02/08/83) (television); *Benson: Katie's Cookies* (11/18/83) (television); *CHiPs: Fast Company* (03/20/83) (television); *Emerald Point N.A.S.* (television); *The Fall Guy: Manhunter* (01/19/83) (television); *Knight Rider: Short Notice* (05/06/83) (television); *The Outsiders*; *Rumble Fish*; *Seven Brides for Seven Brothers: The Killer* (01/12/83) (television); *Simon & Simon: I Heard It Was Murder* (10/13/83) (television); 1984: *Masquerade: Caribbean Holiday* (01/12/84) (television); *The Master: Juggernaut* (03/16/84); *Red Dawn*; *Riptide: The Hardcase* (02/28/84); *The Yellow Rose: The Far Side of Fear* (05/12/84) (television); *Scarecrow and Mrs. King: Fearless Dotty* (03/26/84) (television); *The Jerk, Too* (television); 1985: *Fever Pitch*; *Hardcastle and McCormick: There Goes the Neighborhood* (01/07/85) (television); *Hunter: Think Blue* (12/14/85) (television); *The Mean Season*; *Simon & Simon: Quint Is Out* (12/05/85) (television); *T.J. Hooker: Outcall* (02/02/85) (television); *When Nature Calls* (a.k.a. *The Outdoorsters*); *Wildside* (television); 1986: *The A-Team: The A-Team Is Coming, The A-Team Is Coming* (01/21/86) (television); *Airwolf: The Girl Who Fell from the Sky* (03/15/86) (television); *Downtown: The Outlaws* (11/29/86) (television); *Eye of the Tiger*; *Highway to Heaven: The Torch* (03/12/86) (television); *Murder, She Wrote: Deadline for Murder* (11/16/86) (television); *The Phantom Empire*; *The Twilight Zone: Shadow Play* (04/04/86) (television); 1987: *Airwolf: Welcome to Paradise* (08/07/87) (television); *The Badd One* (video); *Commando Squad* (video); *Hell Comes to Frogtown*; *Houston Knights: Lady Smoke* (10/20/87) (television); *Moon in Scorpio*; *O'hara: Silver in the Hills* (12/19/87) (television); 1988: *B.O.R.N.* (a.k.a. *Merchants of Death*) (video); *Bulletproof*; *Danger Bay* (11/28/88) (television); *Emperor of the Bronx* (video); *Hunter: Honorable Profession* (12/10/88) (television); *The Kill Machine* (a.k.a. *Nightmares of Nam*) (video); *Maniac Cop*; *Memorial Valley Massacre* (a.k.a. *Valley of Death*) (video); *Paradise: Founder's Day* (11/10/88) (television); *Platoon Leader*; *Red Nights* (video); *Supercarrier: Common Ground* (03/20/88) (television); 1989: *Action U.S.A.* (video); *Deadly Breed* (video); *East L.A. Warriors* (a.k.a. *Guerrero Del Este De Los Angeles*) (video) [Mexico-U.S.]; *Empire of Ash III* (a.k.a. *The Last of the Warriors*) (video) [Canada]; *Evil Altar* (video); *Hell on the Battleground* (a.k.a. *Battleground*) (video); *Hunter: The Fifth Victim* (12/09/89) (television); *Jungle Assault* (video); *L.A. Vice* (video); *The Last Battle* (video); *Slow Burn* (video) [Canada]; *Spirit of the Eagle*; 1990: *Cartel* (video); *Chance* (video); *The Final Sanction* (video); *Forgotten Heroes* (video); *Highway Warrior* (video); *Instant Karma* (video); 1991: *Kiss and Be Killed* (video); *Merchant of Evil* (video); *The Roller Blade Seven* (video); *Shades of L.A.: Cross the Center Line* (01/23/91) (television); *Terror in Beverly Hills* (video); *The Young Riders: A House Divided* (09/28/91) (television); 1992: *American Me*; *Cybernator* (video); *Feast* (video); *Dark Secrets* (video); *Hard Time Romance*; *The Last Riders* (video?); *Legend of Skull Canyon* (video); *The Legend of the Rollerblade 7* (video); *Shadow of the Dragon* (video); *The Third Rail* (video?); *Vinnie & Bobby: Vinnie Gets Sued* (06/20/92) (television); 1993: *Return of the Roller Blade Seven* (video);1994: *Due South: Manhunt* (10/06/94) (television); *Manosaurus* (video); *Maverick*; 1995: *Big Sister* (video); *Judee Strange* (video); *Raw Energy* (video); *Taken Alive* (video); *Walker, Texas Ranger: Final Justice* (11/11/95) (television); 1996: *The Malibu Branch* (television) [Canada-U.S.]; *Neon Signs* (video) [Canada]; *Rasputin* (a.k.a. *Rasputin: Dark Servant of Destiny*) (Voice only) [U.S.-Hungary]; 1997: *Doublecross on Costa's Island* (video); *Ground Zero* (video); *Hollywood Cops* (video); *Interview with a Zombie* (video); *The Shooter* (a.k.a. *Desert Shooter*) (video); *Uncle Sam* (video); 1998: *Blood of His Own* (video) [Australia-U.S.]; *Broken Vessels* (video); *No Rest for the Wicked* (video); *Warriors of the Apocalypse* (video); 1999: *Deadly Currency* (video); *Nash*

Bridges: Power Play (04/16/99) (television); *Star Trek: Deep Space Nine: Badda-Bing, Badda-Bang* (02/24/99) (television); 2000: *Beyond Belief: Fact or Fiction: The Devil's Tattoo* (08/11/00) (television); *Dangerous Highway* (video); *Never Look Back* (video); *Plastic Boy and the Jokers* (video); *Vice* (video); 2001: *The Elite* (video); *The Erotic Rites of Countess Dracula* (a.k.a. *Scarlet Countess*); *The Vampire Hunter's Club* (video); 2002: *Body Shop* (video); *Jumper* (video); *Justice League* (animated): *War World: Part 1* (02/24/02), *War World: Part 2* (03/03/02) (voice only) (television); *The Killing Point* (video); *Y.M.I.* (video); 2003: *God Has a Rap Sheet*; *Rock n' Roll Cops 2: The Adventure Begins* (video); *Zombiegeddon* (video); 2004: *Grave Tales* (a.k.a. *Killer Story*); 2005: *Hell to Pay*; *No Fear*; 2006: *Dead Man's Bluff*; *Inner Rage*; *Rapturous*; 2007: *Her Morbid Desires*.

Austin Stoker

Austin Stoker was born on October 7, 1948, in Trinidad, West Indies. The African American performer is also a very recognizable face to fans of some high-profile genre films of the '70s. Long before the current era of the superstar black movie actors, before there was the entertaining, wisecracking Will Smith and other comedians who smirked their way through action movies, there were the real men: Black action heroes like Fred Williamson, Woody Stroode, and others. In addition, of course there was Austin Stoker.

One of his first such roles was as MacDonald, the sympathetic human and eventual aide de camp to Roddy McDowall's simian Caesar character in 1973's *Battle for the Planet of the Apes*. (The character was played by Hari Rhodes in that film's predecessor *Conquest of the Planet of the Apes* [1972].) Stoker reprised the part in the short-lived television version of the series titled *Planet of the Apes*, and also provided the voice for the character in the equally short-lived Saturday morning animated version of the series, *Return to the Planet of the Apes* in 1974. Not eschewing the popular blaxploitation film craze of the era, he appeared as Pam Grier's lover and action sidekick (named Brick Williams!) in *Sheba Baby* (1975), directed by William Girdler. In the grindhouse *Exorcist* manqué *Abby*, again directed by exploitation specialist Girdler, he portrayed a detective. In William Girdler's thriller *The Zebra Killer* (1974), he co-starred as a tough police officer on the trail of a serial killer in Louisville, Kentucky. That same year, Stoker portrayed another heroic police officer in the gritty low-budget thriller *The Twisted Brain*. Stoker's love for performing on the live stage keeps him involved in the theatre.

Nowadays, he is best remembered for his leading role as Lt. Ethan Bishop in director John Carpenter's seminal action-horror film *Assault on Precinct 13* (1976), where, with the assistance of a few felons, he leads a ragtag group of people against a horde of seemingly hundreds of youth gang members when they lay siege to a nearly deserted police station on its last night. The world that Carpenter sets his film in is one that was not too alien to the culture of the seventies, although in a rather amped-up way he manages to make the ordinary seem foreboding, even scary. In this film, Carpenter's society is one of horrible neighborhoods, where people are strangely absent from the streets and an ice cream vendor carries a gun. The police have been driven to extremes, and there may even be a possible state of emergency taking place in the city (according to brief onscreen police patrol car radio announcements). Stoker's Bishop is a man who still believes in heroism, a man who emerged from the ghetto, to help others no matter what their skin color, religion, background, or deeds and/or misdeeds. His need/quest for heroism during a crisis is what makes the best kind of cinematic heroes. Napoleon Wilson meanwhile is an atypical urban action

Austin Stoker appears with Roddy McDowall (center) and Paul Williams (left) in *Battle for the Planet of the Apes* (1973) (Apjac International/20th Century Fox Film Corporation).

film anti-hero with his own moral code. He is en route to prison for an unspecified series of crimes, but in the world that Carpenter creates, Bishop (Stoker) and Wilson (Darwin Joston, eerily channeling actors Gary Cooper and Alan Ladd) join forces to combat the unknown (not unlike a western) and a seemingly endless horde of gun-toting psychopathic youths. This is one of the best films of the seventies, and Austin Stoker makes a fine cinematic hero you will not soon forget.

Q: Can you tell me about your earliest acting roles?

Austin Stoker: I entered the College of Our Lady of Fatima at fifteen years of age. Two years later, I joined a troupe formed by Geoffrey Holder, who not only achieved later fame as an interpreter of West Indian dance and music, participating in festivals in San Juan, Puerto Rico, but went on to become a highly respected dance choreographer as well as an actor. [To genre film fans, he is most memorable as one of the main henchmen, Baron Samedi, in the 1973 Roger Moore James Bond film *Live and Let Die*.] I was but one of a smaller group of performers retained by Holder for an exclusive engagement at the Caribe Hilton hotel. In addition, having been a movie fan since childhood, fantasizing myself as some sort of a Bogart or Olivier, I finally got my chance when I appeared in a travelogue produced by the producer Sol Hurok. My biggest break at that time came when Holder had the company journey to New York for a few club dates. After that, we were signed to the production *House of Flowers* on Broadway, and that show lasted for six months. That was during the end of 1954, beginning of 1955.

Q: You stayed in the United States?

Stoker: I teamed with a singer named Vivian Bonnell in a musical and comedy act. I played the bongos and steel drums, sang and danced. I joined the Army in 1957, and after my discharge two years later; we resumed our act, and then married that same year. We continued this way, as a club act, for about eight years, and then decided, in 1968, to go to California and try our hand at straight acting careers. I concentrated on drama, while Vivian concentrated on comedy. Before we left for California, though, I studied with Herbert Berghof, and later with Paul Mann, two well-regarded New York–based acting teachers.

Q: When you arrived in the West Coast, was it difficult finding work as an actor?

Stoker: Things were slow at first. I worked at various jobs to support my family, including a stint with a telephone company. However, I continued to study acting at the Theatre East Workshop, and then things gradually came around for me. I began to get parts in a variety of television shows like *The Mod Squad*, had small, tiny roles in motion pictures like *The Aquarians* [1970], and did a few Movies of the Week such as *Trouble Comes to Town* [1973]. I also worked a lot in commercials to supplement my income. When the road company of the play *The Boys in the Band* came to Los Angeles, I was first signed as an understudy, and then as a principal player. We toured the States for the better part of a year.

Q: Was the role of MacDonald in the movie *Battle for the Planet of the Apes* your first leading role in a major motion picture?

Stoker: Another actor [Hari Rhodes] had been set for the part of MacDonald, an African-American human who is sympathetic to the plight of the apes in their period of enslavement and now for the most part, the most valued human in a time of ape ascendancy. The original actor who had been signed for the part was unable to commit to the role due to some prior commitment, so my agent sent me over to 20th Century–Fox and I met with the producer Arthur P. Jacobs and the director J. Lee Thompson. Within days, I was working on the set of *Battle for the Planet of the Apes*.

Q: What was it like working on that production?

Stoker: I thought to myself, I have always known acting was a volatile profession, but this was ridiculous. However, I had studied hard and worked hard, and I knew I was as well-prepared as I would ever be. Fortunately, we started the production with the phys-

Stoker plays a trustworthy ally of the ape colonists in *Battle for the Planet of the Apes* (1973) (Apjac International/20th Century Fox Film Corporation).

ical sequences, the action stuff, and got into the dramatic material some time later. I had gotten the sense that the script was not quite polished, possibly not even finished by the time we started filming.

Q: How did you get the role of Lt. Bishop in *Assault on Precinct 13*?

Stoker: A mutual friend introduced me to John Carpenter, and he gave me the role without even an audition. Darwin Joston [who played Napoleon Wilson in *Assault on Precinct 13*] was a very good friend of mine; we had even studied acting and performed in the theatre together, and so it was great to work together in that film. I am saddened nowadays whenever I see that film because I miss him so much; he was a dear, good friend of mine. [Joston, who also appeared in Carpenter's *The Fog* as a character named Dr. Phibes, also acted on-screen with Stoker in 1982's *Time Walker*. He succumbed to leukemia in 1998.]

Q: Has the notoriety of appearing in *Assault on Precinct 13* affected your life, it being considered a cult classic?

Stoker: Once, while I was performing in the play *Detective Story* at LA's Lee Strasberg Theatre, Quentin Tarantino ran up to me in the lobby, and he ran off my whole résumé to me! Then, there was a time where I was receiving physical therapy and a nurse who immediately started to hum Carpenter's signature theme music from that film recognized me.

Q: What do you recall most about *Assault on Precinct 13* when you view it nowadays, nearly thirty years since its production?

Stoker: A sense of sadness because I miss Darwin Joston so much, and a sense of accomplishment. Even though it is a low-budget movie, it is still very, very effective, and you can't make that kind of film nowadays the same way. Even though there was a remake with Ethan Hawke and Larry Fishburne, it may share the same title, and even be based on the same core material, but there is no way that you can duplicate the feeling of the original film... although I suspect that they tried very hard.

Q: You also worked three times with revered exploitation filmmaker William Girdler. What can you recall about the man who directed you in *Abby*, *Sheba, Baby*, and *The Zebra Killer*?

Stoker: Well, we hit off immediately, having shared the same birthday. I have to tell you that I turned down a lot of work in those so-called blaxploitation films, because I felt that the stories were lacking, and that the character development was non-existent. However, I found exception in Girdler's films. He allowed you to show much more of a multi-faceted character. If you portrayed a bad person, you had to show what part of that bad guy is good. If you portrayed a good guy, you had to show what part of you was bad, and then find some way to put it all together. If you are allowed to do that, it makes the role that much more satisfying. Bill Girdler allowed me to do that. Actually, if I may add, Carpenter and Girdler were similar in a way. They were both from Kentucky, both had a passion for music, and both composed their own music for their films, which is interesting to me because there is such a tight correlation between music and acting.

Q: Do you still act?

Stoker: I continue to act, I still love learning my craft, there's so much more to know. Anyone who is interested in films, television, theatre, you are always a student of the art form, you are learning every day.

Credits: 1969: *The Mod Squad: In This Corner—Sol Albert* (12/16/69) (television); 1970: *The Aquarians* (television); 1973: *Battle for the Planet of the Apes*; *Love Thy Neighbor: Let's Have a Baby* (09/05/73) (television); *Trouble Comes to Town* (television); 1974: *Abby*; *The Blue Knight: Point of View* (television); *McCloud: The Colorado Cattle Caper* (02/24/74) (television); *Kojak: Before the Devil Knows* (02/27/74) (television); *The Twisted Brain* (a.k.a. *Horror High*); *The Zebra Killer*; 1975: *Airport 1975*; *Bronk: Betrayal* (12/14/75) (television); *Police Story: Incident in the Kill Zone* (01/07/75) (television); *Return to the Planet of the Apes* (animated) (voice only) (television); *S.W.A.T.: Death Carrier* (04/28/75) (television); *Sheba, Baby*; 1976: *Assault on Precinct 13* (a.k.a. *John Carpenter's Assault on Precinct 13*); *The Gemini Man* (television); *Jigsaw John: Dry Ice* (03/01/76) (television); *Riding with Death* (television); *Victory at Entebbe* (television); 1977: *Roots* (television); 1978: *The Hardy Boys Mysteries: Dangerous Waters* (10/29/78) (television); 1979: *The Incredible Hulk: Like a Brother* (01/31/79) (television); 1981: *Terror Among Us* (television); 1982: *Time Walker*; 1984: *Hotel: Intimate Strangers* (09/26/84) (television); 1985: *Robert Kennedy & His Times* (television); 1986: *Cagney & Lacey: The Man Who Shot Trotsky* (03/03/86) (television); *Scarecrow and Mrs. King: The Eyes Have It* (02/17/86) (television); 1988: *Uninvited*; 1989: *Falcon Crest: Ties That Bind* (05/05/89), *The Last Laugh* (05/12/89) (television); 1990: *A Girl to Kill For*; 1998: *Arli$$: Whatever It Takes* (06/07/98) (television); 2000: *Two Shades of Blue*; 2001: *Mach 2*; 2003: *The District: A House Divided* (11/08/03) (television); 2005: *Black Leather Soles*; 2007: *Twixter*.

Don Stroud

If you lived through the seventies as an avid movie buff, then you know the face of Don Stroud, the tall, blonde actor who was adept at playing beach bums, lotharios, and psychos. Stroud came from a real-life background as a sports enthusiast and surfer in Hawaii, and was cast as a body double surfer for early television heartthrob Troy Donahue in the television show *Hawaiian Eye*. He journeyed to the mainland in the sixties, and a succession of jobs led him to Hollywood where he landed roles in a variety of television westerns like *The Virginian*, before being cast in the thriller *Games*.

Movie roles as psychotic, nearly unstoppable villains cemented Stroud's movie persona in the public eye. In the early seventies, on television he was often seen trying to kill *Hawaii Five-0*'s Steve McGarrett (Jack Lord) or attempting to murder *Ironside* (Raymond Burr). The eighties bought better parts in *The Buddy Holly Story*, the James Bond thriller *Licence to Kill*, and a major role as a good guy: Police Captain Pat Chambers in the CBS television program *Mickey Spillane's Mike Hammer*. Nowadays, Stroud performs less in front of the camera but seems genuinely excited about relating tales of his life and career for those who appreciate his work as one of the great movie and television villains.

Don Stroud was born on September 1, 1944, in Honolulu, Hawaii, the son of the vaudevillian performer Clarence Stroud (of the Stroud Twins team) and singer Ann McCormack. Stroud grew up on the beaches of Honolulu where his stepfather Paul Livermore and his mother owned and operated a popular eatery and nightclub where she performed. As a teenager, Stroud worked on the beaches teaching tourists how to surf, one of the very few Caucasians, among native Hawaiians, Filipinos, Polynesians, Chinese, and Japanese. In an interview with *Drama-logue* magazine in 1984, Stroud said, "I was the only *Haole* [Caucasian] kid in school, and it was tough."

In 1960, teenager Stroud placed fourth in the Duke Kahanamoku World Surfing Championship, and that same year became Troy Donahue's stunt double. The television series *Hawaiian Eye* was partly filmed on the island, and Donahue's character had to surf. As he was unable to do it, the physically similar Stroud was discovered in true Hollywood style; the strapping youngster, all 6'2", 175 pounds of him, became Donahue's surfing double. "In the opening, you would see me on a surfboard, riding a big wave, and then there would be a close-up of Troy Donahue with water being thrown in his face. The close-up was shot in Hollywood."

On Donahue's advice, Stroud left Hawaii and journeyed to Los Angeles to try to make it further into the Hollywood limelight. He became a bouncer and then manager at the world-famous Whiskey a Go-Go nightclub on the equally famed Sunset Strip. Nightly, famous and infamous musical acts (and Hollywood celebrities) walked through the doors of the Whiskey a Go-Go. On occasion, Stroud even sat in on the drum kit, being a musician himself, and became good friends with many of the performing musicians including Frank Zappa. When not at the club, Stroud was still attempting to get steady work as an actor. He told *The National Enquirer* in an interview in the spring of 1974, "I auditioned for every part I heard about, and I got turned down, time, and again. But I finally broke through." On the advice of Sidney Poitier, a regular at the nightclub, Stroud began his acting career in earnest. "[Poitier] was in there all the time and I talked to him about acting, and he steered me in the right direction."

Stroud's acting agent was the same person who also represented famous movie stars Jane Fonda, and Sean Connery. "The very first thing I was up for was *Midnight Cowboy*, and they flew me to New York to read with Dustin Hoffman. There I was with Michael Sarrazin and Jon Voight [also vying for the role], and I didn't even know how to read a script." He told *Drama-logue*.

In 1968, Universal put him into five films as a contract player. He made his movie debut in Curtis Harrington's thriller *Games*, which starred Simone Signoret, Katharine Ross, and James Caan. "The contract system was great, being paid, and going to school in front of the camera."

After a villain part in the film *Madigan*, Stroud worked with Clint Eastwood in the urban action film *Coogan's Bluff*. The introduction to the Big Apple (the film's location) also introduced him to a wilder New York lifestyle, He told interviewers Bruce Earl Bowell and Nicarnor Loreti in *Psychotronic Video* magazine in 2003, "Clint Eastwood was one of the nicest guys I've ever met. I did *Coogan's Bluff* and *Joe Kidd* with him. However, *Coogan's Bluff* was my first trip to New York. Wow! That's the first thing I can say about my first trip to New York because I was drinking in those days. You see, I have been sober for twelve years now. Clean and sober by the way, clean and sober for twelve years. But those days, I was drinking a lot, taking a lot of drugs, doing cocaine, smoking a lot of marijuana...."

Of his over seventy television credits, Stroud is most proud of his work as a villain in a number of popular shows of the sixties and seventies. As he also told *Psychotronic Video*, "I was called back to Hawaii, to do *Hawaii Five-O* by Jack Lord, because he liked my work. He was a fan of mine, and we became very good friends.... [M]any actors did not really like Jack that much, but Jack and I got along fine. The first *Hawaii Five-O* role that I got, I was this hit man that came from Chicago, and came to the islands to murder this girl. Then I fall in love with this girl, and had to murder another girl, and dump the body in the river. I [used to] get all kinds of parts like this. Therefore, I fell in love with a girl, and then the Mafia made me shoot this girl who I was in love with. It was a great part. The next *Hawaii Five-O* that I did, I used a local accent. The third one I did was the best role. I was a sniper, at night, who got to shoot cops from this car. Those were wonderful, wonderful days."

Stroud also starred in two of the last three films Roger Corman directed. In *Bloody Mama* (1970), he had the male lead role opposite Shelley Winters; the supporting cast included Robert De Niro, Bruce Dern, and Robert Walden. "*Bloody Mama* was awesome. It had a great cast, and crew. Shelley and I had quite a love affair in those days...." He nearly married his co-star. In 1971, he appeared in the WWI action film, *Von Richthofen and Brown*, also directed by Roger Corman. It was plagued by accidents that took place during the filming of aerial dogfights.

In 1973, Stroud posed nude for *Playgirl* magazine's popular celebrity centerfold. (In a 1984 interview with the *San Francisco Examine* he said, "I'd like to do another centerfold now. I'm in the best shape I've ever been in my life.") At the same time, he was still being chased by his own demons. "I drank a lot, half gallon of vodka a day, and all the coke I could get my hands on! I could afford an eight ball of cocaine a day so that's what I did. I remember driving around Hollywood with a bottle of vodka between my legs. It was a great time in my life but it was a bad time in my life...."

He received some of the best critical notices of his career for his portrayal of the title character in *Murph the Surf*, a film based on the true-life exploits of Jack Murphy (Stroud) and Allan Kuhn (Robert Conrad), real-life serial robbers who eventually became infamous for the theft of the rare Star of India sapphire from the American Museum of Natural History in New York. *Variety*, in its September 4, 1974, review stated, "Stroud has the makings of a super villain. Even nattily attired, as was (the real) Murph's style, he looks like the perfect candidate for Mr. Amorality. Provocative and with great skill he creates the feeling of loathing for the Murphy character."

In 1976, he co-starred with his then live-in partner, Brenda Vaccaro, in *Death Weekend*, a.k.a. *The House by the Lake*, a brutal, nasty Canadian film, about a group of sadists terrorizing a couple in their isolated cabin in the woods. One of Stroud's best roles in years came via *The Buddy Holly Story* (1978). In the biographical picture about the pioneering rock 'n' roll singer, Stroud co-starred with Gary Busey and Charles Martin Smith, and played the drums. (All three stars played their own instruments in the critical and box-office hit.)

His association with the television shows based on famous noir novelist Mickey Spillane's Mike Hammer, private eye, began a completely new career for Stroud as Hammer's police lieutenant friend, Captain Chambers. The program had an on again, off again, start-and-stop schedule plagued by threats of cancellation. Star Stacy Keach's arrest for possession of drugs led to a smuggling charge and imprisonment.

In 1985, Stroud appeared as The Great Kahuna in the television program (and busted pilot) *Gidget's Summer Reunion*. One of

Don Stroud and a rather large gun appear menacing in the Don Siegel film *Coogan's Bluff* (1968) (Malpaso Company/ Universal Pictures).

the largest budgeted and biggest movies of his life, the James Bond film *Licence to Kill* (1989) found him as a heavy alongside the chief villain Robert Davi. It was the first Bond film ever to be considered for an R rating by the MPAA, before being shorn of several minutes of violent footage.

Don Stroud had a real-life run-in with violence on the streets of New York. Sometime in 1989–90, he attempted to assist a young man who was being mugged in Greenwich Village, but was stabbed several times for his good deed as the mugging victim disappeared into the night. Stroud suffered partial facial paralysis and the loss of an eye. Even with the many operations and therapy that resulted, the incident did not slow him down much; he has appeared in numerous films in the years since, mainly in lower budgeted B movies. As he told the Internet site www.terrortrap.com in a recent interview, "Well, I live on this Screen Actors Guild pension now. Every man in the world should have it. However, I have earned it, doing all the crap that I did... I did a lot of B movies that I didn't want to do." The 1997 Spanish thriller *Perdita Durango* (*Dance with the Devil*) contained one of his best roles in years as a crime boss. After appearing in *National Lampoon's Men in White* in 1998, he has remained semi-retired from acting.

Q: I read that you were the fourth-place winner in a surfing contest in Hawaii when you were seventeen.

Don Stroud: Being both born and raised in Hawaii, instead of playing pool, etc., my friends and I hung around the beach. I started surfing when I was just three years old, and when I was a little older, I believe when I was seventeen years old, I came in fourth in the Duke Kahanamoku World Championship. Surfing is fun, but I like to surf big waves. I surfed some twenty-footers when I was younger at the Banzai Pipeline, which at that time was located in a place that wasn't even called the Banzai Pipeline. We had nine-, ten-foot surfing boards in those days, made out of balsa wood, and we had no leashes, and wore no wet suit. Even in California, when you surfed you wore no wet suits, so when you lost your board you had to swim. However, kids down there today, they got the leash on the boards, they got the wet suits on, and it's a whole different thing. I ride short board now in a place near Malibu.

Q: You still surf?

Stroud: I still surf—of course, not like I used to, I'm sixty-three years old now. But I like to go out; I've got my nine-footer. I've enjoyed surfing all my life. I highly recommend it for anybody looking for something besides tennis, and baseball, and football, and those kinds of sports. Surfing, it is a great, great sport.

Q: Is it true that actor Troy Donahue discovered you because he needed a surfing double?

Stroud: Yes, it is true. I was on the beach at Waikiki. Back in the old days, the sixties, I was just out of high school, and I had long blonde hair. I was six foot two, and sported a real dark tan. Troy had long blonde hair. I was a great surfer at that time; Troy could not surf. They were shooting *Hawaiian Eye* in Hawaii. (Bob Conrad was a co-star on the show, and he became a dear friend of mine, we worked on *Murph the Surf* together years later.) That's when I started doubling for Troy, on *Hawaiian Eye*. That was one of those old, old television shows that shot some footage on location, and that's me surfing in what's supposed to be the long shot of Troy Donahue, then they cut to Troy and Bob in the studio, standing on some inner tubes, doing the close-ups. That was my first experience with Hollywood. Later on, I became a sort of stand-in for Troy on the show. Then

I became his bodyguard, and then his double, and stuff like that. Later on still, I eventually moved to Hollywood, and got a job parking cars as an attendant. Then I worked at the Whiskey a Go-Go.

Q: You were a manager there as well.

Stroud: I was about twenty-one, twenty-two, and I started out as a bouncer, and I eventually became the manager there. When I was working there, bands like The Byrds, Janis Joplin and Big Brother, Buffalo Springfield, Jefferson Airplane, who became Jefferson Starship, The Doors, The Young Rascals, The Turtles, The Grateful Dead, all those kids were around. I could go on and on and on with a list of names. There was a wonderful group of people there, and many unknowns as well. Many, many bands came through the doors of the place, and countless times that amount came there to hear the music. Sometimes even the then-unknown bands became stars after performing there.

Q: You must have been almost the same age as many of the musical acts that performed there...

Stroud: Well, a lot of them were all in their late teens, early twenties. We were also all of the state drinking age at that time, but nearly everybody took LSD in those days. We drank Coca-Cola too, massive amounts of the stuff, probably because of all the drugs. Nearly everybody seemed stoned in those days. God rest my soul, I have not had a drink or smoked in almost fourteen years now, but I had some trouble fighting the booze. I had to straighten out my act. However, back then, those days were crazy days. I hung around a lot with Frank Zappa and the Mothers of Invention. They were among the first long-haired groups who played at the Whiskey a Go-Go, and at first, not a lot of people gave them their due. People would go, "Get them off the stage, they stink," while they were performing songs like "Suzy Cream Cheese," and others. He had some great stuff, Zappa. At that time, nobody really liked Frank Zappa in great numbers. Years later, down the line, he did finally become a major player. *Freak Out!*, what a record that was, I still recall how amazing that record was. God rest his soul, Frank Zappa. It's a shame; he died way too young, Frank. He was a real good guy. You know, to my knowledge he never did drugs or anything like that. A lot of people think that Frank and the Mothers of Invention were a bunch of drug addicts, but Frank was straight all the time when I knew him back then. Frank didn't drink, he didn't smoke, and he was always a really good family man. I wouldn't say he was a spiritual type of man but he was different from the average group in those days. In those days, pretty much everybody got loaded in a real heavy way, especially on acid. Frank was a different breed of man, and I really liked him a lot. We got along great, and I knew Frank for years; he became a dear friend of mine. A lot of those guys who played the Whiskey are dead now.

Q: It must have been a great experience to be there nightly.

Stroud: It was a wonderful experience because we were all about the same age, and everybody seemed like they were into rock 'n' roll music. Up in San Francisco all the vibes were music, music, music all the time. There were always constant music jams going on up in Haight Ashbury and all those places. Let me tell you, it really was something, everywhere you went there was music, and people jamming.

Q: Is it true that Sidney Poitier went to the Whiskey and encouraged you to get into acting?

Stroud: In those days, all kinds of people came to the Whiskey. I recall Richard Burton, Elizabeth Taylor, Sidney Poitier, and Donald Sutherland. You name 'em, they came into the Whiskey a Go-Go. The Beatles, The Stones, all those guys used to come in. They used to have their own private booths, back tables, whatever. Burton and Elizabeth Taylor came in there all the time, the Queen of England came in there once when I was working there. She came to visit the Whiskey a Go-Go. It was a world-famous place, and usually there was a standing room only crowd. I made about $100 a night, which was a lot of money in those days, and the experience was incredible. I recall that I was telling Sidney Poitier that I was interested in acting, and I told him about what I had done on *Hawaiian Eye*. He introduced me to the same Hollywood agent that represented people like James Dean and, later on, Burt Reynolds, and I think Al Pacino. This agent had big name acts on his roster, and he took me on. Eventually, I got a contract with Universal Studios, and from there on, I have had a terrific career. I believe that I am one of the most fortunate actors to have worked in Hollywood in those days. I got into character acting right away, so I didn't have to go through that "I don't want to do this" and "I don't want to do that" kind of crap. I did everything I was offered. I worked on episodes of *CHiPs* and then I appeared in a supporting role in a James Bond movie—what a difference! I'd come back from working overseas, and then I'd work on a *Barnaby Jones* episode on television, and then I'd go off and do a film with Clint Eastwood, and then I'd go to Europe, and do a film for whoever. I worked all the time or it seems like it now. You know, there are these actors who say "I can't do this" and "I don't want to do that." Well I just loved the work I did. It was no problem for me to appear on *Ironside, Marcus Welby, The Virginian, The Name of the Game*, etc.

Q: Was the western series *The Virginian* one of your first roles on television?

Stroud: Actually, I think *The Virginian* was my first role. It featured Pernell Roberts as a guest star; he'd quit *Bonanza* as a regular. They were doing these terrific television series back then because color had just come in, and Universal was producing like twenty to thirty shows, one after the other. As an actor, I would just go from show to show to show. During this period, I was only making a couple of hundred a week tops.

Q: You were making more money working at the Whiskey a Go-Go?

Stroud: Actually, I was making twice, three, five or six times as much. I was making $100 a night, five to six nights a week, and the broads, oh! The broads were so, so worth it. Women are still nice nowadays, but in those days, with the flowers in their hair, and the free love happening and everything... wow. One cannot put it all into words if you were not there to live through it. I used to live in Laurel Canyon right near Canned Heat, the band. They were my neighbors, and at the time they lived there, they had a great hit song, "Going up the Country." It was free love everywhere you went at that time out on the West Coast, and everybody hitchhiked. Free love is a thing of the past, and nowadays, very few people hitchhike—too dangerous. Frank Zappa lived up in Laurel Canyon as well. He lived in the same old house that Houdini used to live in.

Q: *Games* in 1967 was your first feature film.

Stroud: I had never done any work in a feature film before. Curtis Harrington directed it. I was still under contract with Universal; I was under contract with them for seven years, and somehow I was moved onto this feature film project. I never read a script, and was just offered this part, in *Games*.

Q: What can you recall about *Coogan's Bluff* with Clint Eastwood, directed by Don Siegel?

Stroud: I recall that I got to ride my own motorcycle in the movie. I was one of the first actors who could bring his motorcycle on to the lot at Universal; at that time, you could not really drive a motorcycle on the lot, it was not allowed. I was into motorcycles in a big way back then. It was also because of my love for motorcycles that I went into the movie *Angels Unchained*. Later on, I had a terrible accident on a motorcycle, and after that, I was somewhat spooked from riding on one. Working on *Coogan's Bluff*, *that* was back in my motorcycle riding days. I also worked on the movie *Joe Kidd* with Clint Eastwood after that. I did a couple of films with Clint.

Q: Looking back, do you think that *Coogan's Bluff* may have been your introduction to everyone in the audience as a major heavy?

Stroud: No question about it. Because after that I appeared in *Madigan*, which starred Richard Widmark, and it just went on from there. There was the film *...tick...tick...tick...* [1970] and others where I played a heavy. I just got these really great bad guy parts. I was co-starring with all of these really great guys, and I made all of the stars look terrific. I was a big, tough-looking kid, so when the leads beat me up, I always made them look pretty good. I got beat up by Barnaby Jones. Marcus Welby beat me up, Cannon, hell, even Raymond Burr in his wheelchair [on *Ironside*] beat me up. He's in the wheelchair fighting me, and beating me up, and I'm holding on to the wheelchair, I tip over the wheelchair, I grab a hold of a pillow, and I'm trying to strangle him, and he beats me up... this went on, and on, and on. Aaron Spelling was a big fan of mine. He produced *Charlie's Angels* and so on, he had about five or six shows on television at that time and he hired me often. The producer Quinn Martin also had some great shows back then, *Cannon*, *Barnaby Jones*, and *The Streets of San Francisco*, and I worked for him a lot. I appeared on *The Streets of San Francisco* four times. *Hawaii Five-O*, I did five times. Jack Lord and I got on wonderfully. Remember, I was a big guy, and at the end of the particular episode, when he caught me, I always made him look good. I made all those guys look good. Those were great days, especially on *Hawaii Five-O*, because I got to go back to Hawaii. When I guested on that show, I stayed at the Hilton hotel. When I lived there as a teenager, I was the towel boy at the pool. Here I am, it's years later, fifteen years later, and I am staying at the penthouse. It was quite a great experience for me.

Q: Did you see any of your friends, people, surfers, etc. from the old days?

Stroud: The guys on the beach? They are still there today, the ones that are still alive. Those guys will always be my dear friends. We're all a bunch of old surfers. You have to understand that I was the only white boy in my school when I grew up—they called us *Haoles* [pronounced hollies] over there. I grew up with the Samoans, the Filipinos, the Hawaiians, the Japanese, the Chinese, and so on and so on. There were no other *Haoles* hanging out around there at that time but me. The only other *Haoles* that I was even aware of went to another school, the good school. I went to the bad school. However, I didn't go to school much, I surfed. I grew up in a whole different world when I grew up in Hawaii. In those days in Hawaii, it was different, really spectacular. It was a wonderful world to grow up in. I'm really glad I grew up in Hawaii.

Q: What can you recall about *Von Richthofen and Brown*, where you had one of your first co-starring roles. It was produced and directed by Roger Corman, and it wound up being his last picture [as a director] for nearly twenty years.

Stroud: I almost was killed making it. I was actually in a plane crash while making that film. We were in Ireland, shooting a scene where the camera was mounted on the

Stroud as he appears in *Von Richthofen and Brown* (1971) (The Corman Company/United Artists).

wing. We had to shoot all of the aerial footage in the air. A bird came through the cockpit and hit the pilot. It was a double wing cockpit, and it hit him in the face. The plane went down and crashed into a levee. We were both underwater, the pilot and I. When I realized that I was still alive, but in the water, I took my parachute off, and then my seat belt off, and then I took the pilot's seat belt off, and found that he was unconscious. I held him up for forty-five minutes and saved his life. I think it was all due to the surfing the big waves in Hawaii that gave me the strength to make it, it helped me to live, and to save this guy too.

Q: It took them that long to reach you?

Stroud: For a few minutes, they didn't even know that we had crashed. We were ten, fifteen miles from where we took off from the airport, when we were out there shooting. We were shooting out in the countryside, we crashed... boom, just like that, and we were down. It took them a long time to find us. It was quite an experience.

Q: You had a very different kind of role in that film.

Stroud: I thought the aerial photography was better than many of the big films that they were making at the time—you know, the more expensive World War I films like *The Blue Max*, etc.

Q: Do you think that maybe the film was too ambitious for Corman?

Stroud: Whatever it was, it turned out to be a Roger Corman movie. Roger Corman is in a world where he makes the movies that he wants to make. Believe me, he made money on that film. He makes money on all of his films. I've made about twenty-five films for Roger Corman, and most of them are bad films, but I got paid every time and to this day, I get residuals on them. *Von Richthofen* is probably playing somewhere tonight, maybe in Yugoslavia or some place like that, but I will get a residual payment off it. I mean [*laughs*], Roger's films play all over the world. Working for Roger, he has his own style, no doubt about that. He does not even care if he makes hits because he makes so much money on all these films. It is partly because of how little they cost to make. Back in those days, nobody made any money on these kinds of films except for Roger. If Roger directed it, he usually produced it at the same time, so he managed to be on top of everything. Most of the time, he also had a hand in the distribution as well.

Q: What's it like to work with Clint Eastwood?

Stroud: Clint's a wonderful guy. Clint and I had to get along in the first place; otherwise he wouldn't have called me back. Last time I was going to work with him, I auditioned for a role in a film that he directed. The one he made in Savannah, Georgia, the one that did not do box-office...

Q: *Midnight in the Garden of Good and Evil*?

Stroud: Right. I didn't get the part, but I wound up getting a role in another movie around that same time. It was something else, a film called *Perdito Durango* with Rosie Perez. I think it's a nasty little film. I played a weird part in that, a really weird part.

Q: But he's good to work with, Eastwood?

Stroud: Who wouldn't want to do a Clint Eastwood movie? You know you're going be seen, that it's going to lead to another gig, which is what making a good movie is all about.

Q: A higher profile?

Stroud: A higher profile definitely. The character of Ringerman was a great, great character in *Coogan's Bluff*. He was a psycho, a blown-out kind of guy. The part I had in *Joe Kidd* was a great role too. It was work, good work, and that's where I'm at, character acting.

Q: What can you recall about *Murph the Surf* with Robert Conrad?

Stroud: *Murph the Surf* was a lot of fun because I also got to meet the real Murph the Surf, the guy himself. I went down to the prison to meet Jack Murphy, the real Murph the Surf, and we had so much in common. It turned out that he knew a lot of the same people that I did, because he ran with that old surfer crowd that I knew. He was pretty much my age. He got out of jail, he beat the rap, he turned born again Christian, and then Hollywood bought his story. He was not arrested for stealing that ruby, and he beat that rap. Unfortunately, later on, he was doing a double life sentence for murdering two girls who he took out water skiing. The story goes that he killed these two girls, and that was what he was doing in prison. When I went down to the prison, I even went to death row, and I got to sit in the electric chair. Then the warden took us down to death row, I asked, "Could I sit in that chair?" He said, "Go ahead." I sat right in the electric chair. It was like a big antique chair.

Prison on television is not real life. *Oz* is a pretty hardcore show, but that is like a country club compared to the real deal. It's freaking scary just to be there, man. You are on your own there, man. It's really something. So working on *Murph the Surf* was more than just doing the usual movie stuff. I researched this guy, went down to the prison to meet him... what a place, what an experience.

Q: He had a personal life that was similar to yours.

Stroud: He surfed. I am also a musician, I play drums, and he was a musician too. He played the violin. As I said, he knew a lot of the same people that I knew. Back in those days, I was sort of a hustling type of guy myself, so of course, with our personality similarities, we got on pretty good. I worked out how I was going to play this part before meeting him, which is usual for most actors; they study the character before the film is shot. I kind of invented my own character version of Murph, but when I met him, and saw how he was, I decided that it worked out pretty well after all and wound up staying in the character type that I invented, rather than playing the real person. I don't think people would want to meet the real Murph the Surf.

Q: Was there a television show that you worked on that you were particularly fond of?

Stroud: Working on the *Hawaii Five-O* episodes were great. The *Streets of San Francisco* episodes I recall were good too... Ida Lupino directed me in one of those. In another episode of *Hawaii Five-O*, I played a sniper who was confined to a wheelchair. In yet another, I played a hitman who fell in love with a girl who I was supposed to murder. In that episode, I murdered another girl, and then I had an affair with another girl that the mob hired me to murder. I just remember getting these great parts, and even in the *Cannon* television episodes with William Conrad, and the *Barnaby Jones* episodes with Buddy Ebsen, I didn't just play a bad guy, I played these weird, weird villains. I always got that Son of Sam–type of stuff, those strange roles, and I think I played them pretty well. In real life, I'm not a bad guy at all. I never really got in trouble for my being bad. In real life I got into some trouble for my use of booze, and all the other bullshit in life, but like I said, in almost fifteen years now, thanks to God, I haven't smoked, drank or taken any form of drugs. However, in the past, I used to really take a lot of drugs, and drink a lot. I used to like to work when I was loaded. In fact, I used to work loaded all the time. I used to enjoy having roles where I would play drunks, drug addicts, and the director would say, "You were great in that scene." Do you know why? I was drunk, and loaded on drugs—how great can you be? Moreover, I got away with it.

Q: But you remember all this stuff very clearly.

Stroud: I was playing them great, because I was playing that kind of a part. If I played a drug addict, I would go get loaded, if I played a drunk, I would be drunk. They would go, "Oh, you played that scene good." I would be, "Yeah, great." Good days, those were great days. However, I'll tell you, I'm very happy to be sober. Kids today, who want to become actors, they've got to watch the booze, and all that stuff. It doesn't work like it used to. Look at what happened to the careers and lives of some of my poor friends. The young popular actors of today, they have got all the breaks in the world, and they shouldn't screw it up. It's a different world nowadays. I'm not like that any more, I'm a different person.

Q: The movie *The House by the Lake* seemed like it was influenced by the popular European thrillers of that time period. However, this movie seemed way too intense for most American audiences.

Stroud: I thought that was a pretty good little nasty film.

Q: I thought that it also contained one of your best villainous roles.

Stroud: It was a great film, and I got to work with Brenda Vaccaro in it too. Brenda and I were almost going to get married at one time. We've known each other for years. At one time, we lived together for at least six years. In fact right around the time we made this movie together. It was a rough time because I was drinking a lot in those days, and that period was my cocaine usage days. They were pretty crazy times, and we were both kind of half-assed movie stars. As far as star power, she was bigger than I was sometimes, and I was bigger than she was sometimes, and that got in the way of our relationship. It is said that it's very hard for two working actors to get together, and I will tell you it is. It takes a lot of whatever that is... that "how come you're working and I'm not" type of thing, and if you're off for two months or something like that, and in acting, that's a long time, it seems like two years. The other person is going, "What time are you coming home?" and you go, "What do you mean? I'm working in China on a movie." It's a rough, rough thing to do to have a relationship with another actor.

Q: Do you remember anything specific about *The House by the Lake*?

Stroud: We shot it in Canada, and I heard that it was based on a true story. Me and the other guys in that film, we were portraying our roles as flat-out evil, just evil. Brenda was great. When her character turned around, and got everybody back at the end, seeking her revenge, she became as evil as everybody else did, and she was the perfect actress to play that part. It was such a low-budget film, and maybe it was too violent after all. It should have been a better film. And it did not get that much TV play because it is not much for television, too violent...

Q: *The Amityville Horror* was a huge box-office hit.

Stroud: I had a small part in that, but I got to work with Rod Steiger and James Brolin, who's remained a dear, dear friend of mine all these years. I appeared in his television show, *Pensacola*, and it was a terrific role for me. I played the father of a Marine, and I even got to have a crying scene in the hospital. Jimmy Brolin and I, we go back to the *Marcus Welby* days.

Q: *The Buddy Holly Story*—did you enjoy your role in that film?

Stroud: As a member of Buddy Holly's band, the drummer in the movie, we played live as a band—did you know that? I had the role of the frustrated drummer in that film, and I really played the drums, so it wasn't much of stretch for me. During the filming of that movie, Gary Busey and I became like brothers. And Charlie Martin Smith, I thought he was terrific. When we had to shoot the concert scenes, and got up in front of two or three thousand kids and performed—that was great. They'd bring in all these kids in buses, we would give concerts, and they'd just go crazy dancing in the aisles for real because we really played. We also recorded the soundtrack live right there. What fun to do a film like that with that music. When I was a kid I saw the real Buddy Holly on television, on *The Ed Sullivan Show*, and years later I got to be involved and recreate that show for real. I'd think, "I remember watching this on TV, and here I am on *Ed Sullivan*..."

Q: How did you guys get to play live? It's usually not done too much, often it's music mimed to prerecorded tracks...

Stroud: We played live. You had to be able to play live to get the part. The original Buddy Holly musical recordings, we could not use them. The Buddy Holly music was recorded in hi-fi, and was old scratched-up music. We played live, full, blown-out live.

They had the 24-track recording trucks outside the venue and recorded everything. It was a great, great experience.

Q: You portrayed Police Captain Pat Chambers in the *Mike Hammer* television show.

Stroud: Yeah, that was another great program that somehow fell apart for everyone concerned, especially when Stacy Keach was arrested for cocaine and everything changed. We had twenty-two shows ordered by the networks and then he was arrested. Do you know what it is to have twenty-two shows ordered by a big television network? After a pilot, most programs usually only get requests for thirteen episodes or something like that. We lost all that work. What a shame. I don't know if you know anything about the money people make, making television series, but I was making some serious money. Some *serious* money...

Q: And you had a great part, a good guy part.

Stroud: Captain Chambers was a great part, but when that fell apart, it fell apart bigtime because CBS crucified Stacy. It's a shame because it took Stacy many, many years to recover from that bust. Some of these guys, like Gary Busey—they had movies waiting for him as he got out of jail. Where Stacy was concerned, it didn't work out that way for him; they crucified him. He's doing much better these days, but I think Stacy should have been one of the big, big stars, I think that hurt him a lot. I think the timing... I think they thought he was a little too old, a little too smart for that shit, and it's a shame, man. Stacy was not into hard drugs at all, he was working hard, he was writing and stuff, and just took a little hit to do this and that, trust me, I know all about it. We should have all got busted together. He's one of the nicest guys I've ever known.

Q: What can you tell me about *Licence to Kill*?

Stroud: James Bond! My agent called me up and said, "How would you like to go to Acapulco for twenty weeks and do a James Bond movie?" I was like, "Where do I sign up?" My character, Heller, wasn't the biggest part in the world, but it was twenty weeks worth of work in Acapulco. There's one thing about doing a James Bond movie: if you want to know what first-class moviemaking is like, what it's all about, [James Bond] it's first-class all the way. On that film, I even had a nice trailer. None of that stuff had ever impressed me before, but when you get it, I'll admit it, it's nice. When you are out in the middle of the desert, and you are in a trailer with no air conditioning, making a low-budget film, you feel it. When you are on a Bond film, in between scenes, you can be out in the middle of the desert in an air-conditioned trailer watching a ball game. I probably only worked six or seven weeks out of the twenty weeks. The rest of the time I was in the penthouse of a hotel on a $100-a-day per diem, instead of $20. Then the limousine picks you up to take you to the set. As I said, it does not normally impress me, but when you do a movie of that caliber, that's the life you live. You get to see what the jet-set type of thing really is like.

Q: That film is fondly recalled by James Bond fans, partly because it was so violent. Some say it was fairly close to the way that author Ian Fleming had originally written the character, and that it had a good story too.

Stroud: It also had a dark side to it. Timothy Dalton's portrayal of James Bond was a little darker than the usual type of thing. It had a little bit more of an edge to it. I also thought that Robert Davi was terrific in it. It also had things like drugs and stuff like that in it; usually James Bond is a lot more about espionage, so it was darker than usual, no doubt about it.

Q: What was Timothy Dalton like to work with?

Stroud: Timothy was very quiet, and he stayed by himself a lot. We worked very hard, a lot of hours; sometimes one shot would take two days. One shot. Just being down in Acapulco, and down in the Florida Keys, it was fun, a lot of fun, and I made a tremendous amount of money.

Q: *Perdita Durango*—how did you get that part?

Stroud: It just kind of fell into my lap. The producers were running out of choices for whoever was going to play that part, and then they asked me to play it. I read the script, and I said, "He's a child molester type of guy, a really nasty type of guy." I was hesitant to do it because they had this one particular scene with my character and a little kid that I thought went a little too far. I wasn't about to do anything with a little kid, even if it's only implied—it's just not in my genes or in my soul, and I just couldn't do it, not even acting. I said to them I would only do the movie if they could tone that scene down. When I talked about that scene with the producers and the director, I said, "You're not going to have me fool around with this little kid. I don't think I want to do the movie." They said, "We'll handle it right," and we did. I thought the director was pretty good too. I also did a film in Buenos Aires called *Two to Tango* with Hector Oliviera, a good director.

Q: What is Don Stroud doing nowadays?

Stroud: I'm into the stock market. I work whenever I want to. I'm also doing some film convention appearances, for mostly fun. I did not realize so many people remember me.

Credits: 1959: *Hawaiian Eye* (stunt double for Troy Donahue) (television); 1966: *The Virginian: The Long Way Home* (12/14/66) (television); 1967: *Banning* (uncredited); *The Ballad of Josie*; *Bob Hope Presents the Chrysler Theatre: Wipeout* (04/26/67) (television); *Games*; *Ironside: An Inside Job* (10/19/67) (television); *The Road West: Eleven Miles to Eden* (03/13/67) (television); *Run for Your Life: Fly By Night* (12/22/67) (television); *The Virginian: Paid in Full* (11/22/67) (television); 1968: *Coogan's Bluff*; *A Hatful of Rain* (television); *Ironside: Epitaph: Part 1, Epitaph Part 2* (09/26/68) (television); *Journey*

Stroud on the set of the film *Bloody Mama* (1970) (American International Pictures).

to Shiloh; *Madigan*; *The Name of the Game: Pineapple Rose* (12/20/68) (television); *The Outsider: A Time to Run* (10/30/68) (television); *Something for a Lonely Man* (television); *Split Second to an Epitaph* (television); *The Virginian: Image of an Outlaw* (10/23/68) (television); *What's So Bad About Feeling Good?*; 1969: *Explosion* [Canada-U.S.]; 1970: *Angel Unchained* (a.k.a. *Angels Unchained*); *Bloody Mama*; *The F.B.I.: The Savage Wilderness* (10/18/70) (television); *Hawaii Five-O: The Late Louisiana* (11/11/70) (television); *Marcus Welby, M.D.: The Other Side of the Chart* (02/24/70) (television); *...tick...tick...tick...*; 1971: *The Bold Ones: The New Doctors: The Convicts* (11/21/71) (television); *D.A.: Conspiracy to Kill* (television); *The Deadly Dream* (television); *McMillan and Wife: Death Is a Seven Point Favorite* (12/08/71) (television); *Von Richthofen and Brown* (a.k.a. *The Red Baron*) [U.S.-Ireland]; 1972: *Adam-12: The Surprise* (11/15/72) (television); *The Daughters of Joshua Cabe* (television); *Ironside: Nightmare Trip* (11/09/72) (television); *Joe Kidd*; *O'Hara, U.S. Treasury: Operation: Smokescreen* (03/10/72) (television); *Rolling Man* (television); 1973: *The ABC Wide World of Mystery: Nightmare Step* (television); *Banacek: No Stone Unturned* (10/03/73) (television); *Cannon: Come Watch Me Die* (10/24/73) (television); *The F.B.I.: Break-In* (10/07/73) (television); *Gunsmoke: Jesse II* (02/19/73) (television); *Hawaii Five-O: The Flip Side Is Death* (12/18/73) (television); *Hec Ramsey: The Mystery of the Yellow Rose* (01/28/73) (television); *Ironside: The Best Laid Plans* (03/15/73) (television); *Marcus Welby, M.D.: The Problem with Charlie* (01/30/73) (television); *Scalawag* [Italy-Yugoslavia-U.S.]; *Slaughter's Big Rip-Off*; 1974: *Barnaby Jones: Programmed for Killing* (01/27/74) (television); *The Elevator* (television); *The Manhunter: The Ma Gantry Gang* (09/11/74) (television); *Gunsmoke: A Town in Chains* (09/26/74) (television); *Kung Fu: Cry of the Night Beast* (10/19/74) (television); *Police Woman: Warning...All Wives...* (09/27/74) (television); *The Streets of San Francisco: Blockade* (01/24/74) (television); *I Ain't Marchin' Anymore* (10/10/74) (television); 1975: *Harry O: Group Terror* (11/13/75) (television); *Murph the Surf* (a.k.a. *Live a Little, Steal a Lot*); *Petrocelli: A Fallen Idol* (01/22/75) (television); *Police Story: The Return of Joe Forrester* (05/06/75) (television); *Police Woman: Blaze of Glory* (11/11/75) (television); *The Return of Joe Forrester* (a.k.a. *Cop on the Beat*) (television); *The Rookies: The Saturday Night Special* (01/13/75) (television); *S.W.A.T.: Deadly Tide: Part 1* (09/13/75), *Deadly Tide: Part 2* (09/20/75); 1976: *Death Weekend* (a.k.a. *The House by the Lake*) [Canada]; *Hawaii Five-O: Target—A Cop* (12/23/76) (television); *High Risk* (television); *Hollywood Man*; *The Killer Inside Me*; *Police Woman: Task Force: Cop Killer: Part 1* (03/02/76), *Task Force: Cop Killer: Part 2* (03/09/76) (television); 1977: *The Choirboys*; *Sudden Death*; 1978: *The Buddy Holly Story*; *Katie: Portrait of a Centerfold* (television); 1979: *The Amityville Horror*; *Express to Terror* (television); *Mrs. Colombo* (a.k.a. *Kate Colombo*) (television); *Search and Destroy* (a.k.a. *Striking Back*) [Canada-U.S.];1980: *Charlie's Angels: Angel in Hiding* (11/16/80) (television); *The Dukes of Hazzard: Carnival of Thrills* (09/16/80) (television); *Fantasy Island: Aphrodite/Dr. Jekyll and Miss Hyde* (02/02/80), *The Don Quixote/Sex Symbol* (11/15/80) (television); *Insight: God in the Dock* (11/10/80) (television); *More Than Murder* (a.k.a. *Mickey Spillane's Mike Hammer: More Than Murder*); 1981: *CHiPs: Crash Course* (01/04/81) (television); *Hart to Hart: Homemade Murder* (03/03/81) (television); *The Incredible Hulk: Danny* (05/15/81) (television); *The Night the Lights Went Out in Georgia*; *Trapper John, M.D.: The Ego Experience* (11/08/81) (television); *Vega$: The Andreas Addiction* (01/07/81) (television); 1982: *CHiPs: Trained for Trouble* (04/04/82) (television); *Fantasy Island: The Beautiful Skeptic/The Lost Platoon* (11/27/82) (television); *Knight Rider: Good Day at White Rock* (10/08/82) (television); *Knots Landing: Cricket* (02/18/82), *A Brand New Day* (09/30/82) (television); *Simon & Simon: Rough Rider Rides Again* (11/18/82) (television); 1983: *The A-Team: A Nice*

Place to Visit (05/10/83) (television); *I Want to Live* (television); *Matt Houston: Get Houston* (02/20/83), *Heritage: Part 1* (09/09/83) (television); *Murder Me, Murder You* (a.k.a. *Mickey Spillane's Mike Hammer: Murder Me, Murder You*) (television); *Sweet Sixteen*; 1984: *Mike Hammer* (a.k.a. *Mickey Spillane's Mike Hammer* a.k.a. *The New Mike Hammer*) (television);1985: *The A-Team: Knights of the Road* (02/26/85) (television); *Gidget's Summer Reunion* (television); *Hunter: The Biggest Man in Town* (10/05/85) (television); *Murder, She Wrote: Murder Takes the Bus* (03/17/85) (television); 1986: *Armed and Dangerous*; *Hotel: Shadows of a Doubt: Part 1* (01/08/86), *Shadows of a Doubt: Part 2* (01/15/86) (television); *The Return of Mickey Spillane's Mike Hammer* (television); 1987: *Jake and the Fatman: Body and Soul* (11/03/87) (television); 1988: *Two to Tango* (a.k.a. *Matar Es Morir Un Poco*) [Argentina–U.S.]; 1989: *Dragnet* (a.k.a. *The New Dragnet*) (television); *Hyper Space*; *Licence to Kill* [Great Britain–U.S.]; *MacGyver: Renegade* (05/08/89) (television); *Mike Hammer: Murder Takes All* (television); *Paradise: A House Divided* (02/16/89) (television); 1990: *Cartel* (video); *Down the Drain*; *Mob Boss* (video); *Twisted Justice* (video); 1991: *The Divine Enforcer* (a.k.a. *Deadly Avenger*) (video); *Father Dowling Mysteries: The Moving Target Mystery* (02/07/91) (television); *The King of the Kickboxers* (a.k.a. *No Retreat, No Surrender 4*) (video) [U.S.–Hong Kong]; *MacGyver: High Control* (02/11/91) (television); *Prime Target* (video); *Quantum Leap: Play Ball—August 6, 1961* (09/25/81) (television); *The Roller Blade Seven* (video); 1992: *Baywatch: Dead of Summer* (11/23/92) (television); *The Legend of the Rollerblade 7* (video); *Murder, She Wrote: The Big Kill* (03/07/92) (television); 1993: *The Adventures of Brisco County Jr.: Riverboat* (10/01/93) (television); *Cyber Seeker* (video); *Dr. Quinn, Medicine Woman: Running Ghost* (02/27/93) (television); *The Flesh Merchant* (video); *Hell Comes to Frogtown II* (video); *In the Heat of the Night: Even Nice People* (04/28/93) (television); *It's Showtime* (video); *Ned Blessing: The Story of My Life and Times: Oscar* (09/08/93) (television); *Renegade: Windy City Blues* (11/15/93) (television); *Return of the Roller Blade Seven* (video); 1994: *Babylon 5: TKO* (05/24/94) (television); 1995: *The Alien Within* (television); *Carnosaur 2*; *Courthouse: Pilot* (09/13/95) (television); *Criminal Hearts* (video); *Dillinger and Capone* (video); *Sawbones* (a.k.a. *Prescription for Murder* a.k.a. *Roger Corman Presents Sawbones*) (television); *Walker, Texas Ranger: The Guardians* (10/07/95) (television); 1996: *Babylon 5: Ceremonies of Light and Dark* (04/08/96) (television); *Precious Find* (video); *Soldier Boyz* (video); 1997: *Haunted Sea* (video); *Little Bigfoot* (video); *Nash Bridges: Out of Chicago* (03/28/97), *Wild Card* (04/25/97) (television); *Perdita Durango* (a.k.a. *Dance with the Devil*) [Spain–Mexico–U.S.]; *Wild America* (video); 1998: *Detonator*; *Men in White* (a.k.a. *National Lampoon's Men in White*) (video); *Pensacola: Wings of Gold: Lost Shipment* (04/20/98) (television); 1999: *L.A. Heat: Death House* (04/09/99) (television).

Cary-Hiroyuki Tagawa

Cary-Hiroyuki Tagawa was born in Tokyo, Japan, in 1950. With his family, he moved from one U.S. army base to another (his father was a U.S. service member, his mother, a Japanese actress). He studied Kendo in junior high school, and also had fascination with the cinema at an early age. In 1985, at age thirty-six, he made his feature film debut in the cult film *John Carpenter's Big Trouble in Little China*. Cary subsequently appeared in director Bernardo Bertolucci's *The Last Emperor*. His lithe appearance, dramatic rugged facial features, deep voice, and martial arts abilities have made him a movie villain favorite over the years. Notable as the sinister, nearly unstoppable Shang Tsung in the popular film *Mortal Kombat* (based on the equally popular video game), he can be seen in countless fan favorites, including the James Bond movie *Licence to Kill* (as Kwang, 1989), *The Perfect Weapon* (as Kai, 1991), *Showdown in Little Tokyo* (as Yoshida, 1991), *Rising Sun* (as Eddie Sakamura, 1993), *The Phantom* (as The Great Kabai Sengh, 1996), *Provocateur* (as Captain Jong, 1996), *John Carpenter's Vampires* (1998), and *The Art of War* (2000).

Tagawa has also appeared on the genre television programs *Star Trek: The Next Generation*, *Mission: Impossible*, *Space Rangers*, *Babylon 5*, *Stargate SG-1*, and *Poltergeist: The Legacy*. Recent high-profile films include *Pearl Harbor* (2001) and the Tim Burton–directed *Planet of the Apes* (2001).

Q: What can you recall about appearing in John Carpenter's *Big Trouble in Little China*?

Tagawa: It was my first role in film. It has the distinction of being my only extra job, and it was the kind of thing where I waited all my life to be in the business so when I walked on the 20th Century–Fox lot I was so excited. I believe that my life has always been the kind of life where everything happens for a reason, I have certain feelings about things when they happen, and sure enough when I walked on the Fox lot, I had the feeling, "Now is the time for me." To me, life is not about whining about what isn't happening, but preparing for that moment when it does, and I was certainly prepared at that moment. They moved me to the front of the line, from the back, of the bad guys. The assistant director turned around and said; "Now everybody look at this face. Everybody should look like that." I thought, "Yes, now I'm here." That is how my career began.

Q: What steered you towards acting?

Tagawa: I had an inspiration from my mother. She was a Japanese actress. Then when I actually started moving towards acting, I was really surprised when my mother discouraged me, saying, "Asian roles aren't that good, please wait." I thought, "That makes sense."

My career did not start for another nineteen years. I never heard of anybody being that patient, but it did start later.

Q: What can you recollect about being selected by Bernardo Bertolucci for *The Last Emperor*?

Tagawa: That was my first actual film role. I went from a being an extra working with John Carpenter to working as a supporting player with Bertolucci. It was like "What a career!" It did not have anything to do with talent; it was just being in the right place at the right time. Bertolucci was the most down-to-earth person. When I first walked in for an audition for a role in the film, and I had on these stylish pants, he said, "Oh, I have those pants" and he really made me feel comfortable. Then we got into the process of discussing my role. Of course, I had never done an interview with him before, and he just tripped me out. I really did not know what to do in the audition. Every time something did not happen right with an audition, or if I did not get the role, I would think to myself, "Oh, I really must have messed up." That is what I was thinking with Bertolucci because he wanted me to read for another part as well as the one that I went in to audition for. We kept going through roles, about five different parts actually, and I thought to myself, "I must have really been a failure here," and finally, I read for the Eunuch role versus the bad Japanese guys that I had been reading for him, and subsequently I got that part. I was so nervous, I was not quite sure how to go about it, and Bertolucci said to me, "You're an actor, make it up." I thought, in my mind, "If you only knew." And then I thought, "Forget it, I can do this." So I just pretended, and sure enough, that was the beginning of my acting career.

Q: What do you think was the reason for the popularity of your role in *Mortal Kombat*?

Tagawa: *Mortal Kombat* the video game was something special. Playing the game, I liken that to a bunch of kids who are monks. Monks who every day are on their own, are kind of in a religious experience after school. You figure they're afraid of going to school. They don't know if they are going to come home. It gave them a sense of power to play this game in a communal atmosphere. Therefore, you have all of these monks who finally had a church to come to, and see *Mortal Kombat*, the movie.

Q: You also appeared in a number of genre films, including *The Perfect Weapon*, *Showdown in Little Tokyo*, and *Rising Sun*, which contained a larger role for you at that time. Why do you think you were cast so often in villainous roles?

Tagawa: One thing that you have to understand about villains in Hollywood: John Wayne was a villain. All those guys, except Clint Eastwood and Tom Cruise. Actually, even Tom Cruise played a bad guy once—remember the movie *Taps*? Bad guys are a very convenient way for any actor to get into the business. They always have the good guy, the hero, already, so if you are starting out, you've got to either play wimps or the bad guys, especially in my case. At one time, roles for Asians in Hollywood films consisted of Asian businessmen with glasses, with a camera saying [*adopts subservient tone*] "Yes, yes," and I hate that. I thought, "I want to come off as a more masculine role model, for young boys." I would rather have them look at that, rather than a businessman or something like that. I have been proud of that kind of part. Of course, because of my strength, my martial arts abilities, I am able to present a stronger counterpoint to the racist stereotypes. But in general I would say that most of the good guys I have ever met, who play good guys in Hollywood, are wimps. I have found that most of the bad guys that I have ever worked with in

Cary Hiroyuki-Tagawa promotes his appearance in the television series, *Space Rangers* (1993) (Photo courtesy Cary-Hiroyuki Tagawa).

Hollywood are really cool. I do not know if it's the look, but typically, the bad guys that I have met have all had a lot of life experience, and have been through some tough times. Typically, it is true in life, that when you do that, you have a most different perspective on life. You appreciate your career in Hollywood a lot differently. Therefore, I have always had the best time portraying the villains, or being one of the stunt bad guys. I can deal with that. The rest of that ego kind of good-guy nonsense just drives me nuts, and that is why I do not live in Hollywood.

Q: Do you think that having a martial artist's determination and attention to detail that can help one to excel in other things in life?

Tagawa: Absolutely, it helps one deal with everything. I would recommend it for all kids. But, I would say that it would be wise to be very cautious of who your teacher is. Teachers are so often critical. We are having an education problem in this country today, but I think that the martial arts in their truest form could help. Martial arts are a great thing which every child should experience at some point. Certainly, I believe that martial arts should be offered as an additional teaching tool for many different reasons; it certainly helped me. I did not enjoy the competition part of it; that sort of took me out of it for a little bit, and I was fine with that. However, I later developed my own style, which is not about fighting. I would say that there is a way to get that concentrated focus, all of those things, without the fighting, and that is what I have developed with my own martial arts style. I am going to start teaching my style to whoever wants to learn it. Basically, I am a teacher.

You do not hear actors talking like this all the time. They want to tell you what they have eaten for breakfast, but I do not give a heck about that. Another thing that I want to teach is martial arts athletics. I do believe that martial arts can move into sports with a greater impact with our understanding of how the body works. [Setting aside] all the concentration and focus that it will take, it is about getting past that hype. I am really sad to see that our pro athletes today prove such a poor examples for our children. Not all of them of course, but a great [many] of them. It is an American thing: you get a lot of money, and you go nuts. I have certainly seen my share of that.

Q: Robin Shou and Talisa Soto, your *Mortal Kombat* co-stars, returned in *Annihilation*, the sequel. Were you asked to return?

Tagawa: Yes, I was in the script. In the first movie, I was supposed to not be seen getting beat up, but a big cloud, a shadow was supposed to come over. In the [*Mortal Kombat*] script, we were to never see me dying or anything like that. I assumed that I did not. Then I had a discussion with the producers about it and they were very clear about me not coming back for another film. My character of Shang Tsung was a classic kind of character. If he dies, he will always be remembered. I didn't really want to bring him back; I would not bring him back.

Q: Is it true that the Japanese-co-produced motion picture, *Picture Bride* (1994) contains one of your own favorite roles?

Tagawa: Yes, absolutely. As in the movie, my family did immigrate to Hawaii. My grandfather was a farmer; I never met him. It is one of those films every actor should do just for the hell of it. Well, not for the hell of it, but for the heaven of it. Because it was a generation that really was overlooked, I think everywhere in the world. They were the immigrants, the first-generation guys, and I owe it all to them. Without them, everything

Tagawa as the villain in the action film, *Soldier Boyz* (1996) (Motion Picture Corporation of America/HBO).

I have attempted in my life, I could not have done, it could not have happened. I feel very strongly about family.

Q: *The Art of War*—what can you tell me about working on that film?
    Tagawa: I appeared as a favor to Wesley Snipes, and I owe him nothing any more, and that's all I'll say about that movie.

Q: Did it do very well box office–wise?

Tagawa: You would think so, with his name attached, and with the subject matter, but it did not. Overall, I think it made something like $30 million, which is horrible nowadays. Although, you would probably be surprised to hear that actually they did make money, because they made it for a really cheap budget. It did crazy business on video, so they also eventually made more money on that end as well. Wesley is a very interesting person, because he had such an explosive beginning as an actor. They had him so set up, he had his opportunities, and to have a $30 million gross, it kind of says something about what the fans feel about him at this point in his career. I know he had a lot of fans but I think at a certain point... they will wait for another *Blade*.

Q: *Pearl Harbor?*

Tagawa: Acting in *Pearl Harbor* was very emotional for me, because half my family was in the Japanese Imperial Navy and the other half was in the U.S. Army. My father was a lifer, twenty years. Every Pearl Harbor day was not a holiday for me. I really dreaded going to school on Pearl Harbor day. It is something that has been a very personal, emotional issue all my life. I was hoping to get out of the last millennium without hearing that this is the thousandth anniversary of the bombing of Pearl Harbor. If there were an example of two countries that could not be more dependent on each other, it would be Japan and the United States. I think we are still not clear about what the importance of that alliance is. I played Lieutenant Commander Genda, who was a national hero in Japan. He was a pilot. Probably, never in the history of Japan has a lieutenant commander worked with an admiral. It was a very renegade sort of combination. Japanese pilots in those days were very much cowboys, as were the American pilots. They had respect for each other. The Japanese pilots were no slouches, the Americans certainly had the animosity, but they had a level of respect for each other in the sky—the sky was a completely different place. I was very proud to play his character. It was very emotional putting on the uniform, watching Zeros go off into the sky, and take off from the aircraft carrier. I just got very emotional. I was really anxious to see how the younger generation might have been affected by the movie, but of course, it turned into another event movie, and at the box-office it didn't fare as well as anyone connected to it had hoped. Of course, being born in 1950, five years after the war, my whole life has been World War II–influenced, especially Pearl Harbor–influenced, and I know that today's kids are not. They are going to see films like this as a kind of action movie.

Q: *Planet of the Apes?*

Tagawa: I loved the original version. The remake was not the original. To me, it was the *Star Wars* version of *Planet of the Apes*. The first one was originally written by a Frenchman, and was very philosophical. The remake had nothing to do with anything philosophical about the future. It was very much an action adventure film concentrating on merchandising heaven. Originally, I was supposed to play Michael Clarke Duncan's role, that of Attar, the army general. While it was exciting on one hand to work with Tim Burton, on the other hand, it was another bad-guy role. Originally, I was being fitted for the Attar costume, and then they announced a little bit later that Michael Clarke Duncan was cast as a general. I was thinking, "Wait a minute. How am I going to be a general next to Michael Clarke Duncan?" Then I started to think, "Oh my God! What if they gave him *my* part?" I already had a contract, so we went down to the studio, and waited, and sure enough, they said, "There's a new script coming, and we're not sure if he's [*Tagawa*] in it." Tim said, "We want to have him in the film," and I ended up playing a good guy. I was on the heroic side then. Originally, the character was not as full as it became, but Tim was very gracious, and creative, and allowed me to sort of bring other aspects to the role. I am very proud of this character. Not unlike our misunderstanding of people—we have misunderstandings about Silverback apes, that they are just ferocious. They are actually very intuitive, they are very instinctive of course, which gives them great street smarts. The other thing is their sensitivity, which I tried to bring out. These character traits were not in the original script as it was written. I created these things on the set, as we were shooting.

Q: Did you do research for this role?

Tagawa: Oh yes, very extensively. There is a lot of footage on apes that is available. The order probably has to be somewhere between cat, dogs, and apes. There is a lot of material available, and I exhausted every possible thing that I could to do research for my role. It is somewhat sad, the way that they have become an endangered species where their hands have been cut off, all because of their ferociousness. We should be studying them for their sensitivity, and here we are with this misunderstanding of them. It really distorts who we are.

Q: Who was the best director that you have worked with?

Tagawa: I have to say that there are three of them. Tim Burton was certainly—maybe a little bit *too* easy to work with. He's just such a nice guy. Phil Kaufman on *Rising Sun*, and Bertolucci on *The Last Emperor* are the other two.

Q: So far, what is your favorite film that you have made?

Tagawa: My two favorites are *The Last Warrior*, which is a story about two soldiers during World War II, one Japanese and one American. It meant a lot to me at the time in 1988 to work on this movie. We went to South Africa, which at that time was very much still Apartheid-oriented; Screen Actors Guild discouraged us [the production] from going there to make the movie. In fact, they were talking about blacklisting us, as if it was the fifties or something. But I met the director, he was a businessman who was getting into film, who went on television in South Africa to talk about the film, and ended up blasting the government there. I thought this guy has got some chutzpah. I thought, if there's any reason that I should go, then this is it. In fact, he said, "Cary, please, I understand. I appreciate it. We need to have voices like yours come, and talk to us. We're isolated. We need people to come." So, I thought, "I'm going." He really allowed me to help create the character. The other film is *Johnny Tsumani* [1999], a Disney Channel movie—one of the highest rated Disney Channel movies ever. I played a surfing grandfather. It was the best time that I ever had making a movie, really. I didn't have to hurt anybody. I couldn't stop smiling. It really is the closest to my own nature.

Credits: 1985: *Big Trouble in Little China* (a.k.a. *John Carpenter's Big Trouble in Little China*); 1986: *Armed Response*; 1987: *The Last Emperor* [France–Italy–Great Britain]; *MacGyver: Dalton, Jack of Spies* (02/23/87) (television); *Miami Vice: The Rising Sun of Death* (12/04/87) (television); *Star Trek: The Next Generation: Encounter at Fairpoint* (09/26/87) (television); 1988: *Bulletproof* (uncredited); *Hotel: Double Take* (01/02/88) (television); *Spellbinder*; *Twins*; 1989: *Alien Nation: The First Cigar* (10/23/89) (television); *The Last Warrior* (a.k.a. *Coastwatcher*) [Great Britain–South Africa]; *Miami Vice: Asian Cut* (01/13/89) (television); *Mission: Impossible: Countdown* (10/26/89) (television); *Moonlighting: Perfect* (04/09/89) (television); *Superboy: Terror from the Blue* (03/11/89) (television); 1990: *Hard-

ball: Wedding Bell Blues (06/01/90) (television); *Jake and the Fatman: Chinatown, My Chinatown* (05/16/90) (television); *L.A. Takedown*; *Licence to Kill* [Great Britain–U.S.]; *Murder in Paradise* (television); *Vestige of Honor* (television); 1991: *Kickboxer 2: The Road Back*; *Mission of the Shark: The Saga of the U.S.S. Indianapolis* (television); *Not of This World* (television); *The Perfect Weapon*; *Showdown in Little Tokyo*; 1992: *American Me*; *Baywatch: War of Nerves* (02/13/92) (television); *Raven: Return of the Black Dragon* (06/1992), *Reunion* (07/08/92) (television); *Renegade: Samurai* (01/25/92) (television); 1993: *Nemesis* [U.S.–Denmark]; *Rising Sun*; *Space Rangers* (television); 1994: *The Dangerous*; *Day of Reckoning*; *Lives in Hazard* (television); *Mortal Kombat: Behind the Scenes* (video); *Natural Causes*; *The Picture Bride* (a.k.a. *Bijo Photo*) [Japan-U.S.]; 1995: *Babylon 5: Convictions* (11/13/95) (television); *Mortal Kombat*; *Thunder in Paradise 3* (video);1996: *Cybill: Cybill and Maryann Go to Japan* (09/30/96) (television); *Nash Bridges* (television); *The Phantom* [U.S.–Australia]; *Sabrina, the Teenage Witch: Sweet & Sour Victory* (12/06/96) (television); *Soldier Boyz*; *White Tiger*; 1997: *Danger Zone* (video) [Canada–South Africa–U.S.]; *Stargate SG-1: Emancipation* (08/08/97) (television); *Showdown* (a.k.a. *Top of the World* a.k.a. *Cold Cash*); 1998: *American Dragons* (a.k.a. *Double Edge*) (video); *Assignment Berlin* (a.k.a. *Babyhandel Berlin—Jenseits Aller Skrupel*) (television—Germany) [U.S.-Germany]; *Poltergeist: The Legacy: The Internment* (07/17/98) (television); *Provocateur* (a.k.a. *Agent Provocateur*) [Canadian]; *Vampires* (a.k.a. *John Carpenter's Vampires*); *Vengeance Unlimited: Ambition* (10/29/98) (television); 1999: *Bridges of Dragons* (video); *Fixations* (video); *Johnny Tsunami*; *Netforce* (television); *Seven Days: Walter* (05/19/99) (television); *Snow Falling on Cedars*; 2000: *The Art of War* [U.S.-Canada]; *Walker, Texas Ranger: Black Dragons* (02/26/00) (television); 2001: *Code of the Dragon* (a.k.a. *The Ghost*) (television); *Pearl Harbor*; *Planet of the Apes*; 2003: *Batman* (animated): *Rise of Sin Tzu* (voice only) (television); *Baywatch: Hawaiian Wedding* (television); 2004: *Bushido* (video); *Elektra*; *Faith of My Fathers* (television); *Fallacy* (video); *Hawaii* (television); 2005: *Memoirs of a Geisha*; 2007: *Balls of Fury*; *Duel of Legends*.

Dee Wallace Stone

Dee Wallace Stone, who also performed as Dee Wallace prior to her marriage to actor Christopher Stone, is an actress who will be best remembered for her genre film roles, particularly as the besieged mother in Wes Craven's disturbing *The Hills Have Eyes* (1977); a beleaguered news journalist battling a werewolf cult in Joe Dante's *The Howling* (1981); a harried mother facing a hound from hell in *Cujo* (1983); the mom of little Drew Barrymore who befriends an alien from another world in Steven Spielberg's *E.T.: The Extraterrestrial* (1982); and a scary psycho killer from hell in Peter Jackson's *The Frighteners* (1996).

Born December 14, 1948 in Kansas City, Kansas, Dee moved to New York City in 1975. There she studied acting and ended up in a touring production of *Annie Get Your Gun*.

One of her earliest roles was on the television show *The Streets of San Francisco* in 1975, followed by an appearance in the strange genre film *The Stepford Wives* (1975). A co-starring role in Wes Craven's demented and intense *The Hills Have Eyes* (1977) led to a starring role in Joe Dante's *The Howling* in which she appeared alongside Christopher Stone (her then-fiancé). The Spielberg blockbuster *E.T.: The Extraterrestrial*, *Cujo*, *Critters* (1986), and *Alligator II: The Mutation* (1991) followed. This led to a succession of more prominent roles in other productions.

During the eighties and nineties, Dee Wallace Stone became a familiar face on American television, appearing in a staggering number of made-for-TV movies including Tobe Hooper's *I'm Dangerous Tonight* (1990) and Joe Dante's *Runaway Daughters* (1994). She still is in demand as an actress, partly because as one keen observer on the Internet Movie Database noted, "All-American looks and an easy going demeanor has seen Dee often cast as a typical suburban mother, a sympathetic friend or a trusted ally." She has also released a line of motivational video and audio cassettes (available through her website) covering such topics as *Body, Mind and Spirit* and *Creating Success Now*. Dee continues to perform (she returned to series television in 2006 with a featured role on *Sons and Daughters*), and keeps in touch with her fans through her website: http://www.deewallacestone. She has also begun to create her own online acting studio (http://dwsactingstudio.com).

Q: What are your earliest remembrances of working in the entertainment industry?

Dee Wallace Stone: Well, I got my start back home in Kansas City. My mom worked on all the plays at church, my dad would be involved with scenery, my grandmother did the costumes, and I started out dancing when I was very young. A lot of my fans don't know this, but I worked on a lot of publicity with the Walt Disney Production company in the Midwest, and so every time Walt Disney himself would come in, or Robert Wagner would come in promoting something, or Gene Autry would come into town promoting something, I would help them with all the publicity for the Walt Disney films that they appeared in. I would appear as myself, then a young girl of seven or eight years old, and be photographed with them. The acting bug really bit me early on [because of] this, and by watching my mom. As far as films are concerned, my earliest remembrance was working on the television show *Lucas Tanner*, and I got the part because I had baked cookies and taken them around to the studios to give to all the casting directors. I was in one particular producer's office, and I guess the girl that they had sent over to do the waitress part didn't fit into the costume, and he looked at me—you know, timing's everything. He said, "What size do you wear?" and I said, "What size do you need?" They sent me over to the set, and I began working as an actress, that day, on an episode of *Lucas Tanner*.

Q: Another one of your earliest credits is an appearance in the original version of *The Stepford Wives*.

Wallace Stone: For *The Stepford Wives*, I was sitting in the casting agent's office, ready to be interviewed by... I think it was the director. The director walked out of the office, and looked at me, went back in, came back out and looked at me again, and said, "Are you an actress?" I said, "Yes." He said, "Do you want to be in a movie?" and I said, "Sure." I think I had one line or no lines, I cannot even remember at this point but I just had the look that he wanted.

Dee Wallace Stone and Christopher Stone in Joe Dante's *The Howling* (1981) (AVCO Embassy Pictures/International Film Investors/Wescom Productions).

A mother always protects her child: Stone in *Cujo* (1983) (Sunn Classic Pictures Inc./TAFT Entertainment Pictures Inc./Warner Bros.).

Q: The original version of *The Hills Have Eyes* is a very disturbing movie. What do you recall about the production of that film?

Wallace Stone: It was a very difficult film to make. We shot it in the Mojave Desert and of course, it was a super, super, super low-budget production, so they weren't putting anybody up in a place to stay nearest to the location. I had to drive from the Valley to the Mojave Desert every day there were shot scenes that I appeared in. It was incredibly hot during the day, and freezing at night. There were a lot of great people to work with, but the one thing I recall the most, is that it was an extremely low-budget film.

Q: Were you aware of the intensity of the film at the time?

Wallace Stone: You had to be aware of the intensity, because you were in it! I was screaming and crying and doing a lot of this... yes, it was an intense film, and we were all aware of it.

Q: *The Howling* was your next major role in a genre film.

Wallace Stone: We had a ball working on *The Howling*, we just had an absolute ball. Again, like *The Hills Have Eyes*, it was a very low-budget film. There was little money around for the production, but we all loved Joe Dante. There were a lot of people who were very talented, who hadn't made it yet, who were just at the beginning of their careers and they put us all together, and it was just fun, we all had this "Let's put on a show" attitude. A lot of us also shared the only trailer on the set. For one scene in *The Howling*, in order to light it for the cameras, everybody pulled up in their cars and literally lit it up by turning on their headlights; we also lit some of the other outdoors scenes that way. As well, I got to appear in a film with my husband, Christopher Stone. We were married in 1980. The production of *The Howling* was so low-budget that often times some of us would get together and purchase donuts for the crew because there wasn't enough money for the crafts services that we really needed.

Q: Was the werewolf makeup that you wore in the film difficult to apply?

Wallace Stone: That is not me onscreen. I had it in my contract that I would not appear as a werewolf in the film. Back then, stuff like that for an actor or an actress was important, or we thought it was. Joe Dante called me after the studio saw all the screening cards and he said, "Dee, everybody wants to see the character as a werewolf" and I said, "I can't Joe, I'm shooting *Cujo* now." He said, "I can get somebody else. It's going to be full makeup, but I have to get your okay." I said, "Okay, but she needs to be different from the other werewolves. She fought so hard; she needs to be vulnerable. If you promise me...." They came up with this wonderful Bambi-looking werewolf.

Q: *Cujo* involved many sequences of the rabid dog attacking. Was it difficult to set up those sequences?

Wallace Stone: What I recall most about the filming of *Cujo* is that they had to treat me for exhaustion for three weeks afterwards. It was a horrendously difficult shoot, but I must say that I am very proud of my work in that film. They were all very nice dogs in real life. They used five dogs for the main one for that movie—stunt dogs I guess you would call them. All of them were trained to go after toys. So, from the waist up, they all looked terribly ferocious, but they had to tie their tails, because they were so happy, wagging their butts all over the place. The dogs were very well cared for, very well protected. I do a lot of work for animal rights, so that was of big importance to me when I took on the film, was that they were not going to be abused in any way. Carl Miller, who trained the dogs, was just phenomenal. However, I just remember it being a very difficult and, emotionally, an incredibly draining experience.

Q: We all know how acclaimed *E.T.* has become over the years, but what were your thoughts at the time you were making this movie? Did you think that possibly, this film might become something special?

Wallace Stone: I think you knew for sure, even when you were reading the script, that it was going to be an incredibly special film. I didn't think that appearing in the film was going to do anything special for me in terms of my career. I remember calling my agent and saying, "I don't think it's going to do anything for my career, but I want to be a part of it because it's such a positive, uplifting film."

Q: What was it like to work with Spielberg?

Wallace Stone: He's an absolutely wonderful director. He was great with the kids. I think one of Steven's greatest assets is that he is just brilliant at casting. He finds the right people, and puts them in the right roles.

Q: What are your favorite films?

Wallace Stone: I would definitely have to say hands down *Cujo, The Frighteners*, and a little movie of the week that I did for television called *The Texas Cadet Murders*.

Q: *The Frighteners* is a film that I believe is underrated. I also firmly believe that you gave a great performance in it. What did you think of Peter Jackson as a director?

Wallace Stone: Peter was just his own man. Fortunately, sometimes when you get out of the country, directors do not care so much how much money the film will make, what their peers are going to think, etc. They stay [true] to their own vision. It was really refreshing to me to work in New Zealand and to work with a director that cared not only for his actors, but also about his crew. Everyone was always treated with great respect. There were many guys on the crew who had wives who gave birth while we were there. Everybody was allowed three days off, with a guarantee that their jobs would be there when they got back, no pressure, no guilt. This kind of thing does not happen in America. I have to tell you that I lost my husband during the shooting of *The Frighteners*, and I could not have been surrounded with more love and more support, and more understanding. I had to travel back and forth from and to New Zealand so many times, and at the end I went to settle up with him and the production company as a payback for all the kindness that they extended towards me in my time of grief... for all the airline flights, etc. But the production company said that Robert Zemeckis, the producer, and Peter Jackson wanted to give me all the airline flights free, as a gift to help me through the difficult time.

Q: Do you also have any thoughts on why the film did not perform as well as it should have in America upon its initial theatrical release?

Wallace Stone: I know why it did not do as well: Universal, in their infinite wisdom, did not stick to the original plan of distribution. It was always meant to be a Halloween film, to be released at that time of the year; it was a perfect Halloween film. It would have done great business had it come out then. But they rushed Peter to finish the movie, they threw it together before it was really ready for the screen, they made him get it ready for a July release and then they brought it out against two huge summer blockbusters and it was buried. It's really too bad because it is a wonderful film.

Q: What are you doing nowadays?

Wallace Stone: In 2000, I appeared in a movie called *Killer Instinct*, which my late husband wrote. We sold it, and they called and asked if I would come in to do the part that he wrote for me, which was really nice. I worked on one of the last *Ally McBeal* episodes. I did a movie of the week last year. I own an acting studio in LA, and I am doing motivational speaking all over the world. So, I'm very busy, not the least of which is raising a beautiful daughter.

Q: How do you feel about the fact that there are many fans of your work?

Wallace Stone: One really gets a sense of how you are not just a commodity. That there are many times when I have touched people's lives and their hearts with my work. For me, that's what it's all about.

Credits: 1974: *Lucas Tanner: Merry Gentlemen* (12/25/74) (television); *Ellery Queen: The Adventure of the Chinese Dog* (09/25/74) (television); 1975: *The Stepford Wives*; *The Streets of San Francisco: The Programming of Charlie Blacke* (02/06/75) (television); 1977: *All the King's Horses*; *The Hills Have Eyes* (a.k.a. *Wes Craven's The Hills Have Eyes*); *The Man from Atlantis: Melt Down* (09/22/77) (television); *Police Woman: Do You Still Beat Your Wife?* (10/25/77) (television); *Starsky and Hutch: The Crying Child* (10/22/77) (television); 1978: *Barnaby Jones: Terror On a Quiet Afternoon* (02/09/78) (television); *CHiPs: Return of the Turks* (11/25/78) (television); *Lou Grant: Hooker* (10/16/78) (television); *Police Story: A Chance to Live* (05/28/78) (television); 1979: *Hart to Hart: Jonathan Hart Jr.* (10/06/79) (television); *Mrs. Colombo: Ladies of the Afternoon* (10/18/79) (television); *Taxi: Alex's Romance* (11/20/79) (television); *10*; *Trapper John, M.D.: Deadly Exposure* (10/07/79) (television); *Young Love, First Love* (television); 1980: *The Secret War of Jackie's Girls* (television); 1981: *Child Bride of Short Creek* (television); *The Five of Me* (television); *The Howling*; *Making a Monster Movie: Inside "The Howling"* (television); *Saturn Awards* (television); *Skeezer* (television); *Take These Men* (television); *A Whale for the Killing* (television); 1982: *E.T.: The Extra-Terrestrial*; *Jimmy the Kid*; 1983: *Cujo*; *Happy* (television); *Wait Till Your Mother Gets Home!* (television); 1984: *Hotel: Intimate Strangers* (09/26/84) (television); *The Sky's No Limit* (a.k.a. *The Sky's the Limit*) (television); 1985: *Club Life* (a.k.a. *King of the City*); *Finder of Lost Loves: Mister Wonderful* (03/09/85) (television); *Hostage Flight* (television); *Secret Admirer*; *Simon & Simon: Love and/or Marriage* (10/03/85) (television); *Suburban Beat* (television); *The Twilight Zone: Wish Blank* (10/18/85) (television); 1986: *Circus of the Stars #11* (television); *Critters*; *Hotel: Facades* (02/12/86) (television); *Shadow Play*; *Sins of Innocence* (a.k.a. *Two Young People*) (television); *Together We Stand* (television); 1987: *Bialy Smok* (a.k.a. *The Legend of the White Horse* a.k.a. *White Dragon*) [Poland-U.S.]; *An Enemy Among Us* (television); *Happy 100th Birthday Hollywood* (television); *Hotel: Desperate Moves* (11/14/87) (television); *Miracle Down Under* (a.k.a. *The Christmas Visitor*) (television); 1988: *Addicted to His Love* (television); *Stranger on My Land* (television); 1989: *Murder, She Wrote: Fire Burn, Cauldron Bubble* (02/19/89) (television); *The New Lassie* (television); 1990: *Alligator II: The Mutation*; *I'm Dangerous Tonight* (television); 1991: *Murder, She Wrote: Tainted Lady* (05/05/91) (television); *P.S. I Luv U: Pilot* (09/15//91) (television); *Popcorn*; 1992: *F.B.I.: The Untold Stories: Mommie Dearest* (television); *L.A. Law: Wine Knot* (11/12/92) (television); 1993: *Discretion Assured* [U.S.-Brazil]; *Huck and the King of Hearts*; *Lightning in a Bottle*; *My Family Treasure* (a.k.a. *Sokrishche Moey Semi*) [Russia-U.S.]; *Prophet of Evil: The Ervil LeBaron Story* (television); 1994: *Moment of Truth: Cradle of Conspiracy* (television); *Rescue Me* (a.k.a. *Street Hunter*); *Runaway Daughters* (television); *Search and Rescue* (television); *Temptress*; *Vanishing Son IV* (television); *Witness to the Execution* (television); 1995: *Brothers' Destiny* (a.k.a. *The Long Road Home*) (television); *Cops n Robbers*; *High Sierra Search and Rescue* (television); *The Phoenix and the Magic Carpet*; *The Skateboard Kid II*; 1996: *Best of the Best 3: No Turning Back*; *The Frighteners* [New Zealand–U.S.]; *The Making of "E.T.—The Extra-Terrestrial"* (video supplement); *Skeletons*; *Subliminal Seduction* (a.k.a. *Flash Frame*) (television); 1997: *Black Circle Boys*; *Invisible Mom*; *JAG: Crossing the Line* (01/31/97) (television); *Love's Deadly Triangle: The Texas Cadet Murder* (television); *Mutual Needs*; *Nevada*; *The Perfect Murder* (television); *Touched by an Angel: A Delicate Balance* (05/18/97) (television); *Women: First and Foremost* (television); 1998: *Bad As I Wanna Be: The Dennis Rodman Story* (television); *The Christmas Path*; *The Making of "The Frighteners"* (video supplement); 1999: *Ally McBeal: Buried Pleasures* (11/01/99) (television); *Deadly Delusions*; *Invisible Mom II* (video); *Nash Bridges: Resurrection* (02/19/99) (television); *Pirates of the Plain* (video); *To Love, Honor & Betray* (television); 2000: *Flamingo Dreams* (video); *Killer Instinct* (video); 2001: *Adjustments*; *18* (video); *I Love 1980's: I Love 1982* (02/03/01) (television); *Felicity: The Storm* (11/21/01), *A Month of Sundays*; *Out of the Black* (a.k.a. *Buried Lies*); *A Perfect Match* (12/19/01) (television); 2002: *Artie*; *The Division: Beyond the Grave* (03/17/02) (television); *"E.T.: The Extra-Terrestrial": 20th Anniversary Celebration* (video supplement); *The E.T. Reunion* (video supplement); *Fish Don't Blink*; *Live at the Shrine! John Williams and the World Premiere of "E.T.: The Extra-Terrestrial": The 20th Anniversary* (video supplement); *Sex and the Teenage Mind*; *She Spies: First Episode* (07/02/02) (television); 2003: *The Agency: Our Man in Korea* (05/10/03) (television); *Looking Back at "The Hills Have Eyes"* (video supplement); *The 100 Scariest Movie Moments* (television); *Paradise* [Switzerland-U.S.] (unreleased?); *Scream Queens: The E! True Hollywood Story* (television); *The Ultimate Film* (television); *Unleashing the Beast: Making "The Howling"* (video supplement); *Welcome to Werewolfland* (video supplement); 2004: *The Blue Rose*; *Boo!*; *Dead Canaries*; *Dead End Road*; *Paradise*; *The Perfect Husband: The Laci Peterson Story* (television); 2005: *Cold Case: Strange Fruit* (04/03/05) (television); *Expiration Date*; *Headspace*; *Kalamazoo*; *The Loch Ness Monster* (short film), *The Lost*; *The Magic 7* (animated) (television) (voice only); *Scar*; *She's No Angel* (television); *Spice of Life* [India-U.S.]; *Yesterday's Dreams*; 2006: *Abominable*; *Bone Dry*; *The Plague*; *Sons & Daughters* (television); 2007: *Between the Sand and the Sky*; *Halloween*; *The I-Scream Man*; *J-ok'el*; *Little Red Devil*; *The Ocean*; *Soupernatural*; *The Stalker Within*; 2008: *The Magic 7*.

Mel Welles

Mel Welles was born in New York, New York in 1924. Prior to his Hollywood acting career, Welles held a variety of jobs, including that of a clinical psychologist (holding a Ph.D. in Psychology), writer, and radio deejay. After appearing on the stage in a variety of small roles, he wound up in Hollywood, where he appeared in his first film, *Appointment in Honduras*, in 1953. His best, most fondly remembered, and own personal favorite role was that of the flower shop owner Gravis Mushnik in director Roger Corman's 1960 horror comedy *The Little Shop of Horrors*. This film was also one of Welles' last in the U.S. for many years; he left the country in the early sixties and forged a long acting-producing-directing career in Europe.

As an actor, Welles appeared in approximately sixty feature films and amassed something in the range of over three hundred television credits. As a voice actor, he has committed his vocal intonations to literally hundreds of radio shows, cartoons, television commercials, business industry shorts, documentaries, and feature films, many of them not even documented for posterity by Welles himself. As a voice actor, he was renowned for dubbing a great many foreign films into the English language. He also worked as a consultant for many of the major Hollywood studios including Columbia, MGM, 20th Century–Fox, Universal, and Warner Bros. For years, Welles was known in the industry as a film doctor for his creative input talents. He produced and directed twelve films during his eighteen years in Europe and Southeast Asia. More recently, he spent more than ten years creating, and then conducting, an assortment of seminars and experimental workshops for business industry executives and professionals. As of 2003, he was associated with the Center for Executive Re-Invention in Austin, Texas, and continued to work with other Fortune 500 companies in a variety of roles.

On Welles' website www.melwelles.com, he wrote, "Some years ago, my publishing company Robertsbridge published two award-winning children's books in a series entitled *Wiki, Tiki,* and *Krapachnek*. The Brandeis Institute and several others hailed these stories as the best example of non-violent fun. The author, Howard Andreola, had created a body of work, which boasts 325 of these adventures. I am now in the process of securing financing and distribution for animated episodes of these stories to be syndicated. As well, the original title of this website and of one of its portals is *House of a Hundred Horrors*. This is [also the title of] a truly relentlessly horrifying Gothic art cum horror flick, which I [am planning to] produce in the coming spring or summer in Ireland or Hungary. I am hoping that [*Little Shop of Horrors* colleague] Chuck Griffith will agree to direct it. It is, of course, not a comedy, but it is every bit the love project that *Little Shop of Horrors* was. At this present time, I am [also] busy putting together a Jewish stage musical called *Beyond the Pale*. I call it my 'Jewsical,' as it is based, loosely, on the novella *Mottel, the Cantor's Son* by the great [author-playwright] Sholem Aleichem. [The story] is joyous, and full of fun."

However, none of these projects came to fruition, as Welles died of heart failure on August 19, 2005. This interview dates from the late nineties.

Q: After first working with Roger Corman, how did you come to work in the Italian film industry?

Mel Welles: Well, I was rather fed up with the movie industry here in the United States. I had purchased a short story from *Playboy* magazine called *The Skin Diver and the Lady*; it was kind of an erotic story. I had originally made a deal with a German film producer to direct a movie he had called *The Maid from Nymphenburg*, and he, in turn, would produce my film of *The Skin Diver and the Lady*. I packed up my family, I went to Germany, we went to the Berlin film festival and the Cannes film festival, we hung out in hotels, and nothing ever happened. Finally, [the German producer] was arrested, and sent to jail. I said [to my family], "Before we go home, I want to go to Italy"—the round-trip tickets had gone through Rome anyway. I said, "We'll go to Rome, I want to see the Coliseum and all of those things." We went to Rome and I checked my family into a villa, and hit the streets. I went to a place that I had been told about called The Colony where British and American people hung out. I got in there, and I got to talking with a Scottish agent named Malcolm Carswell. He happened to be the agent for John Drew Barrymore, who was also a very good friend of mine at the time, I became kind of like his surrogate father. Barrymore's agent asked me if I would like to direct a film there in Italy, so I said yes. So, that's how I came to be stuck in Europe for all those years.

Q: What was the first film that you directed there?

Welles: *La Teste Calde*, which means *The Hot Heads*, in English. It was with John Drew Barrymore, Mark Damon, and Nino Castelnuovo, who was a new actor at the time... he was like a budding star. The film also featured a kid named Franco Nero. The actual star of the picture was a character actress named Alida Valli, who used to be known in America, only using the name Valli. After that, I went into the English dubbing of films. I had a dubbing company in Rome and one in Madrid, but the one in Rome was the headquarters.

Q: At the same time, Eduardo Ciannelli was doing the same thing over there.

Welles: Eduardo and his son Louis had their own company. There were a lot of us. Lionel Stander was there, and there was a nice colony of people there.

Q: You worked on all kinds of films that were being exported to America.

Welles: I dubbed something like eight hundred European films. One of the most successful ones imported to America was a French film called *Z*. I would write the literal translations from the original scripts and direct the dubbing of the English-dubbed versions for export myself. Often, I would also perform one or more of the voices for the actors being dubbed; the same thing for the film that I directed, *Lady Frankenstein*. In *Lady Frankenstein*, I dubbed the voice of Herbert Fux, who played the grave robber. I made a very handsome living dubbing foreign-language films into English. Then I directed some films. I directed this picture called *Island of the Doomed* with Cameron Mitchell.

Mel Welles and Allison Hayes appear in a scene from the Roger Corman film, *The Undead* (1957) (Balboa Pictures/American International Pictures).

Q: Which is also known as *Man-Eater of Hydra*.
   Welles: That was an alternate title. This film was an Italian, Spanish, and German co-production. I also directed an espionage-themed picture called *Hello Glen Ward*, which was also retitled something else, with Ray Danton. This was a Spanish-Italian co-production. I directed another spy film with Phillipe Lemaire, and there have been others. You know, it's hard for me to remember all of this stuff.

Q: You worked on the English-language dubbing for some of the Mario Bava films.
   Welles: I worked on all of the Mario Bava films. All of those films I dubbed into the English language.

Q: *Lady Frankenstein* was an Italian movie that probably had more of a cult following than the others.
   Welles: My other film, *Island of the Doomed*, never made any noise whatsoever at the box-office, although it made some money for Allied Artists on its first release in the U.S. It's thought of as kind of a cult film to dyed-in-the-wool horror film buffs who, as you know, collect bad films as well as good films. I mean, they will go see a bad horror film four or five times; the same amount of times as they would go and see a good horror film. That's what's really good about it, although Gothic horror is hard to get financing for. Actually, *Lady Frankenstein* has become a cult film. It has had a renaissance of late.

Q: Did you choose Rosalba Neri for the lead in this film?

Welles: There is a story there. You will notice the name Harry Cushing in the credits. Harry Cushing was a rich American who lived in Italy, and he was in love with Rosalba Neri. He was always looking for something to do, to get her to love him back, which she did not. He brought me a script called *Lady Dracula*, and he said, "Let's do this picture." In this business, when somebody comes and says, "Here's the money, let's go do a film," that is the greatest thing that can happen to you. I said okay, and I worked for a few months trying to put it together, and discovered he did not own the script, and the person who owned the script did not want to sell the rights to the script. So, I figured *Lady Dracula* could become *Lady Frankenstein*. I went to England, got together with a friend of mine named Eddie Di Lorenzo, and wrote *Lady Frankenstein*. To this day, I still believe that *Lady Dracula* was the better script though. *Lady Frankenstein* was a fair script, and I bettered the script in that I made the film with a real passion.

Q: What can you tell me about Mickey Hargitay, who had a featured role in that film?

Welles: I just thought that he was right for that part. I didn't really care if he was any good as an actor because I was going to dub him anyway. I know he looked good physically.

Q: Well, he did have presence.

Welles: But that's not his voice at all; at that time, he had a thick Hungarian accent. These days, he does not have much of an accent at all.

Q: You have said that *Lady Frankenstein*'s English-language version is missing about twelve minutes.

Welles: This was because Roger Corman's company New World released it. In fact, he bailed me out. What happened was Harry Cushing gave me only so much money for the picture, and the rest of the money came in from a letter of credit from a person who had a company called Heritage Films. When I went to cash the letter of credit in a bank in Italy, they said that it was bogus. It had too many clauses on it, that it was a trick. I got on a plane very fast. In Italy, I had 126 people on the payroll and the studio hired, everything was ready to go, and suddenly I was short $90,000. I got on a plane, flew to California, and went to see Roger Corman, and he said okay. And of course, his letter of credit is always good and he took up that portion of the budget. He did get a lot for his help though. He got the rights to the film in America, in perpetuity. Nobody ever gives that away but I was stuck, so I gave it away. Otherwise, the film would be mine again, and I could do what I want with it.

Q: You don't own any of it?

Welles: Well, he has to give me 25 percent of the revenue, but he is not doing anything with the picture nowadays, so there *is* no revenue really. But, if I had still owned the picture, I would figure out a way to exploit it.

Q: Whatever happened to Rosalba Neri?

Welles: She was one of the premier actresses in Italy, but unfortunately she made some very bad decisions. When censorship blew up, she made some very erotic films that bordered on pornography—they were what we would call soft-core porn. They were like stories like *The Story of O*, things like that. She made a few of those, which kind of hurt her career a little, and then that all blew over and she returned to acting. I understand she worked for a period again, as a character actress, before retiring. She is about sixty nowadays.

Q: How was it to work with Joseph Cotten on that film?

Welles: Wonderful. When working with Joseph Cotten, one worked with an actor that had discipline because he came from the theater, he was one of the original members of the Mercury Theater, and because of that, there was a lot of discipline there. You did not have to tell him anything twice. He came to the set, always prepared with his lines ready to be said. He was never a problem. I was a great friend of his wife, Patricia Medina. As an actor, I had done a picture with her, and we had become very close. Therefore, working with Joseph Cotten was a happy filmmaking relationship.

Q: After you stopped working dubbing foreign-language films and working as a filmmaker abroad, how did you change your focus to leave Europe and sort-of change careers?

Welles: I never actually stopped filming because what I do a lot, is to help other people make their films. I do not get any credit for this at all, although I make some money, and I have some fun. I help other people make their films, even today, I am involved in at least two films a year, and some of them are in the thirty to fifty million-dollar category. What I do is rightly called problem solving. I do creative consultations, things like that. During the period that we were just discussing, which was before the seventies, I was beginning to look to leave Italy, anyway. In 1971, I left Italy, and went to Southeast Asia, I went to Australia, and I went with the idea of going into the film business there. I had a film script called *House of 100 Horrors* that I wanted to make, and Roger Corman was going to distribute it. I had a friend who opened a studio in Sydney—he was the guy who produced the old *Inner Sanctum* series on the radio. However, when I got to Australia, the Australians made it so difficult for an outsider to get into the film business that I got out of the film business altogether, and I started a company which did multi-screen slide shows for big corporations, with up to thirty-six screens working at one time. I made a very good living at that. I also produced thirty-eight concerts at the Sydney Opera House. I did not get back into the film business until I came back to the United States in 1976.

Q: What happened when you came back to America in 1976?

Welles: I came back to America, and of course everybody was very nice, they welcomed me back. I had a terrific reputation; I had done so many things when I was abroad. I immediately went back to work as an actor, as a voice-over person. In fact, I was given the title of the Godfather of the Voice Industry when I came back.

Q: Did you work for Roger Corman again?

Welles: No, interestingly enough. Although my youngest son was the distribution manager for Corman, almost two years passed before Corman knew that he was my son. One day he said to him, "Are you any relation to Mel Welles?"

Q: What is your favorite performance as an actor?

Welles: Gravis Mushnick. It was based on a character that I did for ten years before the film was even made. I would be Gravis Mushnik at parties and stuff like that. It was a character that I knew so well because it was based on three Jewish merchants who lived in the theatrical district of New York. Chuck Griffith, who was my best friend, wrote a part in *Little Shop of Horrors* which incorporated all of the things that I used to say when

I was interpreting this Mushnik character, specifically for me, that never happened again in my life.

Q: Your performance in *The Undead*—do you consider that among your better performances?

Welles: Not among my better performances, but among my favorites. Actually, I got a terrific review in *Variety*. *Variety*, which was not very prone to giving Roger Corman any good reviews, compared me with Stanley Holloway in Shakespeare's *Hamlet*. He had played a gravedigger at some time, apparently, in *Hamlet*. I have never seen that film version, but they compared me to him. I thought that was somewhat marvelous. I have had a few really good roles. I loved the part I had in a film called *Soldier of Fortune*. The weird thing about this is, I have done sixty-five films, only about six of these films could be considered in the genre of horror or fantasy, and yet I have become a horror film icon, when my major body of work has nothing to do with horror films. As a director, it is the same thing, I have directed twelve films, and only two of them are horror films.

Q: Many people have had difficulty researching your acting credits, but even more trouble researching films that you have directed overseas. Do you think that one of the reasons for the confusion may be the use of pseudonyms on the films that you directed?

Welles: I did not use any pseudonyms personally.

Q: But why are some of your films attributed to other people? It is very difficult to know what films you actually directed. Except for *Lady Frankenstein*, for which the direction is credited to Mel Welles, there are a number of titles with other names listed as the director.

Welles: I know now what is that you are talking about. The primary reason is that when you are working in Europe, in order for the countries that are involved in a co-production to garner financial incentives from the government, the director had to be from one of the co-producing countries. The government gives premiums, financial support; without it, the films could not be made.

Q: Like a tax break?

Welles: No, better than a tax break, *money*. In Italy, they gave you premiums based upon the box-office of the film, and in Spain, they gave you premiums based upon the budget of the film. The U.S. had the only movie industry that did not have government support, which was a good thing, because we also did not have government interference. However, getting back to the original question, the director had to be from one of the co-producing countries, except in the case of *Lady Frankenstein* because on that film, we only had one American actor, so there was room for a director. We did all the studio work and all of the laboratory work in Italy, and we had an American financier as well. Therefore, the Italian producers, Alexia Film, could qualify for premiums because they didn't give that many profit points away to foreigners. However, in the case of the Jamaican picture, *Our Man in Jamaica* with Larry Pennell, where I was billed as the director Julio Salvador, and in the case of *Island of the Doomed*, where I was Ernst Von Theumer, things were different. Ernst Von Theumer was the German producer of the film, and Julio Salvador was a former Spanish director who became the office boy at Aragon Films where I made the picture.

Q: So, they took credit as the director?

Welles: Only in the countries of the co-production; in the rest of the world it was always Mel Welles. But on the IMDb, Internet Movie Database, it gets a little screwed up when they begin to investigate these things, and the name pops up as Ernst Von Theumer. In fact, they had it really screwed for a while. They had him doing *Little Shop of Horrors* as an actor, because they thought that Ernst Von Theumer and Mel Welles were the same person. Fortunately for me, I was able to get them straight on that, but there are still some errors in the IMDb. If you want an accurate picture of my background, go to my website. The bio and the credits are mostly accurate, plus the fact that you will be interested to know about some other things that I have done, and am doing. I am connected with the Executive Center for Re-invention in Austin, I have an MBA as well as a Ph.D., and I have done many other things.

Q: What brings you to the cult genre conventions?

Welles: Ego, I think, number one. Doing this stuff [conventions], it just validates your body of work. When we were making these films, we thought they were the biggest pieces of crap on the Earth. *Attack of the Crab Monsters*, we made that film for twenty-seven thousand dollars, and it affected three generations of people.

Q: The Italian director Joe D'Amato told me pretty much the same thing. I was asking him similar questions and people were coming over to him, and he said to me, "This is what it's all about."

Welles: It validates your body of work. I feel that I have not wasted my time. I mean, whole generations of people were frightened by *Attack of the Crab Monsters* and by a four hundred dollar Styrofoam crab. A whole generation of people who are now doctors, and lawyers, and politicians... they were frightened by that picture, and they all remembered the character of Dr. Jules Deveraux because the crab talked with my voice after it devoured me.

Q: As a kid, I always thought that *The Undead* was a very scary film, because of the whole idea of going back in time, and the climax of the film when the camera zoomed in on the body of the hypnotist...

Welles: And just the clothes were there.

Q: It was the idea of the clothes propped up, as if someone had been there once.

Welles: That was somewhat strange, that whole thing, because that was a typical Roger Corman move. At that particular time the regression craze...

Q: Bridey Murphy?

Welles: Paramount made the picture, *The Search for Bridey Murphy*, based on the real-life incidents surrounding a woman who had supposedly regressed through a number of past lives and recalled them all in hypnotherapy, and Corman immediately had to jump on the bandwagon. What I liked about the film was everything but the hypnotic suggestion theory regression part. It was the whole Hansel and Gretel feeling of the rest of the picture that I liked more, and I would have adored seeing him leave it alone as it was, because it could have been a classic for all time. See, he missed that. In fact, *Little Shop of Horrors*, that one that is a classic for all time, and it is the one that Roger had the least to do with. First of all, it was shot in two days and two nights. Chuck Griffith wrote the script, I rehearsed the actors. We were there two days on the set; and the two nights that we were doing the exteriors scenes, there was no Roger Corman involvement at all because we were stealing the exterior shots, on the sly, ourselves. Corman didn't have anything to do with that film for the most part. So, in reality, if you look at it, all he did was stand around on the set for two days. We had two cameras, it was an early sitcom technique, and there was nothing for him to do. In a way it kind of sticks in his craw that his most famous film is a film that he had little to do with. Many of his other films, he had a lot to do work with. It was lock, stock and barrel, whatever the film was. But, he would have had another classic if he had let *The Undead* go, the way it was, without adding in the regression therapy material. It would have still been around, and getting raves, because Chuck really wrote a brilliant, brilliant script.

Q: What did you think of the remake of *Little Shop of Horrors*?

Welles: To me, they didn't remake *Little Shop of Horrors*. I mean, that's a lot more important story than a remake. First of all, if you are talking about the live musical, I love the live musical; it's just a totally different project. The musical was created by the late Howard Ashman and Marty Robinson, and they both saw the original picture when they were kids, and both were independently obsessed with making a musical of it. They met in New York; one was broke, and looking for something to do. The other was making money hand over fist working for *Sesame Street* as a puppeteer. They got together and they said, "Well, why don't we do it?" They got Alan Mencken to write the music, and they put together a shoestring budget version in order to put it on for twenty-four performances, as a showcase. They didn't have a clue that there was something magical about the whole thing. They didn't have a clue about what was going to happen. The music is not that memorable, but it's good, and entertaining. The lyrics are good and entertaining, but there were no hit songs, nothing crossed over into a hit song.

Q: So, I gather that you did not like the Frank Oz film too much?

Welles: Well, I did not like it for two reasons. One was that I wasn't in it, and I was pissed off at the way that it was handled because they evidently wanted me in it. They called me for my availability, and Frank Oz, when he was brought aboard, he made an arbitrary decision, which had nothing to do with me, just that he said, "No, I don't think it's a good idea to have anybody from the original picture in there." I think it would have been a terrific idea, in that I was the only one who could have conceivably reprised his part, because age didn't make any difference. So, that was the first reason. The second reason was that they went so overboard with Oz and his cronies, like Steve Martin, Bill Murray and John Candy, that they hurt the

Welles and the author in the late 1990s.

story of the play a lot, and were spending too much time on those sequences. In fact, they cut two songs from Vincent Gardenia, and I am sure he was very upset about it. People even wrote me on my website, and they said, "Was it because he couldn't sing?" He was a glorious singer, he was a trained opera singer, and he was Italian. What Italian do you know that does not sing? He must have loved the idea that he was going to have a couple of songs, and a funny little dance, and then they cut it, leaving him with his Mafia personality, and the fact that in that movie you didn't care very much whether he lost the shop or not because he didn't have the chance to show you any pussycat warmth. He had the chance to show you the grub, curmudgeonly values of the part. I performed in the live musical, just recently, I brought all of the ethnic warmth back into the role, and I even snuck in many of the original lines from the original movie to try to bring back the flavor, but the main thing is the difference between the two projects. There's a chemistry difference. In the musical version, the plant is stone evil, it's Mephistophele, it's Satan, it corrupts, and it corrupted Seymour. You watch the dentist die, and he feeds Mushnik to the plant. In the original film, the plant was just hungry, that's all. There was nothing evil about it, just hungry. Seymour never lost his innocence, everybody died by accident. That's a big chemistry difference. The chemistry is so different now with the Hollywood big-budget remake, which did not do as well financially that I'm sure they all hoped for. You start with a farce and by the second act, you're getting really dark, perhaps too dark.

Credits: 1953: *Appointment in Honduras* (uncredited); *The Golden Blade* (uncredited); *Gun Fury*; 1954: *Bengal Brigade* (uncredited); *Captain Midnight: Trapped Behind Bars* (10/16/54) (television); *Jesse James Vs. the Daltons* (uncredited); *Massacre Canyon*; *Pushover* (uncredited); *The Racers* (uncredited); *The Silver Chalice* (uncredited); *Wyoming Renegades* (uncredited); *Yankee Pasha* (uncredited); 1955: *Abbott and Costello Meet the Mummy*; *The Big Knife* (uncredited); *Captain Midnight: The Invisible Terror* (02/12/55), *Peril from the Arctic* (02/26/55) (television); *Duel on the Mississippi*; *The Fighting Chance*; *The Ford Television Theatre: Mimi* (05/19/55) (television); *Hold Back Tomorrow* (a.k.a. *No Tomorrow*); *Kismet* (uncredited); *The Lone Ranger: Counterfeit Redskins* (09/01/55) (television); *The Pirates of Tripoli* (uncredited); *Soldier of Fortune* (uncredited); *Spy Chasers* (uncredited); *Stage 7: The Long Count* (03/27/55) (television); *Tales of the Texas Rangers: Blood Trail* (09/24/55) (television); *Topper: Topper in Mexico* (01/28/55) (television); 1956: *The Adventures of Dr. Fu Manchu: Dr. Fu Manchu's Raid* (10/22/56) (television); *Calling Homicide* (uncredited); *Flight to Hong Kong*; *The Ford Television Theatre: Journey by Moonlight* (01/05/56), *The Payoff* (05/03/56) (television); *Meet Me in Las Vegas* (uncredited); *Outside the Law*; *Private Secretary: Dollars and Sense* (11/25/56) (television); *Tales of the Bengal Lancers: The Regiment* (10/21/56) (television); 1957: *Attack of the Crab Monsters*; *Code of Silence* (a.k.a. *Killer's Cage*); *Designing Woman* (uncredited); *Hell on Devil's Island*; *Hold That Hypnotist*; *Rock All Night*; *Tales of the Bengal Lancers: The Glass Necklace* (03/24/57), *Ten Thousand Rupees* (03/31/57) (television); *Tip on a Dead Jockey*; *The 27th Day* (uncredited); *The Undead*; 1958: *The Adventures of Rin Tin Tin: Border Incident* (03/28/58) (television); *Alfred Hitchcock Presents: Flight to the East* (03/23/58) (television); *The Brothers Karamazov*; *Hakuja Den* (a.k.a. *Panda and the Magic Serpent*) (animated) (voice only) [Japan-U.S.]; *Have Gun—Will Travel: The Protégé* (10/18/58) (television); *High School Confidential!* (a.k.a. *Young Hellions*); *Maverick: The Judas Mask* (11/02/58) (television); 1959: *The Deputy: The Deal* (12/05/59) (television); *The Texan: The Ringer* (10/19/59) (television); 1960: *The Little Shop of Horrors*; *Mr. Lucky: Election Bet* (06/18/60) (television); 1962: *Hemingway's Adventures of a Young Man* (uncredited); *The Reluctant Saint* (uncredited) [Italy-U.S.]; *Lo Sceicco Rosso* (a.k.a. *The Red Sheik*) [Italy-France]; 1963: *The Keeler Affair* (a.k.a. *The Christine Keeler Affair*) [Great Britain–Denmark]; 1964: *Panic Button*; 1966: *La Sorella Di Satana* (a.k.a. *The Sister of Satan* a.k.a. *Revenge of the Blood Beast* a.k.a. *The She Beast*) [Great Britain–Italy]; 1968: *Die Grosse Treibjagd* (a.k.a. *The Last Mercenary*) [Spain–Italy–West Germany]; *Llaman De Jamaica, Mr. Ward* (a.k.a. *Our Man in Jamaica, Mr. Ward* a.k.a. *Flatfoot* a.k.a. *Hello Glen Ward, House Dick*) [Spain-Italy]; 1977: *Joyride to Nowhere*; 1980: *Dr. Heckyll and Mr. Hype*; 1981: *Body and Soul*; *Faeries* (animated) (voice only) (television); *Wolfen* (voice only); 1982: *The Last American Virgin*; 1982: *Homework*; 1986: *Chopping Mall* (a.k.a. *Killbots*); 1987: *Commando Squad*; 1988: *Invasion Earth: The Aliens Are Here* (television); *Rented Lips*; 1989: *Wizards of the Lost Kingdom II*; 2002: *Raising Dead* [Canada].

Fred Williamson

Fred Williamson, the world's first black action movie superstar, crashed through the gates of Hollywood racism previously left ajar by the efforts of Sidney Poitier and Harry Belafonte. In the seventies and eighties he became one of the leading male stars in the cinema, years before Wesley Snipes and Ving Rhames did the same. He also supplanted Woody Strode as a formidable presence in European-financed and -lensed action and adventure films. In the early eighties, he was considered one of the world's foremost sex symbols by a poll conducted in Sweden.

Williamson has been called "one of America's most durable tough guys" by the *New York Daily News*, "The first black film producer in history to actually make hit movies" by the *New York Amsterdam News*, and "The Black Clark Gable" and "Almost unbelievably handsome" by a variety of film press journalists. Even the usually staid *New York Times* said of him (in 1977), "His face and physique ... look as though they were chiseled to order in heaven by Michelangelo for some customer who had requested the perfect man."

As a director-producer in his heyday he also had as much clout if not more than Sidney Poitier did, and definitely more than pioneering African-American filmmaker Oscar Micheaux years before him. In an interview with the *New York Daily News* (November 1983) he stated, "I'm one of the few producers left who can make a movie that's competitive with the major motion pictures for under a million dollars."

Williamson was born on March 5, 1938, in Gary, Indiana. The son of a welder Williamson grew up in a tough Chicago neighborhood. In a press release for the 1974 film *Three the Hard Way*, he said, "I used to get my lunch money taken away so regularly that I finally just went down to the corner, and said, 'Line up for the lunch money everybody.' Finally, I hit six feet tall, and started getting a little lunch money back." In an interview with the *New York Times* in March of 1972, he recalled of his later teenage years, "I became what I am because I was a jock. When I was a kid, pimps, gambling, stealing, and robbery surrounded me. That was in the fifties, and we never knew what a junkie was. One time, we were living in Chicago, and I was the leader of a gang called the Red Tops. Finally, I discovered girls, and when I found out girls dug football players, all that gang stuff went down the tubes."

Williamson excelled in scholastic sports like basketball, track, and football, and reportedly was offered forty athletic scholarships, settling for one with Northwestern University. In 1960, he was signed by the professional football team, the San Francisco 49ers, but was traded before the start of the upcoming season to the Pittsburgh Steelers. In 1961, he played for the Oakland Raiders and, in 1965, the Kansas City Chiefs. He even appeared in the very first Superbowl in 1967, when the Chiefs played the Green Bay Packers. Williamson retired from pro sports in 1968, and for a brief time worked as an architect out of Montreal, Canada. During the latter part of his football career Williamson was nicknamed The Hammer by sports journalists and fans because he had an aggressive style of playing. "One day, I decided that, since I was bigger than most of the pass receivers I was covering, I'd just knock them down as they came off the scrimmage line," he said. After nearly ten years of pro football, he had played with four teams, in ninety-three games, and intercepted over thirty passes.

Seeking a new career and a new life, Williamson packed everything and headed to Tinsel Town, waltzing into the offices of producer Hal Kanter; "I had seen this show on television, the *Julia* show, and I decided I would become Julia's boyfriend." Williamson so impressed the producer of the *Julia* TV series starring Diahann Carroll, that he was immediately cast as the lead actress' boyfriend, Steve Bruce. Afterwards, filmmaker Robert Altman recruited Williamson to appear in the role of Spearchucker, the football ringer in the film *M*A*S*H**. He got his first taste of directing when he handled the choreography and directing chores of the film's famed football sequence. He then landed a small role in *Tell Me That You Love Me, Junie Moon*, directed by Otto Preminger.

As the seventies began, Williamson became one of an elite team of black actors who were former (or, in some cases, still active) professional athletes. The list also included Jim Brown, Bernie Casey, Jim Kelley, D'Urville Martin, and Richard Roundtree.

In 1972, Williamson began appearing in gritty urban action-adventure films as the maverick hero and, in some cases, anti-hero. Barnstorming through roles with unmatched verisimilitude and glee, the world's first Black action star was born. Most of the early films, defiantly anti-establishment, fulfilled the suppressed fantasies of millions of African-American youths. Many Caucasians also became fans of the new genre. As Williamson told a press representative for the film *Black Caesar*, "Most of my fans are kids in ghetto areas. They cannot relate to my university degree, that's too far removed from what's possible for them. But they can relate to my athletic career, that's possible, and to the characters I play, the guy who overcomes all the obstacles, and spits in the establishment's eye."

In titles like *Hammer* (1972), *The Legend of Nigger Charley* and its sequel *The Soul of Nigger Charley* (both 1973, and both westerns), *Black Caesar* (1973), *That Man Bolt* (1973), *Hell Up in Harlem* (1973), *Black Eye* (1974), *Three the Hard Way* (1974), *Three Tough Guys* (1974), *Boss Nigger* (1975), and *Bucktown* (1975), Williamson meted out his own brand of justice. He had box-office success with his films, and earned himself a special place in the history of action films. He even began his own production company, Po' Boy, to produce the films that he wanted to make, personally financing most of his productions in the late seventies through today, and giving up his own salary to keep production costs down; "I'm a guy who still associates with moviegoers."

When controversy reared its head during the peak of the Blaxploitation film cycle, Williamson was there to meet it head-on. In the early eighties he told the *New York Daily News*, "Black people weren't being exploited, because the movies were providing jobs for a lot of blacks who never had a chance to show their talents before. Nobody was twisting people's arms to get them into the theater. It is embarrassing when groups like the NAACP and CORE ... are fighting among themselves about whether black movies should be censored or scripts should be reviewed. It's embarrassing to black people... I do not make educational films. I make entertainment films. Sex and violence have been around way before we started making films. Nobody, when I was a kid, said, 'Don't watch James Cagney,

Fred Williamson blows away the action movie competition.

because he definitely will kill a whole flock of people.' Now black people are doing the same thing, but we've got black people crying 'blaxploitation.'" Critical praise in the press was rare, Williamson was a star where it counted... in the cinemas, and on the streets.

In 1973, he became the highest-paid African-American actor in the movies, securing a one million dollar contract to star in the (ill-fated) Universal film *That Man Bolt*, an action film intended to be the first of a series about a globetrotting adventurer. However, indifferent and lackluster direction guaranteed the film mediocre box-office. That October, he appeared (mostly) nude in *Playgirl* magazine.

In 1974, Williamson replaced Don Meredith, and joined Howard Cossell and Frank Gifford on the ABC television network's *Monday Night Football* program as a commentator. His co-anchor stint was brief. Said Williamson in 1977 to the *New York Amsterdam News*, "My deal with ABC was very costly for them. I was supposed to do three Movies of the Week for them as producer, director, and star. However, they wouldn't give them to me unless I did *Monday Night Football*. I did not need football anymore, but that's what they really wanted me for. So, I said you have to keep me in my acting, and film production bag. [But] nobody told Cossell. [He] did not like the idea of having someone in the booth he might lose to... someone wittier than he was... Cossell ignored everything that I said. So, I didn't need it. I am a movie star. They paid me off in cash."

Williamson never did make the three ABC films. On the heels of this debacle, he hosted a karate tournament in New York, and told the *Amsterdam News* that he had been studying karate for eight years and had attained the rank of first-degree black belt in the martial art form.

In the eighties, Williamson journeyed to Europe to star in a number of Italian-financed or co-financed films. His gung ho characterizations in *The Bronx Warriors* (1982), *Warriors of the Wasteland* (1982), *Delta Force Commando* (1987), and *Black Cobra* (1988) elevated those lower budgeted science fiction and adventure films. Even though some of these films only played briefly on American screens, they enjoyed a lucrative afterlife on videocassette, and The Hammer was introduced to a completely new cadre of fans. Williamson even co-financed some of the European made films (like 1988's *Black Cobra 2*), and appeared as recurring lead character Detective Malone in a series of European films produced until 1990.

Williamson came back to U.S. screens with a vengeance, stronger than ever as a one-man industry, through his Po' Boy productions. He gave work to former Hollywood stars whose careers were suffering. The likes of Christopher Connelly, Robert Forster, Henry Silva, and Bo Svenson were often cast in his productions. As his film production and acting roles started to slow down, his strengths as a filmmaker and actor showed little signs lessening. In Robert Rodriguez's unusual horror movie *From Dusk Till Dawn* (1996), he was given a shining cameo role (with a monologue by the film's screenwriter and co-star, Quentin Tarantino) that was intended as a special gift to Fred Williamson fans. (Then his character met his fate head on by attacking a group of vicious vampires!) In the years since, he has produced the Larry Cohen–directed film *Original Gangstas* (1996), which featured a who's who of the best of the best from the Blaxploitation era: Jim Brown, Pam Grier, Richard Roundtree, and Ron O'Neal. Yes, we had in this film The Hammer, Slaughter, Sheba/Coffy, Shaft, and Superfly.

In 1998, Williamson co-starred with action movie icon Dolph Lundgren in John Woo's *Blackjack*. However, the Canadian-U.S. film, intended as a pilot for a television series, floundered in the ratings, and became more successful in the video rental markets. Williamson directed and appeared in his most recent production, the action movie *Down 'n Dirty* in 2000, but his career may be headed for a revival as he has had a major supporting role in the updated feature film version of the seventies television show *Starsky and Hutch* (2004), and may even appear in director Quentin Tarantino's long-in-gestation remake of *The Inglorious Bastards*, the 1977 WWII adventure film in which Williamson co-starred with Bo Svenson. As Williamson told *The New York Times*, "The people I admire most are me, and the cat I see in the mirror everyday. They are 100 percent for me, and I am 100 percent for them. I have never failed in life; I have never failed in anything. That's because I always give 105 percent effort into whatever I do. I hang in there, and eventually I win what I want."

As for his fans, Williamson always keeps them in mind close to his heart. "When people think of me, I'd like them to think of a handsome sexy serious actor idol."

Q: Your football career turned into a movie career around 1970. What compelled you to go into movies?

Fred Williamson: After I retired from pro football, I became an architect. That was my trade. During the off-season each year that I played pro football, I was an architect for a steel corporation. I had a divided lifestyle. One was six months of nine-to-five, behind a desk. The other was six months of freedom playing football, with not having my time regulated, having my hour off for lunch and all that. Once I started playing football, I realized, after nine months, that, for the rest of my life, it was going to be nine-to-five, with an hour for lunch, and I could not make that adjustment smoothly. One night I was watching television and saw the *Julia* show. I said to myself, "Shit, I could do that." So, I went to Hollywood and became Diahann Carroll's boyfriend on the *Julia* show.

Q: Did you audition for that part?

Williamson: I didn't audition. I went and bullshitted my way in. I drove up to the 20th Century–Fox lot and they would not let me in the gate without a pass. Therefore, I drove around the corner, picked up a pay phone, and called the front gate. I told them that this was Mr. Hal Kanter's office calling from the *Julia* show, and that we are expecting Mr. Fred Williamson. Would you please let him drive through the gate? I hung up the phone and drove right back around, and they said, "Oh yeah, we are expecting you." I drove in, and I got to the secretary. I said, "I'd like to see Mr. Hal Kanter," and she said "Well, who's here?" I said, "Just tell him, it's… The Hammer." So, she got on the squawk box, and she said, "Mr. Kanter, there's a Mr. Hammer here." I said, "No, no, no, not Mr. Hammer. It's The Hammer." Kanter said on the squawk box, "Football player?" I said, "Yeah." He said, "All right, come right in."

Q: You received some good notices for those early appearances on *Julia*.

Williamson: Well, I'm not a bad actor. I'm due notice when I do good work. As long as I know that I did well, I don't really care.

Q: Then you went into *M*A*S*H**.

Williamson: That was filmed on the same lot as the television show. I was working on *Julia* at 20th Century–Fox, and one day I was in the commissary room and Robert Altman came up to me and he said, "You're The Hammer, right? The football player? I'm doing a movie and I don't know shit about football, so I need your help to come and do the football sequences, and also be in the movie. You can handle all the directing for the football sequences." So, that was my first directing job.

Q: [Assistant director] Andy Sidaris has claimed responsibility for directing the football sequence. Isn't he credited with that?

Williamson: Andy Sidaris started it, but when he came in with this overhead crane camera, I said, "You're not going to like that look." I told Altman, "You're not going to like that look." First of all, we were not shooting on a real football field; we drew lines on the grass in Griffin Park. You had temporary bleachers and, once you get up high, you're going to see that it's all fake and phony. I said, "You need to do it like the NFL and put that camera like twelve inches off the ground and shoot down the line. Then, everything in the background is out of focus, and everything in the foreground is in focus." Altman said, "So, why don't you do it?" I said okay. After that, Ingo Preminger, the producer on *M*A*S*H**, was trying to help his brother find an actor to play a role in a film called *Tell Me That You Love Me, Junie Moon*. Ingo took me over and introduced me to Otto Preminger and I got that part.

Q: And you played the Beach boy, right?

Williamson: The Beach boy [laughter], yeah, that was my role. And, from that, I went on to say, "Well, shit, this is easy. I should have left football and been doing this a long time ago." Then I took ideas to Paramount Pictures and said, "Listen, you never made a black cowboy movie before." So we did *The Legend of Nigger Charley*. Then I went to American International Pictures and said, "You've never done a black gangster picture before..." and I did *Black Caesar*.

Q: With Larry Cohen, the writer?

Williamson: Well, I did it for AIP. They hired Larry Cohen to write the script because they liked his writing style at that time. However, it was my idea, my concept to do this movie. When I approached [AIP] about a film about a black gangster, they had never done it before. So, they bought Larry Cohen in, based on my idea.

Q: That was a very successful film for you.

Williamson: Part of that success was due to the genre. I knew what was happening. Heroes were needed at that time, both black and white, even more so in the black area. So, that's what I became to the blacks at that particular time... their hero.

Q: I believe you were a hero to a lot of Caucasians as well. I grew up in New York, in Brooklyn, which is an urban area, and I used to travel out of my way to see your movies when I was a youngster.

Williamson: Well, stand-up guys are always liked and appreciated by people of every color, and that's the kind of roles that I play, the kind of roles that I try to pick up. A stand-up guy [is] what I am in real life. I try to keep my real life as close to the movie without killing people. I beat up a few now and then, but I don't kill anybody.

Q: In person, you have an easygoing and charming manner... yet onscreen...

Williamson: That's what makes the heroes. I never confuse being the tough guy with being the hero. I never start fights; I never hit first. I always get hit first, get beat up first. Then, I'm allowed to make a comeback. Then, the public is always on my side. The tough guy who hits first, breaks down doors, and turns over cars is not really necessarily a tough guy. He may be the loudest guy, but not necessarily the toughest guy.

Q: I think of these films as action films. I always have had a problem with the term Black Exploitation or Blaxploitation.

Williamson: I do not understand how they could use that terminology, because I don't know who was being exploited. People came to the movies because they enjoyed it. Everybody who worked in them was paid, their checks cleared. It was providing work. Therefore, I never understood what the terminology meant.

Q: However, unfortunately, it got to be a problem and...

Williamson: It got to be a problem, and it contributed to the demise of the industry.

Q: The two Westerns that you made, *The Legend of Nigger Charley*, and *The Soul of Nigger Charley*—were there marketing problems with that word in the title?

Williamson: No and this was my idea again. I went to Paramount Pictures and I said to them that they never made a black Western, and let's do one. They said, "Okay, how much is the budget?" I said, "I can make it for $600,000." They said, "What are you going to call it?" I said, "*The Legend of Nigger Charley*," and they just about jumped out of their chairs. I said, "Listen, that's the advertising campaign, that's what I want. The reaction that you just gave me is the reaction that I want from the public and the people." What we did is we put up big billboards in Times Square [in New York]. The first billboard

Williamson gets the ranch, the girl (Marcia McBroom), and the bad guys in *The Legend of Nigger Charley* **(1972) (Paramount Pictures).**

said, "He's coming." Nothing else, just "He's coming." The next one, about two weeks later, featured my picture, and it said, "He's here." It was a photo of me standing with my shirt off in a town dressed in a Western outfit, and a gun on my side, with my arms folded. Two weeks later, there was another billboard and it said, "*Nigger Charley* has arrived." In addition, I'm standing there [on the poster] with two sidekicks in Western gear. We set 'em up. We set 'em up, so when the picture came out, people were anticipating what the hell is this *Legend of Nigger Charley* going to be about? The only problem we had was that not every newspaper would carry that advertising. They carried advertising that said *Black Charley*. They carried ones that said *Charley*. In the main markets, New York and Chicago and LA, they carried the title *The Legend of Nigger Charley*, but throughout the South, it was *Black Charley*, or just *Charley*.

Q: Was *That Man Bolt* devised because of the international success of the James Bond movies?

Williamson: Universal wanted to get into the arena of the secret agent films, but with a black star, but they didn't want to get into other stuff. Whatever film they made, they didn't want to call it exploitation. They wanted to stay away from portraying black urban life. They chose me as the star because I had the dashing, debonair, suave look and style to do their James Bond movie. Then, they ran out of guts. After we made the movie, and the movie did very well, they called me into the office and they said, "Listen, we don't know what to do with you next." I had a three-picture deal for a series of movies featuring the Jefferson Bolt character, but the movie was not without its difficulties being made. We had two directors, Henry Levin and David Lowell Rich. When the studio saw the initial rushes and saw the potential, they replaced one director who made it seem like a glorified TV movie, and brought in another one to make it more like the globetrotting action film that it was intended to be. Naturally, I gave my percentage of input into the filmmaking process as well. Since they didn't know how to follow-up *That Man Bolt*, they just paid me off. They gave me a check for two movies.

Q: That is a shame, because I would have liked to see more of those. I am sure many people would have liked to see another *Bolt* film.

Williamson: It was a great filmmaking experience. We shot it in Hong Kong, in Las Vegas, in Los Angeles, it was great. It got good reviews, and made a lot of money. However, Universal just was not ready to take that step, to make a series of major action features with a black star. Other studios were willing to take that step, but at that time, not Universal.

Q: What was it like to work with director Jack Arnold in the film *Black Eye*?

Williamson: I always believed that the film was very good. Jack was a very good director. The problem with the film was that when we made it, it was titled *Shep Stone*. By the time it was finished and ready for distribution, it got up to the seventieth floor and thirty-five movie studio executives looked at it, and they decided that this was their jumping-on point, that they were going to jump into exploitation films, and they changed the title to *Black Eye*. That hurt the film. It hurt the film severely when it came out as *Black Eye* because the name of my character was Shep Stone, and when we made the movie, it was called *Shep Stone*.

Q: It is a very slick-looking film.

Williamson: Everything I have done in my life, I have always been ahead of my time. Most of the time, innovators never get full credit, or get their full due. None of the movies I ever made in the seventies were "Get Whitey" movies. I was an equal opportunity employer, I killed white people, and I killed black people, yellow people, and pink people. I beat up everybody that was bad so that they can never call my movies "Get Whitey" movies, as some of those movies were in the seventies. Those movies were vindictive movies, creating racial problems. I wasn't about that. I was about being a gangster; I was about being a cowboy...

Q: You were the hero.

Williamson: Yes.

Q: Tell me about *Crazy Joe*. Even though that was a smaller part for you, that certainly was a successful film.

Williamson: For the film *Crazy Joe*, the studio wanted a black person who had some street credibility and the strength to portray the real black guy who really lived during the time that Crazy Joe Bonnano had lived. This character [that I played] really did meet Crazy Joe. They met when Crazy Joe got out of prison. Crazy Joe used his friendship with this black guy, to use his gang, to get some of his powers back in a mob struggle. They wanted somebody in that part that I played, that the public would accept and buy with believability. To pull it off as this person did in real life that is why they chose me for that.

Q: Do you have any remembrances of working with Peter Boyle on that film?

Williamson: Peter was a great guy. It was a fun shoot. My greatest experience working on that film was going to Rome, Italy. The majority of it was filmed on the streets of New York, and the rest was shot in Rome so we had a hell of a time.

Q: I thought *Three Tough Guys* was your first European film.

Williamson: No, it was *Crazy Joe*, then *Three Tough Guys*, but what happened was, once I got exposed to working in and living in Italy, I stayed there for five or six years. I made a lot of pictures in Italy.

Q: Your first film with the director Antonio Margheriti was the western *Take a Hard Ride*.

Williamson: Actually, one of my first Italian pictures was *The Inglorious Bastards*; then, after that, I did a whole slew of films, *Black Cobra*, *Black Cobra 2*. The Margheriti film came a couple of years after *Three the Hard Way* because there was Jim Brown, Jim Kelly and me. On the strength of *Three the Hard Way*, we did *Take a Hard Ride*.

Q: Those Westerns did very well for you. I believe that you were responsible for kickstarting the revival of the genre, because the traditional Spaghetti Westerns had peaked in popularity by the beginning of the seventies...

Williamson: I think that there is always a place for the western. If we don't have westerns today, just think of all of the history that the kids today are going to miss. We cannot do the cowboys and Indians any more because it is politically incorrect, but we can do cowboys and cowboys, that's for sure.

Q: Then there is *Joshua*, which is a Western that I think is underrated.

Williamson: *Joshua* is one of my own personal favorites. It is probably my favorite film. It never really got the exposure that it was due. Nobody really got to see it. However, I think it had a hell of a story, better than some of these twenty and thirty million dollar things that they are making nowadays.

Q: You have made a number of films featuring the character Jesse Crowder. Which is your favorite?

Williamson: I kind of like everything that I do. There is nothing that I really, really like that I make, because I always see something that I can make better. There is always a scene that I could have improved on. I like them all. There's none that I dislike. The Jesse Crowder series is really strange because Jesse Crowder was the name of a person who

I went to high school with, who I respected a great deal, and after I did like five of these films featuring the character of Jesse Crowder, I got involved in a lawsuit. He sued me for using his name. He said I was using his name. So, I said, "Wait a minute. You are not the only Jesse Crowder in the country, man. There's got to be twenty thousand Jesse Crowders in the country." My lawyer went on my behalf, bought about seventeen pages from different phone books from around the country, and said that there are many Jesse Crowders." Then my lawyer said to Jesse Crowder, "Were you ever a private detective?" He said, "No." "Did you ever kill anybody?" "No." "Did you ever beat up seventeen people in a karate fight?" "No." "Then, how the hell do you figure that he's depicting your life?" I thought I was doing something kind and generous to the guy, and I ended up being sued.

Q: The suit made you end the series?
Williamson: That's why I dropped that.

Q: I thought *No Way Back* was definitely one of the highlights of the series.
Williamson: Yeah, *No Way Back, Death Journey*. I was just getting started and finding the right scripts for that character when this guy came out of nowhere and said I was using his name.

Q: *Vigilante* was a powerful film, directed by William Lustig.
Williamson: It was timely. That's what was happening in society at that particular time. A lot of groups in neighborhoods were getting together, not to fight fire with fire, but to let a lot of the wrong environment in their neighborhood know that they were not going to stand for it. So, all we did was take advantage of what was happening in America.

Q: Woody Strode was in that as well, wasn't he?
Williamson: Woody Strode had a fight scene in the bathroom, saving Robert Forster's behind, literally. I knew Woody before, from Rome, Italy. I used to sit around and talk to Woody and his wife quite often. I knew Woody and respected Woody. In fact, I think that Italy was trying to make me the next Woody Strode because Woody was getting old and not working quite as much. I was the young guy coming up with the muscles, like Woody, and they were trying to make me into the next Woody Strode, except that I had a different image. It was to my advantage in timing to be there at that particular time.

Q: Whereas he was silent and strong...
Williamson: He was on his way out and I was on my way in.

Q: Then you got into the science fiction genre when the Italians were making all of those *Road Warrior* rip-offs.
Williamson: Futuristic. Those films were not so much about science fiction, as they were futuristic. That's when the Italians were making all these movies that featured America as a land covered in dust, everybody had funny-looking cars, and it was kind of a futuristic style.

Q: You appeared in a number of them, including *The New Barbarians, The Bronx Warriors*...
Williamson: And *Warriors of the Wasteland*. Again, that was that Woody Strode look that I was interpreting. I was always standing around half-clothed; my muscles would be bulging. As I became the next Woody Strode, it was timely for them as well, the producers, the studios, the audiences, because that's what they needed.

Q: Do you recall anything in particular about those pictures?

Williamson: I felt kind of stupid doing them [*laughs*]. Other than that, I was in Italy, I was in Rome, I was enjoying the hell out of my life, and I felt stupid doing those movies. Nevertheless, I was enjoying being in Rome so much that it really didn't matter.

Q: In the seventies, the eighties, and to an extent, in the nineties, it has not been always easy for black directors to work in Hollywood. For instance, you work mainly independently, and pretty much have done so as a director for over three decades. The films that you have turned out are generally beyond so much of the schlock that was released by most of the independent filmmakers in the seventies and eighties. And, today, you are still working as a director as well as an actor and yet you have still not received due recognition as a director. How do you feel about all this?

Williamson: Well, I still haven't been accepted. The only place that I have been accepted as a director is in Canada. A couple of years ago, I was working on a television series called *Fast Track*, and they wanted me to direct two of the shows. They knew that I could direct fast and economically, they knew that I could work with multiple cameras, and they knew that, if I did it, it would be something different for the Canadian audiences, because I would give them a motion picture look, rather than a television look. So, they gave me my due in Canada. They still have not given it to me in the United States. However, maybe it's because I'm not really trying to be part of the mainstream. I don't want to get into that kind of controlled environment. I like being an independent filmmaker. I like being free, and I don't want to look up and see the guys in suits and ties standing on the sideline. Once you see them, you know they got something to tell you that you're not going to like. Therefore, I do not want to be part of that infrastructure. I have never really tried to be part of that power structure.

Q: In *One Down, Two to Go* [1983], you resurrected many older themes which were prevalent in seventies films. And you featured actors in supporting roles that mainstream Hollywood seemed to have forgotten.

Williamson: That's what I do. It's not so much resurrecting themes, as resurrecting actors over forty that Hollywood *has* seemed to have forgotten about. All the people who came up with me, and were around when I was starting out, have not been working that much. In addition, if they are working, they are not doing the kind of roles, characters, and images that they portrayed back in their heyday. I have always believed that I have the power to make the change; to give something back, to give them their strength, as I did in *Original Gangstas*, which is the only reason that I made that movie... to bring back Pam Grier, Richard Roundtree, Ron O'Neal and Jim Brown. In addition, look at what happened to Pam Grier's career. It has gone way into the mainstream. Jim Brown is working regularly now. He's just done a football film for Oliver Stone. Spike Lee has made a documentary about his life. My idea was to resurrect the dormant careers of actors. Show the audiences and the studios that we are still marketable, that we are still viable, and that, if you're over forty or over fifty, it doesn't mean that you are dead. You still have an audience out there that is wondering what you are doing, and wants to see you do it again.

Q: Whatever happened to Jim Kelly, the martial artist and actor who co-starred with you in a few films?

Williamson: Jim Kelly disappeared. He cannot be found. I have looked high and low for Jim Kelly and cannot find him. He would have fit perfectly in *Original Gangstas*, because it would have been all of them together.

Q: In *From Dusk till Dawn*, you gave a great showcase performance.

Williamson: Being a friend of Quentin Tarantino, and Quentin being a friend of the movies of the seventies, and being a friend of black actors, he called me and asked me. He had a small role for me and asked if I would do it. I said, "Let me look at the script," then I said, "Let me show you what my interpretation is of what I think this role is about." I created this character and gave him my interpretation of this character and it blew him away. He said, "Man, that's it, you really hit it on the head."

Q: You have a great monologue in that film too.

Williamson: They made me write all that shit. It was perfect for me because the timing in the movie, in that scene, appeared when everybody was now afraid for their lives. Everybody was scared, and all these monsters were knocking on doors and windows and about to come in. It was time for the hero to step up. Now, I know the audience is looking at The Hammer and saying, "The Hammer is going to go out there and kick ass!" Then, I go off into this monologue about Vietnam, and the people are going, "Oh shit! What's wrong with him? He doesn't have it together, what's wrong with him?" It came off stronger, and it came off more funny than probably I intended it to be, all because of the timing... where it was cut into the film.

Q: What do you recall about Robert Rodriguez and his direction on that film?

Williamson: As a director, Robert gave you freedom. Again, a lot of the stuff that I did in that movie was improvised. I had this idea where, being the martial arts guy, when one of these monsters charges me... why don't I just rip his heart out? So, I have his heart in my hand, and he still keeps coming. So I have to stick a pencil or something into it to kill it. Robert said, "Great. Do it." He shot everything, he was his own cinematographer. He was walking around with the camera. Not only was he the director, he was the camera operator too.

Q: You also turned up in a supporting role in a John Woo–directed picture called *Blackjack*, which was made for television via cable and video as a pilot.

Williamson: It was a pretty expensive pilot—six million dollars. It was supposed to have been a pilot for a series. However, when Barry Diller, the producer bought the USA Network, he changed it around, because it was made for the USA Network. Diller sort of backed off from many of the action films that he used to be famous

Fred Williamson: Ageless and still packing a pistol.

for producing, and went off in another direction. I worked in it chiefly because of John Woo, and I figured that Dolph Lundgren and I would have a good time together if it went on to become a series. But, it didn't happen.

Q: Which was a shame, it's not a bad movie, although it had some problems in the pacing. What did you think of Woo as a director?

Williamson: I think that John Woo is a good director and, once he gets full command of the English language, he will be an even better director. He is definitely good. He has many new ideas, fresh ideas. He just has a communication problem and, sometimes, I am sure in his mind he settles for things that are a little less than what he really wanted, only because he has a communication problem.

Q: You also have a television series that you want to produce, *Blue Chicago*.

Williamson: *Blue Chicago* was a series idea that I had. I would like have done it, and I still might resurrect it. It's about a character in a nightclub in Chicago. It is a blues club and the club is called Blue Chicago, and the club is the whole backdrop of the show. It's like the old *Peter Gunn* series. My office is in the club, the club is always filled with blues music, and I had hoped that the show would have featured blues musicians as well—B.B. King and all those kind of people would be seen hanging out in the club.

Q: Sounds like that is the television show for me—I am a fan of blues music. Why does Fred Williamson still keep trying to take a crack at the movie and television market?

Williamson: I'm trying to get the coach potato out of the house, or keep them from flicking the button two thousand times to find something to watch. Hollywood is making stuff for eighteen- to twenty-five-year-olds. They do not care anything for anybody over forty, forty-five. It is like a lost race out there. I also like to get work for my friends, actors who deserve to work today, and who don't get enough respect in the industry. For example, Charles Napier is a friend of mine, and he does not work as much as he could, and should. I want to also be the one to offer actors like that another shot. That is what I do for people I respect. I get actors like Charles Napier, Henry Silva, Wings Hauser... you do not see him that much on film nowadays. Robert Forster worked in nearly every movie of mine until he got an Academy Award nomination for Quentin Tarantino's *Jackie Brown*. Now I am going to have to step away from him, because he is too expensive.

Q: How would you like to be remembered?

Williamson: As the guy who has done everything he wanted to do, whenever he wanted to do it, and as often he wanted to do it. I just want to keep making action films. Keep doing what I am doing. In front of the camera, behind the camera, beside the camera, on top of the camera... same thing.

Credits: 1968: *Ironside: Sergeant Mike* (12/12/68) (television); *Julia* (television); 1969: *Deadlock* (television); *The Outsider: The Flip Side* (02/26/69) (television); *Star Trek: The Cloud Minders* (02/28/69) (television); 1970: *M*A*S*H**; *Tell Me That You Love Me, Junie Moon*; 1972: *Hammer*; *The Legend of Nigger Charley*; 1973: *Black Caesar*; *Hell Up in Harlem*; *Police Story: Dangerous Games* (10/02/73) (television); *The Soul of Nigger Charley*; *That Man Bolt*; 1974: *Black Eye*; *Crazy Joe* [Italy-U.S.]; *NFL Monday Night Football* (television); *The Rookies: Johnny Lost His Gun* (11/04/74) (television); *Three the Hard Way*; *Uomini Duri* (a.k.a. *Tough Guys* a.k.a. *Three Tough Guys*) [Italy-France-U.S.]; 1975: *Boss Nigger*; *Bucktown*; *La Parola Di Un Fuorilegge...E Legge!* (a.k.a. *Take a Hard Ride*) [Italy-U.S.]; 1976: *Adios, Amigo*;

Death Journey; Joshua; Mean Johnny Barrows; No Way Back; Police Story: Thanksgiving (11/23/76) (television); 1977: *Mr. Mean* [Italy-U.S.]; *Quel Maledetto Treno Blindatto* (a.k.a. *Inglorious Bastards*) [Italy]; 1978: *Blind Rage* [Philippines-U.S.]; *Wheels* (television); 1979: *CHiPs: Roller Disco: Part 1/Roller Disco: Part 2* (09/22/79) (television); *Express to Terror* (television); *Fantasy Island: The Pug/Class of '69* (11/24/79) (television); 1980: *Fist of Fear, Touch of Death* (a.k.a. *Fist of Fear*) [U.S.–Hong Kong]; 1981: *Il Cappotto Di Legno* (a.k.a. *Fear in the City*) [Italy]; *Lou Grant: Violence* (04/06/81) (television); 1982: *1990: I Guerroero Del Bronx* (a.k.a. *1990: The Bronx Warriors* a.k.a. *Bronx Warriors*) [Italy]; *I Nuovi Barbari* (a.k.a. *The New Barbarians* a.k.a. *Warriors of the Wasteland*) [Italy-U.S.]; *One Down, Two to Go*; 1983: *The Big Score; The Last Fight; Vigilante*; 1984: *I Guerrieri Dell'Anno 2072* (a.k.a. *Warriors of the Year 2072* a.k.a. *The New Gladiators*; *Rome, 2072 A.D.*) [Italy]; *Impatto Mortale* (a.k.a. *Deadly Impact*) [Italy]; *Vivre Pour Survivre* (a.k.a. *White Fire*) [Turkey–France–Great Britain–Italy]; 1985: *The Equalizer: Reign of Terror* (12/11/85), *Back Home* (12/18/85) (television); *Il Giustiziere Della Terra Perduta* (a.k.a. *Warrior of the Lost World* a.k.a. *I Predatori Dell'Anno Omega*) [Italy-U.S.]; *Half Nelson* (television); 1986: *Foxtrap* [Italy-U.S.]; 1987: *Cobra Nero* (a.k.a. *Black Cobra*) [Italy-U.S.]; *Delta Force Commando* [Italy]; *Eroi Dell'Inferno* (a.k.a. *Hell's Heroes*) [Italy]; *Il Messagero* (a.k.a. *The Messenger*) [Italy-U.S.]; 1988: *Amen: Will You Still Love Me Tomorrow?* (10/22/88) (television); *Deadly Intent* (video); 1988: *Cobra Nero 2* (a.k.a. *Black Cobra 2*) [Italy]; 1989: *The Kill Reflex*; 1990: *Cobra Nero 3* (a.k.a. *Black Cobra 3* a.k.a. *Black Cobra 3: The Manila Connection*) [Italy]; *Cobra Nero 4* (a.k.a. *Black Cobra 4* a.k.a. *Detective Malone*) [Italy]; 1991: *Delta Force Commando II: Priority Red One* [Italy]; *Steele's Law* [Italy]; *3 Days to Kill* (video); 1992: *Deceptions; South Beach; State of Mind* [France-Belgium-U.S.-Netherlands]; 1994: *Renegade: Way Down Yonder in New Orleans* (10/17/94) (television); 1995: *Silent Hunter*; 1996: *Arli$$: Colors of the Rainbow* (09/25/96) (television); *From Dusk Till Dawn; Original Gangstas*; 1997: *Fast Track* (television); *Full Tilt Boogie* (video); *Night Vision; Pitch*; 1998: *Blackjack* (a.k.a. *John Woo's Blackjack*) (television) [Canada]; *Children of the Corn V: Fields of Terror; PSI Factor: Chronicles of the Paranormal: The Kiss* (television); *Ride*; 1999: *Active Stealth; Intimate Portrait: Pam Grier* (television); *Whatever It Takes*; 2000: *Down 'n Dirty; Hollywood Goes to Hell* (television); *The Independent; The Jamie Foxx Show: Super Ego* (01/07/00) (television); *Submerged*; 2001: *A Huey P. Newton Story* (television); *Carmen: A Hip Hopera* (television); *Deadly Rhapsody; The Rage Within; Shadow Fury*; 2002: *Baadasssss Cinema* (video); *Jim Brown All American* (documentary); *On the Edge*; 2003: *Fighting Words; Vegas Vamps*; 2004: *Lexie* (video); *Starsky and Hutch; The N-Word*; 2005: *Soft Target; Spaced Out*; 2007: *Black Kissinger* [Canada-Jamaica-U.S.]; *Fighting Words; Revamped*; 2008: *4-Bidden.*

William Windom

William Windom was born on September 28, 1923 in New York. Renowned as one of *the* most recognizable character actors, he is a veteran of numerous stage, television, and feature film appearances.

After attending a succession of colleges, Windom entered a naval academy where he studied seamanship, which in later years he used when he developed an interest in sailing. He then spent three years in the Army as a paratrooper. After the end of World War II, Windom honed his acting skills and eventually made it to Broadway as an actor in 1946 (appearing in Shakespeare's *Henry VIII*). In 1960 he acted in the show *Viva Madison Avenue*; it closed after only two performances, but led the way to Hollywood. He regularly returned to the stage often in a series of one-man shows (usually based on James Thurber) that toured the college and university circuit in the seventies.

Genre film fans fondly recall him as Commander Decker in the final season (1968) classic *Star Trek* episode *The Doomsday Machine*. He also starred in an acclaimed, eerie episode of *The Twilight Zone* titled *Five Characters in Search of an Exit* in 1961.

Classic film viewers will recognize him as the prosecuting attorney in the movie *To Kill a Mockingbird* (1962); television addicts will recall him in anything from villainous roles in episodes of classic television programs like *Mission: Impossible*, *Ironside*, and others to a starring role in the one-season-only James Thurber–influenced comedy-drama *My World and Welcome to It!* (1969), where he played a fictionalized version of the famous *New Yorker* magazine writer-editor-cartoonist (named John Monroe on the show). Windom excelled as this character who, in the real world, submitted to his wife, feared his daughter, and spent time with his pals... but managed to change things around due to a series of clever animated interludes that found him commenting on the episode in the third-person.

William Windom also had a long run on the mystery show *Murder, She Wrote*. For over ten years (1985–1996), he portrayed Dr. Seth Hazlett, a confidant to Jessica (series star Angela Lansbury), and garnered a whole new generation of fans.

Nowadays, Windom concentrates on the occasional television (chiefly voice work in animated programs), or film appearance. He also enjoys meeting and greeting his fans at conventions. He even tried to teach me the con game three-card monte in between a short bout of questions...

Q: Your first-ever feature film appearance was in *To Kill a Mockingbird*. What can you recall of that film?

William Windom: I recall that there was one day when Gregory Peck just cracked me up. We were sitting on opposite sides of the table. We were on orders to leave him alone because he wasn't to be distracted for the upcoming, very serious scene that we were about to shoot. Days went by as they were shooting this footage with Peck with his head in his hands, almost as if he was saying a prayer, looking really glum. I was sitting opposite him, with one leg draped over a chair, with a pencil in my mouth, trying to loosen my tie, doing anything I could to kill the boredom. One day, Peck said, "Bill, do you think this would be too much?" And he dropped his elbow off the table as if he had fallen asleep. It was very funny, but I also think it was his way of saying, "I'm the star here." I also recall that while I was shooting that movie, I was appearing in a play during the evenings. We did that a lot during those early years. The woman who played the alleged victim in *Mockingbird* appeared in the same play during the nights. Her role in the play called for her to become an elegant socialite, a dame of society, and *Mockingbird* called for her to be a possible rape victim, a redneck kind of girl... it was strange. Funny thing about that movie was I also recall that the actor playing her father seemed to me to be a real redneck kind of guy for real. Funny thing too, he eventually made a living playing those kinds of roles.

Q: What can you tell me about that episode of *Star Trek*, *The Doomsday Machine*?

Windom: Well, before that time, Bill Shatner and I were on Broadway together in the play, *The World of Suzie Wong* [1958–1959]; he was the star, and I was his understudy. Not his fault, but I think in my mind, it caused a little friction on the set when it came a few years later, and here we are again, and he's the star of *Star Trek*. I thought that episode was a piece of crap, really. For what it was, I guess it wasn't bad, and I didn't like the director on that either, a fellow named Marc Daniels. For some reason, that episode has so many fans; for years, people have been coming up to me saying, "That was wonderful... great... what was it like..." I'll tell you, I could not wait to get to lunch, out of there... back to a chess game... whatever.

William Windom, a delightful raconteur as well as a colorful character actor.

Q: Over the years, you worked with a number of now, highly regarded film directors. For example, you worked with John Frankenheimer on *The Gypsy Moths* and with John Sturges on the western *Hour of the Gun*.

Windom: Both of those men, I recall, liked to really crack the whip. They were very serious about everything. Let's just say that I had more fun on other movie sets.

Q: You also worked with Clint Eastwood on the film *True Crime*.

Windom: He is absolutely nothing like the way he comes across on-screen. Clint Eastwood is a real soft gentleman. We've played tennis together many times. He's not the greatest tennis player, so I like to play against him. Being an actor and working with him is another thing, he is great to work for. I had a small part, I think it was as a bartender in *True Crime*, but he is a great director to work for. Not a great tennis player, but a great director.

Q: You have been acting for many years. What is your take on the profession?

Windom: I have a wisdom... wisdom, rhymes with Windom, don't you think? Anyway, try this out... how about if ninety percent of what you do in this world, whether it's eating, wearing clothes, meeting people when you are a child, an adult, plays you go to, are in, same for movies, television... ninety percent is crap. Five percent is awful, and you wish you could forget it, and five percent is memorable. So you enjoy the crap, because that five percent may just be worth everything.

[At this point in the interview, Mr. Windom hands me his résumé, pointing out his various achievements like his sailing trophies, chess tournament accomplishments, and his winning of the best comedy actor Emmy award for *My World and Welcome to It!* He is an engaging and warm individual, a delightful raconteur, and I wish I could remember how to win at three-card monte; it might help me win a few extra dollars on the streets of New York.]

Credits: 1950: *Lights Out: The Heart of Jonathan O'Rourke* (06/05/50) (television); *Masterpiece Playhouse: Richard III* (07/30/50) (television); 1951: *Robert Montgomery Presents: Kiss and Tell* (01/01/51) (television); 1955: *Omnibus: The Lives of Henry Adams and Charles Frances Adams Jr.* (02/27/55) (television); *Robert Montgomery Presents: The Drifter* (05/23/55) (television); *Tomorrow Is Forever* (10/17/55) (television); 1957: *Robert Montgomery Presents: The Grand Prize* (02/11/57) (television); 1958: *Hallmark Hall of Fame: Dial M for Murder* (04/25/58) (television); 1960: *Guestward Ho!: The Christmas Spirit* (12/22/60) (television); *Play of the Week: Seven Times Monday* (10/31/60) (television); *Westinghouse Desilu Playhouse: In Close Pursuit* (television); 1961: *Ben Casey: The Sweet Kiss of Madness* (12/04/61) (television); *Checkmate: Through a Dark Glass* (11/01/61) (television); *Cheyenne: Legacy of the Lost* (12/04/61) (television); *The Donna Reed Show: All Is Forgiven* (11/02/61) (television); *The Detective Starring Robert Taylor: Tobey's Place* (09/29/61) (television); *Gunsmoke: Nina's Revenge* (12/16/61); *Surfside 6: The Affairs at Hotel Delight* (11/06/61) (television); *The Twilight Zone: Five Characters in Search of an Exit* (12/22/61) (television); 1962: *Bus Stop: The Ordeal of Kevin Brooke* (02/25/62) (television); *The Donna Reed Show: The Wide Open Spaces* (03/08/62) (television); *Follow the Sun: Chalk One Up for Johnny* (04/08/62), *A Ghost in Her Gazebo* (03/18/62) (television); *The Gallant Men: Pilot* (10/05/62) (television); *The Gertrude Berg Show: Goodbye, Mr. Howell* (02/15/62) (television); *Gunsmoke: False Front* (12/22/62) (television); *The Jetsons* (animated) (voice only) (television); *Kraft Mystery Theater: In Close Pursuit* (06/13/62) (television); *The Lucy Show: Lucy Digs a Date* (10/08/62) (television); *Seven Times Monday* (television); *77 Sunset Strip: Mr. Bailey's Honeymoon* (01/12/62) (television); *Stoney Burke: A Matter of Pride* (11/05/62) (television); *Surfside 6: Anniversary Special* (01/29/62) (television); *Thriller: Man of Mystery* (04/02/62) (television); *To Kill a Mockingbird*; 1963: *Cattle King*; *Combat!: Off Limits* (02/19/63) (television); *Empire: Hidden Asset* (03/26/63) (television); *The Farmer's Daughter* (television); *For Love or Money* (a.k.a. *Three on a Match*); *77 Sunset Strip: The Checkmate Caper* (06/07/63) (television); *The Twilight Zone: Miniature* (02/21/63) (television); 1964: *The Americanization of Emily*; *One Man's Way*; 1966: *The F.B.I.: The Assassin* (10/09/66) (television); *The Iron Horse: Town Full of Fear* (12/05/66) (television); *Twelve O'Clock High: Gauntlet of Fire*

Windom is an actor who loves boating.

(09/09/66) (television); *The Wild Wild West: The Night of the Flying Pie Plate* (10/21/66) (television); 1967: *Bob Hope Presents the Chrysler Theatre: Wipeout* (04/26/67) (television); *Custer: Under Fire* (11/15/67) (television); *Dundee and the Culhane: The Thy Brother's Keeper Brief* (11/22/67) (television); *The F.B.I.: By Force and Violence: Part 1* (10/22/67), *By Force and Violence: Part 2* (10/29/67) (television); *The Fugitive: The Ivy Maze* (02/21/67) (television); *Gentle Ben: Jennifer* (11/19/67) (television); *Hour of the Gun*; *The Invaders: Doomsday Minus One* (02/28/67), *The Summit Meeting: Part 1* (10/31/67), *The Summit Meeting: Part 2* (11/07/67) (television); *Judd for the Defense: Commitment* (12/01/67) (television); *Mission: Impossible: The Train* (03/18/67), *The Widow* (09/21/67) (television); *Run for Your Life: The List of Alice McKenna* (01/23/67) (television); *Star Trek: The Doomsday Machine* (10/20/67) (television); *The Virginian: To Bear Witness* (11/29/67) (television); 1968: *The Angry Breed*; *Bonanza: Star Crossed* (03/10/68) (television); *Columbo: Prescription Murder* (a.k.a. *Prescription Murder*) (television); *The Detective*; *The F.B.I.: The Nightmare* (11/10/68) (television); *Ironside: Trip to Hashbury* (03/21/68) (television); *Mannix: The Girls in the Frame* (03/16/68) (television); *The Name of the Game: Lola in Lipstick* (11/08/68) (television); *The Virginian: The Orchard* (10/02/68) (television); 1969: *The Gypsy Moths*; *Hawaii Five-O: Which Way Did They Go?* (12/24/69) (television); *Lancer: The Great Humbug* (03/04/69) (television); *Mannix: Shadow of a Man* (01/25/69) (television); *The Mod Squad:*

Hello Mother, My Name Is Julie (01/14/69) (television); *My World and Welcome to It!* (television); *The Outcasts: The Stalking Devil* (04/07/69) (television); *The Outsider: Service for One* (04/16/69) (television); *U.M.C.* (a.k.a. *Operation Heartbeat*) (television); *The Virginian: Halfway Back from Hell* (10/01/69) (television); 1970: *Brewster McCloud*; *Dr. Simon Locke: Losers, Weepers* (television); *The Forty-Eight Hour Mile* (television); *The House on Greenapple Road* (television); *Love, American Style: Love and the Visitor* (10/23/70) (television); *The Name of the Game: The Time Is Now* (10/23/70) (television); *Alias Smith and Jones: Wrong Train to Brimstone* (02/04/71) (television); *All in the Family: Success Story* (03/30/71) (television); *Assault on the Wayne* (television); *Big Fish, Little Fish* (television); *Cade's County: Violent Echo* (10/24/71) (television); *Cannon: Death Chain* (09/21/71) (television); *Escape* (television); *Escape from the Planet of the Apes*; *Fool's Parade*; *Is There a Doctor in the House?* (television); *Love, American Style: Love and the Television Weekend* (10/08/71) (television); *The Man and the City: The Deadly Fountain* (11/10/71) (television); *Marcus Welby, M.D.: Ask Me Again Tomorrow* (10/26/71) (television); *Marriage: Year One* (television); *Medical Center: Blood Line* (09/15/71) (television); *The Mephisto Waltz*; *Mission: Impossible: Blues* (11/20/71) (television); *The Movie Game*; *Night Gallery: They're Tearing Down Tim Riley's Bar* (01/20/71) (television); *Storefront Lawyers: Let the Dier Beware* (03/17/71) (television); *A Taste of Evil* (television); *That Girl: That Script* (01/01/71) (television); *This Is Your Life: Bill Bixby* (11/07/71) (television); *The Virginian: The Politician* (01/13/71) (television); 1972: *Banacek: Project Phoenix* (09/27/72) (television); *Colombo: Short Fuse* (television); *The F.B.I.: The Jug-Maker* (12/10/72) (television); *Ghost Story: The Summer House* (10/13/72) (television); *A Great American Tragedy* (television); *Gunsmoke: The Judgment* (10/02/72) (television); *The Homecoming: A Christmas Story* (television); *Ironside: Achilles' Heel* (02/17/72) (television); *The Jimmy Stewart Show: Old School Ties* (03/05/72) (television); *Love, American Style: Love and the Ghost* (12/08/72) (television); *The Man*; *Medical Center: Vision of Doom* (09/13/72) (television); *The New Healers* (television); *Night Gallery: Little Girl Lost* (03/01/72) (television); *Now You See Him, Now You Don't*; *Pursuit* (television); *The Rookies: Time Is the Fire* (10/16/72) (television); *Second Chance* (television); *The Streets of San Francisco: 45 Minutes from Home* (10/07/72) (television); *The Delphi Bureau: The Terror Broker* (03/17/73) (television); *The Flip Wilson Show* (09/27/73) (television); *The Girl with Something Extra* (television); *The Girls of Huntington House* (television); *Griff: The Last Ballad* (11/10/73) (television); *Hawkins: A Life for a Life* (11/13/73) (television); *Medical Center: Broken Image* (09/24/73) (television); *Mission: Impossible: The Fighter* (09/24/73) (television); *The Partridge Family: Bedknobs and Drumsticks* (02/09/73) (television); *Tenafly: The Cash and Carry Caper* (10/31/73) (television); 1974: *Chopper One: The Drop* (02/21/74) (television); *The Day the Earth Moved* (television); *Hawaii Five-O: Bomb, Bomb, Who's Got the Bomb?* (10/08/74) (television); *McMillan and Wife: The Game of Survival* (10/20/74) (television); *Murder in the First Person Singular* (television); *Petrocelli: The Golden Cage* (09/11/74) (television); *Police Woman: The Beautiful Die Young* (09/20/74) (television); 1975: *The Abduction of Saint Anne* (television); *Barney Miller: Doomsday* (09/11/75) (television); *Doctor's Hospital: Surgeon, Heal Thyself* (12/17/75) (television); *Guilty and Innocent: The Sam Sheppard Murder Case* (television); *Journey from Darkness* (television); *Lucas Tanner: Shattered* (02/19/75) (television); *Mannix: Hardball* (04/13/75) (television); *Petrocelli: One Killer Too Many* (10/01/75) (television); *S.W.A.T.: A Coven of Killers* (03/03/75) (television); *Stevie, Samson and Delilah*; *The Streets of San Francisco: Letters from the Grave* (01/16/75) (television); 1976: *The Bionic Woman: Black Magic* (11/10/76) (television); *Bridger* (television); *Echoes of a Summer* (a.k.a. *The Last Castle*); *The Feather and Father Gang: Two-Star*

Killer (12/06/76) (television); *Doc* (10/02/76) (television); *Gibbsville: Saturday Night* (11/18/76) (television); *Insight: Jesus B.C.* (07/10/76) (television); *Medical Center: If Wishes Were Horses* (03/15/76) (television); *Richie Brockelman: The Missing 24 Hours* (television); *The Streets of San Francisco: Requiem for Murder* (01/22/76) (television); *The Tony Randall Show: Case: Money Vs. Stature* (12/30/76) (television); 1977: *Family: An Endangered Species* (05/03/77) (television); *Hunter: The Lysenko Syndrome* (03/04/77) (television); *Kojak: Once More from Birdland* (10/30/77) (television); *McMillan and Wife: Phillips' Game* (10/23/77) (television); *Police Woman: Silky Chamberlain* (03/08/77) (television); *Quincy: The Hot Dog Murder* (04/22/77) (television); *Seventh Avenue* (television); 1978: *Mean Dog Blues*; *Goodbye, Franklin High*; *Hunters of the Reef* (television); *W.E.B.: Good Night and Good Luck* (09/28/78) (television); 1979: *Blind Ambition* (a.k.a. *The John Dean Story*) (television); *Brothers and Sisters* (television); *The Love Boat: The Critical Success/The Love Lamp Is Lit/Take My Boyfriend, Please/Rent a Family/Man in Her Life: Part 1, Man in Her Life: Part 2* (11/10/79) (television); *Trapper John, M.D.: Taxi in the Rain* (12/02/79) (television); 1980: *Dallas: The Fourth Son* (12/12/80), *The Venezuelan Connection* (12/05/80) (television); *Portrait of a Rebel: The Remarkable Mrs. Sanger* (television); 1981: *Barney Miller: Contempt: Part 1* (12/12/81), *Contempt: Part 2* (12/19/81) (television); *Flamingo Road: The Stranger* (12/08/81) (television); *Foul Play: Play It Again, Tuck* (02/23/81) (television); *The Incredible Hulk: East Winds* (02/20/81) (television); *Leave 'em Laughing* (television); *One Day at a Time: Caveat Emptor* (04/05/81) (television); *Separate Ways* (television); *Side Show* (television); *Walking Tall: The Protectors of the People* (01/24/81) (television); 1982: *Desperate Lives* (television); *Fantasy Island: Daddy's Little Girl/The Whistle* (01/30/82) (television); *Hart to Hart: With This Hart, I Thee Wed* (10/12/82) (television); *Matt Houston: The Good Doctor* (12/12/82) (television); *The Rules of Marriage* (television); *Trapper John, M.D.: You Pays Your Money* (10/31/82) (television); 1983: *The A-Team: Mexican Slayride: Part 1, Mexican Slayride: Part 2* (01/23/83) (television); *Automan: Staying Alive While Running a High Flashdance Fever* (12/22/83) (television); *The Facts of Life: Store Games* (11/30/83) (television); *The Greatest American Hero: Live at Eleven* (01/20/83) (television); *Last Plane Out*; *Lottery: Boston: False Illusion* (12/09/83) (television); *The Love Boat: Captain's Replacement/ Sly as a Fox/Here Comes the Bride...Maybe* (01/15/83) (television); *Mama's Family: Mama's Boyfriend* (03/19/83) (television); *Matt Houston: Heritage: Part 1* (09/09/83) (television); 1984: *Grandview, U.S.A.*; *Hunter: The Hot Grounder* (10/05/84) (television); *Pigs Vs. Freaks* (a.k.a. *Off Sides*) (television); *Reading Rainbow: Hot-Air Henry* (voice only); *St. Elsewhere: In Sickness and in Health* (02/08/84) (television); *Simon & Simon: Under the Knife* (02/23/84) (television); *Velvet* (television); *Why Me?* (television); *The Yellow Rose: The Far Side of Fear* (05/12/84) (television); 1985: *Airwolf: Eagles* (11/09/85) (television); *Hardcastle and McCormick: Surprise on Seagull Beach* (03/04/85) (television); *Highway to Heaven: A Child of God* (02/06/85) (television); *Hotel: Anniversary* (02/20/85) (television); *Knight Rider: Knight Racer* (11/09/85) (television); *Means and Ends*; *Murder, She Wrote* (television); *Prince Jack*; *Space Rage*; *Surviving* (a.k.a. *Surviving: A Family in Crisis* a.k.a. *Tragedy*) (television); 1986: *Magnum, P.I.: All Thieves on Deck* (11/30/86) (television); *Murder, She Wrote* (television); *There Must Be a Pony* (television); 1987: *Dead Aim*; *Dennis the Menace* (television); *Mathnet: The Trial of George Frankly*; *Murder, She Wrote* (television); *Newhart: Good-Bye & Good Riddance, Mr. Chips* (04/06/87) (television); *Pinocchio and the Emperor of the Night* (animated) (voice only); *Planes, Trains & Automobiles* (uncredited); *Sky Commanders* (animated) (voice only) (television); *Square One TV* (02/18-19-20/87) (television); *Welcome Home*; 1988: *Committed*; *Funland*; *She's Having a Baby* (television); *Murder, She Wrote* (television); 1989: *Camp Candy* (animated) (voice only); *Have Faith: Letters from Home* (05/30/89) (television); *Murder, She Wrote* (television); *Street Justice*; *Uncle Buck* (voice only); 1990: *Amen: Miracle on 134th Street: Part 1, Miracle on 134th Street: Part 2* (12/22/90) (television); *Back to Hannibal: The Return of Tom Sawyer and Huckleberry Finn* (television); *Murder, She Wrote* (television); *Parenthood* (television); 1991: *Babes: All Bummed Out* (01/24/91) (television); *Chance of a Lifetime* (television); *The Fanelli Boys: The Wedding: Part 1* (02/09/91), *The Wedding: Part 2* (02/16/91) (television); *Murder, She Wrote* (television); 1992: *Batman: Prophecy of Doom* (10/06/92) (voice only) (television); *L.A. Law: Diet, Diet My Darling* (02/27/92) (television); *Murder, She Wrote* (television); 1993: *Attack of the 50 Ft. Woman* (television); *Murder, She Wrote* (television); *Sommersby* [U.S.-France]; *Sonic the Hedgehog* (animated) (voice only); 1994: *Miracle on 34th Street* (television); *Murder, She Wrote* (television); *Murphy Brown: Be Careful What You Wish For* (10/10/94) (television); 1995: *Burke's Law: Who Killed the Tennis Ace?* (07/28/95) (television); *Murder, She Wrote* (television); 1996: *Children of the Corn IV: The Gathering* (video); *Fugitive X: Innocent Target* (television); *Murder, She Wrote* (television); 1998: *Boy Meets World: Ain't College Great?* (10/09/98) (television); 1999: *Chicken Soup for the Soul: Rescued* (11/19/99) (television); *Judging Amy: Witch Hunt* (10/19/99) (television); *True Crime*; 2000: *Ally McBeal: The Man with the Bag* (12/11/00) (television); *The Thundering 8th*; 2001: *The District: Bulldog's Ghost* (11/10/01) (television); *Early Bird Special*; 2002: *JAG: Need to Know* (11/05/02) (television); *Providence: The Invisible Man* (02/23/02) (television); *Raising Dead* [Canada]; 2003: *Dismembered*; *Dopamine*; *RTX Red Rock* (video game) (voice only); *Star Trek: New Voyages* (independent amateur fan film); 2005: *Yesterday's Dreams*; 2006: *Madness*.

Lana Wood

Lana Wood was born Svetlana Gurdin on March 1, 1946, in Santa Monica, California. She is the younger sister of the late Natalie Wood (who tragically died in a drowning incident in November 1981), and the aunt of actress Natasha Gregson Wagner. Lana Wood's fans best remember her for her brief appearance as the gold-digging Plenty O'Toole in the James Bond adventure *Diamonds Are Forever* (1971) starring Sean Connery. On-screen for only a few scenes, she is one of the most popular Bond girls in the history of the series.

Wood made her acting debut in John Ford's classic western *The Searchers* (1956), also starring her sister Natalie. Lana's role was as the younger version of her own sister. Unlike Natalie, Lana did not really want to act as a small child, and after a spate of roles; she retired early. She then resumed her career when she was 18 with an appearance in a 1964 episode of *Dr. Kildare.* Just as sexy and voluptuous as her more famous sibling (according to *Celebrity Sleuth* magazine, at the time of her appearance in *Diamonds Are Forever*, Lana's measurements were an impressive 36D-24-35), she found herself typecast in sexpot roles. After playing a student in *The Girls on the Beach* (1965), she was signed to the short-lived soap opera *The Long, Hot Summer* (1965–66), and then cast in the television series version of *Peyton Place*.

Her foray into the spy genre began with two roles in the television show, *The Wild Wild West*. In her initial appearance, in the episode titled *The Night of the Firebrand* (1967), she amuses as the cleverly named character Vixen, a runaway from a finishing school seeking to help those less fortunate, but getting mixed up with an outlaw (Pernell Roberts) plotting to incite a revolution in Canada. In another *Wild Wild West* episode, *The Night of the Plague* (the last original *Wild Wild West* before the show's 1969 cancellation) she played the spoiled, headstrong gal who becomes involved with bandits (actually a band of wayward Shakespearean actors infected with a fatal disease) who cross paths with the show's hero James West (Robert Conrad).

After playing a swinging bachelorette in *For Singles Only* in 1968, and a mini-skirted, free-spirited biker girl in *Free Grass* in 1969, Wood posed for a then-controversial nude layout in *Playboy* magazine's April 1971 issue. These photos indirectly helped her land her famous role in *Diamonds Are Forever*. In the film, secret agent James Bond (Sean Connery) is assigned to pose as a diamond smuggler, leading him to a jewel thief (Jill St. John) who has him chasing both her and a cache of coveted diamonds from Amsterdam to Las Vegas. Bond meets bar girl Plenty O'Toole (Wood) at a gambling table in a Vegas casino. After introducing herself to Bond, she goes with him up to his room. Their tryst is interrupted

Lana Wood played her first sex kitten in the movie *Five Finger Exercise* (1962) (Columbia Pictures).

as thugs try to kill Bond and toss Wood out of a 15-story window... naked! Fortunately, she lands in the hotel's pool. A short time later she is discovered murdered. That's about it for Lana Wood's role, but her pulchritudinous self sure made a hefty impression on teenage boys in the early seventies. At the time, there was also much talk about alleged cutting room footage that explained the mysteriously quick demise of her character; not until decades later did this footage finally see the light of day (as a supplementary feature on a special edition DVD of *Diamonds Are Forever*).

Although the film remains one of the lesser Bond adventures (Connery looks tired and paunchy), Wood garnered respectable notices. (*Variety*: "Lana Wood... gets good mileage from her brief exposure as Plenty O'Toole.") Afterwards, she appeared as a guest on one of the later *Mission: Impossible* episodes and received more critical acclaim in 1974 for her role as the mistress of Ben Gazzara in the television miniseries *QBVII*. Wood is also fondly remembered by cult film fans for her appearance as a lesbian prison guard in the controversial 1976 television movie *Nightmare in Badham County*, and for once again baring all in gratuitous nude scenes in the quirky, low-budget soft-core horror film *Satan's Mistress* (1982).

Wood united with two other former Bond girls (Joanna Pettet and Britt Ekland) for a James Bond spy spoof episode of TV's *The Fall Guy* in 1984, and then retired from acting. In 1984, she wrote a book about her late sister, *Natalie: A Memoir*, and in 2004, she appeared in and co-produced a television docu-drama about her sister titled *The Mystery of Natalie Wood*. Nowadays, Lana attends occasional conventions, appears in supplemental material that accompanies re-releases of the James Bond films on DVD, and is writing another book.

Q: What can you recall about *The Searchers*?

Wood: I remember that film a lot better than I remember lots of other things that I did on film. In fact, I remember everything about working on *The Searchers*, absolutely everything. I remember traveling via train to the location where the film was shot; I remember the car rides out to the set at the Indian reservation from the train station. I remember that it was so very hot that they had dry ice in the car. I remember being frightened by it, because my mom would say, "Don't touch it! It'll take the skin off your fingers." I remember the Indians; in the evening you could hear a lot of entertainment going on. While we were shooting the film, we lived above a trading post. I also remember some very bad sandstorms, I recall Ward Bond being bitten by a scorpion, and I will never forget the incredible kindness of Jeffrey Hunter. I remember all of it very, very, vividly.

Q: What did you think of John Ford, director of *The Searchers*?

Wood: I don't think he was very big on kids. He spoke to me, and gave me direction, when it was time for me to do what I was supposed to, and that was about it.

Q: Did you continue to perform as a child actress prior to your appearance as a teenager on an episode of *Dr. Kildare* years later?

Wood: I also did two episodes of *Playhouse 90*, I was on the stage in the prologue scene of the play *Summer and Smoke*, and I did a lot of television, *Have Gun—Will Travel*, stuff like that.

Q: Jumping ahead to films like *The Girls on the Beach* and the television series *The Long, Hot Summer*, did you feel at any point that you were becoming typecast in the role of a sexpot?

Wood: I did not feel that way at the time. I did not feel that way until I hit my mid-twenties. At the time, I just thought I was doing the roles that were being offered to me. It wasn't until later on that I said to myself, "Wow, I really am being typecast." Actually, it didn't really bother me, other than I wish there were more roles like that at the time.

Q: The films and TV show in which you played the sexy femme fatale or the sexy damsel in distress—were there any particular favorites?

Wood: I really liked appearing in the *Wild Wild West* episodes. Robert Conrad was an old family friend, so I felt very comfortable working alongside him, overly comfortable in fact. And [co-star] Ross Martin was a lovely man. I adored him, he was really super. He was very professional, and a quite brilliant actor. I just had a lot of fun, and I got along great with the crew. They had a fabulous cast and crew that literally applauded me on my last day. It was a great, great group of people that worked on that show, both in front of the camera and behind the camera. It meant a lot to me to have them applaud. It meant a lot more to me than probably a lot of other things that have happened when I was working as an actress in the entertainment industry. Another show that I liked was *Police Story*. Working on *Baretta* was a great deal of fun. Working in the television miniseries *QBVII* was an experience I enjoyed, and it was a role I liked a lot.

Q: How did you get the role of Plenty O'Toole in *Diamonds Are Forever*?

Wood: Tom Mankiewicz, who co-wrote it, contacted me. He said that I was being discussed for the role of Tiffany Case, and would I come and meet with "Cubby" Broccoli, the producer and Guy Hamilton, the director. I said, "Of course." I did so, and then I had to leave town shortly thereafter to start working on another film. I was called by my agent who said. "They really want you in the film, but there's a bit of pressure to use someone else in that role. Would you consider doing another role in that film if you didn't get the Tiffany Case part?" I said, "Yes, absolutely." So, then they called back and said would I play Plenty O'Toole and I said, "You got it."

Q: Sean Connery at the time was one of the world's biggest box-office attractions and one of the movie idols that everyone wanted to be seen with.

Wood: We started dating while I was filming my role in *Diamonds Are Forever*... we had a lovely time. I adore him, I still do. I think he's quite a sensational guy.

Q: Why do you think they excised a number of your scenes from the final print of the movie at the time of the initial release in 1971?

Wood: Well, first of all, they really did not help the plot of the story to move along well—that was what Guy Hamilton said to me. He said he was really sorry, but they weren't helping to keep the pace of the film up. The producers stated that *Diamonds Are Forever* sort of went off into Plenty's story on the side, and it really didn't have anything to do with the main plot. They were already worried about the length of the film. At the time, they wanted to keep the running time down to a certain amount of minutes, so that they could have an extra screening per day. They had to cut everything that wasn't germane to the plot, and unfortunately part of that involved my character, Plenty. I was really upset about it at the time, but I'm not upset about it now.

Q: Now the restored footage can be seen on the special edition DVD of the film.

Wood: Nowadays, I agree with them that it was a good thing for them to cut those scenes. I know that to leave them in made sense for the character of Plenty but I don't really think that keeping those scenes in the film would have been terrific for the movie as a whole. It did not really help the film in any way. It helped the character, but then again, the film was not about my character.

Q: Did you go on a promotional tour with the film?

Wood: I did, I went all over the world, all over Europe and the Orient. It was exhausting, but it was a terrific experience.

Lana Wood bewilders and bewitches secret agent 007, James Bond (Sean Connery), and the world with her voluptuous figure in *Diamonds Are Forever* (1971) (Danjaq Productions/Eon Productions/United Artists/MGM).

Q: You followed your role in this film with an appearance in an episode of *Mission: Impossible*.

Wood: We filmed some scenes on a boat. It actually got a little rough at sea sometimes, and that's where I learned to play the card game of hearts, which is a gambling game. I was walking by a table, and a couple of the members of the cast yelled in my direction,

"Do you know how to play hearts?" I said, "No." They said, "Great. Sit down. A nickel a point and a quarter for the queen." I said, "What does that mean?" They said, "You'll figure it out!" I figured it out real fast. I won for a few days, and then I think I lost quite often.

Q: What can you recall about the television miniseries *QBVII*?

Wood: I wanted that role, to work in that show so badly, that I actually lost an agent over that show. The role was offered to me, and my agent thought it was a mistake for me to take it. The producers were setting up all of these meetings for me to go to Italy... my agents felt that the part was too small. I said I really, really wanted to be in that show. I wanted to be with those people, I wanted to be a part of that cast. They said to me that if I insisted upon doing it that they were going to release me from my contract, and I said, "Go for it, what do I care."

Q: And you consider that one of your finest roles, is that correct?

Wood: I just really liked the experience. I liked working with the director Tom Gries. They really listened to my opinions about the character when I had comments and suggestions to make about her. I also got to work very closely with Ben Gazzara. It meant a lot to me to work on *QBVII*, it really did.

Q: What can you recollect about appearing on the *Captain America* television program?

Wood: Reb Brown was adorable. He was about as smart as a brick, but really adorable. Still, I had a lot of fun working on *Captain America*.

Q: What about the cult film *Satan's Mistress*?

Wood: It was a very low-budget film. It was shot on a shoestring budget. The monster was this poor guy who they had to keep gluing hair on to make him appear like a hairy devil. Often they had to keep stop shooting to glue more hair on him, or part of his monster suit would fall off. They were also rigging fire effects scenes with no idea of what the heck they were doing. Overall, it was a nice try, but the movie didn't really happen for me.

Q: In 1984, you appeared with two other James Bond movie alumni in an episode of *The Fall Guy*.

Wood: That was great, I loved that. I just dearly adored Joanna Pettet. She is really one of the terrific people and it was a lot of fun. At first, I was concerned because I did not know how to play me, I always played a character. I thought, "What do I do?" Then, I decided to be the most out-there me that I can possibly be.

Q: In 1999, as they prepared special edition DVDs of the James Bond films, you began to appear in photographic layouts in *Vanity Fair*, *TV Guide*, etc., with other actresses who had appeared in Bond films. How did it feel to have all that the media attention, the celebrity status? To once again be in the public eye?

Wood: I thought it was absolutely wonderful. I never expected at the time that I was making *Diamonds Are Forever* that it would sort of live forever. It is just one of these wild phenomena. It's sensational. I could not be more pleased to be a part of it, I think it's great.

Credits: 1956: *The Searchers*; 1957: *Playhouse 90: Winter Dreams* (television); 1958: *Have Gun—Will Travel: The Teacher* (03/15/58) (television); *Marjorie Morningstar* (uncredited); 1962: *Five Finger Exercise*; 1964: *Dr. Kildare: Man Is a Rock* (09/24/64) (television); *The Fugitive: Detour on a Road Going Nowhere* (12/08/64) (television); 1965: *The Girls on the*

Beach (a.k.a. *Summer of '64*); *The Long, Hot Summer* (television); 1966: *The Long, Hot Summer* (television); *Peyton Place* (television); 1967: *Bonanza: The Gentle Ones* (10/29/68) (television); *Peyton Place* (television); *The Wild Wild West: The Night of the Firebrand* (09/15/67) (television); 1968: *Felony Squad: The Last Man in the World* (12/18/68) (television); *For Singles Only*; 1969: *Rowan & Martin's Laugh-In* (10/13/69) (television); *Scream Free* (a.k.a. *Free Grass*); *The Wild Wild West: The Night of the Plague* (04/04/69) (television); 1970: *Black Water Gold*; *The Over-the-Hill Gang Rides Again* (television); 1971: *Diamonds Are Forever* [Great Britain–U.S.]; *O'Hara, U.S. Treasury*: (television); 1972: *Justin Morgan Had a Horse*; *Mission Impossible: The Deal* (09/30/72) (television); *Night Gallery: You Can't Get Help Like That Anymore* (02/23/72) (television); *A Place Called Today*; 1974: *Police Story: Countdown: Part 2* (01/23/74) (television); *QBVII* (television); 1975: *Sons of Sassoun*; *Who Is the Black Dahlia?* (television); 1976: *Baretta: Shoes* (10/27/76) (television); *Nightmare in Badham County* (television); *Starsky and Hutch: Running* (02/25/76) (television); 1977: *Corey: for the People* (television); *Little Ladies of the Night* (television); *Police Story: Ice Time* (03/08/77) (television); *Speedtrap*; 1978: *Fantasy Island: Fool for a Client/Double Your Pleasure* (05/15/78) (television); *Grayeagle*; *Police Story: No Margin for Error* (04/30/78) (television); *A Question of Guilt* (television); 1979: *Captain America* (television); *Captain America II: Death Too Soon* (television); *David Cassidy—Man Undercover: Nightwork* (01/11/79) (television); *Starsky and Hutch: Ninety Pounds of Trouble* (02/06/79) (television); 1981: *Nero Wolfe: Might As Well Be Dead* (02/13/81) (television); 1982: *Capitol* (television); *Satan's Mistress* (a.k.a. *Dark Eyes* a.k.a. *Demon Rage*); 1984: *The Fall Guy: Always Say Always* (02/22/84) (television); 1985: *Mike Hammer* (a.k.a. *Mickey Spillane's Mike Hammer*): *Deadly Reunion* (01/12/85) (television); 1999: *The James Bond Story* (television-video) (uncredited); 2000: *Inside "Diamonds Are Forever"* (DVD video supplement); 2003: *Biography: Natalie Wood* (television); 2004: *The Mystery of Natalie Wood* (television); 2006: *Wild Michigan*.

Celeste Yarnall

Celeste Yarnall was born on July 26, 1944, in Long Beach, California. From her lengthy career as a model, specialty products spokesperson, and actress, Celeste has managed to keep herself in the public eye for decades. In 1968, she was named the Foreign Press's Most Photogenic Beauty of the Year at the Cannes Film Festival. That same year, the National Association of Theater Owners voted her Most Promising New Star.

Besides her entertainment career, she has managed her own commercial real estate business, became a cat breeder, and appears regularly as a lecturer. Earning a Ph.D. in nutrition in the late nineties (she serves as an adjunct professor of nutrition at Pacific Western University), Celeste Yarnall has also written books on holistic health care for cats and dogs.

However, it is Yarnall's acting achievements that have brought her the most notoriety. In early roles in such films as *The Nutty Professor* and *Around the World Under the Sea*, she stood out from the usual array of glamour girl extras, and began to forge a career as a stunningly beautiful and talented actress. An early highpoint was an appearance on the original *Star Trek* series (the episode *The Apple*). Her other early genre credits include the starring role as a female Tarzan in *Eve* (1968) and the heroine in the Philippine shocker *Beast of the Dead* (1970). In the seventies, she had the starring role in *The Velvet Vampire* (1971); appeared alongside Charles Bronson and Jan-Michael Vincent in the violent action film *The Mechanic* (1972); and co-starred with Alain Delon and Burt Lancaster in the espionage thriller *Scorpio* (1973).

Q: What are your earliest remembrances of becoming involved with the entertainment industry?

Celeste Yarnall: Well, you surprised me with that question. I am hardly ever asked that. My earliest memories of getting into the entertainment industry were dancing in my pajamas when I was about five years old. I always wanted to be in entertainment. I always wanted to sing and dance. The way that I actually got my break was that I walking to one of my first commercial auditions and I took a short cut through General Service studios, which was where they shot *The Ozzie and Harriet Show*. I must say that I believe I looked very cute that day because I caused a minor riot; no, I am going to be bold and say I caused a major riot on the studio lot that day. The guys were whistling and catcalling, and those guys were Ricky Nelson and his star football player friends who were out on the lot playing football. They caused a ruckus, and Ozzie Nelson came out of his bungalow and said, "What's going on out here? What is this all about?" He looked at me and said, "Hey

Yarnall in her sixties heyday (Photograph from the collection of Louis Paul).

little lady, anybody that can stop traffic on this lot deserves to be on this show. We're going to give you a part on this show." I said, "But, I'm not a member of the union." He said, "Don't worry, we'll get you in." So, he got me my Screen Actors Guild card and got me in the business. He gave me two lines on the show and they were, "Are you coming with us Roberta? Okay, see you later." I managed to get those two lines out.

Q: You remember the lines?

Yarnall: Oh my God, you can never forget something like that. I did go on to a commercial audition afterwards, and I hooked the commercial and the resulting print ads for a hairspray called Show Curl. I still have a picture of myself from the photo shoot wearing rollers and a bouffant bonnet, which was like a wave set. I believe all this took place around 1962.

Q: What do you recall about *The Nutty Professor*?

Yarnall: That was shot during that same time. I always looked much older than I really was, because I started in the business when I was seventeen. I was always looking like a thirty-year-old, even when I was seventeen. They sent me on this call for a one-day shot, where I was supposed to be a glamorous model type. I was cast; Jerry Lewis himself selected me from hundreds of other girls, right there on the spot. They didn't have the videotaping and all of the agony that you have to go through nowadays to do a screen test and get a job. Back then, they just went, "Okay, I like her, let's sign her up." I did my one-day shoot, and it was a very difficult shot for Jerry. It was the entrance that the Nutty Professor [Lewis] makes as his alter ego Buddy Love [also Lewis], into the nightclub. So, Jerry was directing while in his Buddy Love persona and performing onscreen, making his entrance into the nightclub. Jerry is a real perfectionist, and I was very enamored of him and he was struggling, struggling with this shot and he said, "Okay, release them all. Give them five minutes." The director said, "You can sit down, Miss Yarnall," and I went "No, I'll stay." They didn't bring in any of the stand-ins, he caught my eye, and he smiled at me and kind of nodded like that was very professional. The next thing that I knew, I was hired onto the film for six weeks. I became one of the main kids in the film. It was like a miracle. It was like a gift from God, through Jerry Lewis, that I got that break. Then I did *A New Kind of Love*; I had a little tiny role in that. Then shortly thereafter, my agents entered me in the Miss Rheingold contest which some of the middle-aged Eastern folk might remember. They paid us our hourly modeling rate while we competed to be a contestant in the Miss Rheingold contest. I made the first cut in Los Angeles, and then they sent me to New York to audition and do interviews with Rosalind Russell and Irene Dunne and Bob Cummings and William Wellman and, really, just a star-studded group of people. I kept making the cuts, and finally I was selected as one of the six girls to go on tour. Ultimately, I got twenty million votes and became New York's Miss Rheingold 1964.

Q: What do you recall about the movie *Around the World Under the Sea*?

Yarnall: That was fun to work on. The role actually came about when I was in New York and [producer] Ivan Tors was auditioning and screen-testing me for a continuing role on *Flipper*. This was in 1965; I was still doing some Rheingold promotions. Tors thought that I was a little too young for the part in the *Flipper* series, but he pushed forward and still did the screen test, and offered me this part in *Around the World, Under the Sea*. What I remember especially about that is that they put me in the tank with Flipper, and Flipper was really two dolphins named Daisy and Cathy, and I got to swim with the dolphins. That was just amazing. They're very strong; I was covered with bruises, because they can give you a little nudge. What the dolphins did was, as soon as I got in the tank, they'd come up to say hello and it was a trick; they'd come up to you and almost stand in the water and then they'd soak you when they splash and you would then take off. They put me in the tank with a surfboard to act as my floatation but it was scary and mystic and I will never forget that as long as I live.

Ivan Tors had a great facility down there in Florida. I was still so young, and we were not as sophisticated as people are today. To hit your mark, you worked with hundreds of people in a crew, and I was just getting it together. It took me into the late sixties until I was completely comfortable with which angles photographed best but at that time we worked so hard, and so fast, we were lucky to just get it out and over with.

Q: One of your earliest genre credits is an appearance on *Star Trek*, in the episode *The Apple*.

Yarnall: I loved it. I did not know much about the show when I was cast; only a few episodes had aired and I really did not understand too much about it. The greatest recollection that I have is that Leonard Nimoy scared me to death, because he stayed in the character of Mr. Spock, which had that satanic feeling to it, you know, the ears, the color, and the stoic look. With *Star Trek*, I was twenty-three and it was daunting. The person that made it really wonderful was Bill Shatner. I have wonderful memories of Bill. Today, we are still good friends and I absolutely adore him. He is one of the funniest people I have ever known; he just does me in. I cannot keep a straight face around him. He is also a brilliant actor; he was a Shakespearean actor...

Q: He also did a lot of Broadway and other stage work before *Star Trek*.

Yarnall: He is a brilliant, brilliant actor, although he cannot sing a note... he tries. If you ever want to see the greatest stand-up comedian you have ever seen in your life, come to one of the conventions when Bill is on, and when Bill does Bill. He looks wonderful, I think he feels good. Bill is a brilliant writer, I love his books. *Ashes of Eden* I thought was spectacular. I'm becoming a *Star Trek* fan. I'm so honored and I'm so happy to have anyone remember anything that I ever did, let alone this role.

Q: What do you recall about the seldom-seen production *Eve*?

Yarnall: The big news is that I turned down a role in *Funny Lady* with Barbra Streisand due to a written contract to do *Eve*. There was a threat against my life if I didn't show up on the set to do *Eve*. The story of doing that movie is a book. You need a two-hour interview to get that story. They ran out of money, I was completely written out of the film and a whole other character was created to cover the time when I would not come to the set because there was no money. If you remember the movie, there was a false Eve. All of that was going on when they were trying to find the money to pay me. It was stuff like my hotel bill, my airfare, and the common courtesies of starring in a movie. It wasn't like a trailer; it was like, just pay my hotel bill.

Q: Was that a Harry Alan Towers production?

Yarnall: Yes it was! The fun thing that I love to tell people is that the bikini that I wore in the movie, according to the costume company, was one of Raquel Welch's bikinis from *One Million Years B.C.* They re-cut it cut the strap off, and fixed it up for me. I still have that bikini; one day I will sell it on eBay.

Celeste Yarnall as a female Tarzan in the 1968 film *Eve* (Ada Films/Harold Goldman Associates/Hispamer Film P.C./Sargon Entertainment/Towers of London Productions/Udastex Films/Commonwealth United).

Q: Where was *Eve* filmed?

Yarnall: *Eve* was shot on in locations in and around Madrid. One of the locations was the actual location where Tyrone Power had died. He died in Spain, and we were filming exactly where he was filming. I remember that we had an accident on our set when an electrician died. During the shooting, an electrician caught an arc and was blown away and died. It was a frightening experience. I was almost killed in one of the stunts myself.

The girl who played the false Eve didn't take the instructions from the stunt coordinator and she used the wrong foot to do a kick, which was right into my stomach that was casting me off into the arms of a stuntman. She used the wrong foot, which threw me out over a cliff, and the stuntman took a flying dive, caught the back of my head, and caught me before I was bashed against the rocks.

Q: It sounds like it was a difficult film to shoot.

Yarnall: It was really a difficult shoot. I didn't have the arm strength to really swing from vines. Whenever I tried to swing up to my platform, I would go cascading into the platform and be covered with bruises. I had to walk across logs that were over waterfalls, and I am terrified of heights. They thought I was a wuss. In Brazil, gigantic mosquitoes ate me up, I had dysentery, I had to be given staphacellin shots, and that drug isn't even on the market any more, it causes blindness. It was hell! I was promised that there were going to be sequels and I would be really known for what I was, which was the cinema's first female Tarzan. I don't know if anybody realizes that, but I am supposedly the cinema's first female Tarzan. Irish McCalla, who played Sheena, Queen of the Jungle, was television's first. I was supposed to be the first female Tarzan, being a child born and being raised in the jungle by apes and so forth. It was rough.

Q: Was the Philippines location filming for *Beast of the Dead* just as rough?

Yarnall: Yes I had just found out that I was pregnant, the day before I got on to the flight to the Philippines. Try doing that kind of a shoot with morning sickness. If you have seen that movie with the drowning in the quicksand sequence, there is a scene where a rifle slipped over the shoulder of a stuntman as he was pulling me out of the quicksand... and it split my face open. We were four hours from the nearest dirt road. However, I have always grown up with the mentality that the show must go on. No matter what was ever wrong with me, I have never canceled a shoot.

Q: What were the Philippine cast and crewmembers like?

Yarnall: Wonderful, wonderful. In fact, I loved the Filipino cast. You know, we often had two luncheons served, a Filipino luncheon and then one with American food. The American English food was just appalling, so I went and sat on the ground with the Filipinos and ate off banana leaves just as they did. [Actor] Victor Diaz was a very nice man. Eddie Garcia, who played Lorca, was a gentleman, and the Filipino girl who was one of the leads was very sweet. I had a Filipino bodyguard that I just adored who was one of the stuntmen. Oh yes, the stuntman. One day, I was being lit for a shot and this stuntman saw me being set up for a shot, being lit, being prepared for my camera angles, all in preparation and all of a sudden, he jumped in with a machete. With his bare hands, he grabbed this snake, which was just about to come down and get me. There are two kinds of snakes, a pit viper and a mock pit viper, and the only way you know which is which is if you die after it bites you. He risked his life to catch this viper with his bare hands to save me, and he killed it. It was very primitive on these locations. Where we were shooting was hours from the nearest dirt road, and when we shot on an island location, to get there and back we took this horrible boat that had no facilities, it had no restrooms, just buckets. And remember that all during this I was pregnant. We got to the island and there was no electricity, no running water. It was wild. I thought I was going to lose the baby, but by the grace of God, I got through it. My beautiful daughter Camilla was born on July 4, 1970.

Q: *The Velvet Vampire* contained a more explicit film role for you, in terms of the violence and the nudity that you were required to do.

Yarnall: I was newly divorced; I had a brand new baby. My baby was about six months old when I was cast in that film. I had to stop breast-feeding at about seven months to quickly drop ten pounds because I had to do the film. It was a pleasure working with Roger Corman and the Rothmans' were wonderful to work with. Stephanie Rothman was the director and the cinematographer was the French gentleman who photographed *A Man and a Woman*, so it was brilliantly lit. They closed the set when I did the nude scenes, so I really was not uncomfortable. I had to eat raw chicken liver onscreen to depict my vampiric cravings, which was interesting, but not as bad as you would think. My memories of John Ashley from the Philippine horror movie and other leading men are wonderful, but my memories of working with Michael Blodgett, my [*Velvet Vampire*] co-star, were not so great. Michael knows who he was and what he was doing at the time and the producers actually brought in his girlfriend to try to get him under control. Case in point, if you are familiar with the movie, there is a scene where I bite his neck. Well, he grabbed my back and dug his nails into my spine. I was black and blue and purple all down my back and I just screamed in horror. I was not really hurting his neck at all, but the more he squeezed my back, the more I bit down. That was a rough shoot also. But nothing, nothing like *Beast of the Dead*. *The Velvet Vampire* was filmed in civilization, Yucca Valley in fact, and there were lunch wagons for food. Believe it or not, Roger Corman was high-budget compared to working on *Eve* and *Beast of the Dead*.

Q: What do you think of *The Velvet Vampire* today?

Yarnall: I would have to see it again today. I feel that I am a much better actress today. I think that my performance is a reflection of the direction that I was given.

Q: It seems to have a macabre atmosphere.

Yarnall: I agree, it does. It was a very sophisticated vampire film, using the guise of me having the rare blood disease and no fangs. There is a lot about it that I like and I'd like to see it brought out on video again so that we can expose the new generation of fans to more of my work. Perhaps someone can find a way to bring *The Velvet Vampire* back into circulation. I know many younger fans have been intrigued by the pictures and the name and would enjoy adding me to the collection that they have, but they cannot find it.

Q: What about the Charles Bronson movie *The Mechanic* and the Burt Lancaster–Alain Delon thriller *Scorpio*?

Yarnall: *The Mechanic* was interesting. That was another perhaps-wrong decision that I made. I made many poor career choices in my life. Just to segue for a moment, my manager, before my baby was born, turned down a term contract with Universal, which would have been one of the highest term contracts that they had offered anyone at that time. My agents turned down the contract that Universal had offered me. With the contracts most studio systems offered, you made no money, which is all the agents ever care about, making money, but for themselves. The heck with building a career, the greedy people... I should have been in the hands of the studio system, because the girls that they built instead of me were Katharine Ross and Susan St. James. I'm not saying that those would have been my roles, the ones that I would have gotten instead of them, but I am saying that I could have been like them with a major television career. However, even without a term

Celeste Yarnall today (Photograph courtesy Celeste Yarnall).

contract I made out all right. Universal was very good to me for casting me in television shows like *The Bold Ones* and *The F.B.I.*, I did a lot of good work for them. However, losing that term contract meant all the difference; I would have been groomed for stardom. Instead, I did *The Velvet Vampire*. Roger Corman had another film that he wanted me to immediately go into. It was the role of a lesbian. There was a little lesbian overtone to *The Velvet Vampire* as well; but this other film was going to be a prison picture and I was going to play a very sophisticated lesbian in Costa Rica. But at the last minute, Michael Winner offered me a part in *The Mechanic* shooting on the Malta coastline with Charles Bronson and Jill Ireland. He said, "You come with us, darling. We will do something wonderful for you. You'll not go with Roger Corman, we'll take care of everything." I said yes, and they did take care of me... I was given a very, very small part. Then I was promised a part in *Scorpio* [also directed by Winner]. I was then told that the studio wanted Gayle Hunnicutt instead. I was thinking that I was going to have a very good role in *Scorpio* and I ended up in another small role. When we were filming *Scorpio*, we were staying at the same hotel in Washington that happened to be the location of the Watergate break-in. We were also the ones with all of the CIA–Hollywood ballyhoo, because the CIA gave us special clearance because we filmed in their headquarters. We were right there, at the exact same time as the Watergate break-in occurred. I am honored to have worked with Paul Scofield, Alain Delon; I had the pleasure of knowing Burt Lancaster, so I have fond, fond memories of those two movies. However, was it the right career choice? On the other hand, would have I have been a bigger scream queen had I stuck with Roger Corman? Perhaps.

Q: What are some of your favorite recent roles?

Yarnall: There is a movie called *Midnight Kiss*. That was at least a challenging film. The more grandiose films that I had small parts in were the remake of *Born Yesterday* with Melanie Griffith, Don Johnson, and John Goodman. Luis Mendoki, one of my favorite directors, filmed that and it was a pleasure to work with him. Leonard Nimoy and I worked together in *Funny About Love*, even though I was mostly cut out of the film. I worked with Farrah Fawcett who was the actual star of the film, but all of her scenes got cut out. It was fun to see Farrah again, and it was incredible to see Leonard whom I had been so terrified of in *Star Trek*. I also turned up twice on the television show, *Melrose Place*.

Q: In retrospect, what is your own personal favorite role?

Yarnall: *Star Trek, Land of the Giants, It Takes a Thief, The Man from U.N.C.L.E., Hogan's Heroes.* The director John Ford once came to the set of *Hogan's Heroes*; he was a huge fan of the show. He loved my performance and complimented me when I was filming. I did another TV show where I did some comedy and that was *Love, American Style*, and I really enjoyed that.

Q: You really liked many of these roles?

Yarnall: Especially *It Takes a Thief* and *The Man from U.N.C.L.E.* When I went on the audition for the role for *U.N.C.L.E.*, my character had to speak French, so I affected a French accent and said, "Please don't speak French to me, I am in this country to learn the English language." It was not until day three that I broke out with my American accent and then they learned that I was not from France. I am French, but not from France. Funny business, eh?

Credits: 1962: *The Adventures of Ozzie & Harriet: Rick and the Maid of Honor* (09/27/62) (television); 1963: *Burke's Law: Who Killed Beau Sparrow?* (12/27/63) (television); *A New*

Kind of Love (uncredited); *The Nutty Professor* (uncredited); 1965: *The Wild Wild West: The Night of a Thousand Eyes* (10/22/65) (television); 1966: *Around the World Under the Sea*; *Bewitched: And Then There Were Three* (01/13/66) (television); *Gidget: Independence—Gidget Style* (03/17/66) (television); *The Man from U.N.C.L.E.: The Monks of St. Thomas Affair* (10/14/66) (television); 1967: *Captain Nice: May I Have the Last Dance?* (04/17/67) (television); *Star Trek: The Apple* (10/13/67) (television); 1968: *Bonanza: Queen High* (11/24/68) (television); *The F.B.I.: The Mercenary* (04/28/68) (television); *The Face of Eve* (a.k.a. *Eve*) [West Germany–Spain–Great Britain–U.S.]; *Hogan's Heroes: LeBeau and the Little Old Lady* (02/24/68), *Will the Blue Baron Strike Again?* (12/14/68) (television); *It Takes a Thief: Locked in the Cradle of the Keep* (04/16/68) (television); *Land of the Giants: The Golden Cage* (12/29/68) (television); *Live a Little, Love a Little*; 1969: *Bob & Carol & Ted & Alice*; *The Bold Ones: The Protectors: Draw a Straight Man* (12/14/69) (television); *In Name Only* (television); *Mannix: Eagles Sometimes Can't Fly* (09/27/69) (television); 1971: *Beast of Blood* (a.k.a. *Beast of the Dead* a.k.a. *Horrors of Blood Island*) [Philippines-U.S.]; *Colombo: Ransom for a Dead Man* (television); *The Velvet Vampire*; 1972: *The Judge and Jake Wyle* (television); *McMillan and Wife: Terror Times Two* (12/13/72) (television); *The Mechanic*; 1973: *Love, American Style: Love and the Postal Meter* (03/09/73); *Scorpio*; 1987: *Fatal Beauty*; 1990: *Funny About Love*; *A Shattered Dream*; 1991: *Ambition*; *Daughters of Privilege* (television); *Driving Me Crazy*; 1993: *Civil Wars: Split Ends* (01/26/93) (television); 1993: *Born Yesterday*; *Midnight Kiss* (a.k.a. *In the Midnight Hour*); 1994: *Metaltech: Earthsiege* (video game) (voice only); *Sisters: Chemical Reactions* (01/22/94) (television); 1995: *Melrose Place: Oy! to the World* (12/11/95) (television); 2002: *That's My Baby: Mimosa* (television); 2003: *Shrink Rap* (video); 2005: *Skinwalker: Curse of the Shaman* (video); 2007: *The Two Sisters*; *Star Trek: Of Gods and Men* (video).

Bibliography

Tom Atkins
Fangoria. Interview, 1986
Paul, Louis. "The Chiller Interviews." *Chiller Theatre* magazine #23 (2005): 42–46
Variety. Review of *Halloween III: Season of the Witch*, January 17, 1980
Variety. Review of *Night of the Creeps*, September 3, 1986

Adrienne Barbeau
Paul, Louis. "The Chiller Interviews." *Chiller Theatre* magazine #23 (2005): 46–49
Variety. Review of *Swamp Thing*, March 24, 1982
Variety. Review of *Open House*, November 25, 1987

Michael Berryman
Fangoria. Interview, 1984
Variety. Review of *The Hills Have Eyes*, December 27, 1978
Variety. Review of *The Hills Have Eyes II*, February 19, 1986

Samson Burke
Paul, Louis. "The Chiller Theatre Interviews." *Chiller Theatre* magazine #21 (2004): 48–50
Variety. Review of *The Three Stooges Meet Hercules*, January 24, 1962

David Carradine
The New York Post. October, 1973
The New York Times. December 19, 1976
The New York Post. Interview, October 29, 1982
The Newark Evening News. Interview, June, 1966
Paul, Louis. "The Chiller Interviews." *Chiller Theatre* magazine #16 (2002): 49–53
People. June, 1978
TV Guide. Interview, 1974
Variety. October 27, 1976
Variety. Review of *Death Race 2000*, May 7, 1975
Variety. Review of *Bound for Glory*, December 8, 1976
Variety. Review of *Circle of Iron*, January 24, 1979

Robert Davi
Paul, Louis. "The Chiller Interviews." *Chiller Theatre* magazine #23 (2005): 50–54

Brad Dourif
Paul, Louis. "The Chiller Interviews." *Chiller Theatre* magazine #22 (2005): 42–43

Keir Dullea
Paul, Louis. "The Chiller Interviews." *Chiller Theatre* magazine #20 (2004): 44–47
Variety. Review of *The Hoodlum Priest*, February 22, 1961
Variety. Review of *David and Lisa*, September 9, 1962

Tippi Hedren
Paul, Louis. "The Chiller Interviews." *Chiller Theatre* magazine #17 (2002): 58–63
Variety. Review of *The Birds*, March 27, 1963
Variety. Review of *Marnie*, June 16, 1964

Gloria Hendry
The New York Amsterdam News. 1973
Variety. Review of *Black Belt Jones*, January 30, 1974

Richard Herd
Drama-Logue. March, 1989

Brion James
Variety. Review of *Crimewave*, May 22, 1985

Ed Lauter
The New York Daily News. February, 1986
Variety. Review of *Family Plot*, March 24, 1976

Valerie Leon
Paul, Louis. "The Chiller Interviews." *Chiller Theatre* magazine #19 (2003): 46–47
Variety. Review of *Blood from the Mummy's Tomb*, October 27, 1972

Richard Lynch
Variety. Review of *Invasion U.S.A.*, October 2, 1985
Variety. Review of *Bad Dreams*, April 6, 1988

Charles Napier
Paul, Louis. "The Chiller Interviews." *Chiller Theatre* magazine #18 (2003): 42–43

Steve Railsback
Paul, Louis. "The Chiller Interviews." *Chiller Theatre* magazine #20 (2004): 40–43

Tura Satana
Lisanti, Thomas and Louis Paul. *Film Fatales: Women in Espionage Films and Television, 1962–1973*; McFarland (2002): 264–67
Variety. March, 1959
Variety. Review of *Faster Pussycat! Kill! Kill!*, February 9, 1966
The Village Voice. April, 1996

John Saxon
Paul, Louis. "The Chiller Interviews." *Chiller Theatre* magazine #16 (2002): 55–58
Variety. Review of *The Appaloosa*, September 14, 1966
Variety. Review of *Enter the Dragon*, August 22, 1973

Madeline Smith
Paul, Louis. "The Chiller Interviews." *Chiller Theatre* magazine #20 (2004): 48–50

William Smith
Cinefantastique. September, 1981
Variety. Review of *Run, Angel, Run*, April 23, 1969
Variety. Review of *The Losers*, April 23, 1969
Variety. Review of *Darker Than Amber*, August 19, 1970
Variety. Review of *C.C. and Company*, October 21, 1970
Variety. Review of *Seven*, October 3, 1979

Austin Stoker
Paul, Louis. "The Chiller Interviews." *Chiller Theatre* magazine #22 (2005): 45–46

Dee Wallace Stone
Paul, Louis. "Interview: Dee Wallace Stone." *Chiller Theatre* magazine #13 (2000): 43–45

Don Stroud
Drama-Logue. 1984
Psychotronic Video. 2003
The San Francisco Examiner. 1984
Variety. Review of *Murph the Surf*, September 4, 1974

Cary-Hiroyuki Tagawa
Paul, Louis. "The Chiller Interviews." *Chiller Theatre* magazine #14 (2001): 37–39

Fred Williamson
The New York Amsterdam News. 1977
The New York Daily News. November, 1983
The New York Times. March, 1972
The New York Times. 1977
Variety. Review of *The Legend of Nigger Charley*, May 17, 1972
Variety. Review of *Hammer*, September 20, 1972

William Windom
Paul, Louis. "The Chiller Interviews." *Chiller Theatre* magazine #22 (2005): 43–44

Lana Wood
Lisanti, Thomas and Louis Paul. *Film Fatales: Women in Espionage Films and Television, 1962–1973*; McFarland (2002): 308–10
Paul, Louis. "The Chiller Theatre Interviews." *Chiller Theatre* magazine #21 (2004): 46–48
Playboy. April, 1971

Celeste Yarnall
Lisanti, Thomas and Louis Paul. *Film Fatales: Women in Espionage Films and Television, 1962–1973*; McFarland (2002): 311–13

Web Sites
All Movie Guide [www.allmovie.com]
The Astounding B-Monster [www.bmonster.com]
Brian's Drive-In Theatre [www.briansdriveintheater.com]
Chiller Theatre [www.chillertheatre.com]
Internet Movie Database [www.imdb.com]
The Official Site of Adrienne Barbeau [www.abarbeau.com]
The Official Site of Samson Burke [www.samsonburke.com]
The Official Site of David Carradine [www.davidcarradine.org]
The Official Site of Brad Dourif [www.dourif.net]
The Official Site of Sid Haig [www.sidhaig.com]
The Official Site of Tippi Hedren [www.shambala.org/tippi.htm]
The Official Site of Richard Herd [www.richardherd.com]
The Official Site of David Hess [www.davidhess.com]
The Official Site of Brion James [www.geocities.com/Hollywood/Movie/2919/]
The Official Site of Valerie Leon [www.valerieleon.com]
The Official (Fan) Site of Richard Lynch [http://officialrichardlynch.tripod.com]
The Official Site of Charles Napier [www.charlesnapier.com/index.htm]
The Official Site of Linnea Quigley [www.linneaquigleycircle.com]
The Official Site of Tura Satana [www.turasatana.com]
The Official Site of John Saxon [www.hollywoodnetwork.com/Saxon]
The Official (Fan) Site of William Smith [www.williamsmith.org]
The Official Site of Dee Wallace Stone [www.deewallacestone.com]
The Official Site of Don Stroud [www.donstroud.com]

The Official Site of Cary-Hiroyuki Tagawa [www.carytagawaonline.com]
The Official Site of Mel Welles [www.melwelles.com]
The Official Site of William Windom [www.timem.com/starwebs/williamwindom/index.htm]
The Official Site of Lana Wood [www.lanawood.net]
The Official Site of Celeste Yarnall [www.celesteyarnall.com]
The Official Site of The Roar Foundation / Shambala Preserve [www.shambala.org]

Index

Abby 234, 238
Across 110th Street 91, 96
Adler, Stella 55, 60, 110, 118, 125
Airport '77 144
Albert, Eddie 138–139
Aldrich, Robert 137–138, 229
Aleichem, Sholem 270
Alexander, Jason 98
Alfred Hitchcock Hour 46
Alfred Hitchcock Presents 81
The Alien Factor see *Zeta One*
Alien Resurrection 63
All in the Family 18
Allen, Ginger Lynn 77
Allen, Woody 7
Alligator II: The Mutation 262
Ally McBeal 266
Altman, Robert 118, 280, 283
American Reel 44
American Strays 118
Americana 44, 49
The Amityville Horror 249
Anderson, Pamela 193, 196
The Andersonville Trial 100
Angels Unchained 245
Ann-Margret 224–225
Annie Get Your Gun 262
Annis, Francesca 217
Another 48 Hours 118, 121
Another Man, Another Chance 25, 27–28
Ansara, Michael 203
L'Anthologie du Plaisir 132
Any Which Way You Can 223, 227
The Appaloosa 204, 207–208
Applegate, Royce 106
Appointment in Honduras 269
The Aquarians 236
Argento, Dario 63, 149, 205, 209–210
Armed Response 44
Arnold, Jack 286
Around the World Under the Sea 307, 309–310
The Art of War 254, 258–259
Arthur, Bea 16
Ashby, Hal 42–43
Ashley, Elizabeth 73
Ashley, John 313
Ashman, Howard 276
Askwith, Robin 169

The Asphalt Jungle 224
Assault on Precinct 13 234, 237–238
The Astro-Zombies 199–200
Atkins, Tom 7–15
Attack of the Crab Monsters 275
Auto Rosso Sangue see *Hitchhike*
Autry, Gene 45, 263
Avalanche Express 111
The Avengers 165

Babylon 5 63, 65, 254
Baciamo le Mani see *I Kiss the Hand*
Bad Company 138
Bad Dreams 173
The Bad Seed 44
Bad Timing 193
Badler, Jane 104–105
Baker, Roy Ward 215
Balsam, Martin 83
Barb Wire 193, 196
Barbeau, Adrienne 7, 10, 16–23
The Bare-Breasted Countess 190
Baretta 8, 137, 303
Barker, Ronnie 219
Barnaby Jones 244–245, 248
Barnes, Priscilla 77
Barrymore, Drew 262
Barrymore, John Drew 270
Basic Instinct 60
The Basic Training of Pavlo Hummel 174
Batman 77, 223–224
Battle Beyond the Stars 205
Battle for the Planet of the Apes 234–237
Bauer, Michelle 186, 188–189
Bava, Mario 204, 206–207, 271
Beast of the Dead 307, 312–313
The Beatles 45, 110, 244
Beeson, Luc 118, 124
Belafonte, Harry 279
Belasco, David 137
The Belle of New York 164–165
Belmondo, Jean-Paul 58
Belushi, John 182
Ben Casey 224
Berger, Helmut 133
Berghoff, Herbert 236
Bergman, Ingmar 44, 48
Berry, Halle 91
Berryman, Michael 24–31, 77, 112

Bertolucci, Bernardo 254–255, 260
Beyond the Valley of the Dolls 180–182
The Big Bird Cage 76
Big Brother and the Holding Company 243
The Big Doll House 75
Big Trouble in Little China 154
The Bionic Woman 81
Bird 107
Bird on a Wire 44, 49
The Birds 10, 80–85
The Birds II: Land's End 81, 85
Black, Shane 12
Black Belt Jones 91–92, 96
Black Caesar 91–92, 96, 280, 283
Black Christmas 69, 73, 205
Black Cobra 282, 287
Black Cobra 2 282, 287
Black Eye 280, 286
Black Kissinger 92, 97
Black Mama, White Mama 75
The Black Room 189
Black Samson 222
Blackjack 282, 290–291
Blade 258–259
Blade Runner 108, 117–118, 120–122, 125
Blair, Linda 190
Blatty, William Peter 10
Blind Date 71
Blind Target 189
Blodgett, Michael 313
Blood and Guts 227
Blood from the Mummy's Tomb 164, 166–170
The Bloody Judge 148–149
Bloody Mama 240, 251
Blue Chicago 291
The Blue Max 246
Blue Monkey 192, 196
Blue Sunshine 117–118
Blue Velvet 63
The Blues Brothers 182
Bochco, Steven 175
Body Count 111, 114
Bogart, Humphrey 139–140
Bohus, Ted v
The Bold Ones 205, 315
Bonanza 244
Bond, Ward 302
Bonnell, Vivian 236

Boothe, Powers 120
Born Yesterday 315
Boss Nigger 222, 227, 280
Bound for Glory 42–43, 49
The Box 197
Boxcar Bertha 41, 46–47
Boyle, Peter 101, 287
The Boys in the Band 236
Brainwaves 71
Brando, Marlon 58, 60, 85, 204, 207–208
Brave New World 71
Breakheart Pass 139
Bresslaw, Bernard 165
Briant, Shane 218
The Bride of Chucky—Child's Play 4 64
Bridges, Beau 91
Bridges, Jeff 142
Brigade des Moeurs 128
Broccoli, Albert "Cubby" 56, 58–59, 169, 303
Brolin, James 249
Bronson, Charles 139, 307, 313–315
The Bronx Warriors 282, 288–289
Brosnan, Pierce 57, 142
Brown, Jim 91, 280, 282, 287, 289
Brown, Reb 305
Bruiser 13–14
Brynner, Yul 223, 227
Buck at the Edge of Heaven 111
Bucktown 280
The Buddy Holly Story 239, 241, 249–250
Buffalo Springfield 243
Bugliosi, Vincent 194
Bujold, Genievieve 27
Bullitt 174
Bunny Lake Is Missing 68, 71–72
Burke, Michelle 173
Burke, Samson 32–39
Burke's Law 200
Burr, Jeff 96
Burr, Raymond 239, 245
Burton, Richard 243
Burton, Tim 144–145, 147, 254, 259–260
Busey, Gary 12, 241, 249–250, 250
Busting 78
Butterflies Are Free 73
The Byrds 243

Caan, James 25, 27–28, 240
Cabaret 99
Cabin Fever 112
Caffaro, Cheri 91
Cagney, James 100, 280=281
Calvaire 129
The Canary Sometimes Sings 219
Candy, John 142, 276
Canned Heat 244
Cannibal Holocaust 172
Cannon 137, 245, 248
Cannonball 42
Capp, Al 99
Capri, Ahna 226
Captain America 305
Carnivale 16, 21
Carpenter, John 7, 10–11, 16, 19–21, 234, 237–238, 254–255

Carradine, David 1, 3–4, 40–52, 223
Carradine, Keith 44, 51
Carradine, Robert 44, 51
Carreras, Sir James 166, 215
Carreras, Michael 168
Carroll, Diahann 280, 283
Carry On Again, Doctor 165
Carry On Camping 165
Carry On Girls 165, 217
Carry On Matron 165, 216–217
Carry On Stuffing 165
Carry On Up the Jungle 165
Carry On Up the Khyber 165
La Casa Sperduta nel Parco see *House on the Edge of the Park*
Casey, Bernie 280
Castellari, Enzo G. 112, 114, 210
Castelnuovo, Nino 270
Cat on a Hot Tin Roof 73
C.C. & Company 221, 224–225
Cecil B. DeMille—A One-Man Show 98
Chain Dance 65
Chan, Jackie 158
Chaney, Lon, Jr. 224
Chaplin, Charles 80, 85
Charlie and the Chocolate Factory 145
Charlie's Angels 77, 144, 200, 203, 245
Chase, Brandon 175
Chateau, Rene 132
Chekov, Michael 55
Cherry, Harry and Raquel 180–182
The Cherry Orchard 197
Cherry 2000 118
Child's Play 63–65
Child's Play 2 63
Child's Play 3 63
Chiller Theatre v, 3, 77, 118
The China Syndrome 101, 103, 107
CHiPs 118, 244
Chrichton, Michael 69
Christie, Agatha 217
Christopher Columbus 59–60
Ciannelli, Eduardo 270
Ciannelli, Louis 270
Il Cinico, l'Infame, il Violento see *The Cynic, the Rat, and the Fist*
Circle of Iron 44
Clark, Bob 69
Clarke, Arthur C. 69, 71
Clement, Kevin v, 3
Cleopatra 35
Clery, Corrine 111
Clouse, Robert 226, 229
Coburn, James 200, 203
Coffy 75
Cohen, Larry 42, 174–175, 282–283
Coleman, Dabney 101
Collins, Kevin v, 189
The Color of Night 63
Conan the Barbarian 223, 227–228
Connelly, Christopher 282
Connery, Sean 80, 93, 164, 169, 240, 300–305
Connors, Michael 111
Conquest of the Planet of the Apes 234
Conrad, Robert 241–243, 247–248, 300, 303
Conrad, William 248

Contract on Cherry Street 53, 55–56
The Convent 16, 21
Conway, Kevin 101
Coogan's Bluff 240–241, 244–245, 247
Cooper, Gary 235
Coppola, Francis Ford 229
Corbett, Ronnie 219
Corigliano, John 110
Corman, Gene 207
Corman, Roger 48–49, 69, 73, 75, 205, 207, 240, 245–247, 269–276, 313, 315
Cossell, Howard 281
Costner, Kevin 142
Cotton, Joseph 273
Count Dracula 148
A Countess from Hong Kong 80, 85
Le Couteau sous la Gorge 128
Coward, Noel 71, 219
Craven, Wes 16, 20, 24–27, 110–111, 210, 262
Crazy Joe 287
Creepshow 7, 13, 20
Crime and Punishment 173, 176
Crimes of Passion 193
Crimewave 118, 121, 123
The Critic 182
Critters 262
Cronenberg, David 205, 227
Crosby, Bing 224
The Crow 25, 27–29
Cruise, Tom 255
Cujo 262, 264–265
Cummings, Robert 309
Cunningham, Sean 123
The Curse of Frankenstein 144
Curtis, Jamie Lee 7, 10–11, 19
Curtis, Tony 214–216
Cushing, Harry 272
Cushing, Peter 107, 144, 146, 150, 168, 218
Cut and Run 25
The Cynic, the Rat, and the Fist 209

Dale, Jim 165
Dallas 105
Dalton, Timothy 53, 58–59, 96, 250–251
Damon, Mark 270
Dance with the Devil 242, 251
Danger Route 168
Dangerfield, Rodney 53, 61
Daniel Boone 224
Daniels, Gary 158
Dante, Joe 262–265
Danton, Ray 271
D'Antoni, Phil 174
Dark Eyes see *Satan's Mistress*
Dark Mission—Operacion Cocaina 128, 133
Darker Than Amber 222, 226–227, 229
Darren, James 104
Davi, Robert 1, 53–62, 242, 250–251
David and Lisa 68, 72–73
Davis, Ossie 99
Davis, Rochelle 29
Deadly Blessings 25
The Deadly Trackers 226

Deadwood 63, 65
Dean, James 206, 244
Death House 210
Death Hunt 139
Death Journey 288
Death Machine 63
Death Mask 187
Death Race 2000 42, 48–49
Death Trip see *Three Green Dogs*
The Death Weekend see *House by the Lake*
Death Wish 3 139
Deathsport 42, 48–49
Dee, Ruby 99
Dekker, Fred 8, 12
De Laurentiis, Dino 37, 139, 169
Deliverance 24
Delon, Alain 128, 131, 307, 313–315
Delta Force Commando 282
Del Toro, Benicio 59
Delusions 115–116
Demme, Jonathan 181–182
Demon Rage see *Satan's Mistress*
De Niro, Robert 240
Dennis, Sandy 73
Deodato, Ruggero 27, 111–112, 114, 172, 175–176
Depp, Johnny 147
De Rita, Joe 33
Dern, Bruce 140, 240
De Sade 69, 73
The Detective 7–9
Detective Story 237
Les Deux Orphelines Vampires 128, 133
Devil in the Brain 69
The Devil's Agent 149
The Devil's Daffodil 149
The Devil's Rejects 75, 77
Devil's Three 157, 162
Diamond Zero 82, 87
Diamonds Are Forever 96, 300–305
Diaz, Victor 312
Dick, Philip K. 117
Die Another Day 91
Die Hard 53, 57–58
Diller, Barry 290–291
Dillon, Matt 229
Dillon, Melinda 101
Distortions 192
Dobson, Tamara 158
Doc Savage—The Man of Bronze 24, 30
Dr. Jekyll and Sister Hyde 168
Dr. Kildare 300, 302
Dr. No 96
Dr. Wong's Virtual Hell 148
La Dolce Vita 207
The Doll Squad 199–200, 203
Don Quixote 147
Donahue, Troy 239, 242–243
Donnor, Richard 53, 57
The Doomsday Flight 205
The Doors 243
Dostaly, Rhony v
Douglas, Michael 24
Dourif, Brad 63–67, 197
Down 'n Dirty 282
Dracula 144
Dracula Has Risen from the Grave 145

Dracula, Prince of Darkness 150
Dream On 81
The Drew Carey Show 16
Duke, Patty 100
The Dukes 55
Dullea, Keir 68–74
Duncan, Michael Clarke 259–260
Dune 63
Dunne, Irene 309
Duvall, Robert 125
Dylan, Bob 45
Dynamite Johnson: Bionic Boy 157, 160–162
Dynasty 105

Eagan, Richard 181
East Side/West Side 46
Eastside 176
Easterbrook, Leslie 77
Eastwood, Clint 107, 205, 223, 227, 240, 244–245, 247, 255, 294–295
Ebsen, Buddy 248
The Education of Private Slovik 58
Edwards, Blake 53
Edwards, Vince 224
Eight Men Out 173
Ekland, Britt 302
The Electric Horsemen 205
Ellery Queen 140
The Empire Strikes Back 106
Endfield, Cy 69, 73
Enemy Mine 118, 125
Enter the Dragon 41, 205, 208–209
ER 141
Escape 2000 192, 195
Escape from New York 7, 11, 16, 20–21
Eszterhas, Joe 60
E.T.: The Extraterrestrial 262, 265
Eve 307, 310–313
The Evil Eye see *The Girl Who Knew Too Much*
Excalibur 175
L'Executrice 128, 131
Exorcist III 64–65
The Eyes of Laura Mars 63

Faceless see *Les Predateurs de la Nuit*
Falcon Crest 105
Falk, Lee 99
The Fall Guy 302
Family Plot 139–141
Farina, Dennis 13
Farmer, Mimsy 114
Farrow, Mia 47, 71
Fascination 128, 131–132
Fassbinder, Rainer Werner 111
Fast Company 205, 227
Fast Track 289
Faster Pussycat, Kill Kill 4, 199–200, 202–203
Fatal Beauty 63
Fatal Frames 189
Fawcett, Farrah 19, 315
The F.B.I. 315
La Femme Nikita 118, 124
La Fiancee du Dracula 129
The Fifth Element 118, 124
The Fifth Floor 25
Film Fatales v

Fine, Larry 33
Finney, Albert 125
First Blood: Part 2 57, 182
Fishburne, Laurence 238
F.I.S.T. 101, 107
Five Finger Exercise 301
Five for Hell 37
Fleming, Ian 59
Flipper 309
Foch, Nina 125
The Fog 7, 10–11, 16, 19–20, 237
Fonda, Henry 223
Fonda, Jane 205, 240
For Singles Only 300
For the Love of Ivy 91
The Forbidden Dance 173
Ford, Harrison 117
Ford, John 300, 302, 315
Foree, Ken 77
Foreman, Carl 168
The Forgotten 193
Forman, Milos 24, 63–64
Forster, Robert 282, 288, 291
Forsythe, William 77
48 Hours 117, 121
The Four Musketeers 144
The 4th Tenor 53, 61
The Fox 73
Foxy Brown 75
Franco, Jess see Franco Jesus
Franco, Jesus 128, 131, 133, 147–149, 187–190
Franju, Georges 128
Frankenheimer, John 294
Frankenstein and the Monster from Hell 214, 218–219
Free Grass 300
Free to Be ... You and Me 44, 49
The French Connection 174
The Frighteners 262, 265–266
Frith, Christopher v
From Dusk Till Dawn 282, 290
From Russia with Love 96
Fruet, William 192–193, 196
Frye, David 139
Fuchsberger, Joachim 149
Funny About Love 315
Funny Girl 165
Funny Lady 310
Fux, Herbert 270

Gabor, Zsa Zsa 223–224
Games 239–240, 244
The Gangster Chronicles 56
The Ganzelresa 200
Garcia, Eddie 312
Garner, James 14
Gaynor, Mitzi 100
Gazzara, Ben 99 , 302, 305
Gein, Ed 193, 196–197
Gentleman B 142
The Ghost of Frankenstein 221, 224
Gibson, Mel 12, 44
Gidget's Summer Reunion 241–242
Gifford, Frank 281
Girdler, William 234, 238
The Girl from U.N.C.L.E. 200, 203
The Girl I Want 190
The Girl Who Knew Too Much 204–207

The Girls on the Beach 300, 302
Girolami, Enzo *see* Castellari, Enzo G.
Glen, John 58–60
Glenn, Scott 193
Glover, Danny 12, 60
God Told Me To 174–175
The Godfather 60
Goldfinger 96
Goodman, John 315
The Goonies 53, 57
The Grateful Dead 243
Grave of the Vampire 227
Grier, Pam 75, 77, 92, 158, 234, 282, 289
Gries, Tom 305
Griffith, Chuck 269–270, 273–275
Griffith, Melanie 80, 315
Guerrero, Franco 159
Guinness, Sir Alec 217
The Guns of Will Sonnett 221
Gunsmoke 77, 221, 224
Guys and Dolls 99
The Guyver 25–27, 190
Gwynne, Fred 73
The Gypsy Moths 294

Habeus Corpus 217–218
Hackman, Gene 75, 125, 175
Hagitay, Mickey 272
Haig, Sid 75–79
Haji 200
Halloween 10
Halloween III: Season of the Witch 7, 11
Hamilton, Guy 91–93, 303
Hammer 222, 227, 280
Hampton Wick 219
Hansen, Gunnar 30
The Happy Anniversary 100
The Harrad Experiment 81
Harrington, Curtis 240
Harris, Brad 36
Harris, Richard 226
Harry and Walter Go to New York 117–118
Harry-O 8
Hauff, Reinhardt 111
Hauser, Wings 291
Have Gun—Will Travel 302
Hawaii Five-O 223, 239–240, 245, 248
Hawaiian Eye 239, 242–244
Hawdon, Robin 166
Hawke, Ethan 238
Hawtrey, Charles 165
Hayes, Allison 271
Head, Edith 83
Hearn, George 10
Heckart, Eileen 99
Hedren, Tippi 4, 80–89
Hell Up in Harlem 91, 280
Hello Glen Ward 271
Helter Skelter 192–193
Hemingway, Mariel 7
Hendry, Gloria 90–97
Henrickson, Lance 123
Henry and June 128, 133
Henry VIII 293
Hess, David 110–116

Heston, Charlton 106
Hercules in New York 100–101
Herd, Richard v, 98–110
Herrington, Rowdy 13
Hickey and Boggs 138
High School Confidential 224
Hill, Debra 11
Hill, Jack 76
Hill, Walter 44, 49, 117–120, 123
Hill Street Blues 175
The Hills Have Eyes 24–25, 30, 262, 264
The Hills Have Eyes: Part II 25
Hitchcock, Alfred 10, 80, 82–85, 139–141, 181
Hitchhike 111, 113
Hitters 53
Hobson's Choice 99
Hoffman, Dustin 63, 174, 240
Hogan's Heroes 315
Holder, Geoffrey 236
Holbrook, Hal 20
Holloway, Stanley 274
Hollywood Chainsaw Hookers 187
Holt, Seth 168
The Hoodlum Priest 68, 73
Hooper, Tobe 192, 195–196, 262
Hopper, Dennis 205
Hornsby and Rodriguez 182
The Horror Show 118, 123
The Host 75
The Hot Chick 53, 236
The Hour of the Gun 294
The House by the Lake 241, 248–249
House of 1000 Corpses 75–77
House on the Edge of the Park 111, 114
Howard, Moe 33–35
Howard, Ron 141
Howard, Trevor 40
Howerd, Frankie 217
The Howling 262–265
Hunnicut, Gayle 315
Hunter, Jeffrey 302
Hunter, Ross 73
Hurok, Sol 236
Hurt, John 176
Huston, John 63–64, 73
Hutton, Lauren 19
Huxley, Aldous 71
Hyams, Peter 71, 78

I Am a Camera 99
I Kiss the Hand 205, 209
I, Spy 37
I Woke Up Early the Day I Died 81, 87
I'm Dangerous Tonight 262
In the Light of the Moon 193, 196–197
The Inglorious Bastards 282, 287
Inner Sanctum 273
Innocent Blood 187
Invasion of the Flesh Hunters 209
Invasion U.S.A. 172–173, 175, 177
Irma La Douche 200–203
Ireland, Jill 315
Ironside 239, 244–245, 293
Irvin, John 57
Island of the Doomed 270–271, 274
It Takes a Thief 315
The Italian Job 58

Jack O'Lantern 189
Jackie Brown 77, 92, 291
Jackson, Peter 145, 262, 265–266
Jacobs, Arthur P. 236
JAG 142
Jagger, Chris 192
James, Brion 1, 117–127
Janssen, David 11
Jason King 214–216
Jaws 92
Je Brule De Partout 128, 131
Jefferson Airplane 243
Jefferson Starship 243
The Jericho Mile 141
Jeunet, Jean-Pierre 63
Jewison, Norman 101
Jinnah 145, 149
Jodorowsky, Alexandro 144
Joe Kidd 205, 240, 245, 247
John Carpenter's Big Trouble in Little China see Big Trouble in Little China
John Carpenter's Vampires 254
Johnny Belinda 47
Johnny Tsunami 260
Johnson, Arch 224
Johnson, Don 315
Johnson, Tom v, 146, 150
Jonathan degli Orsi 112, 114, 210
Jonathan of the Bears see Jonathan degli Orsi
Jory, Victor 99
Joshua 287
Joston, Darwin 235, 237–238
Julia 280, 283

Kanter, Hal 283
Kaplan, Gabe 139
Karloff, Boris 25
Kate Bliss and the Ticker-tape Kid 101, 106
Kaufman, Philip 133, 260
Kazan, Elia 100, 192–193
Keach, James 193
Keach, Stacy 241, 250
Keir, Andrew 168
Kelly, Grace 80, 84–85
Kelly, Jim 91, 205, 208, 287, 289–290
Kennedy, Burt 101, 106
Kerr, Walter 99
Kershner, Irvin 68, 106
Kidder, Margot 69, 176
Kiel, Richard 169
Kill Bill: Volume One 44, 158
Kill Bill: Volume Two 44, 158
Killer Instinct 266
King, B.B. 291
King, Stephen 13, 20
King Kong 139, 169
Kinski, Klaus 37, 107, 148
Kiss Meets the Phantom of the Park 118
Klein, Robert 139
Kneale, Nigel 192
Knots Landing 105
Kojak 137
Konchalovsky, Andrei 123
Kotto, Yaphet 91
Kove, Martin 110

Kubrick, Stanley 68–69, 72
Kung Fu 40–41, 46–49, 223
Kung Fu: The Legend Continues 42, 137
Kung Fu: The Movie 42
Kung Fu: The Next Generation 42
Kurosawa, Akria 115

Ladd, Alan 235
Ladd, Cheryl 19
Lady Frankenstein 270–274
Lahaie, Brigitte 4, 115, 128–136
Lake, Veronica 99
The Lambada Forbidden Dance see *The Forbidden Dance*
Lancaster, Burt 307, 313–315
Land of the Dead 12
Land of the Giants 315
Landis, John 181
The Landlord 91, 96
Lansbury, Angela 293
The Last American Hero 138
The Last Emperor 254–255, 260
The Last Hours Before Morning 139–140
The Last House on the Left 110–114, 116
The Last Warrior 260
Lauter, Ed 4, 137–143, 221
Lawson, Leigh 217
Leachman, Cloris 141
Lear, Norman 18
Ledbetter, Craig 3
Lee, Brandon 25, 27–29, 42
Lee, Bruce 41, 48, 160, 205, 208–209, 223
Lee, Christopher 3–5, 107, 144–156
Lee, Marrie 3, 5, 157–163
Lee, Sally 137
Lee, Spike 289
The Legend of Nigger Charley 280, 283–286
Leibman, Ron 58
Leigh, Janet 19
Lelouch, Claude 25, 27–28
Lemaire, Phillipe 271
Lennon, John 45
Lenzi, Umberto 182
Leon see *The Professional*
Leon, Valerie 3, 164–171, 217
Lethal Weapon 12
Levin, Henry 286
Levinson, Richard 58
Lewis, Jerry 309
Licence to Kill 53–54, 58–59, 239, 242, 250–251, 254
Lifeforce 192–193, 195–196
Light Up the Sky 100
Lincoln, Abbey 91
Link, William 58
Lisanti, Tom v
Lister, Tiny 118
Liston, Sonny 181
Lithgow, John 8, 10, 71
Little Shop of Horrors 269–270, 274–277
Live and Let Die 91–96, 214–216–218, 236
The Living Daylights 96
Locklear, Heather 102–104
Lockwood, Gary 68–69, 72

Lolly-Madonna XXX 138
Lommel, Ulli 71
Londale, Frederic 219
Lone Wolf McQuade 42
The Long, Hot Summer 300, 302
The Long Riders 44, 49, 51
The Longest Yard 137–139, 142
Lord, Jack 223, 239–240, 245
The Lord of the Rings: The Fellowship of the Ring 145
The Lord of the Rings: The Return of the King 63, 65–66, 145
The Lord of the Rings: The Two Towers 63, 65–66, 145
The Losers 221, 225
Lou Grant 60
Love, American Style 315
Love, Suzanna 71
LSD: Trip to Where? 172
Lucas Tanner 263
Ludlum, Robert 99–100
Lundgren, Dolph 282, 290–291
Lupino, Ida 248
Lustig, William 12, 288
Lynch, David 63–64
Lynch, Richard 112, 172–179
Lynley, Carol 68, 71–72

Macarthur, James 223
Macho Callaghan 41
Mad Max 192
Madame X 73, 137
Madigan 240, 245
The Magnificent Seven 118, 137, 205
The Magnificent Seven Ride 137
Magnoli, Albert 124
Magnum P.I. 32, 37, 137
Maibaum, Richard 58
The Man from U.N.C.L.E. 200, 203, 315
The Man with the Golden Gun 144
Man-Eater of Hydra see *Island of the Doomed*
Mane, Tyler 77
Maniac Cop 7, 12
Mankiewicz, Tom 303
Mann, Paul 236
Mannix 111, 137, 141, 180
Manson, Charles 192–193
M.A.N.T.I.S. 118
Mao-ying, Angela 158
Marcus Welby, M.D. 244, 249
Margheriti, Antonio 182, 209, 287
Margolin, Janet 68
Mari-Cookie and the Killer Tarantula 187–190
The Mark of the Astro-Zombies 200
Marnie 80, 84–85
Martin, Dean 200
Martin, D'Urville 280
Martin, Pamela Sue 192
Martin, Quinn 245
Martin, Ross 303
Martin, Steve 276
Marvin, Lee 111
*M*A*S*H* 280, 283
Mastorakis, Niko 71
Mastroianni, Armand 192
Mata Hari 44, 49
Maude 16, 18

Max Ernst—Mein Vagabundieren Meine Unruhe 111
May, Mathilda 192, 196
McBroom, Marcia 285
McCalla, Irish 312
McDonald, John D. 222
McDowall, Roddy 234–235
McGrory, Matt 77
The McMasters 41
McQueen, Steve 47
McTiernan, John 53, 57–58
The Mean Season 229
Mean Streets 48
The Mechanic 307, 313–315
Medina, Patricia 273
Melrose Place 315
Memoirs of a Geisha 4
Men in Black 182
Mencken, Alan 276
Mendoki, Luis 315
Meredith, Don 281
Meyer, Russ 4, 180–182, 199–200, 202–203
Miami Vice 112
Micheaux, Oscar 279
Mickey Spillane's Mike Hammer 239, 250
Midler, Bette 16–17
Midnight Caller 107
Midnight Cowboy 240
Midnight in the Garden of Good and Evil 107, 247
Midnight Kiss 315
The Migrants 141
Mikels, Ted V. 199–200, 203
Milian, Tomas 209
Milius, John 227–229
Miller, Jason 175
The Mindbenders: Scary Drug Education Films from the 60's: Volume One 172
Mineo, Sal 110
Mission: Impossible 77, 181, 254, 293, 302, 304–305
Mississippi Burning 63
Mitchell, Cameron 270
Mitchell, Gordon 35–37
Moby Dick 146–147
The Mod Squad 236
Monday Night Football 281–282
The Monster Squad 8
Moon, Sherri 77
Moonfire 181
Moore, Roger 58, 91–96, 164, 169, 214, 215–218, 236
Mortal Kombat 4, 255, 257
Mortal Kombat: Annihilation 257
Moseley, Bill 77
Mulligans! 81
The Mummy's Curse 25
Munro, Caroline 133
Murder, She Wrote 141, 293
Murder Weapon 190
Murph, the Surf 241, 247–248
Murphy, Eddie 117
Murray, Bill 276
Murray, Don 73
Mutator 118
My Partner, the Ghost see *Randall and Hopkirk Deceased*

My Science Project 25
My World and Welcome to It! 293, 295
Myers, Cynthia 200
The Mystery of Natalie Wood 302

The Naked Carmen 110
Namath, Joe 224–225
The Name of the Game 244
Napier, Charles 4, 114, 180–185, 221, 291
Nash Bridges 230
National Lampoon's Men in White 242
Natividad, Kitten 200
Natural Born Killers 188
Neeson, Liam 142
Nelkin, Stacy 7, 9, 11
Nelson, Ozzie 307–308
Nelson, Ricky 307–308
Neo Ned 197
Neri, Rosalba 272–273
Nero, Franco 111, 113–114, 270
Never Say Never Again 164, 169
Never Steal Anything Small 100
The Next One 71
The New Barbarians 288–289
A New Kind of Love 309
Newmar, Julie 168
Nibelungen, Die 36
Nicholson, Jack 63
Nickelodeon 117–118
Nielsen, Leslie 25
Night Caller from Outer Space 207
Night of the Creeps 7–8, 12, 14
Night of the Demons 187
Nightmare at Noon 118
Nightmare in Badham County 302
A Nightmare on Elm Street 173, 187, 205, 210
Nightwatch 63
Niki de Saint Phalle: Wer Ist das Monster—Du Oder Ich? 111–112
Nimoy, Leonard 310, 315
Nine to Five 101
1941 144
The Ninth Configuration 10, 172
Niven, David 100
Nixon, Richard 47–48
No Way Back 288
Noi Siamo Angeli 112, 114–115
Nolte, Nick 117
Nomads 57
Norrington, Stephen 63
Norris, Chuck 92, 172–173, 175, 177
Not Another Teen Movie 139
Notorious 83
La Nuit des Traquees 128
The Nutcracker 112
The Nutty Professor 307, 309
NYPD Blue 142, 175

O'Barr, James 29
The Odyssey 37
O'Herlihy, Dan 7
Olivier, Laurence 71
Oliviera, Hector 251
One Down, Two to Go 289
One Flew Over the Cuckoo's Nest 24, 63–65
One Million Years B.C. 310–311
O'Neal, Ron 282, 289

Oregon Trail 181
Original Gangstas' 282, 289–290
O'Toole, Pete 144, 192, 194–195
Our Man Flint 202–203
Our Man in Jamaica 274
The Outlaws 181
Oz 8, 247–248
Oz, Frank 276–277
The Ozzie and Harriett Show 307

Pacific Heights 81
Pacino, Al 172, 174–175, 244
Page, "Diamond Dallas" 77
Paint Your Wagon 99
Pal, George 24, 30
Palance, Jack 55
Palmieri, Phil v
Pantoliano, Joe 197
Paperback Hero 69, 73
Parker, Alan 63
Parker, Ed 223
Pataki, Michael 227
Pearl Harbor 254, 259
Peck, Gregory 293–294
Penn, Arthur 197
Pennell, Larry 274
Penrod 99
Pensacola 249
Percy's Progress 217
Perdita Durango see *Dance with the Devil*
The Perfect Weapon 254–255
The Persuaders 214–216
Peter Gunn 291
Peterson, Wolfgang 125
Pettet, Joanna 302, 305
The Phantom 254
Philadelphia 182
Picture Bride 257
Pitt, Ingrid 214, 216
Planet Earth 209
Planet of the Apes 234, 254, 259–260
The Player 118
Playhouse '90 302
Pleasance, Donald 189
Please Sign It Love 200
La Plus Belle Nuit du Cinema 128
Poitier, Sidney 91, 240, 243, 279
Police Academy: Mission to Moscow 144
Police Story 303
Poltergeist: The Legacy 254
Pour la Peau d'un Flic 128, 131
P.O.W. The Escape 44
The Practice 61
Les Predateurs de la Nuit 128, 133
Predator 2 60
Preminger, Ingo 283
Preminger, Otto 71, 280
Presley, Elvis 110
Preston, Robert 75
Price, Vincent 8, 106–107
Priestley, Jason 197
The Professional 118, 124
Profiler 53, 57, 60–61
The Progeny 63
Prophecy III: The Ascent 63
Provocateur 254
Prowse, Dave 218
Pryor, Richard 139

Psycho 83
Psycho from Texas 186
Pulp Fiction 75
Pumpkinhead II 96, 187
Puppetmaster III: Toulon's Revenge 173
Purple Rain 124
Puzo, Mario 60
Puzzle of the Red Orchid 149
Pyun, Albert 175

QBVII 302, 305
Quaid, Dennis 125
Quantum Leap 98, 106–107
Queen Gorilla see *Queen Kong*
Queen Kong 168–169
Queen of Blood 207
Quigley, Linnea 186–191
Quinn, Anthony 55, 60, 91

Rabe, David 174
Ragtime 63, 65
Raiders of the Lost Ark 92
Railsback, Steve 4, 77, 192–198
Raimi, Sam 8, 121
Rain, Douglas 68
The Rainbow Thief 144
Rains, Claude 99
Les Raisons de la Mort 128, 131
Rambo II see *First Blood: Part 2*
Randall, Tony 101
Randall and Hopkirk Deceased 165
Rashoman 115
Raw Deal 53, 57
Rebecca 83
Rebel Yell: The Billy Idol Story 25
Red Dawn 229
Red Heat 123
Red Scorpion 118
Redford, Robert 205
Redgrave, Vanessa 176
Reeves, Steve 35, 37
Reservoir Dogs 188
Ressler, Robert 60
The Restless Years 204
Return of Captain Invincible 144
Return of the Living Dead 186–187
Return to the Planet of the Apes 234
The Revenge of the Pink Panther 164
Reynolds, Burt 46, 137–139, 244
Rhames, Ving 279
Rhodes, Hari 234, 236
Rich, David Lowell 286
Rich Man, Poor Man 222
Rising Sun 254–255, 260
The Road Warrior 288
Roar 80, 85–86
Roberts, Pernell 244, 300
Robinson, Marty 276
Rock, Chris 142
Rock Pretty Baby 204
The Rockford Files 8, 14, 137, 181
Roddenberry, Gene 209
Rodriguez, Robert 282, 290
Rogers, Peter 216
Rogers, Roy 45
Rollin, Jean 4, 128–129, 131, 133
The Rolling Stones 244
Romay, Lina 189
Romero, George A. 7, 12–14, 16, 20–21

Rooker, Michael 197
Ross, Katherine 240, 313
Roth, Eli 112
Rothman, Stephanie 313
Roundtree, Richard 280, 282, 289
Rourke, Mickey 229
The Royal Hunt of the Sun 40, 46
Rubin, Jennifer 173
Rugrats 182
Rumblefish 229
Run, Angel, Run 221–222, 224–225
Runaway Daughters 262
Runaway Train 123
Rush, Richard 192–195
Russell, Kurt 21, 123–124
Russell, Rosalind 309
The Russellresa 193, 197
Russo, James 197

Sailor of Fortune 147
The Saint 93, 165
Saint, Eva Marie 99
Saint James, Susan 313
Saltzman, Harry 91–93
Salvador, Julio 274
Sanders, Ed 194
Sandler, Adam 142
The Sands of the Kalahari 73
Sarrazin, Michael 240
Satana, Tura 4, 199–204
The Satanic Rites of Dracula 151
Satan's Mistress 302, 305
Satan's Playground 25
Saturday Night Live 144
Savage Sisters 90–91, 95–96
Savage Streets 190
Saxon, John 69, 204–214, 227
Scarecrow 172, 174–175
Scarlet Pimpernel 147
Schamoni, Peter 111–112
Scheider, Roy 71, 105–106, 174
Schizoid 107
Schneider, Rob 53
Schow, David 29
Schwarzenegger, Arnold 57, 100–101, 227–229
Scofield, Paul 315
Scorchy 222
Scorpio 307, 313–315
Scorsese, Martin 41, 46–48
Scott, George C. 46, 65
Scott, Ridley 108, 117
Seabiscuit 139, 142
SeaQuest DSV 105–106
The Search for Bridey Murphy 275
The Searchers 300, 302
Seed of Chucky 63, 66
Seinfeld 98
Sellers, Peter 164
Seraphim Falls 142
The Serpent's Egg 44, 48
Seven 222, 228
The Seven Minutes 181–182
The Seven-Ups 172, 174
The Seven-Year Itch 100
Seymour, Jane 94
Shane 41, 45–47
Sharif, Omar 144
Shatner, William 98, 100–106, 294, 310

Shaw, Robert 77, 111
Sheba Baby 234, 238
The Shoes of the Fisherman 58
Shore, Sig 192
Shou, Robin 257
Showdown at the Equator 159
Showdown in Little Tokyo 254–255
Showgirls 53, 60
Sidaris, Andy 283
Siedelman, Alan Arthur 100–101
Siegel, Don 241, 244–245
Signoret, Simone 240
The Silent Flute see *Circle of Iron*
Silent Running 69
Silva, Henry 282, 291
Silver, Joel 57, 60
Silverado 118
Simon and Simon 224
The Simpsons 182
Sinatra, Frank 7–9, 53, 55–56
Sing Out, Sweet Land 99
Sizemore, Tom 13
The Skin of Our Teeth 197
Slash 197
Slaughter's Big Rip-Off 91, 96
Sleepy Hollow 144–145, 147
Slice 25
Smashing Time 165
Smith, Alexis 99
Smith, Brian-Trenchard 192
Smith, Charles Martin 241, 249–250
Smith, Madeline 4, 214–220
Smith, Paul L. 118, 121
Smith, Will 234
Smith, William 4, 221–233
Snipes, Wesley 258–259, 279
Snodgrass, Carrie 196–197
Soldier Boyz 258
Soldier of Fortune 274
Soldier of Orange 60
Soles, P.J. 77
Sollima, Sergio 69
Someone's Watching Me! 16, 19
Sommers, Suzanne 19
The Son of the Pink Panther 53
Sonny Boy 44, 63
Sons and Daughters 262
The Sorcerer's Apprentice 61
Soto, Talisa 257
The Soul of Nigger Charley 280, 283–285
South Bureau Homicide 96
Southern Comfort 117–120, 123–124
Space Rangers 254, 256
Spacek, Sissy 141
Spelling, Aaron 105, 200, 203, 245
Spencer, Bud 112, 115
Spider Baby 75, 77
Spielberg, Steven 53, 57, 106, 144, 262
Splendor in the Grass 100
Spy Hard 25
The Spy Who Loved Me 96, 164, 169
The Spy Within 193
Stack, Robert 106
Stalag 17 71
Stallone, Sylvester 101, 107, 123–124
Stander, Lionel 270
Star Trek 77, 98, 106, 180, 293–294, 307, 310, 315

Star Trek: The Next Generation 106, 254
Star Trek: Voyager 63, 65
Star Trek IV: The Voyage Home 25
Star Wars 92, 106, 209, 259
Star Wars: Episode II—The Attack of the Clones 144
Star Wars: Episode III—Revenge of the Sith 144
Stargate SG-1 254
Starlost 69
Starship Troopers 2: Hero of the Federation 139
Starsky and Hutch 181, 282
Steel Dawn 118
Steiger, Rod 101, 249
Stensgaard, Yutte 166
The Stepford Wives 262–263
Stevens, Brinke 186
Stewart, James 139–140
Stewart, Patrick 192
Stiller, Ben 181
Stoker, Austin 230–238
Stone, Christopher 262–263, 265
Stone, Dee Wallace 4
Stone, Oliver 289
Stone Cold Dead 186
Storey, David 8–9
Strasberg, Lee 55
Strauss, Peter 141
The Streets of San Francisco 137, 172, 174, 245, 248, 262
Streisand, Barbara 165, 310
Striking Distance 13, 118
Stritch, Elaine 139
Strode, Woody 234, 288
Stroud, Don 1, 4, 221, 239–253
Struthers, Sally 18
The Stunt Man 192–195
Sturges, John 294
Suarez, Bobby 159, 162
Summer and Smoke 302
Summer Love 204
Superman 92
Supervixens 181–182
The Survivalist 192
Sutherland, Donald 243
Svenson, Bo 282
Swamp Thing 16, 20, 111
Swashbuckler 77
Sweet Jesus, Preacher Man 222, 227
The Swiss Conspiracy 111, 113
The Sword and the Sorcerer 172, 175

Tagawa, Cary-Hiroyuki 4, 254–261
Taggart 41, 45–47
Take a Hard Ride 287
A Tale of Two Cities 98–99
Tango and Cash 118, 123–124
Taps 255
Tarantino, Quentin 3, 44, 61, 75–77, 158, 188, 237, 282, 290–291
Taste the Blood of Dracula 214
Taylor, Elizabeth 243
Taylor, Rod 181, 222–223, 226–227
Tea with Grandma 81, 87
Tell Me That You Love Me, Junie Moon 280, 283
Tenebrae 205, 209–210

Termination Man 193
The Terrorist on Trial: United States vs. Salim Ajami see *The United States vs. Salim Ajami*
Le Teste Calde 270
The Texas Cadet Murders 265
The Texas Chainsaw Massacre 30, 75
That Man Bolt 280–281, 286
Theater Macabre 147
They Call Her ... Cleopatra Wong 157, 160–161
The Thin Red Line 68, 72
Thirteen Days 142
Thomas, Philip Michael 112, 114
Thomerson, Tim 107, 117–118
Thompson, J. Lee 236
Three Green Dogs 36
The Three Musketeers 144
The Three Stooges Meet Hercules 32–34, 39
Three the Hard Way 279–280, 287
Three Tough Guys 280, 287
Thurber, James 293
...tick...tick...tick 245
Tim Burton's Corpse Bride 145
Time Walker 237
T.J. Hooker 98, 100–105
To All a Good Night 111
To Catch a Thief 83
To Kill a Mockingbird 293–294
Topol 106
Torchlight 198
Tors, Ivan 309–310
Total Recall 121
Toto 35
Toto Contro Maciste 35
Tout Est Bien Qui Finit Bien 128
Tower of London 25
Towers, Harry Alan 148, 310–311
Trancers 107, 117
The Transgressor Rides Again 41
Trauma 63
Trejo, Danny 77
The Triumph of Robin Hood 35
Trouble Comes to Town 236
True Crime 294–295
Trumbull, Douglas 69
Turkel, Joe 108
Turner, Lana 73
Turkey Shoot see *Escape 2000*
The Turtles 243
Tushingham, Rita 165
21 Hours at Munich 111, 113
Twiggy 217
The Twilight Zone 293
Twilight's Last Gleaming 229
The Twisted Brain 234
Two Evil Eyes 7, 12, 16
The Two Ronnies 219
2001: A Space Odyssey 68–73
2010 71–73

Two to Tango 251
Tyree, Jack 175

The Ugly American 58
The Ultimate Warrior 227
The Undead 271, 274–276
The Unguarded Moment 204
The Unholy 21–22
The United States vs. Salim Ajami 53
Up Pompeii 216–217

V 98, 104–105
V: The Beginning 104–105
Vaccaro, Brenda 241, 249
Valkenburgh, Deborah Van 77
Valli, Alida 270
The Vampire 175
The Vampire Lovers 214–216
Van Cleef, Lee 11
Van Doren, Mamie 224
Van Eyck, Peter 149
The Velvet Vampire 307, 315
The Vengeance of Cleopatra Wong 158–159, 162
The Vengeance of Ursus 35
Verhoeven, Paul 53, 60
Vibrations Sexuelles 129
A View from the Bridge 99
A View to a Kill 96
Vincent, Jan-Michael 307
The Virginian 46, 221, 239, 244
The Visitors 192–193
Viva Madison Avenue 293
Voight, Jon 240
Von Richthofen and Brown 240, 245–247
Von Theumer, Ernst 274–275

Wagner, Robert 263
Wagon Train 46, 221
Wagon's East 142
Walden, Robert 240
Walker, Ally 61
Wallace, Edgar 149
Wallace, Tommy Lee 11
Wallace Stone, Dee 262–268
Wandering Samurai 159
Warbeck, David 189
Ward, Fred 120
Warden, Jack 72, 224
The Warrior and the Sorceress 42
Warriors of the Wasteland 282, 288–289
Waterston, Sam 58
Wayne, John 255
Weaver, Fritz 20
Weaver, Tom v, 1, 146, 150
Weird Science 25
Welch, Raquel 310
Welcome to Blood City 69
Welles, Mel 1, 4, 269–278
Welles, Orson 146–147

Wellman, William 309
We're No Angels see *Noi Siamo Angeli*
Wes Craven's New Nightmare 210
Westworld 69
The White Buffalo 139
White Hot 56
White Hunter 147
Who's Been Sleeping in My Bed? 200
Why Didn't They Ask Evans? 217
Widmark, Richard 245
The Wild Bunch 77
Wild Palms 63
Wild Wild West 300, 303
Wilder, Billy 200–202
Willard 227
William Tell 147
Williams, Cindy 141
Williams, Esther 204
Williams, Lori 200
Williams, Paul 235
Williams, Spice 27
Williamson, Fred 1, 4, 91–92, 96–97, 222, 227, 234, 279–293
Willis, Bruce 13, 118
Wilson, Colin 192
Winchester '73 205
Windom, William 293–299
Windsor, Barbara 165
Winner, Michael 315
Winters, Shelley 240
Wise Blood 63–64
Wiseguy 53
Woo, John 282, 290–291
Wood, Ed 81
Wood, Lana v, 300–306
Wood, Natalie 300
The World of Suzie Wong 294
Woronov, Mary 77
Wrong Is Right 205
Wyngarde, Jason 214, 216

The X-Files 63, 65, 137, 193

Yap, Johnson 157
Yarnall, Celeste v, 307–316
Les Yeux Sans Visage 128
York, Francine 200
Young, Doris (a.k.a. Doris Young Siew Keen) see Lee, Marrie
Young, Robert 75
The Young Rascals 243
The Young Riders 118

Zappa, Frank 239, 243–244
The Zebra Killer 234, 238
Zeta One 165–166, 169
Ziegfeld, Florenz 137
Zmed, Adrian 102–104
Zombie, Rob 75–77
Zorro's Black Whip 45
Zulu 73

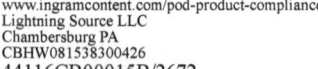